PENGUIN BOOKS

HANCOX

Charlotte Moore is an author, lecturer and freelance journalist. She has published four novels, three historical biographies for children, and *George and Sam*, a highly acclaimed account of life with her autistic sons. She contributes to many newspapers and magazines, including the *Guardian*, the *Daily Telegraph* and the *Spectator*. She grew up at Hancox, where she and her three sons now live.

By the same author

Fiction
Promises Past
Martha's Ark
My Sister, Victoria
Grandmother's Footsteps

Non-fiction
George and Sam: Autism in the Family

For children
Who was Florence Nightingale?
Who was Elizabeth I?
Who was William the Conqueror?

Hancox

CHARLOTTE MOORE

PENGUIN BOOKS

PENGUIN BOOKS

Published by the Penguin Group
Penguin Books Ltd, 80 Strand, London WC2R ORL, England
Penguin Group (USA) Inc., 375 Hudson Street, New York, New York 10014, USA
Penguin Group (Canada), 90 Eglinton Avenue East, Suite 700, Toronto, Ontario, Canada M4P 2Y3
(a division of Pearson Penguin Canada Inc.)
Penguin Ireland, 25 St Stephen's Green, Dublin 2, Ireland (a division of Penguin Books Ltd)
Penguin Group (Australia), 250 Camberwell Road,
Camberwell, Victoria 3124, Australia (a division of Pearson Australia Group Pty Ltd)
Penguin Books India Pvt Ltd, 11 Community Centre, Panchsheel Park,
New Delhi – 110 017, India
Penguin Group (NZ), 67 Apollo Drive, Rosedale, Auckland 0632, New Zealand
(a division of Pearson New Zealand Ltd)
Penguin Books (South Africa) (Pty) Ltd, 24 Sturdee Avenue, Rosebank, Johannesburg 2196,
South Africa

Penguin Books Ltd, Registered Offices: 80 Strand, London WC2R ORL, England

www.penguin.com

First published by Viking 2010
Published in Penguin Books 2011

1

Typeset by Jouve (UK), Milton Keynes
Printed in England by Clays Ltd, St Ives plc

ISBN: 978-0-141-02175-1

www.greenpenguin.co.uk

This book is dedicated to the descendants of
Alan and Mary Moore and to their spouses:

Norman and Janet Moore; Richard Moore;
Ann Moore; John and Meriel Oliver.

Peter Moore and Pam Edwardes; Caroline Moore;
Helena Moore and David Alexander; Charles and
Caroline Moore; Simon White; Rowan Moore and
Lizzie Treip; Tom and Catherine Oliver;
Henry and Emily Oliver.

Paul and Esther Edwardes Moore; Toby, Mary and
Guy Cohen; Rose, Catherine and Harriet Alexander;
Will and Kate Moore; George, Sam and Jake Smith;
Helena and Stella Moore; Isaiah Oliver,
and his sibling *in utero*.

Also in memory of Anne Norris, late of Crowham
Manor, who took great interest in the progress
of this book but did not live to see its completion.

'These little bits of driftwood washed up on the beach of the present time from the vast illimitable ocean of the past always touch me'

— Norman Moore to Amy Moore, 30 June 1890

List of Contents

List of Illustrations   xi

Family Tree   xiv

Map   xvi

Acknowledgements   xix

Prologue: A trust for my ancestors   xxi

1. 'Except the Lord build the house . . .'   1

2. 'Still she talks and laughs!'   15

3. 'Every old house must have its ghost'   41

4. 'A high forehead and the highest principles'   54

5. 'He is unstained by the common vices of youth'   69

6. *A cœur valiant rien impossible*   84

7. 'Aunt Barbara's Amy'   114

8. '*Eira* is awa''   144

9. 'Free-minded Albion's daughters'   178

10. 'Looking after the farming business'   204

11. 'A question of life or death'   230

12. 'My dear Papist'   252

13. 'Your tiresome Mil'   276

14. 'Hancox is the place'   294

15. 'The Land of Love'   327

16. *Arma virumque cano*   350

17. 'A monstrous inconceivable war'   386

18. 'England best my heart contents'   406
19. 'I feel he is happy somehow'   430
Epilogue: An old silk nightgown   459

Bibliography   469
Index   471

List of Illustrations

1. Marble bust of Bella Leigh Smith

2. Major-General John Ludlow

3. Ben Leigh Smith on board the *Eira*

4. Bob, the *Eira*'s dog, with a member of the crew, probably Captain Lofley

5. Anne Leigh Smith (Nannie) and Isabella Blythe (Isa)

6. Georgina Leigh Smith (Jenny)

7. Sketch of Willy Leigh Smith

8. Barbara Leigh Smith before her marriage

9. Milicent Ludlow at about the time she moved into Hancox

10. Mabel Ludlow

11. Ludlow Coape Smith at the time of his engagement to Mabel

12. Scalands Gate, 'Dr Bodichon's cottage'

13. Yotes Court, Milicent's childhood home

14. Glottenham Manor, with whale's jawbone in grounds

15. Crowham Manor, Willy and Jenny's home

16. Amy Moore, née Leigh Smith, in her twenties

17. Amy, aged 19, in theatrical costume

18. Daguerrotype of Robert Ross Rowan Moore

19. Rebecca Moore with son Norman

20. NM at about the time of his marriage

21. Uncle Ben with his sons, Valentine and Philip

22. Aunt Charley in 1892

23. Rose and Ike Smith on their wedding day

24/25. A postcard from Rose's collection

26. Hancox from the south, 1909

27. Repairs to the north end, 1915

28. The kitchen garden, 1909

29. The hall being renovated, 1907

30. The hall with its new panelling

31. The parlour fireback

32. The main staircase

33. NM speaking to an audience, including Milicent

34. NM as President of the Royal College of Physicians, 1918

35. Ethel Portal

36. East End girls on a visit to Hancox in the 1890s

37. Alan, Ethne and Gillachrist in 1897

38. Gilla with his nurse, Eliza Brown

39. Ethne with her first child, Johnnie, in 1911

40. Alan riding a penny-farthing at Hancox

41. Gilla at Hancox in 1914

42. Mary Haviland, around 1911

43. Alan on board HMS *Sagitta* in 1915

44. Mary Burrows at the time of her engagement

45. Alan and Mary's wedding, April 1922

All photographs courtesy of Charlotte Moore.

A Family

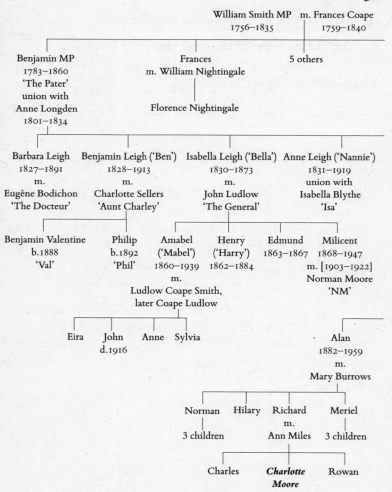

William Smith MP m. Frances Coape
1756–1835 1759–1840

Benjamin MP
1783–1860
'The Pater'
union with
Anne Longden
1801–1834

Frances
m. William Nightingale

Florence Nightingale

5 others

Barbara Leigh
1827–1891
m.
Eugène Bodichon
'The Docteur'

Benjamin Leigh ('Ben')
1828–1913
m.
Charlotte Sellers
'Aunt Charley'

Isabella Leigh ('Bella')
1830–1873
m.
John Ludlow
'The General'

Anne Leigh ('Nannie')
1831–1919
union with
Isabella Blythe
'Isa'

Benjamin Valentine
b.1888
'Val'

Philip
b.1892
'Phil'

Amabel
('Mabel')
1860–1939
m.

Henry
('Harry')
1862–1884

Edmund
1863–1867

Milicent
1868–1947
m. [1903–1922]
Norman Moore
'NM'

Ludlow Coape Smith,
later Coape Ludlow

Eira

John
d.1916

Anne

Sylvia

Alan
1882–1959
m.
Mary Burrows

Norman

3 children

Hilary

Richard
m.
Ann Miles

Meriel

3 children

Charles

*Charlotte
Moore*

Rowan

Tree

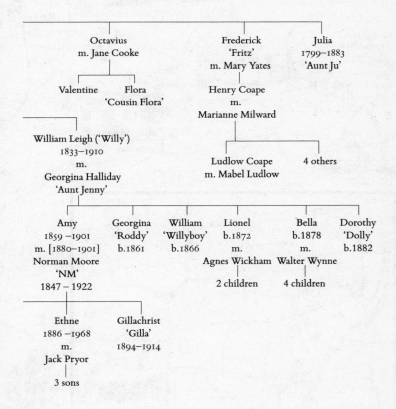

Octavius
m. Jane Cooke

Frederick
'Fritz'
m. Mary Yates

Julia
1799–1883
'Aunt Ju'

Valentine

Flora
'Cousin Flora'

Henry Coape
m.
Marianne Milward

William Leigh ('Willy')
1833–1910
m.
Georgina Halliday
'Aunt Jenny'

Ludlow Coape
m. Mabel Ludlow

4 others

Amy
1859 –1901
m. [1880–1901]
Norman Moore
'NM'
1847 – 1922

Georgina
'Roddy'
b.1861

William
'Willyboy'
b.1866

Lionel
b.1872
m.
Agnes Wickham

2 children

Bella
b.1878
m.
Walter Wynne

4 children

Dorothy
'Dolly'
b.1882

Ethne
1886 –1968
m.
Jack Pryor

3 sons

Gillachrist
'Gilla'
1894–1914

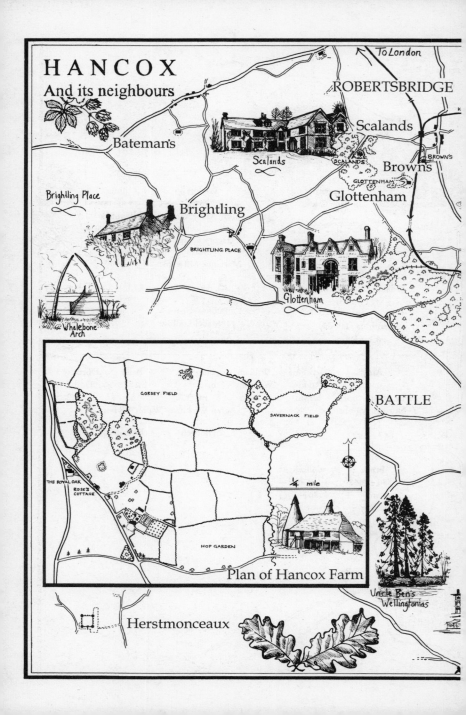

HANCOX

And its neighbours

Bateman's

Brightling Place

Brightling

Scalands

SCALANDS

GLOTTENHAM

To London

ROBERTSBRIDGE

Scalands

BROWN'S

Browns

Glottenham

Glottenham

Whalebone Arch

GORSEY FIELD

SAVERNACK FIELD

BATTLE

THE ROYAL OAK

ROSE'S COTTAGE

¼ mile

HOP GARDEN

Plan of Hancox Farm

Uncle Ben's Wellingtonias

Herstmonceaux

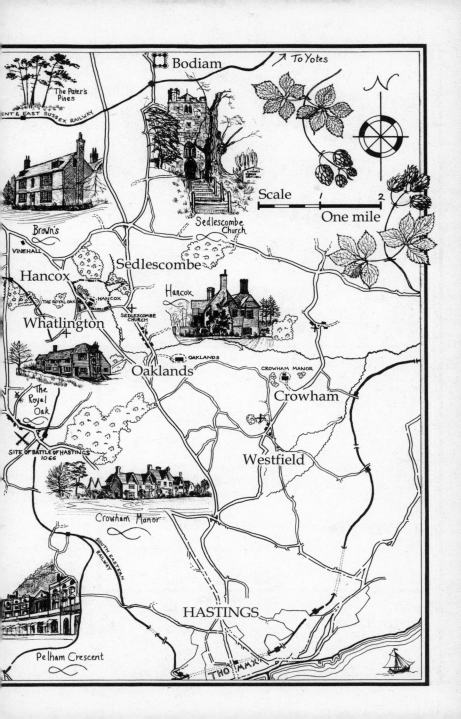

Bodiam

To Yotes

The Pater's Pines

ENT & EAST SUSSEX RAILWAY

Sedlescombe Church

Scale
1   2
One mile

N

Brown's

VINEHALL

Sedlescombe

Hancox

Hancox

THE ROYAL OAK

HANCOX

Whatlington

SEDLESCOMBE CHURCH

Oaklands

OAKLANDS

CROWHAM MANOR

Crowham

The Royal Oak

SITE OF BATTLE OF HASTINGS 1066

Westfield

Crowham Manor

SOUTH EASTERN RAILWAY

HASTINGS

THO MMX

Pelham Crescent

Acknowledgements

My mother, Ann Moore, catalogued thousands of family letters; if she had not done so, it would hardly have been possible to write this book. My thanks also go to her for reading and annotating the manuscript.

My uncle Norman Moore, my father Richard Moore and my aunt Meriel Oliver also commented on the manuscript and supplied me with their memories. I thank them for this, and for their generous approval of this intrusive project. My thanks are also due to Christopher Leigh Smith for similar reasons.

Several others have read the manuscript and made helpful and encouraging suggestions, most particularly Charles Moore, Kate Moore, Tom Oliver, Elspeth Sinclair, Cathy O'Neill, Caroline Barrett and Simon White. Very many thanks, also, to Tom for his beautiful map, and to Simon for his Googling and chauffeuring, and for listening to me talk about family history night and day for the last four years.

The Cherry family – Ethne's descendants – unearthed Ethne's memoir and diary, for which I am deeply grateful. Thanks also to the Sutton family, Rosemary and Jeremy Goring, Kevin Ades and Pete Capelotti for sharing points of information. I'm grateful to the Norris family and to Amanda Helm for giving me access to Crowham, and to Simon and Katherine Weston-Smith for allowing me to peer at the fireplace at Scalands.

Many thanks are due to my agent David Godwin, who helped shape the idea, to my patient and good-natured editor Tony Lacey and his assistant Ben Brusey, to Sarah Day for her careful copy-editing, to the rest of the team at Viking/Penguin, and to Mark Reed for his painstaking photographic work.

Eva Littna has typed all my manuscripts, but this was by far the

most complicated. I am deeply grateful to her for the cheerful sacrifice of so much of her time.

A Note on the Text

Errors of punctuation and spelling have not been corrected in original material.

Prologue: A trust for my ancestors

I live in the house where I grew up. Hancox has a Tudor hall house at its core, but each century has added or subtracted a layer, so that it is a living history of East Sussex architectural vernacular, an organic unplanned pile of tile and timber and russet brick in which nothing quite fits, a house of unnecessary corridors and pointless landings and doors that lead nowhere. There are thirteen windows on the side that faces north-east, and not one of them matches another. The materials that made the house would almost all have come from within a five-mile radius; perhaps that's why it looks like a natural outcrop, something cast up from the undulations of the Sussex Wealden landscape in which it sits. It's not a silent house. It sighs and rustles. Windows rattle, hinges squeal, floorboards groan. Squirrels, mice and worse career across the roof; starlings jabber in their nests under the hanging tiles, jackdaws quarrel in the chimneys. The water pipes hum and drone; the house is a gigantic Aeolian harp.

My three sons, George, Sam and Jake, have grown up with the same sights and sounds that formed the background to my own childhood. They are the fifth generation of their family to live at Hancox. Such continuity would once have been common; now, it's unusual though not extraordinary. What is extraordinary is the extent to which my sons and I are surrounded by evidence of the lives of those five generations. I spread the table with a cloth monogrammed with the initials of my great-grandfather. My sons have all ridden Queenie, the rocking horse belonging to their great-great-grandmother. The copy of *The Jungle Book* I read aloud to Jake is inscribed by his great-great-grandfather Norman Moore as a gift to his wife Amy. Jake stirs his cocoa with a silver spoon engraved with the name 'Gillachrist', a christening present for his great-great-uncle, who died at the first Battle of Ypres. Sam sleeps beneath a frieze of waterbirds chalked on to the bedroom wall by that same Gillachrist in his Edwardian boyhood. George's room, once the night nursery, has been liberally graffitied by children of several generations sent upstairs to 'rest', including me and my brothers, Charles and Rowan. The walls of this room are covered with lining paper, honey-coloured with caramel blotches. There are many holes in the paper, evidence of childhood games and fights. Underneath, you can see brown hair, the hair of Sussex cattle, mixed in with the old plaster; when I was a child I knew that my great-grandfather had had more than one wife, and I believed that this hair was the hair of these wives. I didn't feel that they'd been murdered and walled up; it was more a sense that those wives of the past, with their long, old-fashioned hair, were somehow still here in the house.

Hancox seems to house the dead as well as the living. I grew up with such a strong idea of the people who had lived here or been connected with it that I almost thought of them as living presences – Milicent, who first bought the house, Uncle Ben who got shipwrecked in the Arctic and had to eat polar bears, poor Bella who went mad, beautiful Amy carrying a sheaf of rushes, Aunt Charley who gave me my name, Aunt Barbara who invented university for women, my grandfather Alan, who walked round the top of factory chimneys without feeling giddy but couldn't bear to have cooked cheese in the house. I always felt that these, and many more, lived on at Hancox somewhere, and in a sense my research for this book has proved me right.

All families are potentially interesting. Every human life is full of drama, it's just that, in most cases, the evidence is destroyed. Most families would have thrown out the frayed tablecloth, sold or lost the christening spoon, redecorated over Gillachrist's swans and geese. My own family tend towards a strong historical sense and a reverence for the written word. They are disinclined to throw anything away, especially anything that's been written on. If you live in a house as large as Hancox you don't have any pressing need to dispose of stuff; it just silts up. Stamped on our DNA is a dislike of change, an inability to generate or to hang on to much money – there's never enough for 'home improvements' – and an unusually high threshold for tolerating, even welcoming, shabbiness and inconvenience in our living arrangements. 'Odd that so many of our relations tend to discomfort,' my grandfather wrote to his sister Ethne, though he himself tended that way. He would routinely make a note in his diary when the temperature in his dressing room fell below freezing point, but he never felt it was within his powers to do anything about it.

What all this means is that, since Hancox came into the family in 1888, remarkably little has changed, inside or out. It's not so much that we live in the past as that we live in parallel with the past. I can't see any reason not to use the pots and pans that came with the (new!) Aga in 1934, when the kitchen range was replaced (I'm sure that was controversial). The pans still function. And I enjoy the thought that so many other hands have touched them, used them for homely, kindly things like boiling eggs and potatoes and Christmas puddings, or stuck them under drips when the roof can't stand up to the pressure of stormy nights.

As I sit writing this, the view from my window is much the same as it has been for several hundred years, before my family's time, even. The shakes and ripples in the ancient glass distort it for me just as they would have distorted it for all those who went before. I can see a glimpse of our farm, the great roof of our cathedral of a barn, the stables, the old coach house, the brewhouse where the beer was made, the hut in which the butchering of pigs took place – a series of pyramid shapes, all hung with the same warm fox-coloured tiles. I can see the crumbling walls that frame what were once the kitchen garden and the bowling green, the culinary rose bushes planted in the 1890s, the flowers of which were harvested to make rosewater and pot-pourri, the hops, the last of those once grown for beer, now preserved for sentimental and decorative reasons. I see the wobbly brick paths that converge at the cover over the brick-built well shaft that drops seventy feet to an underground stream that never dries up.

The most modern construction I can see is a loosebox built in the late 1880s to house the hunters belonging to Mabel Ludlow, a valiant rider-to-hounds, a lively but often unhappy woman whose life was overshadowed by what her fearsome Aunt Nannie called 'the family taint'. Mabel was, with her sister Milicent, the first of my relations to live at Hancox, but it's with Milicent that this story begins, because it's due to Milicent that I'm here today.

On the mantelpiece in this room, a room which Milicent and her husband Norman called the 'Scriptorium', is a little grey plaster cast not much bigger than my hand. It shows, in profile, the bas-relief portrait of a young woman wearing a hooded cloak, her long hair loosely coiled in a bun. The flowing lines of the cloak and hair give her a romantic, adventurous air; the firm outline of her nose and chin correctly suggest determination and a sense of purpose. This is Milicent Ludlow; it was made in Rome in 1893 when she was visiting her Aunt Nannie.

I'd always known about Milicent. I knew that she was the second wife of my great-grandfather, and that she was also the cousin of his first wife, Amy, which makes her my first cousin three times removed as well as my step-great-grandmother. I knew that it was Milicent who bought Hancox; childless, she later handed it on to my grandfather Alan. He brought up his four children here; one of them was my father, Richard, and in turn it became our family home. But it only struck me a few years ago, as I inspected more closely the little image I'd always taken for granted, that when Milicent took on Hancox she was extraordinarily young – only twenty when she moved here in 1888. True, her sister Mabel, Mabel's husband and their children lived here with her for much of the time, but it was Milicent who bought the house, Milicent who set about enlarging it, built cottages for farmworkers and tenants and – most surprising of all – Milicent who decided to manage the farm herself.

This Victorian girl's impulsive, brave, foolhardy decision has shaped my life, for Hancox is a place that shapes lives. I wanted to find out more about the place and the people who made me, so

I began to work my way through the vast archive that fills the house. Every drawer, every cupboard, every trunk, shelf, box, is filled with letters, memoirs, journals, notebooks, sketchbooks, photograph albums; there are prescriptions, bills, invoices, school reports, recipe books, even chequebook stubs.

I am not the first to attempt to weave a narrative out of this tangle of domestic archaeology. Milicent's husband, Norman Moore, was the dominant ancestor, a man of whom it is appropriate to use the well-worn description 'larger than life'. An Irishman, the only child of a hard-up single mother, he had risen to the top of the medical profession. He was a scholar, an author, a linguist, a naturalist, a bibliophile, an antiquarian, and the friend of almost any eminent late Victorian you can think of. His son Alan tried to write his biography, but was defeated by old age and ill health. My mother, Alan's daughter-in-law, took up the challenge in the 1960s; I remember her surrounded by drifts of Victorian letters – from, among others, Darwin, Kipling, Florence Nightingale – sorting them into categories and storing them in turquoise Clark's shoeboxes. She was overcome by the sheer mass of information and by the pressure of other demands on her time, but those early investigations have been the most tremendous help to me. Without the shoeboxes full of ordered letters, without the painstaking family trees drawn up by my grandfather, I would never have threaded my way out of the tangle.

I didn't want to write Norman Moore's biography. His was a marvellous life, and arguably an important one – 'He is a very good representative of an environment and a society which has now passed, and without him the history of the [late Victorian] age would be incomplete,' wrote a younger colleague of his – but my mind isn't scientific enough to do justice to his medical career, or scholarly enough to follow his antiquarian researches. I wanted, instead, to piece together the whole picture, explore the context in which he and Milicent and the others lived their lives, at Hancox and elsewhere. I wanted to take a good look at the forebears who peopled my childhood imaginings; I wanted to see them move, hear them talk. This is a book about a house, but it's also about what the house holds in storage, the human stories that are hidden in those shelves and trunks and shoeboxes. Every little thing in the house is a clue to somebody's story. As Norman Moore himself wrote to his first wife, Amy, 'These little bits of driftwood washed up on the beach of present time from the vast illimitable ocean of the past always touch me.'

I was unsystematic at first, noting things in no particular order, imagining this book as a series of vignettes rather than a full narrative, but the more I unearthed, the more I understood how it all hung together. Marriages, love affairs, bereavements, triumphs, failures, travels, illnesses, friendships, rivalries – I had access to the minutiae of the lives of my forebears, even to the clothes they wore, the food they ate, the animals they kept. And to it all clung the indefinable glamour of the past.

An archive such as the one Hancox holds won't ever be gathered again. The lives I've written about span the best-documented age in our history. The formidable Victorian postal system meant that a letter written in London at breakfast time would arrive by lunch time in Sussex; the penny post meant that everyone could afford to use it. Now, of course, we send emails or make telephone calls; unlike these, letters survive, especially in a highly literate age, when the written word was respected. These post-Romantics believed that expressing their thoughts and feelings in writing was the right thing to do. The affordability of domestic servants meant that the upper middle classes to which my family belonged had enough leisure to write, diaries as well as letters. They sketched, because they wanted to record what they saw, and taking photographs was still expensive and rather complicated. They kept their sketches so that they could discuss them with other people. When photographs were taken, their relative rarity meant that they were reverently stored in albums rather than left to languish in the depths of a computer.

We have a far more intimate knowledge of our Victorian and Edwardian past than we do of that of any earlier age, and no future generation will have anything like so full a picture of us, thanks to our throwaway habits. 'I am myself but I am more. I have received a sort of trust for my dead ancestors,' wrote Norman, again to Amy, and that's just how I feel. This book is my attempt to acknowledge that trust, to make sense of the limitless wealth of evidence that, washed up from the ocean of the past, has gathered under this roof, and to breathe life into the men and women who left it there for me to find.

1. 'Except the Lord build the house . . .'

A carved inscription, set into the panelling, runs the length of our dining-room wall: *NISI DOMINUS ÆDIFICAVERIT DOMUM IN VANUM LABORAVERUNT QUI ÆDIFICANT EAM*. My great-grandfather, Norman Moore, chose the Clementine Vulgate version of this line from the 127th Psalm: 'Except the Lord build the house, they labour in vain that build it.'

Three letters are picked out in gold – N, M, M, standing for Norman and Milicent Moore. The letters that signify the year the inscription was made are larger than the others – MCMVII (1907). The panels bearing the inscription were made in London by an East End woodcarver Milicent had come to know in the course of her mission work at St Margaret's, a settlement in Bethnal Green; my grandfather, Norman's son Alan, brought them down on the train from London and walked the four miles from Robertsbridge station to Hancox with them tied in a bundle on his back. The work cost £3.10/–, which even in 1907 seemed a bargain.

1907 was the year in which Norman and Milicent Moore moved into Hancox. (Norman is always referred to in the family as 'NM', so I'll do the same, not least to distinguish him from my uncle, another Norman Moore.) The association of Hancox with the family goes back a little further, to 1888, long before Milicent's marriage to NM. Milicent Ludlow, then only twenty, and her older sister, Mabel, were the only survivors of their immediate family; both parents and two brothers predeceased them. The girls had inherited plenty of money, but they had no home; Yotes Court, the grand house in Kent in which they had been brought up, was only rented. Mabel had suffered a serious mental breakdown in her early twenties. Though she had officially recovered, when it was decided that the two sisters should set up home together the

burden of responsibility was inevitably placed on the young shoulders of the more stable Milicent. Early in 1888 they started house-
hunting, and by July they had found Hancox. They rented it, in
Milicent's name, from Earl de la Warr.

Family associations drew them to this corner of East Sussex.
Their late mother's family, the Leigh Smiths, had inhabited the
area since the 1820s, and Mabel and Milicent had spent many holidays with these aunts, uncles and cousins. There were plenty more
cousins in London, and the girls could have taken a house there,
but fresh air and physical exercise were vital to Mabel's well-being.
She was a fearless huntswoman, a skilful tennis player and an
enthusiastic cyclist; strenuous exertion was the best way of keeping her mental demons at bay. So Sussex it was. Hancox provided
stabling for Mabel's hunters, a ready-made social network, and
picturesque opportunities for watercolour sketching, a passion
which Mabel and Milicent shared with most female members of
their extended family.

They had been at Hancox for two apparently harmonious
years when Mabel accepted an offer of marriage. Her fiancé was
a lieutenant in the 9th Bengal Lancers. His name was Ludlow
Coape Smith; he was related to Mabel through both her father's
and her mother's families, and on his marriage he changed his
name, strikingly, to Ludlow Coape Ludlow. The wedding took
place in March 1891. In October, Mabel and Ludlow set off
for India, leaving 23-year-old Milicent as head of the Hancox
household.

Not only was Milicent undaunted by the prospect of running
the large house and its grounds single-handed, she immediately
took on additional challenges. She bought the house from Lord de la
Warr for £5,000 – he had taken out twenty-three mortgages on it, so
he must have been glad to get rid of it. The tenancy of Hancox farm
was due to expire. Milicent searched, briefly, for a new tenant, but the
hunt was fruitless. On 1 December 1891 she noted calmly in her
diary, 'I heard that Crump would not take the farm – so must farm
it myself.' Her complete lack of training or experience troubled her

not at all. 'Milicent talked as if the world was hers,' her future husband had once unflatteringly remarked.

Milicent's time in sole charge proved short. Mabel and Ludlow gave up on India after only a few months and returned to Hancox in 1892, assuming that they would be received with open arms. Perhaps because Ludlow was a cousin as well as a brother-in-law, no one foresaw any difficulties with this triangular family structure. Ludlow, who was quietly ducking out of a military career on the grounds of poor health, was eager to be of use. He managed the farm jointly with Milicent, but he had no more expertise than she – rather less, even – and expensive mistakes were made. The Ludlows produced four children in brisk succession; in the wake of childbirth Mabel's mental health began to deteriorate.

Milicent found her independence compromised and her enjoyment of rural life curtailed by domestic cares that were not strictly her responsibility. She was strong-willed and courageous, possibly ruthless, and she made a snap decision. Family legend says that one morning in 1900, at breakfast, Milicent announced to Mabel and Ludlow that she had let Hancox to the Church of England Temperance Society. It was to be used as a drying-out home for 'inebriates'. The Ludlows had no option but to pack their bags.

For some years, Milicent had divided her time between Hancox and Bethnal Green, where she worked at St Margaret's, a branch of the Oxford House settlement set up for the welfare and education of East End girls. Once the Temperance Society had taken Hancox, 'St Mag's' became her main base. But she also spent a lot of time with her cousin Amy, who was dying of tuberculosis. Amy was the first wife of NM. Milicent became such an integral part of the afflicted family that it is not surprising that in 1903, two years after Amy's death, NM asked Milicent to marry him.

On her marriage, Milicent left St Mag's, though she continued to some extent with her good works for the settlement. She became mistress of 94 Gloucester Place, NM's large, rented house in Marylebone. NM's life as one of the country's leading physicians was extremely busy, but Milicent, small, wiry, adventurous and

energetic, threw herself eagerly into her new role as hostess, housekeeper, amanuensis and stepmother. Her reverence for her husband and his profession was boundless; everything was organized
for his convenience and comfort. His work tied him to St Bartholomew's Hospital during the week, but Milicent worried about
what would now be called his stress levels. The need was increasingly felt for a country retreat. It made sense to reclaim Hancox
from the inebriates.

When NM was sixteen years old, he had walked from his home
in suburban Manchester to admire the collection of stuffed birds
and beasts at Walton Hall, near Wakefield in Yorkshire. NM's
fascination with natural history began early and remained with
him all his life. The great naturalist Charles Waterton, the squire
of Walton Hall and owner and stuffer of the creatures NM had
come to inspect, was immediately taken with the spirited and well-
informed boy. Despite the great disparity in their ages – Waterton
was eighty-one when they met – the two became firm friends.
Walton Hall was heaven on earth to NM. Waterton had turned its
park into the first bird sanctuary in England; no gun was to be
fired within its high walls – walls paid for, said Waterton, with the
wine he didn't drink.

By the side of the ancient 'wanderer', as Waterton named himself, the young NM's understanding of natural history grew apace.
NM had never met his own father; the friendship assuaged a need.
Fragments of the old man's conversation would come back to NM
in later years – 'All he said seemed to me true and good.' One such
memory was of Waterton saying, 'I hope when you grow old you
will manage to have a little land of your own & you'll sit in the sun
& now & then think of me.' All his adult life, NM, impecunious,
frantically busy and endlessly curious, had moved from place to
place. Bart's had been more of a home to him than anywhere else
– he had never owned a house. Now, in 1907, at the age of sixty,
he moved into Hancox, put down roots, sat in the sun and thought
of his old friend.

★

Hancox existed by 1433. The name John Handcocks occurs in records of 1492, so it seems likely that the name derives from the surname of an early owner. It is common locally to find houses thus named. The 'x' ending also seems to be a local quirk; Lavix, Platnix, Glorix are all place names found in the area.

When Milicent Ludlow first set foot in the place in 1888, Hancox was half in the small village of Whatlington and half in Sedlescombe, its bigger and more prosperous neighbour. It is the largest medieval 'hall-place' still in existence in the joint parishes. The boundary between the two villages used to run right through what is now our dining room. The old custom of 'beating the bounds' was kept up until 1944; once every seven years the male inhabitants of the parish would walk all round its margins, the older ones showing the young boys the way, pointing out landmarks, crashing through hedges, even ducking them in a ditch or a pond when one came in handy to imprint the boundaries on their minds. This was an age-old way of ensuring that villagers knew exactly what constituted their parish, a rite-of-passage left over from the days before maps were generally available, or even before they existed. When the bound-beaters reached Hancox, they made their way through the middle of the great barn, then knocked at our door for permission to trudge through the dining room. They were given tea and buns. When my parents married in Sedlescombe church in 1955, my grandfather told my mother to sleep in the south-east end of the house the night before the wedding so that she was on the Sedlescombe side of the parish boundary. In 1960 the boundaries were redrawn, and Hancox is now firmly in Whatlington.

The first owner about whom more than a name is known is John Dounton, a lawyer and steward of Battle Manor, who made extensions and alterations to the house in 1569. The original medieval high-roofed hall was divided into separate floors; the upper storey hides the crown-post and roof timbers, though the fine ornamental timbers of the old hall are still visible. On some of the timbers there are painted Roman numerals. These told the builders which piece went where, like flat-pack instructions. The

timbers were erected 'in the green'; as they dried out, they shrank
and warped, which is what gives Tudor houses their wavy, non-
symmetrical, organic look.

The Dounton family was important enough to have a coat of
arms. When John Dounton owned Hancox, '3 score and ten acres
of land' went with it. The general scale of things makes it a gentleman's house rather than an aristocrat's. Dounton's heiress was his
daughter Joan, who married John Sackville in 1589. This was the
beginning of the Sackville connection with Hancox, which lasted
for three hundred years, until Milicent took over. John and Joan
Sackville lived here after their marriage, apparently happily co-
existing with Joan's father. They produced four sons and two
daughters, and presumably felt a little cramped, for they made
two major alterations. First, a central chimney and fireplace were
installed and a ceiling inserted across the great hall, to join the
upper storeys already in existence on either side of it. Second,
what was virtually a second house was added, altering the rectangular ground plan to an F shape. These Sackvilles were a branch
of the important Sussex family, owners of the colossal house,
Knole, near Sevenoaks. Knole, famously, has 365 rooms, as many
as there are days in the year. Though Hancox was of course on a
very much smaller scale, John and Joan's aim seems to have been to
make it one of the most imposing houses in the neighbourhood.

John Sackville died in 1620. His son Thomas succeeded to Hancox and to the flourishing and lucrative furnace situated nearby, off
Brede Lane. In those days, before the Industrial Revolution took
industry to the coal fields, East Sussex was the chief area in the
country for ironworking. There was iron in the soil and, as Sussex
was the most thickly wooded county, plenty to burn in the furnaces. There is a local legend that our streams run red with the
blood of the men killed at the Battle of Hastings, but of course
they actually take their rusty colour from the iron.

Iron helped make Thomas Sackville a prosperous man. By 1626 he
had been created a Knight of the Bath and a Justice of the Peace. His
wife, Elizabeth, provided him with four living sons and five daughters;

two other babies died in infancy. When Elizabeth died (in childbirth, not surprisingly), Thomas remarried and sired another four children. At this time the interior of Hancox was mainly panelled; the panelling would have been brightly painted and patterned. Tiny traces of paint, red and blue, can still be seen.

Thomas's son John succeeded to the property but died childless. His brother, another Thomas, inherited. Colonel Thomas Sackville was perhaps the most interesting of the Hancox Sackvilles. He matriculated at Christ Church, Oxford, aged fifteen, later joined the army, and fought for the Royalist cause in the Civil War. Sussex, however, was predominantly on the side of the Parliamentarians, and Sackville's forge and furnace off Brede Lane were commandeered by Roundhead forces. Thomas left the King's employ and went to France. When he returned to England to claim his inheritance he was fined £400.

After the Restoration of Charles II in 1660 Thomas became a Justice of the Peace and, eventually, a Member of Parliament for East Grinstead. He sold the furnace, and in 1676 he let Hancox for thirteen years at £135 per annum to Thomas Piers of Ewhurst. The colonel lived thereafter at one of his other, smaller, Sedlescombe houses. I assume that by letting Hancox he was hoping to economize by 'down-sizing'.

In the county archive is a list of 'fixtures and fittings' drawn up at the time when Hancox was let, 24 October 1676: 'a schedule of particulars of such goods as were left by the above named Thomas Sackvill in the capitall mesuage mentioned to be devised by him to the above named Thomas Piers in and by the indenture whereunto this is annexed'. It seems that Sackville took his portable furniture with him; this is a list of items of use and value which Thomas Piers would have to account for at the end of his tenancy. The handwritten document is hard to read, but it provides a rare picture of seventeenth-century household items and the uses to which rooms were put:

First in the kitchen, one little iron furnace one little brasse
    furnace, one fender of wrought iron, one rack of cast
    iron for the stove.

<u>Item</u> in the brewhouse two iron furnaces, one iron oven dore & one cooler of firr boords.

<u>Item</u> in the milkhouse one old table with a frame two shelves of firr boords and two little shelves of oaken boords.

<u>Item</u> in the Larder two rows of old shelves round the roome . . .

<u>Item</u> in the Stourhouse two cupboards three shelves and one candle shelf.

<u>Item</u> in the Great Parlour one iron plate . . .

<u>Item</u> in the Buttery one cupboard for glasses . . .

<u>Item</u> in the matted chamber one plate and one plate for the hearth . . .

Other rooms listed are the Lundry (laundry), the Pastry (maybe Pantry, but it really does look like 'pastry'), the chamber over the Bakehouse, the Little Parlour, the closet and the kitchen chamber. Some of these rooms are completely obvious to me and have not changed their function since the seventeenth century or earlier. Others I can't identify. The 'kitchen chamber' is a small space high in one corner of the kitchen accessible only by a ladder; it must have been where servants slept. Though cramped, it would at least have been relatively warm. Now it is used only by spiders. There are still two iron furnaces in the brewhouse. My larder still has 'two rows of old shelves round the roome', and I have no reason to think they are not the ones on the list.

The 'plates' mentioned must be firebacks or braziers. The iron-ware presumably all came from the Brede furnace. The 'firr' (pine) boards were prized above the oak ones because oaks grew all over the place, but 'firr' would have been brought at considerable expense from the Baltic. The slow-growing wood was hard and dense and didn't rot.

Colonel Sackville does not seem to have returned to Hancox, which he eventually sold to his cousin Richard. Richard Sackville was paying rates for Hancox in 1708 but disappears from view by 1712, to be replaced by his brother Charles, Earl of Dorset.

The Earl of Dorset was far too grand to live at Hancox. For the next hundred and fifty years it was let to tenant farmers. Nicholls, Igglesdon, Hook, Russell, Moses Cloke – the names succeed each other rapidly until the Ades family farmed there for three genera-tions. During their long tenancy a drawing of Hancox was made, dated 1785 and entitled 'Seddlescombe Place'. It shows the Jacobean wings, free-standing chimney and oriel windows, now gone. The core of the house is recognizably the same, and you can see the brewhouse and the garden walls, but the feeling of the drawing is very different to that of Hancox today. It's all open and spacious, with only one large tree (an elm?) anywhere near the house. Now-adays, trees crowd and jostle all around – sweet chestnut, yews, sycamores, oaks, hollies, fruit trees, Milicent's rows of Scots pines.

In the early nineteenth century, while the third generation of Ades lived there, the two Jacobean wings were pulled down, the plastered exterior walls were covered with hanging tiles and the front was faced with grey cement, which is now dropping off in large lumps. The Sackville crest over the front door, a coronet composed of a fleur-de-lys with a star above, was covered by a porch.

The Ades' tenancy ended abruptly. This may have been for political reasons. The early decades of the nineteenth century were a time of agrarian unrest. When a local labourer was accused of rick-burning and inciting a riot, Spencer Ades, tenant of Hancox, a well-to-do yeoman and a 'righteous man', held a meeting at Han-cox in support of the accused. Suddenly Lord de la Warr declined to renew the Ades' lease. I like to think of Hancox as having been a site of radical agitation, however fleetingly.

The Ades family was succeeded by John Symes, then John Swift, and in 1865 by Albert Apps, who by 1870 was in arrears with his rent. The last of the tenant farmers boasted to Milicent that he'd

stripped out four wagonloads of old panelling and burned the lot.
It still pains me to think of that. The panelling that was allowed to
remain had been plastered over. During the 1890s Milicent made a
good many alterations, most importantly tacking on an enormous
lump of a drawing room with two bedrooms above it. In 1907 she
and NM set about clearing up after the ravages the inebriates had
wrought and turning the house into both a family home and a fit
place for NM, once a poor Irish boy, now an eminent physician
and man of letters, to study, exercise and entertain his many
friends.

★

The process of removing the inebriates from Hancox began early
in 1907. Milicent, struck down by a lung haemorrhage the year
before, spent the winter at Davos in Switzerland, wrapped in furs
on the hotel balcony. In those days before the discovery of penicillin, the only treatment for TB was fresh, clean air and a strengthening diet. NM wrote to her daily, sometimes twice daily; his
affectionate letters constantly urge Milicent to fatten herself up:

> *11.2.07*   Swallow swallow swallow
>   Never be your inside hollow
>   Outside clothed in garbs of silk
>   Inside filled with mugs of milk.

Having lost his first wife, Amy, to the same disease six years
earlier, his anxiety for Milicent must have been acute. He cheered
both of them with his hopes for their future life at Hancox:

> *22.02.07*   I like to think of our little country seat & hope we
>   may have many a joyful day there together my own
>   dear Mil.

> *23.03.07*   I think it would be nice to encourage birds in our little
>   territory . . . If when the Winters [tenant farmers] lease

falls in we were to take the whole farm we might make a wonderful bird place in a few years.

(This plan did not materialize. The Winters continued as tenants of Hancox Farm until the 1970s; however, the farm has always been rich in bird life.)

On 16 March, NM and his elder son from his first marriage, Alan, then twenty-five, went down to Hancox to see how the land lay. That evening, despite a long and busy day, NM wrote a full account to Milicent. They caught the train from Charing Cross, travelled third class to Robertsbridge and walked:

by that nice old up hill & down dale & by woods & Poppinghole Lane road to Whatlington. We left our coats at the Royal Oak & went straight to Hancox. There are only nineteen drunkards there now. Mr Gott [the superintendent] came & we went in. The house is in a very disordered and rather dirty state. It will want papering throughout . . . Mr Gott says the inebriates could not paint it but seems quite to understand that it must be painted throughout. The big new room is a chapel . . . & it requires a great deal of hyssop. [In other words, it smelled bad.] Was a sort of brown ribbed paper dado round it in your time. If so it looks horrible now. They are scraping the coloured paper off the windows. [Put there to imitate stained glass?] . . . What a lovely old staircase there is. I did not know of it. Upstairs all is horrible at present . . . I almost think every room upstairs should be fumigated with sulphur . . . The garden looks well & it is a dear place & my own I shall like to be there with you.

Alan and I then inspected the fir trees 91 of the 100 are doing well. George [George Dann, tenant of two of the fields and landlord of the Royal Oak] is laying soot on that field. Then we had luncheon. Gott & Mrs Gott begged us to lunch with them but we were very glad we had ordered food at the inn. Roast beef, two kinds of potato, cauliflower & bread & butter pudding.

At 2.30 we rose & walked down to the Hancox stream across the fields . . . & then up the hill to Sedlescomb & looked in its church a sadly restored place & then by way of Oaklands Park to Crowham.

Crowham Manor, Westfield, had been the childhood home of Amy, NM's first wife. Her parents Willy and Jenny Leigh Smith – Milicent's uncle and aunt – still lived there with their unmarried offspring, Roddy, Bella and Willy junior. Before she bought Hancox, Crowham, a large, sleepy old house sitting deep in its own farmland, had been almost a second home for Milicent, and she was very close to her cousins. Reading this letter huddled on her Swiss balcony, Milicent would have been pleased to learn of the warm reception the Crowhamites gave NM, for it had not always been thus: 'They gave us eggs & a noble tea . . . pressed us to stay the night but we couldn't & so started back at five minutes to six.' Willy junior, nearly forty but never to shrug off his 'junior' status and, according to NM, grown 'hugely fat 16 stone I should say,' walked with them to the foot of the Forge Wood, then NM and Alan trudged on:

to Battle station where we arrived at 7.20 so it took us 1 hr 25 m from Crowham. Thus you see we had three good walks. Alan walked well so much better than he used & liked it & was in high spirits & with his great coat on his arm ran at a five barred gate & jumped it clear with ease . . . It was a grey & occasional slight showery day & a tremendous south east wind blowing but in the deep lanes it was quite warm. Very few wild flowers to be seen – Here are the only three primroses I saw . . . even dogs mercury was not out but we saw a few dashes of catkins in the woods.

Alan had arranged for a telegram to arrive about the boat race as he generally sends one to Aunt Jenny [his grandmother]. It came while we were at tea & we cheered that Cambridge had won . . . I like Sussex my own Mil. Oh I am glad you weigh 13lbs more drink milk & make it a stone. A little Milicent is a good thing more Milicent is a better thing & still more Milicent a still better thing in fact you cannot have too much of so good a thing as Milicent . . . Goodnight now my own dearest Mil.

This letter, of which I have quoted less than half, is indicative of the energy that enabled NM to accomplish the work of ten men in a lifetime. The walks he describes amount to more than fifteen miles; more than enough in themselves to tax the strength of most sixty-year-olds, let alone the train journeys, the inspection of Hancox, the family tea at Crowham and the writing of the letter itself.

Work got under way once the inebriates had left – there's no record of what became of them. The ground floor, which had been divided up into many little rooms, was opened up and simplified into library, dining room and front hall, with a little curtained section called the parlour. Once Milicent had returned from Switzerland in better health, she and Alan made regular trips to inspect the work. Her historically minded stepson was excited by the discovery of a recess large enough to hide smuggled goods concealed by a panel. Smuggling had flourished in Sussex for centuries, with landowners, magistrates and clergy involved in it as well as tradesmen and labourers; it was a well-organized industry with numerous hideouts. Smuggled goods could easily be brought to Sedlescombe, which is only six miles from the coast, by means of the tidal River Brede, now a sluggish stream but once a busy thoroughfare. Another welcome discovery had been made when one of the inebriates stumbled and fell heavily against the dining-room wall, causing the ancient deal panelling to be revealed beneath Victorian wallpaper over sacking. Alan and Milicent attacked the wallpaper with knives and found that much of the ground floor was panelled. Restoration was carried out wherever possible, but a new wall of panelling was commissioned for the division between the dining room and the library. This was where the '*Nisi dominus . . .*' chronograph was to go.

Another find was a fine wooden pillar, supporting a ceiling beam. It had been plastered over. The pillar was found to be thirteenth century, a survivor, presumably, of Hancox's first, medieval, incarnation. It stands in the middle of our dining room, a roof-tree, the centre of the house. Attached to its top is a plaster-of-Paris imp, a replica of the imp of Lincoln Cathedral, bought by NM when he was a medical student; he was studying rickets, and thought the imp looked as if he was afflicted by the disease. The grinning bug-eyed creature has amused or alarmed four generations of children. He became a casualty of war; in 1944 a doodlebug shook the house so severely that the imp's leg fell off. But still he grins on, undaunted, ornamented by horns of holly at Christmas.

A wag had stuck a notice saying 'Dipsomania Hall' on the front gate but Milicent and NM were excited by the house, and moved in long before it was ready. They spent their first night together there on 3 September 1907. NM at once began to keep a gardening notebook, noting the plants sent by his friend Miss Willmott, the great gardener of Warley Place. He bought three or four small fields – glebe land – to round off the property. He hung the parlour with handwoven curtains from the William Morris workshop, installed a fireback decorated with anchors and dated 1588, the year of the defeat of the Spanish Armada, the gift of a grateful patient he had successfully treated for gonorrhoea. Then he settled down to cultivate, at last, a sense of home.

2. 'Still she talks and laughs!'

What made Milicent Ludlow decide to buy such a place as Hancox? It was large, dilapidated, complicated and expensive to run. It hardly seems the obvious choice for a very young single woman. But in 1891 Milicent bought not only the house but the farm as well. She set about enlarging the house. She radically restructured the garden. She built or restored several cottages on the farm. And – perhaps most surprising of all – she decided she would be the chief manager of the farm itself.

History books and works of fiction still encourage us to think of Victorian girls as emotionally and financially dependent on men, undereducated, overprotected, physically frail. Milicent Ludlow, it seems, conformed to no stereotype. She came from a family of pioneering women and of men who took pride in them. On the face of it, her childhood had been privileged – plenty of money, plenty of space, plenty of adult attention – but her young life had been beset by tragedy. That's an overused word, but it's not too strong in this instance. Milicent's misfortunes seem to have bred in her a stubborn independence, a brave though possibly blinkered attitude that led her to see no difficulty in organizing building projects and farm management without the slightest architectural or agricultural training.

Milicent died in 1947, twelve years before I was born, but I have a kind of folk memory of her, born of photographs and grown-up conversations. I see her standing on the garden steps under the clematis montana, bony in black with a wide brimmed hat and something in her hand that is either a rolled umbrella or a walking stick. After her husband's death she became Milicent, Lady Moore; Rose Smith, her lady's maid, who lived on to become our cleaner, called her 'Milicent Lady', which changed itself for us children to 'Innocent Lady'.

Milicent was the youngest of the four children of Major-General
John Ludlow and his wife Bella, née Leigh Smith. 'The General',
as Milicent's father was (approvingly) known in the family, came
from a distinguished military line. He was a descendant of Edmund
Ludlow MP, who had fought for the Parliamentarian cause, was
imprisoned several times, and signed King Charles I's death warrant
– the fourteen-year-old Milicent was pleased to spot the signature
when she visited Madame Tussaud's.

The General's father had had a distinguished career in the Indian
Army and was the model for Colonel Newcome in Thackeray's
best-selling novel of 1855, *The Newcomes*. The General himself followed in his father's footsteps. He received his commission in
India, and was praised for his part in very difficult fighting in the
Burmese War of 1824–6. Later he joined the Indian Police Department, in which he exerted a humane and liberal influence. In the
1840s he presided over a Council of Regency that governed Jeypore (as he spelled it; now it is Jaipur) because the prince of that
province was too young to rule.

Unmarried daughters were seen as a disgrace by Indian families,
but the largesse dispersed at a daughter's wedding cost a great deal.
As a result, parents reared just so many daughters as they could
afford to marry off, and destroyed the rest at birth. General Ludlow put an end to this brutal practice by persuading the various
Rajpoot states to agree a common scale of wedding expenditure,
index-linked to the income of the bride's parents, with uniform
penalties for demands in excess. This was the first time that the
jealousies and divisions between the states had been suspended.
The native rulers saw the benefit of acting in unison to abolish an
evil, and their respect for and willingness to co-operate with the
General enabled him to campaign for the abolition of suttee, or
widow-burning.

Suttee was based on the idea that in allowing herself to be
burned to death with her husband's corpse, the widow was hon-
ouring her faith by showing the ultimate chastity and devotion.
The General, operating through his native contacts, pointed out

anomalies in ancient Hindu scriptures that proved the practice to be heretical. Using great tact and caution, he eventually converted the Council of Regency. In 1846 suttee was abolished in Jeypore and eleven of the eighteen Rajpoot states followed suit. General Ludlow was congratulated in the House of Commons.

The General retired from India before the Mutiny. He returned to England and renewed contact with the friends of his youth. These included the enormous family of William Smith, MP for Norwich. William Smith's daughter Fanny had married William Nightingale; their daughter was the soon-to-be-famous Florence. General Ludlow often stayed with the Nightingales. He was also close to Fanny's youngest, unmarried sister, the lively, feminist-inclined Julia, and to their oldest brother Ben.

William Smith's family were Unitarians, powerful in the world of nineteenth-century reforming politics. Unitarians believed in 'Freedom, Reason and Tolerance'; they saw Jesus as a man to be followed rather than a god to be worshipped. Central to Unitarianism was the conviction that actions are more important than words.

William Smith MP was a close associate of William Wilberforce and Thomas Clarkson and was active in the campaign for the abolition of slavery. He sat in the House of Commons for forty-six years, an indefatigable voice of dissent. His Tory enemies composed a piece of doggerel about him:

> At length, when the candles burn low in their sockets,
> Up gets William Smith with his hands in his pockets,
> On a course of morality fearlessly enters,
> With all the opinions of all the dissenters.

William Smith is a presence at Hancox still, partly because of a family pride in his political courage, partly because portraits of him at various stages of his life hang on the walls. Over the drawing-room fireplace, for instance, there's a painting of him as a red-haired boy of about ten being taught by his father, who is resplendent in periwig, knee breeches and frogged coat. The books lie open between them; light from the high eighteenth-century window streams in upon the fresh, intelligent face of the little boy. It is a classic illustration of the Age of Enlightenment.

William's son Ben, the General's friend, followed his father as a politically radical MP for Norwich. He also led a somewhat surprising private life. On a visit to the Nightingales in Derbyshire he impregnated a local working-class girl, a milliner named Anne Longden. Ben brought her south, set her up comfortably in Petley Lodge, a pretty Gothick house not a mile from Hancox – one of at least six properties Ben owned in the area – and supported her throughout her five pregnancies, the third of which produced Milicent's mother, Bella. But Ben and Anne never married.

The Smith family were deeply divided over Ben's behaviour. Some of them would have little to do with the illegitimate family. But Ben himself was a proud and devoted father to Barbara, Ben junior, Bella, Nannie and Willy. He added 'Leigh', his grandmother's maiden name, to their surname, to distinguish them from the sprawling masses of Smiths. Anne Longden died aged only thirty-two, from lung disease; thereafter, Ben lived with the children, dividing their time between Pelham Crescent in Hastings and Blandford Square in London. He was greatly assisted by two single women, his youngest sister Julia Smith ('Aunt Ju') and Anne's only surviving sister, Dolly ('Aunt Longden'). Thus the young Leigh Smiths had the interesting and unusual experience of forming equal attachments to two substitute mothers, one upper class and one working class.

Why did Ben fail or refuse to marry Anne Longden? It would be easy to assume that it was because of the social chasm between them, but it seems the reasons were more unusual and – inevitably, since Ben was a thorough Smith – political. Ben chose to make a stand against the conventions of marriage; he disapproved of the fact that, once married, a woman forfeited any right to property of her own and became little more than one of her husband's chattels. Anne Longden's own thoughts on the subject are not recorded. Ben's stance would seem more honourable were it not for the fact

that, on his death, his Leigh Smith children discovered to their
shock and dismay that after Anne's death he had kept another,
similar ménage, in Hammersmith, the offspring of whom were
named Bentley Smith. There were even rumours of a third family,
here in Sedlescombe. My grandfather Alan said that old Ben's three
families were deliberately upper, middle and lower class, as an
affront to the class system. However, it is difficult to see Ben as a
wholly selfless social experimenter. There is no evidence that the
Leigh Smiths (the 'upper-class' family) attempted to meet their
half-siblings.

General Ludlow was a charitable, tolerant man. Though not a
Unitarian himself – he was a Low Church Anglican – he shared
their ideals of public service. He was much beloved by friends, family and employees. References to him invariably mention his kindness and patience, qualities he was to need in spades once, at the
age of fifty-eight, he proposed marriage to 29-year-old Bella Leigh
Smith. The General must have looked forward to a comfortable old
age with his 'lovely, graceful dear wife elect', as a friend described
her. Such comfort was most emphatically denied him.

By the standards of his time, General Ludlow was unusually
broad-minded in asking an illegitimate woman to marry him. Ben
Smith believed passionately in education for women. At that time
there were few good schools for girls and no university would
admit them, but Ben tried to ensure that his three daughters were
as well read, as well travelled and as independently minded as his
two sons. When the girls came of age, he gave each of them £300
a year, not as a dowry, but so that they could be independent of
men and marriage should they so wish. In the eyes of many,
education and financial ease did not erase the stain of illegitimacy,
but the General was undeterred.

The General knew the family so well that he must have had
some idea of Bella's history of mental illness. As well as being
considered very handsome, Bella had artistic talent and was one of
a circle of female writers and artists. But her twenties had been
disrupted by a series of physical and mental breakdowns.

Bella was both protected and overshadowed by her two powerful older siblings, Barbara and Ben. Barbara was one of the most influential feminist campaigners of her time. As well as co-founding Girton, Cambridge, the first university college for women, she founded a progressive infant school and a night school. She founded and edited *The Englishwoman's Journal* with her friend Bessie Rayner Parkes (later Belloc) and was herself a well-travelled journalist. She campaigned for women's suffrage, and was the architect of the Married Women's Property Act, which enabled women to retain property independently of their husbands.

Barbara divided the year between Algiers, where she lived with her French husband, the politically radical and wildly eccentric Dr Eugène Bodichon, and England. She was a skilful watercolour artist who had studied under Corot, and she had many artistic and literary friends, including the Rossetti family, Dante Gabriel, William and Christina. She had a London house in Blandford Square which she shared with Aunt Ju, and a country house near Robertsbridge which she designed herself, called Scalands Gate. Scalands is about five miles from Hancox. Her friend Gertrude Jekyll helped her lay out the garden. 'Barbara . . . knows every plant she has planted & watches them with a mother's care her garden will be in another year a second volume to her house [and] will present a history of her life & travels in the form of leaves, flowers, fruit from at least three of the world's quarters,' wrote Aunt Ju. Barbara was the first person to guess the true identity of George Eliot when *Adam Bede* was published. She had a great gift for friendship, and was one of the very few women brave enough to continue to visit Marian Evans (George Eliot) once she began her 'sinful' cohabitation with George Lewes. After Lewes's death she invited Marian to come and live with her, showing characteristic disregard for public opinion. The invitation was received gratefully, but declined.

It is easy to imagine that Bella was overwhelmed by her spectacular older sister. Her brother Ben was an even more forceful character. The youngest Leigh Smith sister, Nannie, described Ben as having 'personal <u>influence</u> that subtle thing that makes a person a power without even uttering a word'. He was a scientific explorer who made five expeditions to uncharted Arctic regions. On the fifth, his ship sank. Ben's force of character became evident. Under his command, the entire crew survived eight months of a polar winter unscathed, living off walruses and polar bears.

'Aunt Bar' and 'Uncle Ben' were to be highly influential figures in the young Milicent's life, and she inherited some of their energy and determination. Her mother Bella, however, was not made of the same stern stuff.

As a young woman, Bella was popular and admired – a marble bust by the Pre-Raphaelite sculptor Alexander Munro has something of the Greek goddess about it – and she received and refused offers of marriage. She was liable to hysterical outbursts, which culminated in a breakdown in health in 1856. Barbara, who though sometimes meddlesome was perceptive and sympathetic, was sure that her sister's physical condition was strongly linked to her mental state. She took Bella off to the Isle of Wight to recuperate. From here she wrote to Ben junior, '. . . the mind has so much to do with her disease . . . Her unhappiness is of years' standing.' It seems that Bella was obsessed with unrequited or unfulfilled love, probably for the radical publisher John Chapman, a handsome adulterer who had already had romantic entanglements with George Eliot and with Barbara herself.

'Her mind runs on the subject of love and marriage and all the force of her long pent up passionate nature has burst forth,' wrote Barbara to Ben. 'Twice she has seized and hurt me – today she tried to throw herself out of the window. I caught hold of and pulled her back after she had broken the glass and cut herself . . . I am sure, she will never be well unless she marries.' It was John Chapman who had introduced Barbara to the idea that sexual frustration was bad for women's physical and mental health. But the sad truth was that marriage – or rather its consequence, childbirth – caused Bella's problems to escalate.

One of my great discoveries in researching this book was a series of small notebooks, stowed away in an old suitcase in the attic. The notebooks are filled with tiny cramped pencilled handwriting. They are General Ludlow's diaries; he wrote an entry almost every single day for the last twenty-three years of his life. They provide an unusually complete record of a Victorian gentleman's domestic world; the General noted details about family, friends, servants, horses, dogs, houses, carriages, food, drink, health, weather, trees, money, clothes . . . Occasionally a political event is noted; even more occasionally God is thanked for his mercy, but the General was not given to pious musings or introspection, which makes the diaries all the more valuable from a historical point of view. I've found, in my researches, that feelings can shine through facts but facts are rarely detectable through descriptions of feelings.

The diaries show that the General courted Bella throughout the spring and summer of 1859, three years after her breakdown on the Isle of Wight, and that much of the courtship was conducted on horseback. The General was a fine horseman and was to pass his enthusiasm on to his children, hence Mabel and her hunters, stabled here at Hancox. His rides with Bella were long and adventurous; from central London they rode to Kew, to Sevenoaks, to his relations at Wimbledon and hers, the Bonham Carters, at Ravensbourne, near Bromley. On 6 July he presented Bella with a puppy, and they rode from six thirty until ten. On the eleventh, he made his proposal. The diary entry simply reads, 'Never to be forgotten.'

Bella's acceptance of the proposal must have given rise to a communal sigh of relief. The huge age gap — twenty-nine years — apparently passed without comment. Bella's mental instability did not alter the family's devotion to her. Nonetheless, having the General to shoulder the burden of care must have been a weight off everybody's mind.

I have the letter Bella wrote to her brother Ben about the engagement — one of the very few letters of hers that I have found. The tone is curiously subdued, her own feelings almost submerged in deference to her brother. 'My dear Ben, I want you to write to tell me you are glad. General Ludlow & I are engaged to be married . . .

The Pater is very much pleased about this.' Soon, Ben junior's powerful role in the family was to be strengthened still further. Old Ben, the 'Pater', was dying. He was too ill to attend Bella's wedding at Brightling church (near Robertsbridge), though the bridal party went up to his bedroom at Glottenham Manor after the ceremony to receive his blessing. But it was Ben junior who gave Bella away, escorting her up to the church, where most of the parish was waiting to admire the bride. Local schoolchildren presented bunches of flowers. Aunt Ju described the scene in a letter to her oldest sister, Patty Smith – 'the bride so radiant and her gentle serious benignant bridegroom'.

The Pater died six months after Bella's wedding. His children buried him next to their mother, Anne Longden, in St Edmund's Church, Wootton, on the Isle of Wight, where she had died twenty-seven years earlier, having been taken to the island by Ben senior in a last desperate attempt to cure her lung disease. Barbara, helped by George Eliot, composed the inscription for her father's tomb; it shows how important 'civil and religious liberty' was to the Leigh Smiths:

> He was an ardent advocate of civil and religious liberty and of every measure which could promote the wellbeing of mankind. He supported for twenty years the first Infant School in England. He gave hearty and generous assistance to migration. He loved the arts and sciences and was an active friend to their Diffusion among the people.

It is characteristic of Barbara's courageous disregard for contemporary notions of respectability that she buried her father alongside the woman he loved but never married.

*

It was just as well that the Pater died before the birth of Bella's first child. After the wedding, the Ludlows had a month's honeymoon, first in the West Country and then in Ireland. There are no hints of trouble in the General's diary for the first few months, unless one counts the couple's strange inability to settle. There was plenty of money on both sides, but they moved from house to house, often staying with family, looking for a home but unable to make up their minds. Once, when the General's train was delayed by a break-down, he notes 'poor dear B. alarmed by the ½ hour's delay', which seems an overreaction. More understandably, Bella 'sustained a fright' when a four-wheeler ran into her brougham, but the General was confident that 'a hot bath will restore her comfort and compos-ure.' There was little to warn him of the coming catastrophe.

On 1 December 1860 'my darling Bella gave birth to a little girl – a sweet fair little thing – very lovely – the nose is large for its face and may be considered like Ben's.' The birth itself was easy enough – 'Everything has gone well with the dear mother. God be praised for his goodness.' But after a few days Bella was 'restless . . . excited . . . she wanders . . . rather silent or talks to herself'. Bella became insom-niac: 'No sleep last night. Excitement while the Drs were here.' Mesmerism was tried, but to no avail. Ben came, bringing violets, but could not soothe her. Bella hysterically rejected baby Amabel. A wet nurse was swiftly engaged. Seventy-five-year-old Hannah Walker, who had nursed the Leigh Smith children in infancy and brought them up on Sussex songs and folk tales, was called in to help. It was hoped that her familiarity would comfort Bella. In February she wrote to Bella's sister Nannie, who was in Algiers:

My dear dear Miss I was so glad to hear from your self as I am not rite you on account of our dear Mrs Ludlow but ham trying to tell you she is sertainly better and will son be quite well and love her dear little baby she takes a grate deal more notes of it than she did that will come to her when she gets well for she is a dear good baby and very pretty fair blue eyes you wil love her I know when you see her clearly poor dear I have shed many tears over her and her poor mama to it was very shockin but thank god she has one of the kindes of husbands the ever lived in every way that could be . . . please god to restore her to him quite well it is many years since I felt so fritened . . .

Little Amabel (Mabel) was christened on 1 March at St Margaret's, Westminster. Her mother was well enough to attend. The Ludlows decided to move to 9 Pelham Crescent, Hastings, where Bella had lived as a child; the General hoped the familiar house would make her feel calm and secure. Bella shopped for furniture, went to the dentist and 'to Miss Young's for a bonnet'.

The crisis was over. The Ludlows' new life at Hastings seems to have been active and lively. Nannie, back from Algiers, came to stay and brought a friend, Clementine; they 'dressed themselves up as an Arab woman and a Bey* – and frightened the Nurse – & the Cook – Amabel too woke up surprised with the song & beating of the tamtam'. There was a holiday, in Wales – 'The Welsh fleas are abominable fellows . . . we shall I doubt not enjoy our own home in the contrast.' Amabel was healthy and happy – 'Baby puts things upon her head & plays bopeep of her own accord'; 'Amabel looks charming in her little blue "Pork Pie" hat'; 'Amabel this morning when the early sun came peering in at the Nursery window ambitiously made an effort to puff it out – as she does the candle.'

Bella, though 'easily fatigued' and highly strung, seems to have resumed a normal life. But on 22 January 1862, less than thirteen months after her first confinement, 'her rest', as the General coyly put it, 'was disturbed – and at ½ p 7 a sweet little Boy was given to us – But what perils did both he and his sweet mother endure from his somewhat premature and unexpected birth!' This time, the General was careful to keep Bella as calm and quiet as could be. The only visitor allowed was her younger brother Willy, who lived near Hastings at Crowham Manor in Westfield. 'No other person out of the house has seen her not even her old nurse.'

It is alarming to read that, on the first day of his life, the premature baby 'has partaken freely of food prepared for him in the kitchen'. Bella wanted to breastfeed him, but the doctor decreed that 'her boy's feeding is not to be indulged in though she is very

---

* An Arab ruler or governor.

well and so is he.' The doctor also believed that the baby's early arrival was caused by a falling-out between Bella and the artist Joanna Samworth, a childhood friend. Their spat was thought to have 'startled Bella and caused her unpleasant feelings', inducing labour. An unlikely hypothesis to a twenty-first-century reader, but one which underlines the fragility of Bella's mental state.

Against the odds, baby Henry John (Harry) survived and throve. Bella escaped extreme post-natal depression and was soon drawing once more, and giving her husband sketching lessons. In December, Mabel's second birthday was celebrated with a party for the servants, each of whom invited a friend. Harry, a jolly baby, 'laughs when anyone says "Hot pies"'; Mabel was 'very charming and lovely'. Lady Brassey, wife of the railway tycoon, gave a 'splendid' ball at Beauport Park, near Hastings, where Bella, in her husband's opinion, was the finest looking woman among hundreds. Her mood swings were usually attributed to changes in the weather, or to the sea air, which was said to be 'too relaxing'.

It probably helped that, at this time, Bella's mind was focused on making drawings to sell at an exhibition organized by Barbara in aid of the Lancashire cotton workers. This was a classic Barbara project. In America, the Federal states had blockaded the southern Confederate states in an attempt to force them to put an end to slavery. The Confederates tried to break the blockade by continuing to sell cotton to the mills in the north-west of England. The Lancashire mill hands came out on strike, to show their desire to crush slavery. This was an extremely altruistic decision, as it severely impoverished the mill hands. Barbara, always the champion of those who put principles before self-interest, asked her friends to contribute pictures to her exhibition; the proceeds of the sale went to the relief of the cotton operatives and their families. The General was supportive of the project, and he was delighted to read in *The Times* 'a flourishing account' of the exhibition 'in which Bella has a foremost place and high commendation'.

It doesn't seem that Bella had a great deal of involvement with the day-to-day care of her children, but this would have been normal for a woman of her social position at this time. Any length of time in sole charge of them was a rare event. The General, always considerate to his employees, sent all the servants to watch the 'illuminations and bonfire on Castle Hill' to celebrate the marriage of the Prince of Wales to Alexandra, 'the fair daughter of the Dane', and while they were away, 'B. and I had charge of the Babies – who were disturbed by the firing – I took the Boy in hand and Bella undertook Mabel & we soon got them to sleep again not withstanding the uproar.'

On 16 May 1863, the General's sixty-second birthday, he notes that 'Bella is wonderfully well – she says she has never been so well & happy for years as at present – It is pleasing to hear this from her lips on my birthday.' Bella seemed settled in Sussex, her childhood home; there were frequent visits to her siblings: to Willy and his growing family at Crowham, to Barbara and her studio at Scalands Gate, and to Ben at Glottenham Manor. Nannie, not yet quite the professional invalid she was to become but already anxious to protect her lungs by wintering in hot climates, took a cottage near Crowham for the summer to spend time with her relations. Between them, the siblings did their best to provide a close, protective circle within which Bella could feel secure.

But ultimately, nothing and no one could achieve that for her. On 27 May 'at ¼ past three a fine little Boy was given to us – He is pronounced to be a very large and *well conditioned* infant. His dear Mother is thank God as well as possible – and charmed with her boy.' Mabel, two and a half, was not charmed. Her father noted her reaction on a scrap of paper, which I found in the suitcase with all the diaries:

> I don't like Mama's little baby-boy . . . I like this one (placing a hand on either side of her little brother Henry's face) –
> Funny little Baby, Mama's is – I can't like it – Mary [nursemaid] bought it in Castle St – I suspecks so.

Within a few days the symptoms that had plagued Bella after

Mabel's birth returned. 'She passed a restless night and at 4 a.m. I
sent the carriage for Dr Blundell & he . . . administered something
which . . . produced 2 hours sleep.' Ben, Willy and Barbara were
summoned (but not Nannie, who might 'excite her too much').
Ben and the General took it in turns to stay up with her at night.
Barbara helped by taking the children away and entertaining them.
This time, Bella did not reject the baby, and tried to breastfeed
him, but given the quantities of opiates she was prescribed it was
perhaps best for little Edmund Villeneuve Ludlow that the attempt
failed.

A change of scene was needed. It was also necessary to protect
Mabel and Harry from their mother's frightening and erratic
behaviour. Barbara made Scalands Gate ready for the General, and
for the two nurses who were employed to look after Bella. Ben
loaned Brown's, his pretty farmhouse near Glottenham, for the use
of the children and servants. The two houses are only a mile or so
apart. The General walked or rode over to see the children every
day before breakfast, gave orders to their carers ('I . . . scolded Mary
for allowing the Chn to pull about Ben's books') and played with
the older two in the garden and woods – 'the Girl and Boy had
foxgloves round their hats and looked excessively pretty.' Sometimes Bella went with him, but often she lay in bed, complaining of
a 'chipping' in her head. She began to show signs of paranoia and
sometimes gave her nurses the slip, frightening them by wan-
dering alone into the dense woodland that surrounded Scalands.

In late August she was well enough for a trip to the Isle of Wight
to visit her parents' tomb. She made an attempt to go to church,
but at the end of the second lesson she found the attention too
embarrassing – 'and we had to leave.' By November there was a
real improvement – 'it is pleasing to see her take up her pencil
again with real effect . . . Bella is much amused with Harry's little
tricks – she spoke today of riding about with me and contriving
always to keep well & going where we please.'

The family returned to Hastings. The diary chronicles the dramas of domestic life. 'Mappy [Mabel] had on her new braided

frock & was sick in the carriage'; 'I last evening gave George Snoad
the coachman warning to leave our service in consequence of his
improper intimacy with our late parlourmaid Louisa Clarke.' (Not
long after this the General mentions that Louisa Clarke has found
employment as a wet nurse.) 'Adams Smith [Bella's most eccentric
uncle] blackened the paper in the dining room by rubbing his oiled
wig against it when leaning back on the couch after having partaken
largely of pickled salmon.' (I'm particularly fond of this last detail,
because in one of the Hancox photograph albums there's a picture
of Uncle Adams wearing what must be this same disagreeable wig.)

Bella's physical health began to be more of a worry than her
mental state. Sometimes she spat blood after coughing, and her teeth
gave her much trouble; '[the dentist] deplored the sad condition of
poor dear Bella's teeth – the result of acids having been administered
medically.' Dental appointments were made, which at the last
minute Bella refused to attend. The General made himself a 'corpus
vili' as he called it, undergoing unnecessary treatment in order to
reassure her. At this stage Bella was not suffering from delusions or
extreme paranoia, but she was still a bundle of nerves:

> Dec 8th 1864. Yesterday Mr Ticehurst [the doctor] called he said
> that Bella's pulse was 'as weak as water' – and that she was 'worth
> nothing' – In the evg poor dear she was hysterical.
> 26th Dec. The servants forgot the night light – Poor dear Bella
> cried – but she got some eau de cologne – and was better in the
> last hours of the night and had some sleep.

Though the General never breathed a word of criticism of his
wife, the strain began to tell:

> Bella did not sleep well last night & I had the nightmare and
> fancied I was lying close to a Bis-cobera [cobra] – could not get
> out of its way and was obliged to strike it with my fist as a means
> of killing it! Poor Bella rec'd some thumps on the shoulder from
> my forearm before she could wake me.

There were concerns about little Harry's health, too. He had an inflammation of the eyelids so severe that he couldn't open his eyes for six days, and he was prone to digestive troubles. I doubt the doctor's suggestion that the three-year-old consume a mutton chop every day for breakfast and a glass of wine each evening helped much. In May 1865 the whole family, plus a courier, two nurses and a couple of female servants, set off to the Continent to undergo a series of 'cures'.

By the time they reached Ems, a spa town in Germany, the General himself was suffering, from herpes and an enlarged liver. He was ordered to wear a special belt and to try 'Mr Banting's rusks' – '[the doctor] says he shd like to see my girth brought within narrower proportions.' (Mr Banting was the inventor of a hugely popular weight-loss programme, the forerunner of the many schemes with which the modern reader is all too familiar.) The General stuck to the doctor's orders: '1st July. I have taken today inclusive 26 bottles of Marien-Kreutz [water] – 16 Baths and 14 Douches – enough one wd think to wash out the ills which flesh is heir to tho' their name were legion!' Meanwhile, the children revelled in the strawberries that grew in the hotel garden. When chastised by the gardener for picking them, Harry declared that 'he must have some strawberries and that if they were to go to prison all would have to go together.'

The family moved on by stages to Bern. The General notes all the usual hazards of travelling with small children – motion sickness, broken nights, fussy eating, 'biting flies'. I'm impressed to find how much the sixty-four-year-old father took upon himself, despite the presence of the servants. 'Little Edmund slept with me . . . I hardly closed an eye from anxiety about my dear little charge who looked inexpressibly lovely.' Most of the difficulties, however, seemed to focus on Harry's behaviour:

> 15th July. Harry roared for a Donkey – as he went along the
> streets repeating 'I want a Donkey' about 100 times and crying all
> the while to the surprise of the water drinkers.

19th. We feared that Harry's noise had driven away . . . Princesse
Glyka together with her Lord, a black Poodle, and a <u>superb</u> parrot.
24th. At the table d'hôte . . . Harry a little riotous and we had to
beat a retreat before the cheese was served.
29th August. Little Harry's 'Blanket' from which he was . . .
almost inseparable was left at Lungern.

One can imagine the consequences.

Difficulties escalated when Fanny, the nursemaid the Ludlows
had brought with them from Hastings, became suicidally depressed
and threatened to throw herself into the Rhine. The cause turned
out to be an unhappy love affair with Mr Croft, the ticket collector
at St Leonard's railway station. Fanny feared he would not wait for
her. Since Mr Croft not only had 'inward tumours' but also 'a
child at Etchingham' (a village five stops up the line), he doesn't
sound like much of a catch, but the ever-gallant General left Bella
and the children in the care of the courier and accompanied Fanny
back to her family in Hastings. 'I took the Mother behind the
house . . . I told her that we had done everything in our power to
soothe her and that we did not know how her revelations regard-
ing her conduct took their colour from a disordered brain.'

Leaving one 'disordered brain' behind, the General returned to
another, more familiar one and the family continued their journey
to Bern. 'The scenery . . . must be one of the loveliest spots of the
known world . . . But oh the horror of the legion of creeping
things that infested the beds! . . . at about 6 a.m. we were all in the
small parlour drinking tea and coffee – neither Bella nor myself
has appetite for breakfast after having been preyed upon thro' the
night by the foul insect.' They moved on to Bex, where Bella
'resolutely' embarked on the 'grape cure' – 'she is to eat 6 or 7lb in
a day . . . a work of labour.'

The regime of grapes, beer and medicated baths did some good
and she was able to enjoy walking and experimenting with oil
paints. She and the General chose Tyrolean costumes for the children and had them photographed, but prolonged contact with

them wore her out. Increasingly, she withdrew from them. Mabel befriended some Swiss children; she invited them to her birthday tea, at which the hotelier produced a cake in the shape of a chalet, with 'Mabel's name beautifully written in sugar plums' upon it. Two-year-old Edmund was the life and soul – after downing a bumper of red wine he 'mounted . . . upon the table glass in hand pronouncing that "the wine was good" – He insisted on "hob-a-nobing" with everyone and his animated good fellowship was the admiration of everyone.' But poor little Harry was disturbed by his mother's inability to tolerate his company for long: 'Harry we fear moped a good deal in the absence of his Mama yesterday – Mary says he sat on a couch and told people not to speak to or to touch him'; 'Harry scratched Mary's face a good deal when she took him upstairs yesterday. He pulled her hair.' Unluckily for Harry, Bella punished him by more withdrawal: 'Harry appears to have got into a passion at dinner and to have thrown things at Wirtz [the courier] and Hannah [a maid] . . . His mama will not take him in her lap or give him cakes for some Days and the little Darling seems very sorry for what he has done amiss.' The Ludlows were liberal parents; the General, unusually for a mid-Victorian father, absolutely forbade corporal punishment of any kind. But for Harry, banishment from his mother's lap must have been worse than any slap.

In the spring of 1866 the Ludlows returned to Ems to take the waters once more before leaving for home. They were anxious to get back; they missed family and friends, and besides, war was threatened between Prussia and Austria. This was the Seven Weeks' War, in which Bismarck established Prussian dominance over Austria as the leading German-speaking country. The hotels were emptying fast. 'Great numbers of Prussian soldiers are passing eastwards from the Rhine – and everything now appears to indicate impending war.' Rails were being taken up near Ems, presumably to check the progress of the enemy. The Countess Bismarck, who was staying in the same hotel, told them that her husband had received bad tidings and urged them 'to go away tomorrow by any means'.

With dreadful timing, Bella suffered a swift and sudden relapse. Insomnia, hysteria, muttering to herself . . . all the dreaded symptoms were back. The doctor 'says her illness is <u>nothing</u>' but '<u>exhaltation nerveuse</u>', but it can't have felt like nothing to the General as he filed the rings off her fingers at 1 a.m., fingers that she had injured in her attempts to tear the rings off herself. Sleeplessness wore down the whole family: '15th June. I have kept on my day dress . . . at night since B. has been ill as she has had to take her composing draught every hour or two hours & I have administered it to prevent mistakes . . . I tried to control the agitation and restlessness of my dear patient.' Edmund showed signs of disturbance and refused to sleep: 'I gave him strawberries – I coddled him & told him stories in turn with small effect.' Even the uncomplaining General admitted, 'I felt a little done up from want of rest etc I suppose.'

The political situation was so grave that the General decided they must set off for home, though Bella was hardly fit to travel. The family rallied round to receive them: '21st June. A brilliant morning to welcome us to our native shores . . . Ben met us at [Charing Cross] . . . Barbara came this evening.' They stayed at Ben's London house, 64 Gower Street. Nannie was also in town, with Isabella Blythe, the woman who was to be her life partner. 'Isa', plump and cheery where Nannie was gaunt and prickly, was a great favourite with the children, teaching them to play draughts and taking them to the zoo.

The General was stoutly optimistic: 'When [Bella] has had the requisite amount of repose her poor head will become clear and composed.' But repose was not to be had in London. Ben again lent them Brown's, his Sussex farmhouse. For the children, life at Brown's was an idyll of fishing, haymaking, mushrooming, and visits from their Crowham cousins. The General was in his element with them: 'I brought home a basket of apples to make dumplings for the Children . . . I carried Edmund down Scalands Lane on my shoulders. His head was among the young branches & we walked backwards – to his great delight'; 'Took the chn & Mary in the Fly to Glottenham where I feasted them at supper with Chicken & Ham & Mabel said she was never so happy in her life.'

But they could not stay in Ben's house for ever. The General decided to rent Sir Patrick Colquhoun's house at Penshurst in Kent for £150 a year. Typically, as soon as the deal was done he 'rode to Tunbridge and bought 50 yards of extra-sized wire netting to prevent the Chn falling into the water at the bottom of the grounds'. Bella expressed herself pleased with the house, but she holed herself up in her bedroom, took her meals in bed and sometimes refused to get up even to have the sheets changed. Her sisters were leading active and interesting lives. Nannie bought a beautiful house in Algiers, Campagne Montfeld, where she set up home with Isabella Blythe and took part in the life of the artistic expatriate community. Barbara's myriad activities included publishing her paper, 'Reasons for the Enfranchisement of Women'. She also enlisted her cousin Florence Nightingale's help in an effort to get the General's anti-suttee activities in India formally recognized and honoured. But poor Bella burned her drawings, hacked off her hair, and angrily dismissed servants who got on her nerves. (They were usually quietly reinstated by the General after a short cooling-off period.)

Mabel's sixth birthday was celebrated on 1 December with the usual party for the servants, at which '2 bottles of Champagne 2 of Port & 2 of sherry' were disposed of. 'There was some singing . . .' But Bella did not improve – 'Still she talks and laughs!' The General consulted Dr Tuke, the most progressive psychiatric doctor of his time, who said that he had 'no power over the malady and that he must leave it to nature to work a cure'. This was at least an honest response, and possibly more helpful, or less harmful, than the opiates that had been prescribed for years, but the poor General felt '*ill* with the sad disappointment'. Brother Ben came for Christmas, but Bella locked the door against him. 'We made an effort to be cheerful' but 'it is a sad Xmas day for us.' In the midst of his troubles, the General continued the acts of charity that were habitual to him. 'I gave £5 for the poor . . . poor things they must need coals in this severe weather.'

The weather was at first blamed for little Edmund's indisposition. 'The frost disagrees with him . . . he seems rather sleepy and dull.' His symptoms quickly worsened. He ate and slept little, and his tongue was coated. The General never mentions diphtheria, but this is what it sounds like to me. '14th January 1867. The dear child is very thin and weak – He had 2 Roasted apples & little bits of pheasant today . . . he said "Don't like the doctor, Go away doctor."' Since the doctor prescribed laxative powders and injections of beef tea and port wine, Edmund's reaction is unsurprising. His devoted father sat by his bedside and fed him little bits of boiled chicken, but by 26 January 'the child no longer speaks . . . and he does not open his mouth to take his food . . . I went to Tunbridge for calves feet to make jelly.' Poultices were applied, but to no avail.

On Edmund's third birthday, the year before in Ems, his father had proudly described him as 'A beautiful and fine child as is anywhere to be seen . . . He is perfectly good moreover. The delight of us all and of no trouble to anyone - He is a favourite wherever he goes.' I found a photograph of him from this time, standing on a chair in his tiny Tyrolean costume. But on 30 January it was all over. His father was by his side. 'His end was so peaceful that there was no movement of the body or convulsion to indicate the moment when the breath of life ceased. Bella and I felt, as he lay beautiful in death that we did not desire our glorious child restored to us so fit as he was for Heaven whither his sweet spirit had fled!'

In the aftermath of Edmund's death Bella sank deeper into insanity. 'She covered her head with grease and threw a pack of the chn's cards into the fire.' 'I sat up last night to ascertain whether Bella slept – not a wink!' Self-harming was a risk – 'We got down all the looking glasses and turned the pictures – altogether a wretched day.' She was agitated by Ben's visits and often refused to see him. When the General visited Edmund's grave and planted sweet-briar near it, he did so alone.

With the arrival of bright spring weather, Bella underwent a sudden transformation. On 3 April, 'the children made gardens

for themselves and Bella sat out on the terrace . . . We all went to
Tunbridge & bought spades, rakes etc for the children.' She sewed
a cap for the General; she had done the same thing at the end of
her illness following Mabel's birth. On 26 April Bella's nurse
moved out of her mistress's bedroom and the General moved in –
'a visible sign I trust of my dear Bella's complete recovery'.

The result of this return to normality was the conception of
Milicent. It seems extraordinary to my twenty-first-century sensibility that, since Bella's breakdowns were closely connected to giving birth, it did not occur to the doctors or to the General to take
steps to avoid another pregnancy. But perhaps the desire to fill the
gap left by Edmund was overpoweringly strong. At all events, by
July Bella knew she was pregnant, and I'm glad she was, because if
it hadn't been for Milicent, I wouldn't be living at Hancox now.

It was of course necessary to leave Penshurst and its unhappy
associations. The General engaged Guestling Lodge, a few miles
east of Hastings, for five guineas a week. It was rather small (there
were twelve of them, including servants and the General's middle-
aged niece Fanny Walton, who had arrived from Australia for an
indefinite stay) and the kitchen fireplace smoked abominably, but
it was within visiting distance of Willy and family, Ben, Barbara
and all their old Hastings friends. Bella's pregnancy went smoothly.
She remained on an even keel: she played vingt-et-un in the evenings with the children, escorted her niece Amy back to her Hastings boarding school, and even played the part of a dwarf in a
'pageant' got up for Harry's birthday.

Aunt Jenny, Willy's wife, took Mabel and Harry to stay at
Crowham as Bella's confinement approached. Milicent's arrival
was swift. On 8 March 1868 the General writes:

I went up & found B. standing and leaning on the back of a chair
– she presently said that she thought it must be so, and I ran off to
expedite the dispatch of the Brougham to bring Ticehurst or any
other Dr. and then I ran back to the house – and found the dear
little baby girl had appeared on the stage of existence before the

horses could be put to! – I don't think Bella was ill ten minutes.
She got into Bed and her Baby was born on the instant – a lively
little creature, who promises to be the image of herself.

Aunt Jenny, visiting a few days later, in a rare burst of generous
feeling proclaimed Milicent Bella to be the prettiest baby she had
ever seen.

The General gathered wood anemones and celandines and
brought them home in his hat for Bella. Bella nursed Milicent for
five weeks, until the doctor decided that the breast 'did not afford
sufficient nourishment' and prescribed an Alderney cow. As soon as
the breastfeeding stopped, Bella's troubles began. The ever-patient
General began to express his frustration with the doctors. 'Ticehurst . . . said "I am delighted, Sir, I am delighted – I find her much
better." – But she has not slept for two nights at all – "Never mind
an increased dose will give her sleep. She must be kept like a man
with a broken leg – quiet in bed – and as composed as possible."'

The increased dose gave Bella an eruption on the palms of her
hands. In the past, she had often refused medicine or spat it out.
Now she was inclined to swallow anything and everything, 'so I
had everything in the shape of medicine moved out of the way'. On
the rare occasions when Bella left the house the carriage had to be
kept moving 'so B. was not troubled by anyone speaking to her'. A
dread of being watched was an increasing problem. On 13 June she
ran away, and got herself as far as the Queen's Hotel in Hastings.
But there was to be no escape for her. Dr Ticehurst brought her
home in his carriage. She raged at him, and gave him his professional
dismissal. The tactful General later reinstated him, of course.

On 22 June, Milicent was christened at Guestling church. Her
godparents were Ben, Barbara and Lady Ashburnham, a landown-
ing friend and neighbour. 'Everything was fresh and beautiful.
The Baby uttered a little querulous gabble throughout the service –
and seemed quite in good humour with herself.' Little Milicent,
the youngest member of the family by seven years, was the pet of
all – her father, Mabel and Harry, the servants, her aunts, uncles

and cousins. She spent a comfortable infancy surrounded by natural beauty, breathing clean country air and feeding on the fruit and vegetables that grew abundantly in the garden. There was plenty of money; she was amply supplied with clothes, toys and a state-of-the-art perambulator – they were a recent innovation – costing £4.16/0, chosen by her father in London and dispatched for 'the dainty little lady'. But she never experienced love from her mother. Bella had five years left to live. In that time, her insanity was never in remission for longer than a few weeks; typically, the bright spells were over in a matter of days. The mother Milicent knew was an unpredictable creature who talked to herself, laughed at nothing, banged tunelessly on the piano for hours at a time, smashed windows and ornaments, attacked the portraits in the hall, set fire to her bedclothes, threw her meals on the floor but devoured lumps of coal and wax, rubbed dirt into her hair and skin, and screamed at the people who tried to help her.

For Mabel and Harry, some memories must have remained of Bella the beautiful, the talented artist, the woman who cut a graceful figure on horseback by their father's side, the finest-looking woman at Lady Brassey's ball. They had known, albeit intermittently, a mother who read to them, played cards with them, helped them make their little gardens. For Milicent, there was never any such mother.

Two letters survive, sent by Bella to her nieces Amy and Roddy in the summer of 1868, when she was in London with the General undergoing – or refusing to undergo – yet more dental treatment. The letters are prettily illustrated with pen-and-ink doodles. They suggest a warm, chatty relationship with her two little nieces: 'My dear Roddy, I am sure you do not think that I have forgotten you . . .' 'The harvest has been great fun to you I should not be surprised, we have a parlor maid here as old as sixteen that has never seen a growing wheat field. The other day your Uncle Ludlow and I bought a wedding present for one of the Miss Alves [family friends] . . . Do you think she will like it? It is a necklet a heart in turquoise on a gold chain and can be worn as a bracelet. Your affectionate Aunt my own Amy – B.L.L.' These letters were written during the last patch of almost normal life for Bella, before she became for ever trapped in the endless dark tunnel of insanity.

Her illness caused tensions in the wider family. Aunt Jenny became reluctant to allow Amy, Roddy and Willy-boy to stay with their Ludlow cousins. Even the stalwart Ben expressed reservations about having Bella to stay. Barbara was a generous sister – she offered the Ludlows her London house in Blandford Square, which they declined – but her decided views about the correct treatment for Bella clashed with the General's. 'Barbara in her letter of the 28th writes "My friend Octavia Hill [later, the founder of the National Trust] has got quite well from a nervous and mental derangement by going away from home entirely and putting herself under the Doctor at Brn Rydden." This in Bella's case is the worst advice that could be offered – advice that it is in vain to press upon me and which I must resist – come what may.'

The General continued to record the quotidian detail – the wife of the butcher's man was imprisoned for stealing a turkey; 'the gardener killed his pig today "to save its life". He says he will eat it however! It had been very ill lately – and was off its food and became "cripply-like".' A fox was killed by hounds in the melon-bed opposite the garden greenhouse; the Princess of Wales (Princess Alexandra) visited Hastings, spotted Milicent and said 'What a pretty baby.' But Bella would no longer come down to prayers, nor would she take her meals with her husband.

Once again, it was decided that moving house was the answer. They moved back into Hastings, to Warrior Square Gardens. Ben's visits brought good cheer. He played chess with Bella, who beat him, and took Mabel and Harry on the sands. 'Mabel got her green silk dress splashed & injured so that it must be turned – if not given up! – Ben told the chn that he "wd bear the blame".' A visit from Barbara was less successful. Barbara, deeply distressed by her sister's condition, upset Bella with a stream of intrusive questions. Barbara 'went away crying. There was no doubt much excitement on one side and apparently great want of tact on the other.'

The doctors continued to be of little help. Dr Tuke, the London specialist, 'said a great deal of it was temper and that she could control it if she chose to do so'. Increasingly, the General realized that he was on his own, both in his understanding of his wife and in his determination not to send her away or lock her up but to keep her, as far as possible, at the heart of family life.

He acknowledged, though, that the children sometimes had to be protected from her. They needed more space; it was now unthinkable to do without two full-time carers for Bella. In May 1869, when the General was sixty-eight and Milicent one and a bit, he engaged Yotes Court, near Mereworth in Kent, for £300 a year furnished. The rent was by no means the only expense; three gardeners and a boy had to be employed, at a cost of £153.12/– per annum. Yotes Court was far larger and grander than anywhere the Ludlows had yet lived. It was to be Milicent's home for the rest of her childhood.

3. 'Every old house must have its ghost'

In the drawer of a desk at Hancox I found a pile of exercise books from Milicent Ludlow's days in the schoolroom at Yotes Court. The 'compositions' are written in a copper-plate hand with a neatly ruled margin, very different from the smudgy scrawl, bedecked with doodles, of her two little diaries that survive from 1882 and 1883. The compositions cover the usual incongruous mix of topics: 'The Story of a Thimble'; 'Edward III 1327–1377'; 'The Dog' ('The Dog is of the family of Canidae or Dog, and belongs to the order of the Carnivorous Mamalia', etc). Then there's a lively account of hop-picking, a Kentish activity in which Milicent was allowed to participate each September.

The titles were presumably prescribed by the governess – Miss Northnagel or Miss Kahn – but Milicent managed to slip in some personal and family details. 'The Zoological Gardens' contains a description of Sampson, the polar bear brought back on the *Diana* by Uncle Ben. 'Close behind Sampson's house there rises a path, and when we had reached a certain height above the den we put some bits of bun and bread on an overhanging ledge, and the bear stood up on his hind legs and ate it in a most obliging manner.' Aunt Barbara's influence is apparent in a 'Short Essay on Knotty Points'; the 'knotty points' are women's rights: 'Why were [women] created? Only for the continuation of that poor race called Man? Only to wash clothes, cook food or clean houses? No! emphatically no!!'

When Milicent was twelve she wrote a composition entitled 'Description of Yotes Court':

Part of Yotes Court in the parish of Mereworth was built by James Masters in the year 1658. The rest was added early in the 18th century. The front door opens into a large stone hall, about 60 feet

long. Many family pictures hang on the walls, and there is an old
leather chair, in which Admiral Byng is said to have sat the night
before his execution . . . A door opens into one of the drawing-
rooms, which is now used as a dancing room, and another door
into the little hall, from which a door leads to the second drawing
room . . . From the little hall a square staircase leads to the upper
storey, a morning room (in which there is an old cabinet with
secret drawers), the state room, where the Queen slept, when she
was Princess Victoria, and a few other bedrooms.

The kitchen chimney is very wide, and the meat used formerly
to be turned by spits, and there are still a spit and a few more
kitchen utensils which were used in olden times.

The garden is large and very pretty. Just behind the house it is
laid out in an old-fashioned way. There is a large old stump covered with ivy, which gives a curious appearance; and there is also a
silver fir, which was struck by lightning some years ago. Before it
was struck, it was about 125 feet high, it is said to have been the
highest tree in Kent. 30–35 feet came off. A fine old holly hedge
separates the flower garden from the kitchen garden. There are
two hot houses and a greenhouse.

. . . A beautiful avenue leads up to the house. Close to a large
pond, with a little island on it, are the remains of two walls, where
there might once have been a monastery. Just outside the avenue is
a tributary of the Pilgrim's Road.

Of course every old house must have its ghost, and in Yotes
Court the little hall is haunted!

This was the formative environment for Milicent. Life at Yotes set
the standard for her and helps to explain why, aged only twenty-
one, she wanted to take on Hancox. A house with a history, walled
gardens, fine trees . . . though Yotes is built on a grander scale and
is stately and elegant where Hancox is higgledy-piggledy and agricultural, it's easy to imagine how much the orphaned young woman,
forced by circumstances to give up Yotes, would have enjoyed establishing her own domain at Hancox.

I visited Yotes Court not long ago. It was a dark January day, with traces of snow clinging to the edges of the leaves. First I stopped at Fordcombe church, near Penshurst. I knew that Bella had joined little Edmund in the tomb there, but I was surprised and somehow delighted to find the rest of them there too – the General himself, and Harry, and Mabel, and even Mabel's cousin-husband Ludlow Coape Ludlow. The inscriptions get shorter as space runs out. The only one who's not there is Milicent herself. She's here in Sedlescombe, with NM.

I drove on to Yotes. The internet told me to expect a hotel, but that enterprise had folded; and the big house stood empty. That was perfect for my purposes. Without fear of interruption I trespassed happily in the half light through the garden and peered in through the unshuttered windows. Some melancholy vestiges of the hotel remained – a reception desk, a bar, a bizarre bunker-like 'conference suite' in the grounds – but these twentieth-century scars were quite superficial. I could see the size and scale of the rooms and the staircase, still elegant in abandonment. The 'beautiful avenue' has gone, but the 'fine old holly hedge' is still fine. The lightning-struck silver fir, which Aunt Barbara hurried over to sketch as a noble ruin (I have the sketch), was replaced by a Wellingtonia grown from a seed brought back by Uncle Ben from California. Its planting is recorded in the General's diary. In one of the shoeboxes at Hancox, I found the piece of paper in which Ben had folded the seeds. It has a printed heading – 'Yo Semite Hotel. Yo Semite Valley. Cal.' In Ben's handwriting is simply written '18.10.75 Big Trees.' The Wellingtonia certainly is a big tree now. I wouldn't be surprised if it had replaced its predecessor the silver fir as the tallest tree in Kent.

It was strange and rather wonderful for me to walk round Yotes with the details of the General's diaries so fresh in my mind. I kept thinking, that's where Mabel and her friends played tennis and pretended they couldn't hear the dinner gong; that's where Milicent nearly got her foot run over by the brougham. When an Irish yew was planted in February 1878, nine-year-old Milicent 'put a paper in a bottle with a penny and placed it at the root of the young tree. It was all her own composition – she gave some pieces of contemporary history – relating to the Russo-Turkish War – the inauguration of Leo XIII & begged that the finder of the paper might send it to the British Museum!', the General recorded in his diary. That time capsule was probably still under the ground on which I was trespassing.

I knocked on the door of a neighbouring house, and found out that Yotes had recently been bought by a family planning to carry out an extensive programme of restoration and then move in. I was glad to hear there would be children living there again. Would they, like Milicent, believe in the ghost in the little hall? Or has that ghost been replaced by the spirit of a thin-faced woman with ashes in her hair who stood at the window gazing out at the empty park without prospect of escape?

*

The Ludlows moved into Yotes on 1 June 1869. Some of their old servants came with them, and in July there was an important addition to the household – Mrs Janet MacCreath, baby Milicent's new nurse. 'Creathy' seems to have been tough and practical but also affectionate. Aunts Nannie and Jenny considered her rather common, but the General came to rely on her very much, and every time she visited her sister in Glasgow she brought back a bottle of whisky for him as well as butterscotch and shortbread for the children. Milicent never parted company from her beloved Creathy, who morphed from children's nurse to housekeeper, seamstress and chaperone. Creathy eventually came with Milicent to live at Hancox, died there in 1892, and is buried, like her charge, in the graveyard at Sedlescombe.

The local doctor, Dr Hooker, was as helpless as all the others in the face of Bella's illness. His opinion was that she suffered from 'a Perversion of ordinary moral force'. But he supported the General's wish to keep Bella at home, and became something of a family friend. Bella was able or willing to hold conversations with him after she had almost ceased to communicate with the General or anyone else. Many of the pleasures life at Yotes should have afforded the General were denied him by Bella's condition. If he attempted to shoot, hunt, or entertain friends, often he would be summoned back to help deal with some fresh crisis. Saddest of all, he had no companionship with his beloved wife:

19 January. B . . . much disturbed after breakfast and everything removed from her bedroom as so much has been broken in the past 48 hours . . .
20th. I was called up at abt midnight. Poor B. highly excitable – no sleep for any of us. Wedding ring gone . . . into the fire.

The General worked hard to give his children a normal and happy childhood. He continued to involve himself with the minutiae of their lives, more so than many twenty-first-century fathers. He cut their hair, took them to the dentist, chose fancy-dress costumes for them for Bonfire Night, mended their toys, slept with them when they were frightened. In many ways, life at Yotes was like paradise. The children never knew material want. They had lessons in the schoolroom from a succession of apparently benign governesses, and they went to church twice or even three times on Sundays (and, as Milicent records in her diary in 1882, every day during Passion Week), but beyond these obligations they had plenty of time to ride, play tennis and croquet, fish and even swim in the Boat Pond, climb trees, go on picnics. Whatever the necessary limitations of the General's own social life, he made sure that the children had plenty of opportunity to make friends with the offspring of the local gentry. Harry's letters to his cousin Amy are carefree and typically boyish:

My dear Amy, I am going to have some white mice and some black ones and perhaps some others. You know our double hedge well I ran down from their to the schoolroom door in 15 seconds . . . I have found a great many birds nests and I think all together I must know of ten or more – four of them are robins, and two wrens, three thrushes and some others, we have four dogs now one is mine, one Baby's, and one Mabel's but the other is not ours for we gave her to Miss Bower [the governess]; Don't you remember the pillow-fights that we used to have?

Their many dogs included 'Niger', who used to collect the newspapers in his mouth from the omnibus at the turnpike gate; they had cats, canaries, fish; the sties were always full of sows and their litters (the General took a great interest in his pigs). The hot-houses were bursting with figs, peaches, grapes, nectarines, melons and cucumbers; the General often dispatched hampers of produce to friends, relations and former servants. The children's talents and interests were encouraged. Mabel and Harry were both good sing-ers; first-rate tutors were engaged. Mabel, like her mother and aunts, had artistic talent; Harry wrote poems and was the star bowler of the local boys' cricket team; Milicent, who was regarded as precocious, later also painted, and wrote plays and stories. Their father treated them with unswerving devotion.

But by the end of 1871 Bella was often 'abusive and violent'. Though the General still considered that 'any thing in the shape of Asylum restraint was simply out of the question', he was bending to the idea that something had to be done: 'There are the children to be considered as they cannot be suffered to see their mama should she not get much better very soon.' Mabel showed signs of anxiety by walking in her sleep, Harry suffered from digestive problems and loss of appetite, and Bella's nurses were stretched to the limit. It is almost a relief to read of Bella's physical health going into decline, which made her quieter and less frightening for the children.

She began to lose weight fast. I don't know how tall she was, but the Leigh Smiths were by and large a tall, thin family. In August 1872 she weighed 7 stone 3½lbs fully clothed, which when one considers the weight of a well-off Victorian woman's costume – at least 14lbs – is not very much. By November she had gained 8lbs: 'We drank her health in Champagne on the strength of it and they poured a liba-tion in the Servants Hall.' She rallied a little at this time, and the

General noted, poignantly, 'Bella fondled Baby quite naturally and earnestly this evening. It was quite delightful to see it.'

But in the early part of 1873 her decline was rapid. '31st Jan. I saw by chance B's calf of her leg last Evg. She appears to have become <u>much</u> thinner.' She refused to go to Tonbridge Station to be weighed, so the General ordered a weighing machine for the house. Mabel and Harry enjoyed the new toy and weighed everybody. Mabel sent the results in a letter to Amy: 'Papa weighs 12st 2lbs I weigh 6st 7lbs: Harry 5st 4¾lbs & Baby 36lbs.' Mrs MacCreath and five servants were also weighed. The one member of the household Mabel does not mention is her mother.

Bella began to spit blood. She refused medicine but accepted malt extract and rum-and-milk. By 25 February she weighed only 6 stone 9lbs, still fully clothed. The doctors had always denied that her symptoms were tubercular; now, it was clear that they had been wrong. The one redeeming aspect of these dark days was that the iller Bella grew, the more she seemed like her old self. She called for her writing things, asked the General to buy her the macaroons she particularly liked, and conversed 'more pleasantly than for a long, long period'.

The diary entry for 6 March 1873 is boxed in black:

I was called at 3.20 a.m. as Bella was represented as having been <u>sick</u>. My darling wife had a haemorrhaghic attack and passed away at 3.30 as peacefully as an infant falls asleep . . . We telegraphed to Barbara, Ben & WLS [Willy] . . . Barbara was here about noon. How good how true how loving, how beautiful was my darling – May the Almighty take her into his good keeping – and may her children emulate her goodness.

George Eliot, who had known Bella well before her marriage, wrote to Barbara, 'For her sake – even for the children's – the passing away seems a good,' but the General's diary expresses no sense of relief. His grief was deep and life-long. He lived for another nine years, and always noted the anniversary of Bella's death with sorrow. On 11 March he wrote, 'The people came today and soldered down the leaden coffin – and I had a last look on the face that I so dearly loved – a last kiss – alas – alas!' Three days later the funeral took place:

> Today the mortal remains of my sweet darling wife were consigned to the vault in Fordcombe churchyard and laid beside our sweet boy Edmund Villeneuve whose coffin appeared to be in perfect order – even to its cloth covering . . . Miss Greatorex [Bella's old friend] sent by Barbara the beautiful camellia wreath which was deposited on my loved one's coffin. It was a sweet and touching tribute to the memory of my pure and good and beautiful darling.

Not surprisingly, the General fell ill after the funeral and did not recover for several weeks. But as time wore on he began to enjoy the new freedoms that Bella's absence created. He made trips to London to see old friends and invited people to stay. Early visitors were Barbara and Amy, who 'paddled *nu-pied* in the watercress stream! which they ought not to have done. I was there and was over-persuaded.' This was typical Barbara behaviour. On another visit she brought 'some bottles of dyeing liquid and old ribbons and rags were sought out and dyed. The chn used their hands instead of the sticks and their hands were dyed also.'

Her red-gold hair coiled in a plaited crown, her flowing, loose-fitting clothes coloured by vegetable dyes in soft blues, greens and purples, in contrast to the tight-laced costumes in garish artificial colours favoured by most women of the period, Barbara does not conform to anyone's idea of a childless Victorian aunt. In William Rossetti's memoir he describes Barbara as 'a lady of ample but not very graceful form with a fine animated face, brilliant complexion & superb profusion of flame-golden hair . . . Her manner was replete with energy and heartiness: no woman could be freer from those small femininities which make for affectation. To be frank, straightforward, unprejudiced, generous minded, was a passport to her esteem; there was none other.' At Hancox we have some of that flame-golden hair, plaited into a bracelet. It's greenish-brown now, and a little macabre.

Barbara was on a mission to expand the horizons of all her nieces, but most especially Amy, who, she believed, was stifled at Crowham with her parents, Willy and Georgina ('Jenny'). Amy's parents had a far more conservative outlook than the rest of the family. Barbara said that in his youth her younger brother had been 'very handsome, and witty and merry, and the life of the house'. But now he had buried himself in the country and never travelled if he could avoid it. Neither he nor Jenny had much sympathy with Barbara's ideas about the education of women. True, they sent Amy to school, first in Hastings and then at Hampstead, but these were fairly dim establishments, where the girls were taught little more than the 'accomplishments' intended to make them more marriageable. Aunt Nannie, more outspoken even than Barbara, was horrified to find that Amy's young body was being deformed by the wearing of stays and wrote several fierce letters on the subject: 'I want very much to hear how you are getting on - & particularly that you have left off those horrible stays that make you look so awkward - & would make your back quite crooked if you went on wearing them.'

Amy was beautiful. In 1896, towards the end of her life, Amy and NM stayed at Down House with the Darwin family. Emma Darwin, Charles's widow, wrote of Amy, 'How superior anyone must feel with a nose such as hers!' Henrietta Darwin, editing her mother's letters, adds, 'My mother had a great admiration for chiselled noses.' Roddy, two years younger than Amy, shared her sister's high cheekbones and arched eyebrows, but not her beauty. Amy's features were delicate and ethereal, Roddy's bony and protuberant. Amy was tall (5 foot 7½), slender and graceful; Roddy, also tall, was awkward and spiky. As often happens with beautiful people, others read into Amy what they wanted to find. Ben, Barbara and Nannie all regarded her as special, gifted, a princess who needed rescuing from the prison of dullness in which her parents had confined her. There's no doubt that Amy was a bright girl, but then, so was Roddy. Attempts were made to rescue Roddy too, but they were half-hearted.

The summer following Bella's death, the Ludlows stayed at Glottenham. Nannie and Isabella Blythe were nearby at Scalands with Barbara. Nannie painted a portrait of Milicent in oils and loaded the bereaved children with exotic presents from Algiers; Isa took them to Hastings to bathe in the sea. Barbara got up music and dancing; true to her egalitarian instincts, servants and 'family' danced together. Barbara also organized a 'women's feast' for working-class women in the garden at Scalands; the General noted that there was 'not one even moderately good-looking among them – all looked to me as borne down and subdued by privation and toil.' Barbara was giving the children a taste of the active, benevolent, creative life of which she felt their mother's illness had deprived them.

Not long after Bella's death, Ben had set out for the Arctic in a screw steamer, the *Diana*. When he returned at the end of September, Nannie and Isa were staying at Yotes, soon to be joined by Willy, Jenny, Roddy and Willy-boy. It was an excited family party; Amy, away at school, was missing out. Isa wrote to Amy from Yotes; her letters were jollier and more affectionate than Aunt Nannie's: 'Your Uncle Ben is safe at home isn't that good!!!!! We expect the Crowhamites [Willy and family] . . . I wish my dear old Amyott you were coming too, how jolly it would be! Mabel has written a play and Willy Milicent and all of us take a part. I am at your service the old Count Montreal! In a dressing gown to hide my legs!!' Mabel's play was called *Never Say Die*. She sent Amy the *dramatis personae* and added, 'We are going to perform in the Attic Passage which in the Bill which we have put up on the stairs we have called the Attica Passagia because Attic Passage sounds so very common.' This is characteristic of Mabel, who all her life disliked anything that smacked of 'commonness' and was inclined to make snobbish judgements.

Harry also wrote to Amy: 'It was what you would most likely call very early when a cab drove up to the door and we found to our joy that it was Uncle Ben.' The children quickly altered the play to acknowledge their uncle's recent adventures. 'It introduced the subject of Ben's voyage as reported in a newspaper that was brought in by a page (Willy-boy). It was very effective, and it amused Ben and WLS mightily,' the General wrote in his diary.

This happy little interlude shows the Leigh Smith clan at its best – united in joy at Ben's safe return, inventive and amusing, overturning any notion that 'children should be seen and not heard.' Even Aunt Nannie wrote warmly to Amy: 'Uncle Ben arrived here last night - & everyone was in the greatest excitement . . . All the children here are wishing for you & so are we big people.' The fact that at least four of the party wrote to Amy to let her know that her absence was regretted indicates the strength of the family bond. Milicent, the youngest at this gathering, was experiencing a gaiety and openness that had become impossible in the last stages of her mother's life. The powerful sense of family developed in early childhood never left her; in later life it was to be a source of strength and of distress.

The closeness of the family meant that the aunts and uncles felt that they had a duty to guide, even to control, their nephews and nieces. Both Barbara and Ben organized balls for their teenage relations in London, so that Mabel and Harry could get to know their innumerable second cousins, the offspring of the ten children of William Smith MP – the Shore Smiths, the Nicholsons, the Octavius Smiths, the Coape Smiths, the Bonham Carters. These assemblies also enabled Barbara to observe the social behaviour of her 'chicks', as she called Bella's children. Barbara's own childlessness was a deep sorrow to her, openly expressed.

Fond though Barbara was of the General, she became alarmed at the way he encouraged Harry to drink alcohol. She was also concerned about the boy's lack of intellectual direction. At twelve, Harry had left the schoolroom at home to board at a private school, and had eventually gone on to Rugby, having failed to get into Charterhouse. His tastes were mainly for cricket, football, athletics, hunting, shooting, riding his penny-farthing bicycle, gallivanting with friends and – to Barbara's dismay – smoking and drinking. Harry's school reports, which I found in the same old suitcase that housed the General's diaries, always praise his pleasant nature, but academically he was something of a plodder. Barbara, however, would not allow any nephew of hers to plod.

She enlisted the help of her young protégé, Norman Moore.

Norman was the only child of Rebecca Moore, an old feminist ally of Barbara's. Rebecca lived in Manchester. When Norman moved to London to embark on his medical career at St Bartholomew's Hospital, Rebecca wrote to Barbara to ask her to take her son under her wing. Barbara and Norman hit it off immediately. They had shared interests in natural history and in literature; both were adventurous and unconventional.

A bonus was that Norman Moore – NM – turned out to be one of the few people who got on well with Barbara's peculiar husband, Dr Bodichon. Barbara often invited NM to spend weekends at Scalands. 'Dr Bodichon would like to see a book bound in viper skin if you have one to show us not too big to bring down' is a typical note from Barbara to NM.

NM was an astonishingly well-read and well-informed young man. He was amusing company and a good communicator – the lectures he gave to medical students at Barts were exceptionally well attended. One of his students declared that he would rather go without food than miss one of NM's lectures. NM was also a teetotaller. Barbara decided he was the right person to keep Harry Ludlow on track. Without explaining her full motives to the General, she asked him to invite Norman to Yotes. The visit was a success. She wrote to NM on 3 September 1875:

> I am very glad you liked Yotes and are going again, I want you to be friends to those children very much.
>
> You see their mother was subject to fits of insanity & it is just madness to let a boy like Harry drink wine & he poor boy says it affects his head & just before I left my bedroom at Yotes Ct came in & said he would try and refuse it when it was offered to him at dinner & asked if he took the pledge it would help him. I said your father would not like you to do that but you can refuse & must etc.
>
> You can do a great deal for the boy if you get his love & he is very much inclined to like you so please take the trouble to know him.

Despite his busy life, Norman obliged Barbara by involving

himself with the Ludlows. On 8 September 1875 he wrote to her describing a visit to Yotes:

> I read aloud the 'Tempest' and a few verses of Swift and of Dryden.
> We began the study of architecture at East Peckham church [near
> Yotes]. We talked over Irish history from Cormac MacAist in the
> third century to the year 1800.
>
> The intervals of story telling literature & desultory conversa-
> tion were filled up with athletic sports. The General had a story of
> the East for every one which I could produce from the West . . .
> I think we became friends & I shall be careful to follow the just
> precept in Hamlet & to cultivate the friendship.
>
> I am going to send Harry Waterton's Life. A little example often
> goes far.

Presumably, NM was thinking of the old naturalist's lifelong abstention from alcohol. The General's diary mentions that as well as 'presiding over foot races' in the garden and entertaining dinner guests with 'many Irish stories', NM prescribed for the governess, who had a sore throat. NM was also, most uncharacteristically, an hour late for breakfast, because the manservant had omitted to lay out his clothes.

Though nobody else yet knew, NM was already strongly attracted to Amy Leigh Smith, which may in part account for his willingness to get to know her cousins, but his good nature and desire to please Barbara were also factors. The General liked him; so, it would seem, did Milicent, who (aged seven) wrote to Barbara:

> My dear ant barbar. We got a letter from Harry yesterday he has been
> playing in a match of fut bal. He rights I have a cap WITH A red tas-
> sel . . . I have altogether kicked 3 goals this turm. We hope Dr More will
> come on Saturday Please Tell Him To Do So. I am yr Affec. Milicent.

Unlikely as it seems, the little girl was writing to request – demand, even – the presence of her future husband.

4. 'A high forehead and the highest principles'

The childhood experiences of NM and Milicent were almost diametrically opposed. Milicent, as we have seen, had a strong, principled and loving father; she had attentive siblings, a close extended family, plenty of money, social standing, a rural childhood, a home-based education, and an insane mother who died two days before her fifth birthday. Norman never met his father. He was brought up single-handedly by his mother, Rebecca, an extraordinarily tough, optimistic and intelligent woman who forged a career as an educator and journalist in the face of hardship. There was extended family, but they lived in Ireland; Rebecca brought NM up in Manchester, the nineteenth-century centre of radical intellectual life.

There's a portrait on the stairs at Hancox of Rebecca in old age. It's by John Butler Yeats, father of the poet, and it's said to be a good likeness. It's dark and in need of a clean (that comment could be made about everything in this house), but it conveys a sense of the woman who, as her grandson Alan put it, was 'endowed with a high forehead and the highest principles'. The portrait shows no twinkly granny; the hatchet-faced sitter can only be described as 'formidable'.

The portrait reveals less of Rebecca than does a battered black notebook on the library bookshelf. In this she wrote a brief, incomplete but wonderfully vivid autobiographical sketch, 'The History of Grandmama's Life', for the benefit of her grandchildren, NM's three children Alan, Ethne and Gillachrist. Rebecca was born into a cultured, philanthropic family of Quaker merchants, the Fishers of Limerick. Unusually for Quakers, Rebecca's family were of old Irish stock, not Ascendancy; her great-aunt, 'the Fair Maid of Kerry', was said to be the last educated person in that part of Ireland who spoke Irish as her first language.

Rebecca describes the circumstances of her birth with a story-teller's confidence:

In the city of Limerick, in Ireland, in the evening, there were seven little girls round the fire in their schoolroom. Orah the eldest was just eleven and Constance, the youngest was not quite two years old. Their governess was sitting at the table writing letters, and the children were talking about Christmas, and wondering what presents they would have, when the door was opened, and their papa came in, and said, 'The first Christmas present has come. It is a little Baby Sister for you all.'

Rebecca goes on to describe herself in the third person: 'Baby Rebecca was a great pet. The governess painted a picture of her sitting up in her bassinet playing with her "corling bells" as her favourite toy was called.' Alas, I cannot find this picture, but we have another, quite possibly by the same governess, of Rebecca aged three. It's about five inches high; it shows a very composed little girl, tiny feet crossed at the ankle, sitting bolt upright in a pretty pink-tasselled chair. She wears a full green skirt and an extremely flouncy white blouse. Rebecca's smooth brown hair is parted neatly in the middle; the high wide forehead and strong jaw are already evident. She holds a little book, which she has just put down; her huge, blue-grey eyes hold a level gaze, as if in mild reproach to whoever interrupted her reading. Made before the advent of photography, the little picture is an arresting link with a long-ago childhood.

Raised as a Quaker, in old age Rebecca described herself as a 'scientific atheist'. In her final illness she declined to see a clergyman, declaring, 'I know I shall go out like a candle.' Her parents must have been tolerant people, secure enough in their own beliefs to accommodate and respect the Catholicism of their servants. Her 'dear, kind nurse' Molly was very fond of 'Holy Water' – 'there are wells in Ireland called after the saints & so the water is called "holy water". When we took a drive to see a holy well, &

the pretty glen near it, our Mama used to bring a bottle of the water home for Molly.'

Though Molly could not read, she told Rebecca and her siblings stories about fairies – ' "the good people" she called them, and about mermaids and banshees. She told us how the sun danced on the hills, on Easter morning, but we never could wake up in time to see it.' NM had a deep interest in Irish folklore, perhaps inherited from Molly via Rebecca. Irish airs were the only kind of music that moved him, and this love may also be traced to Molly, who used to sing Rebecca to sleep – 'the sweetest songs I ever heard, though I did not understand the words, for they were in Irish'.

All my life, a little profile portrait has sat on the drawing-room mantelpiece at Hancox. I'd always been aware of it – a blacked-out silhouette, wearing a white lace cap tied with a plaid ribbon, a red shawl draped over the shoulders – but I'd never asked who the sitter was. The other day I turned it over, and to my delight found written on the back ' "Little Molly" – My dear Nurse Molly Vaughan. Rebecca, Her "Darling Becca".'

Rebecca was the eighth Fisher child, but there were more to come. The final tally was thirteen: Deborah (Orah), Mary, Elizabeth, Margaret, Charlotte, Susanna, Constance, Rebecca, Isabella, Amelia, William, Joseph and Sarah Maria. Rebecca, said one of her dozens of nieces, 'was head and shoulders over all the rest in ability'.

Quakers were barred from entering the professions. Rebecca's father, Benjamin Clarke Fisher, ran a linen draper's shop in Rutland Street, the leading business street in Limerick, and it seems likely that he was a good businessman, since all Rebecca's childhood memories are of a life of comfort and pleasure. When she was ten years old the family moved two miles out of Limerick to 'a large house called Lifford, with seven acres of lawns & gardens & splendid trees of all kinds'. Rebecca's account of Lifford overflows with a sense of bounty. Each child had its own patch of garden; they kept rabbits, guinea fowl, cocks and hens, dogs, donkeys and horses. The many varieties of fancy pigeon each had a separate house with a little arched door; Rebecca would sit and read in the clematis arbour cocooned by their cooing.

A scrap of a letter to my grandfather from Rebecca's sister Constance confirms this bucolic idyll. She recalls having 'syllbub and cake on the newly cut grass, raked into "wind rows", a small spoonful of raspberry or strawberry jam was put into a little glass mug, the cow was milked into it, thus stirring & frothing a "caudel" <u>that</u> was syllbub, very luscious, sipped while eating a slice of the dear Grandmother's good homemade cake'. The contrast between this apparently unclouded girlhood and the life the adult Rebecca was to find herself leading as a hard-up single mother in Manchester is extreme, but I can find no evidence that she ever complained. She was, said her grandson Alan, 'indefatigable and undefeatable'.

The Fishers were earnest people, intellectually inclined. Unlike many other middle-class families of the time they made sure that their daughters were well educated and well read. Rebecca and one of her sisters were secretaries of a 'Book Society'; she also enjoyed teaching her little nephews and nieces. Life at Lifford, as recounted by her in old age when the distant view is often rose-tinted, seems an almost ideal balance of learning, good works, socializing and physical activity: 'our 3 cousins, boys, used to come out of town in the early mornings . . . and we used to have grand rides before breakfast, four or five abreast.' The married sisters with their husbands and children came out from Limerick on Sundays for lunch and 'we had a very lively time . . . We often went on excursions & had pic-nics . . . One moonlight night we made a party of friends to walk to Carrig-O'Gunnel, to see the effect of the bright moonlight on the dark ruin. The roads were quite deserted, we met no one, & we held hands & stretched all across the wide road. Some of the party sang together as we went along.'

None of the surviving images of Rebecca suggest that she had inherited the good looks of her great-aunt, the 'Fair Maid of Kerry'. However, she was a high-spirited and intelligent young woman and it is not surprising that when she was nineteen she caught the eye of a brilliant young barrister, Robert Ross Rowan Moore. Robert Moore had a keen interest in radical politics and was making a name for himself as an inspiring orator. In 1839 he came to Limerick to try to prevent a ship called the *Robert Ker* from transporting Irish labourers ignorant of their fate to the West Indies as 'indentured labour' in conditions little short of slavery. His oratory was successful; the *Robert Ker* returned to Glasgow without its human cargo.

Robert Ross Rowan had a letter of introduction to Benjamin Fisher, who shared his political views. Fisher invited the young man to Lifford, and helped him in his campaign. In return, Robert helped with the charitable school the Fishers had set up at Lifford to educate the cottagers' children. To Rebecca, Robert seemed perfect – gifted, eloquent, principled. 'He gave a beautiful lecture about Peace, & Kindness, & Love.'

The drama of the *Robert Ker* over, Robert returned to Dublin – 'he hoped, and we hoped, my sisters and I, that we should meet again.' Soon, Rebecca went to stay with one of her married sisters, Deborah Gough, in Dublin. The voyage took a whole day and a night:

> We travelled from Limerick to Dublin by water, along the grand canal to Lough Derg, & the Shannon, & then the canal again. At Lough Derg we left the canal boat and embarked on board a steamer that plies only on the lake as she is too large for the canals . . . we had a grand steam along the beautiful lake . . . with woods and mountains on each side of the loveliest green & purple. Then we had to descend into a canal boat again. This took us across the Kings County & the counties of Kildare & Dublin, & through the famous bog of Allen, which moves slowly, like a glacier.

NM was to repeat this journey on foot and in reverse; when he was fifteen he left his Aunt Deborah's house equipped with ten shillings, a toothbrush, a comb, a spare flannel shirt and a telescope, and walked the 120 miles to Limerick. It took him four days.

At the Goughs' house, Rebecca renewed her acquaintance with Robert Ross Rowan Moore. 'He was very lively and full of fun and I was always glad to see him.' Rebecca gives a full account of a three-day excursion she made with him and several other young people:

> into the County Wicklow to see its beautiful Mountains & Valleys & Lakes & Waterfalls. We set off on cars [Irish 'outside cars'] at five o'clock in the morning at 6.30 we stopped at a cottage, high up on the mountains near Lough Dan for breakfast. The cottage people had only just got up & they hastened to make up a good fire of turf to boil our kettle . . . we made our tea & brought out our bread & butter & got eggs from the cottage people . . . the men fed the horses and then harnessed them again & we drove off to the Seven Churches of Glendalough. We took a boat & were rowed all round the Lake . . . Music of a bugle & singing sounded beautifully on the water.

It is easy to understand why Rebecca was enchanted with the young barrister, who seems to have been the prime mover in any adventure. I, however, must admit to a prejudice against my great-great-grandfather. His portrait, in crayons, hangs in the front hall at Hancox. His hair is luxuriant, curly, and worn quite long in Byronic fashion, but his nose is bulbous and shiny and his lips look rubbery. Perhaps I only find him unappealing because his later behaviour was reprehensible – his 'beautiful' lectures about Peace, Kindness and Love did not translate into everyday life. Rebecca's comments about him and his family are extremely generous, but one must bear in mind that she was writing this account for her grandchildren, who were given a sanitized version of events.

There is some pathos in the way Rebecca's memories of these far-off summer days are so clear and accurate; she is telling the story of a prelapsarian perfection. No trace remains of any other love interest in her long life, even though she outlived her errant husband by nearly forty years.

After six weeks Rebecca left Dublin and went home to Lifford, but the romance continued.

> I had letters constantly from your Grandpapa, who had gone to live in England . . . Sometimes he would send me a book or a photograph [probably a daguerreotype, in a case with a clasp] & he often sent me newspapers with the speeches he had made at the meetings of the Anti-Corn Law League . . . he wrote about his lectures, & his travels, in England & Scotland, & all the interesting people he met & about doing good for the poor & helping to put down Slavery in America . . . We wrote about the books we were reading, & told each other of new books & fresh discoveries.

In 1844, Robert Moore contested a by-election in the Borough of Hastings on an Anti-Corn Law League platform. This was a safe Conservative seat, but RRRM put up a good fight, and a tradition of his eloquence survived in the area. He was supported by Benjamin Smith MP – the 'Pater' of Barbara, Ben, Bella, Nannie and Willy. Seventeen-year-old Barbara went along to the hustings on Hastings beach with her father and was most impressed by RRRM's speeches. They struck up an acquaintance; a year or so later, when RRRM and Rebecca were in London, Barbara became friends of both. Her friendship with Rebecca was the one that survived, and led, eventually, to Rebecca's son Norman marrying two of Barbara's nieces, first Amy and then Milicent.

The Anti-Corn Law League was formed to protest about the duties imposed by Lord Liverpool's Tory government on imported grain. This kept the price of bread artificially high; farmers benefited but the poor suffered. The League was one of the most powerful radical movements of the nineteenth century. The Corn Laws were finally repealed by Sir Robert Peel in 1846 in response to the Irish potato famine. RRRM's standing in the League was high. His career prospects were bright. It is surprising that he and Rebecca decided to elope. Though Quakers usually opposed marrying 'out', the Fisher parents had always, it seems, made Robert welcome. Perhaps Robert's family made snobbish objections because the Fishers were 'in trade'. Perhaps the idea of elopement just seemed thrilling to the young couple.

Whatever the reasons, after five years of courtship and correspondence, Robert and Rebecca ran away together. Rebecca left behind a letter for her brother Joseph:

My dear Joseph,

In the fullness of feeling, and strength of affection I am at a loss for words heart-reaching enough to speak my farewell to each and all of my beloved name – I am leaving you perhaps only for a time – I have thought right to separate my life from yours but my heart shall often be with you – with the mind's eye I shall look at you continually & hope & pray for you that your lives may be as the holiest rule within dictates – this is my desire for myself & I cannot refrain from expressing it to thee my dear brother in the seriousness & affection that fill my mind while thus writing to thee my earnest Farewell – I know thou wilt believe me when I tell thee there is sorrow at my heart that my parting is such as it is but having made up my mind to go I have judged this mode to be the best & kindest I could adopt – dear Joseph thy truly affectionate sister – Rebecca.

She left similar messages for her other siblings still living at home, but reading the letter doesn't make me feel much the wiser about the elopement.

They were married on New Year's Day, 1845 at St Martins-in-the-Fields in London and spent their honeymoon in Boulogne. 'Your grandpapa,' wrote Rebecca, 'was fond of pretty things & he bought me a fan & some broaches & Gloves & he got for both of us a large musical box that played a great many tunes.' Rebecca's own love of 'pretty things' survived the enforced austerity of her later life, to an extent that embarrassed her grand-daughter Ethne (pronounced, Enna): 'In those days [c. 1900] old ladies usually wore black or dark dresses,' she wrote in her (unpublished) memoir,

'and so I think did Grandmamma, but she would add a purple
shawl or put a purple ribbon in her cap and she used to wear large
brooches and a necklace of enormous amber beads.'

The Moores lived on Camden Hill, London, for a time. Barbara, Bella and Nannie Leigh Smith often called, and took Rebecca
out driving with them in Hyde Park. In the summer of 1845 a
great bazaar, in some respects a forerunner of the Great Exhibition
of 1856, was held at Covent Garden Theatre in aid of the Anti-
Corn Law League, and Robert and Rebecca went many times. 'We
bought several things . . . some of which I have still. Such as the
Rocking Chair, the "Free-Trade" rosewood chair which was carved
by a Working Man for the Bazaar, the brass box & the silver dog.'
(Of these I can only identify the Free Trade chair, now in the pos-
session of my father. It is decorated with a carved sheaf of wheat
growing out of a globe, above the words 'Free Trade'.) The bazaar
ended with 'a great party & Dance . . . the largest I was ever at.'
We have a set of daguerreotypes taken at the bazaar, one each of
Robert, Rebecca, Barbara, Nannie and – I think – Bessie Parkes.
Robert had himself weighed and measured at the same time, and
enclosed the results inside the daguerreotype case. He was 5 foot
8¾ and weighed 10 stone 3lbs.

The summer of jollification was soon over. The Moores moved
to Manchester to further Robert's career; Manchester, almost a
second capital, was the hub of radical activity in the 1840s. 'Your
grandpapa had to go on a lecturing tour . . . and I went to Manchester taking all our pretty things with me to prepare our home.'
RRRM's lecturing tour might better be described as a lechering
tour. John Bright MP, leader of the Anti-Corn Law League, said
to his colleague Richard Cobden, 'For God's sake keep Moore off
our platforms, I do not think there is any man in either party who
he has not cuckolded.' At this stage, this was presumably not
known to Rebecca.

'Home' in Manchester was a rented house in Athol Place, Higher
Broughton, but first Rebecca stayed with friends, the Peacocks, a

theatrical and musical family. 'Mr and Mrs Peacock . . . were like parents in kindness to me,' and their three daughters were 'very pleasant companions'. Two evenings a week, Rebecca and the Peacock girls 'went into Manchester to teach Mill girls & other workers who could not go to day schools'.

It was not long before Rebecca found herself in need of such friends. She was pregnant, and alone. Robert absconded with a Miss Caroline Henderson. Together, Rebecca and Robert had chosen 'pretty papers' for their new house '& had it nicely fitted up with furniture from London', but now he was gone. On 8 January 1847 Rebecca gave birth to her son Norman in this house. RRRM never saw his son, nor ever, as far as I can tell, made any attempt to do so.

'The History of Grandmama's Life' glosses over the painful facts. 'Your grandpapa,' Rebecca cosily tells the grandchildren, 'had to be in London a great deal & up & down the country. But when the Baby came I was never lonely & I had a great many pleasant friends in Manchester.' It seems that Rebecca and little 'Norny' were borne up by a life raft of female friends and relations. They were invited to stay for weeks on end by people who had houses in the country. 'Baby was very good he was greatly admired in his white frocks & blue or red shoes & with his pretty yellow silvery hair & blue eyes & happy smile.'

Rebecca often took the infant Norny to stay at Lifford. The Fisher clan welcomed them, and were apparently uncensorious about Rebecca's marital disaster. It would be interesting to know whether staying on at Lifford indefinitely would have been an option. If so, Rebecca did not take it. She was determined to make a go of independent living at Higher Broughton.

Rebecca was soon able to make a little money from writing. In 1857 a 'Wonderful Exhibition of Art Treasures' was exhibited at Old Trafford. 'I was writing about the pictures & their painters for an illustrated paper & I used to go to study the pictures & Norman often came with me, but he was too young to care much for the pictures he liked better to run at full speed the whole length of the long galleries & when we went in the morning before the other Visitors the policeman allowed him this fun.'

In 1861 Rebecca opened a school. 'I wanted money for Norman's education & for all our expenses of living so I set up a school & got teachers to assist me. The School did very well & brought me plenty of money & I found it very interesting work. It gave me a deal to think about & to study & to arrange for, but I found I could do it very well.' The school, for young children, was run on Froebel's methods; Rebecca kept herself up to date with educational theory. It was housed at 2 Darling Place, Higher Broughton. Rebecca ran it until 1877, but carried on with her journalism too. She became English correspondent of the American paper *Revolution*, writing on such topics as female suffrage, the Married Women's Property Bill (the brainchild of Barbara Leigh Smith Bodichon) and the employment of women. Rebecca's signature can be found amongst those of the 1,499 women who signed Barbara's 1866 petition to parliament in favour of votes for women.

Rebecca was free of the inhibitions that afflicted more genteel Victorian women about the propriety of earning her own living. She seems to have been proud of her independence. Her friendships with feminists such as Barbara would have encouraged such an attitude. A friend of both women, the artist Anna Mary Howitt, described Rebecca as 'a woman who has ideas, and very clever ones too upon policies, morals and literature and education and homeopathy – all alive and full of intellect'.

Rebecca also contributed to *Una*, an American feminist journal. Later in life she travelled to New England, where her friends included Louisa May Alcott, author of *Little Women*, and William Lloyd Garrison, the old hero of the American anti-slavery movement. As Alan put it, Boston was her spiritual home. She was an enthusiastic and adventurous traveller and rode round the Pyramids on a donkey when she was well over seventy.

Beyond her travels, her journalism, her school, her politics, the great project of Rebecca's life was her son. A letter she wrote to her brother William when Norman was five reveals her parenting style:

> Norman [is] always interesting – 'Mama did I improve at all to-day?' was his last question as I laid him in bed this evening. He seems to understand in his small way that '<u>to improve</u>' is the business of life – then I asked him to repeat 'Chief Delight' and he said it :-
>
> > 'Oh that it were my chief delight
> > To do the things I ought!
> > Then let me try with all my might
> > To mind what I am taught.'
>
> Yes I said, you know it very well now, in words, in your memory, but now what other way have you to learn it? '<u>In doing it</u>' he replied, yes I said, in <u>Action</u> as you say.

She adds in a postscript, 'Norman reads a "Fable" every day and often I get him to tell it me out walking to practice him in finding words to use.'

Remarkably, Norman's zest for knowledge and love of books survived this rigour. At Clifton, Bristol, on one of their long visits to friends, the eight-year-old boy 'saw the Bee Orchid growing wild for the first time and dried a specimen of it. The fossils and spar of the neighbourhood were a constant source of interest to me. The old man of the house in which we lodged told me that he remembered well the Reform Bill riots at Bristol. We discussed the Great Rebellion together.' NM was recalling his childhood precocity in his old age, but it rings true. During his stay at Clifton he kept a diary in which he made lists of 'Books I have read' and 'Verses I have learnt'. The twenty-eight books include adventure stories such as *Masterman Ready* by Captain Marryat as well as a *Mythology of Greece and Rome* (which he awards six stars), and *England and Its People* (no stars). The verses include Southey's *Battle of*

Blenheim and Byron's *The Gladiator*. It's a lot for someone who had only just passed their ninth birthday. But the diary also provides moments of simple childhood, as when he bought 'a nice little boat' and sailed it in the bath after tea.

An appealing glimpse of the young Norman is provided by Anna Mary Howitt, in a letter to her sister of May 1853. 'Mrs Moore's little boy . . . is grown a splendid little fellow, who looks as keen as steel.' Six-year-old Norman announced that he lived at 'Vegetarian Villa' (he refused to eat meat, out of respect for animals), but he condoned '"shooting birds for a <u>good</u> purpose! [i.e. to put in a museum]. I mean when I grow up to be a civil engineer by profession and a naturalist for my recreation" . . . and when I left little Norman put on his cap after tea and trudged with me through the rain down to the "The Griffin" where . . . I got into one of the Leviathan omnibuses.'

★

NM wrote to Rebecca almost every day of his adult life. Though he often disagreed with her, he wrote out of affection and respect as well as duty. It is sad, therefore, to find that in old age she became a somewhat marginal figure. NM cannot be accused of abandoning or even neglecting his mother but Ethne's memoir records that he was often short with her – 'He rebuked her for coughing, which he said was unnecessary, and he rebuked her for the way she pronounced Irish.' Both rebukes seem unfair, particularly the Irish dispute; Rebecca, after all, spent a far greater proportion of her life in Ireland than did her son. I'm afraid she simply got on his nerves.

Alan, reliably fair-minded in his attempts to sum up character, balances his praise by saying that 'Her chief failing was a love of giving advice to those to whom she felt she ought to give it,' and one can imagine that this trait would not have made for easy relations with either of NM's wives. The young Ethne certainly found it a strain: 'My brother [Alan] and I paid the visits . . . with reluctance . . . Grandmamma was always pleased to see us but she could never forget what she believed to be her duty, that, being old, she must continually instruct the young.'

Rebecca was often called upon to look after Alan when he was tiny because of Amy's many bouts of illness. She was very fond of him and recorded his early sayings and doings in a notebook headed 'Alaniania', but the urge to educate and inform never left her. On 15 November 1887 she wrote to Alan, 'I am glad to hear . . . that you have begun to learn to read for now you can learn to be of some use in the world.' Alan was five years old.

It seems a shame that the grandchildren, particularly Ethne, were not taught to be proud of this exceptional woman. On the contrary, Ethne's chief feelings were of embarrassment. 'She spoke English with a brogue and this sometimes made me ashamed to be with her. I remember once when waiting in the street for a horse omnibus that she waved her umbrella at each one that came, calling out interrogatively "Marr-able Arr-ach??"' Ethne also records her way of telling the same stories over and over again, though in fairness Rebecca was not the only octogenarian to be guilty of this.

Some of her stories were just dull, like the account of how she broke her little finger, and, because she promptly tied it to the next one, it mended quickly; the moral being 'do the right thing at the right moment,' which she pointed out to us till we were tired of it. But there was a story we liked about sailors adrift in an open boat on the ocean, dying of thirst, who heard a voice from Heaven telling them that if they lowered their bucket at a certain place they would find fresh water. . .

Once my brother and a friend had a bet that she should be made to tell this story during dinner. We led the conversation round to shipwrecks and sure enough in a moment Grandmamma was off; when she came to the crisis in the story, declaiming in her Irish voice: 'Let down your bucket wher' yer *arre*,' we grinned triumphantly across the table and my brother's friend signalled that he had lost the bet.

After the death of Amy, her daughter-in-law, Rebecca took it upon herself to instruct her teenage grand-daughter in the facts of life. But her methods of instruction took such a bizarrely rounda-bout form that they fell wide of the mark:

> She . . . used to write long letters to me about the importance of drying myself properly after my bath, and used to enclose news-paper cuttings about . . . the Wonders of Nature, beginning with plants and leading up to the family life of animals. I had not even read these newspaper cuttings, though at one time, when they had become more numerous than usual, I had bribed a schoolfriend to read them for me, and give me the gist of them so that I could mention them intelligently when answering Grandmamma's let-ters. It was not until many years after her death that one day on finding a packet of these cuttings, I realised on which subject she had been trying to educate me.

Rebecca's educational approaches, then, were not always success-ful. But, undeniably, the central project of her life bore fruit. Across the landing from her stern and shadowy likeness is a three-quarter-length portrait in oils of NM in the red robes and black velvet hat denoting fellowship of the Royal College of Physicians, of which he would eventually become President. Rebecca did not live to see this honour bestowed upon her only child, and she might well have pooh-poohed his baronetcy, but by the time of her death she knew that the boy she had brought up and educated without any help from his father had become the leading physician in the country. The five-year-old who asked, 'Mama did I improve at all to-day?' had taken her lessons to heart.

5. 'He is unstained by the common vices of youth'

The young NM's singularity and obvious intellectual gifts attracted the attention of a wide range of adult mentors. At seven years old, for instance, he struck up a friendship with Michael Healy, a shoemaker from County Clare who had set up shop in Manchester. NM had already learned a few words of Irish from his grandfather, Benjamin Fisher (who, characteristically, had taught himself the language the better to communicate with the workers on his farm at Lifford). Now Michael Healy taught him more: 'I . . . learnt from him the names of birds and beasts and most of the common objects of life as well as a good deal of grammar. He took great pleasure in my progress.' His mother's female friends also took an interest, stimulating him with books and conversation. Barbara Leigh Smith, who was to become so important later in his life, sent him a prescient gift for his fifth birthday – a dried skate fastened to a card, with a long spiny tail. 'She could not have sent a present better suited to my taste & from that day I have grown fonder of her,' NM told his wife Amy years later.

At the age of nine NM started at a small boarding school in Lancaster. The school was run by William Henry Herford, a liberal and a Unitarian who had studied at the University of Bonn, where he had become interested in the educational principles of Pestalozzi and Froebel. Herford aimed to provide his pupils with 'steps from Nature up to Nature's God'. He deplored prizes, competition and corporal punishment, 'viewing as an evil . . . whatever dims the Brightness or checks the Activity of Children'. He regarded it as his duty to 'ensure protection against . . . the Teasing and Bullying, that are ever "waiting at the door" '.

This enlightened approach was in strong contrast to the methods of most early Victorian schools, and it is easy to see why Rebecca chose it for her beloved son. Herford's regime was certainly humane, though teaching methods could be dreary. The class was never allowed to move on to fresh material until the previous lesson had been 'mastered in and out'. NM disapproved of this rigidity: 'We acquire experience in life in fragments and imperfect as they are they help us on to something more and open our eyes to things of interest. Thus we learn from both men and books: an absolute thoroughness in learning retards progress and destroys interest.'

Boys who left their belongings lying about were obliged to chop firewood for half an hour before they could reclaim them. On Sunday evenings each boy recited poetry to the headmaster's wife in her drawing room – not a problem for NM, though his choice of Sir Walter Scott's 'Young Lochinvar' was deemed 'not grave enough for the place and day'. There was something of a family atmosphere. Each boy had a bedroom to himself. NM's vegetarianism was indulged, and he was provided with potatoes with milk poured over them instead of meat; he retained a taste for this all his life. The headmaster's birthday was celebrated with a large cake on which were as many almonds as he had attained years. Inside the cake was a fourpenny piece, a silver groat thought to bring luck to the boy who found it.

The best thing about the school, from NM's point of view, were the excursions to beauty spots. Clapham Cave, near Ingleborough, was explored, each boy carrying a candle. NM admired the stalactites, and notwithstanding the scoffing remarks of his schoolfellows he collected a bagful of bright coloured fungi, which he later ironed in an (unsuccessful) attempt to preserve their colours. It was during his time at the Lancaster school that NM developed his taste for falconry. NM disliked cricket and football, but this was not the problem it might have been for a schoolboy later in the nineteenth century, when team sports became almost a religion. He much preferred the cross-country runs and paper-chases that were allowed as an alternative, and he enjoyed climbing the pear trees in the school garden; the boys were allowed to eat all the fruit they could pick.

Some letters from NM to Rebecca survive from these early school days; aged ten, he described a teacher in tabulated form:

Mr P. P. Carpenter. (Facts about him).

1. He squints.
2. He comes from Warrington every Monday to teach us.
3. He teaches me Agbra.
4. He is a vegetarian.
5. He teaches us Zoology.
6. He can't pronounce his rs.
7. He teaches us Physiology.
8. I like him pretty well.
9. He doesn't sit strait.
10. He's rather coxy [conceited].

The letters are full of his love of birds: '[the starlings] all sing together every morning a short hymn on one or other of the chimneys. The sparrows are the merriest of little birds I think. They twitter and laugh and fight and play like little mad things.' Even at ten, NM was a serious birdwatcher. His fascination with the natural world was throughout his life vivid and emotionally responsive as well as scholarly. Together with his friends, Joe and Arthur, he set up an Ornithological Society. 'The subject of our next meeting is to be the owl's head which George B. gave me. I think it is of the genus Scops or else Scotophilus.'

It says much for the school that a boy as unusual as NM was allowed to pursue his interests unmolested except for a few jibes and taunts. He was passionate about his Irish ancestry, and once got into a fight with another boy on the subject. A master asked about the cause of the quarrel. 'He will not believe,' said NM, 'that three hundred kings were killed in a battle near Derry.' The

master was dismissive: 'A contemptible set of kings,' he sneered;
NM burst into angry tears.

★

Despite Rebecca's assertions in 'The History of Grandmama's Life'
that the school she set up brought in a handsome income, in reality
money was tight. After leaving Mr Herford's school aged thirteen,
NM walked the four miles daily to Chorlton High School for a
year, but his mother made it clear that soon he would have to earn
his own living. He wrote to her, begging to be allowed to continue his education: 'It never will be my object to get rich . . . Leave
school at fourteen! Why I know no Latin, less Greek, hardly anything indeed . . . I wish you would let me stay at school till I am
17 or 16 . . . I almost wish that I had no relations, no friends, because
then I might beat my own track.' But Rebecca was adamant. Perhaps, as well as lacking funds to finance her son's education, she
believed it would be good for him to learn the realities of hard
work. In 1862, aged fifteen, NM began work in a cotton warehouse in Mosley Street, Manchester.

His first job was to sweep the floors after sprinkling them with
moist sawdust. Next he entered in a ledger the names, quantities
and destinations of the cotton prints that were distributed from
the warehouse and loaded the bales into wagons. He earned sixteen
shillings a month; with his first earnings he treated himself to an
eight-volume edition of Chaucer and read it straight through. He
made friends with his fellow workers, who tolerated his oddities.
The discovery of a dead capercailzie in the office safe, put there by
NM pending dissection, was greeted with amusement.

NM joined a working men's Natural History Society; on one
of the Society's excursions he went down a coal mine. He also
helped with the post-mortem examination of a circus camel. His
mother's favourite saying was 'What are the three letters that make
the world go? N R G,' and Norman had certainly inherited
her energy. Several evenings a week, after a long day at the warehouse (work began at 7.30 a.m.) he attended lectures at Owens

College on Latin, Greek, German, English literature, history and mathematics. Owens College, founded in 1851 by a benevolent textile magnate, aimed to provide educational opportunities for those who, like NM, could not afford a conventional school or college education. It evolved into the University of Manchester.

On his days off, NM took long walks into Yorkshire and Lancashire, often with a hooded peregrine falcon on his wrist. Small boys would run after him, shouting 'Eh, is it wick?' ('Is it alive?'). He records the 'longest straight on (except for the dinner time) walk I have ever made' as being 54 miles, from Manchester to Lancaster, via Bolton, Chorley, Preston and Garstang. He walked through the night, and noted the knockers-up going about tapping at the windows of mill hands with long sticks to wake them.

Inevitably, the lecturers at Owens College took an interest in this prodigious student. Whether anyone intervened with Rebecca, or even offered to pay for NM's studies, is unclear, but aged seventeen he was allowed to leave the warehouse and try for a place at Cambridge. The lecturers were extremely important to NM and took great pains with him, but outweighing all other encounters in significance was his meeting on 28 September 1863 with the naturalist Charles Waterton.

NM had heard that visitors were admitted to Walton Hall to see Waterton's collection of stuffed birds. He walked the twelve miles, rang the bell (noticing that the knocker on the left of the double door was fastened to a cheerful face and that there was a sad one on the right) and was ushered in by Mr Waterton himself. The old man left the boy alone to study his specimens – as well as the birds (unusual variants of woodcocks, quail, thrush, sparrows, herons and others, mainly bought alive by Waterton in a Roman market and stuffed by him) there were a chimpanzee, a large snake and the cayman which Waterton had captured by sitting on its back and twisting back its front legs to form handles. At Hancox we have a primitive carving of this incident, made by a Guyanan native out of soft reddish stone, showing Mr Waterton straddling the monster. There were also extraordinary composite creatures which

Waterton, a Roman Catholic, had constructed to caricature the enemies of his religion. John Knox was a black frog, Titus Oates a flat toad, Martin Luther a black gorilla with a humanized face capped with horns, Edward VI and his sister Princess Elizabeth (later Queen) two lizards 'vigorously sucking the teats of Satan who is in the form of a hideous lizard'.

When NM had finished examining the stuffed creatures, a butler appeared with a tray bearing lunch. On his way out, seeing the old naturalist in the grounds, the sixteen-year-old boy went over to thank him for his hospitality. The old man and the boy immediately fell into a conversation that lasted more than two hours. Waterton showed NM the old drawbridge tower and the ancient gates pierced by the bullets of the Parliamentarians, including one shot fired by Cromwell himself before he was driven away by a small gun still in the tower. NM came from a Quaker background and had been brought up in a broadly free-thinking atmosphere, but this encounter planted the feeling for Catholicism that contributed to his conversion forty years later.

Indoors, Waterton showed NM the hammock he had used in his wanderings in South America and introduced him to the Miss Edmonstones, sisters of Waterton's late wife, who kept house for him, and who were to become NM's lifelong friends. Waterton's way of life was austere, as NM recorded in an essay on the naturalist in 1871:

On the top floor . . . was the chapel, and a small room which was at once Waterton's study, bird-stuffing workshop and bedroom, if bedroom it could be called when there was not any bed. The Wanderer always slept on the boards, wrapped in a blanket. His pillow was a block of oak . . . He got up at three, lit his fire, and lay down upon the floor again for half an hour, which he called a half hour of luxury . . . from four to five he was upon his knees in the chapel . . . he read a chapter in a Spanish Life of Saint Francis Xavier, which concluded his early devotions, and he began the secular work of the day with a chapter of Don Quixote in the original. He next

wrote letters or carried on bird stuffing, till Sir Thomas More's
clock struck at eight [Sir Thomas More was one of his ancestors,
which fits] when, punctual to the moment, the household at Walton
sat down to breakfast. His was frugal, and usually consisted of dry
toast, watercress and a cup of weak tea. Breakfast ended, he went
out till noon, superintending his farm, mending fences or clipping
hedges. If the weather was cold he would light a fire in the fields.
From noon till dinner . . . he would sit indoors and read or think . . .
After dinner he walked in the park . . . He retired early to bed . . .
He rose at midnight to spend a few minutes in the chapel, and then
went back to his wooden bed and oaken pillow.

The influence this strange, ascetic man exerted over NM
was profound. Waterton frequently invited him to Walton Hall;
these visits were interludes of perfect happiness. NM slept in a
room looking down the thirty-acre lake towards a large heronry.
Equipped with a telescope, he listed the many hundreds of waterbirds. The old stone house protected by a moat; the willow tree
with twelve trunks known as the Twelve Apostles (the smallest
trunk was St James the Less, and a twisted trunk struck by lightning which groaned as the wind blew was Judas Iscariot); the Cat
Room, in which Waterton kept a fire going purely for the sake of
the cats; the grotto, where an old woman provided cups of tea and
coals for a fire; but above all, the wise old man who put NM in
touch with a greater world than that he had hitherto known . . .
Walton Hall was a place of enchantment. But it was magic with
a moral core. Waterton, said NM, 'gave me an example of charity and kindness to everyone'. The attentive boy took down the
instructions his mentor gave him, noting also the place where the
instruction was given:

When you are able never lose an opportunity of doing charity
quietly. If we only looked into it there is enough misery in
the world to break anyone's heart. (In the turnip field at the far
end of the farm)

Never remain for a moment in the company of those of whose character you are in the least doubtful lest, like the dragon in the ballad you may be obliged to say 'Would I had seen thee never.' (While we were sitting on the old bench by the sunk fence, on the edge of the meadow)

Make one firm resolution never to touch wine, or anything of the kind. Should you be pressed very hard you can say that you promised the old Wanderer of Guiana that you would never do so. If you steadily adhere to this resolution and keep right in the main points you will carry the world before you in anything you undertake. (As we were walking down the Ryeroyd Bank)

Before you undertake anything be sure that it is right. Then consider all the obstacles. If you should then determine to set about it, do so, and you will probably succeed.

Whether you be in sorrow, or in triumph, endeavour always to bear in mind that your stay in this world is very short. I have been living here more than eighty years and when I look back upon my life it seems immeasurably short. (In Mr Waterton's room)

In July 1864, NM wrote:

All the trees are in full leaf and birds abound. The wood pigeons coo all day long. I saw several bats this evening and heard the white owl . . . When the full moon was up the moat looked beautiful. The only sounds to be heard then were from the Canada Goose and the Owl, and fish jumping . . . All morning Mr Waterton was working by the Grotto and I was with him . . . we got into the boat and rowed up to the old oaks where a pier has been made and the stone cross which was on the ruin set up . . . At the foot of this cross between two sister oaks, probably five hundred years old, the brave old Wanderer intends to be buried . . . The Kestrel the carrion crow and the heron will fly over the grave of their protector and the coot will sing his caoine [keen: wailing for the dead, in Irish].

Not all NM's descriptions of life at Walton were quite so lyrical. The following February he and Waterton attempted to stuff a badly preserved gorilla skin:

> After dinner we brought it into the drawing room in a wooden trough . . . but this otherwise fine specimen is a complete wreck. The epidermis (and with it the hair) was peeling off all over, especially on the ears, fore and hind feet. . . . The true skin was very rough thick and had gone quite white . . . After looking at this mournful gorilla skin for some time we looked at the skull and compared it with those of the chimpanzee and howling monky which Mr Waterton brought down.

The Misses Edmonstone, who had taught NM to appreciate the gentle art of drinking fine tea out of Sèvres china, must have been very forbearing.

On 25 May 1865 NM rowed Waterton to the two old oaks. Waterton, carrying a log across a bridge, caught his foot in a bramble; he fell forward heavily on to the log. NM helped him back to the boat and rowed him home on what was to be his last voyage. The old man lay, most unusually for him, on a sofa; his spleen was ruptured and he was in great pain. NM rode to Wakefield for a surgeon.

Leeches were applied. NM and Lydia Edmonstone, Waterton's niece, decided to sit up all night with the dying man. 'I lay on my elbow that I might keep my eyes on Mr Waterton's face. At 12 o'clock [I] went into the chapel to be Mr Waterton's proxy, as of course he could not go.' A priest was sent for. Canon Browne asked if he would have the last sacraments. 'By all means,' said Waterton and sat upright. 'He said all the responses; he said the whole of the Confiteor (in Latin) and the whole of St Bernard's hymn and the first verse and the first two lines of the second verse of the *Dies Irae.*' He was in great pain but struggled hard not to show it. He kissed a crucifix of malachite and bronze that had belonged to the Young Pretender's brother. When he died, just after half past two in the morning of 27 May, Norman went upstairs and stopped Sir Thomas More's clock.

High mass was sung at Walton Hall. The funeral procession rowed across the lake to the two great oaks, headed by a boat containing the Bishop of Beverley and fourteen priests who chanted the Office for the Dead. The last boat, Waterton's own, was empty and draped with black. The cross marking the grave by the oaks was inscribed with the epitaph the Wanderer had composed for himself:

> *Orate pro anima*
> *Caroli* Waterton
> *Cujus fessa*
> *Juxta hanc crucem*
> *Seplientur ossa*
> *Natus* 1782   *Obiit.* 1865

Charles Waterton is still a presence at Hancox. The natural history books he gave NM formed the basis of what was to become a large collection. The inkstand the poet Gray used to write his elegy was another gift. Alas, NM's scruples wouldn't allow him to accept the offer of a first-folio Shakespeare which had been in the Waterton family since the time of its publication. A bust of Waterton broods above the drawing-room door, adorned every Christmas by an ivy wreath. As a child I was intrigued by two stories about this blank-eyed, high-collared, eagle-nosed plaster man. One was that he had no fear of heights, and had climbed to the top of the cross of St Peter's in Rome and left a glove impaled on the lightning conductor. No steeplejack in Rome was willing to retrieve it, so the papal authorities sent Waterton back up to do so. The other was that, on his travels in South America, he had longed to be bitten by a vampire bat, just to see what it was like. He left his big toe sticking out of his hammock every night, but while his companions often woke shouting and cursing, no bat ever took his bait. When my uncle Norman, NM's grandson, went on a scientific expedition up the Gambia river in 1948, he used Waterton's needle book, for stitching up and preserving specimens.

NM remembered and heeded Waterton's precepts all his life, but his influence had a more direct and immediate effect. In the sitting room at Walton Hall hung a picture of St Catharine of Alexandria, which Waterton said reminded him of his dead wife. NM, who had decided to read for a Cambridge scholarship, chose St Catharine's College in honour of this.

He took the exams just three weeks after Waterton's death, and was successful. He went up in October, together with five other men from Owens College, and registered to read natural sciences, then called natural philosophy. His mother managed to find £120 a year to support him. Students had to furnish their own rooms in those days, so NM cut out the expense of a bed by sleeping on the floor, as Waterton had done, with a block of oak for a pillow. One item of furniture he did have was a little African throne, a stool with a curved seat made of dark carved wood. It had been given to his father by General Perronet Thompson, one of the leaders in the Free Trade Movement. General Thompson, who had been a midshipman under Nelson, was a wild card regarded as a nuisance by the authorities, who made him Governor of Sierra Leone in the hope that the climate would kill him. It did not, and he wrote a book on the healthiness of the place. It was here that he was presented with the throne. Later, after an extremely adventurous military career, which included a court-martial, he returned to England and became MP for Hull. His involvement in the Anti-Corn Law League brought him into the orbit of Robert Ross Rowan Moore; he gave Moore the little throne as a token of esteem. It came to have an almost talismanic significance for NM, who possessed so little to connect him to his absent father, most of whose effects had been lost in a shipwreck. The throne went everywhere with NM; my son Jake now sits on it in front of his computer.

NM lived chiefly off bread and marmalade, plus dinner in Hall, at which 'pudding' was free. His mother supplied jam from home, which enabled him to invite people to breakfast and tea. When he entertained twenty friends to tea, he took the door off its hinges and used it as a table. On 12 November he wrote, 'Since I came up I have spent 7d on groceries so you see it is not very ruinous giving teas.'

The lifelong friends NM made at Cambridge were scholarly and serious-minded. His dearest friend was Philip Elwin, whose family were to play a very important part in NM's story, but their first encounter was not promising. Elwin, NM told Rebecca, was 'untidy in his dress and looks somewhat as if he had been baked before a dying fire; his voice is loud and sonorous and he reads like a quaker reading the psalms. He wears an ill-fitting and shabby second, or third hand gown and a decayed looking cap.' Another close friend was Frank Darwin, son of Charles. It is a mark of how quickly ideas changed in the nineteenth century that NM, opposing the motion that 'this meeting view with regret the abolition of slavery' at his college debating society, used the distinctly pre-Darwinian argument that 'since all mankind are sprung from one pair it is manifest that at one time the whole human race was free.'

NM loved Cambridge. No atmosphere could have suited him better. With like-minded companions, he took long walks (Ely was a favourite destination) and experimented on 'velocipedes', an early form of bicycle. Though well-behaved himself, he rather relished tussles between 'town and gown' and rowdy behaviour at a degree ceremony in the Senate House. As well as the college debating society, he joined the Union, where he was the only supporter of a motion to widen the franchise. He belonged to a literary society, wrote poetry, and rowed in the college boat. He attended lectures on history, Anglo-Saxon and classical literature as well as working extremely hard and with great enthusiasm for his degree. He wrote a prize-winning essay on the political situation in Ireland.

The end of his Cambridge career was darkened by an odd incident in Hall. An undergraduate named Hill seems to have picked a quarrel with NM over dinner. What seemed to NM to be nothing more than a little routine sparring became much more serious when, without warning, Hill picked up a heavy glass salt-cellar and flung it at NM's head. NM ducked, and laughed at Hill's furious face. The next day at dinner NM 'chaffed him unmercifully', as he wrote to Philip Elwin. 'He rose with the dignity of a Pecksniff and left the room saying "I leave a society in which there are no gentlemen."' The row rumbled on; the next day Hill struck NM on the ear. NM had the presence of mind not to return the blow, though as he said, 'I should dearly like to thrash the cad.' Dr Robinson, the Master of St Catharine's, recommended a mutual apology. NM refused, as he did not believe himself to have been in any way at fault.

The quarrel seemed to be over. Two months later, for unclear reasons, Carr, the Tutor, revived the subject and gated NM for a fortnight. NM appealed to Dr Robinson, who refused to hear his appeal. NM turned to the man who had replaced Waterton as his mentor and father-substitute, Philip Elwin's father, Whitwell Elwin, clergyman of Booton in Norfolk and editor of the *Quarterly Review*. Elwin told his young friend that if he would stick to his guns he would see him through.

NM wrote to Dr Robinson, but his letters were ignored. NM and Hill were called before the college authorities. The whole university was in a state of uproar; sides were taken according to how one defined the concept of a 'gentleman'. Mr Elwin published a pamphlet in support of NM, entitled 'The Case of Mr Moore'. In it he claimed that NM 'stood alone before a trio, each of whom combined in his own person the complex characters of prosecutor, witness, jury, and judge. I trust that no such defiance of the elementary principles of justice has ever happened before, or will ever be heard of again.'

NM was rusticated, though he was allowed to finish taking his final exams. Mr Elwin expressed his outrage:

The gentleman who is the object of these proceedings is a person of admirable talents, of great and varied knowledge, of a reasoning,

thoughtful mind ... He is unstained by the common vices of
youth. Upright, temperate and diligent, frank, open-minded, and
magnanimous, he would be an acquisition, and an ornament to
any society ... He possesses one quality in a pre-eminent degree
– the courage to speak his convictions whatever they may be ...
This quality has not failed him in the present contest.

The affair reached the national press. Perhaps as a result of anxiety and stress, NM gained a second-class degree rather than the
first that had been expected of him. When he took his degree on
30 January 1869 he was greeted by cheers in the Senate House.

The salt-cellar incident shaped NM's future. He had been asked
to stay on at Cambridge on a research scholarship, to help mod-
ernize and develop the natural sciences course. However, this
scholarship was conditional on residence, so was forfeited by rus-
tication. If this had not happened, NM would never have become
a doctor at all, but would in all likelihood have spent his life as a
Cambridge don.

*

In February, NM started at St Bartholomew's Hospital, to which
he would be attached for the rest of his career. He enrolled to study
comparative anatomy. It was only later that he decided to change
to medicine. His rooms were in the hospital itself; he was told this
would be cheaper than living in lodgings because so much less
would be stolen. The antiquity of 'Bart's' appealed strongly, and
so did its charitable outlook: 'The hospital is open day and night.
All you have to do to get in is to be poor and to be sick.' His fascination with the place was to culminate in his magisterial *History of
St Bartholomew's Hospital*, published in 1919.

Though this was a London where cows were still milked in
Hyde Park, the dirt and noise appalled NM. There were many
factories in central London, as well as the smoke from millions of
domestic fires, and everything was covered in soot. The horse-
drawn traffic – wagons, omnibuses, hansoms, four-wheelers, lan-

daus, victorias, broughams, carts – all had iron-rimmed wheels, and the city streets were paved with stone setts. The roar of the traffic was overlaid by the shouts of hawkers, street bands and barrel organs. The newly opened Underground Railway used steam trains, and the strong-smelling smoke billowed up through the gratings in the street. NM missed wildlife. 'The dragon on the steeple of S. Mary le Bow is the only flying thing I have seen this week,' he wrote to Rebecca. But he was entranced by the City too – by the churches and historical landmarks and teeming human life.

He escaped from the noise into a subterranean storeroom at the British Museum, where he studied comparative anatomy. 'My only companion was an old man . . . who sat at a high desk and brought me the skeletons I asked for.' The old man had only one eye. He dried his boots and cooked his lunch over a fire which was the only bright spot in the sepulchral gloom of the museum's depths. One afternoon, the old man asked if he could have a couple of hours off to go and marvel at the celebrated Siamese twins. 'Sad neglect of parents, Sir, they ought to have been separated as infants,' was his verdict.

It was at this time that the baby Milicent Ludlow took up residence at Yotes Court. The fresh air, the overflowing garden and the grand, spacious house were the inverse of the dark lair in which her future husband pored over the bones of birds, lizards and tortoises.

6. 'A cœur valiant rien impossible'

How is your flower getting on Harry sent you? . . . I had a game of chess with Fanny and checkmated her. Julia sent me more doll's jewelry. Papa says I am improving in my drawing I think so also myself . . . We are going to have a shop – there are going to be penwipers, Harry's little sorts of Boxes & also three open ones. We went to try and see a poney it was lame in a foot – A person came & pulled a piece of stick out of it – He was so little for us he was white.

We have got some little chickens and Scray has five puppies . . .

My dear Amy I send and all your school-fellows my love – I am your

Affectionate

BABY My own signature.

So Milicent wrote to her cousin Amy – or rather, so she dictated to her big sister Mabel. The letter is undated, but my guess is that Milicent was six – young to be checkmating her grown-up cousin at chess, old to be signing herself Baby. Milicent was a spirited little thing. She objected to being called 'a wee darling' on the grounds that 'Wee [oui] is French and I hate the Frenchies.' For Amy, at her lady-like boarding school in Hampstead, the quaint little missive must have been a welcome change from Aunt Nannie's harangues about the danger of wearing stays, or from her own mother's epistolary grumbles about lack of money, worn-out carpets, the cold, or the boredom of life at Crowham.

Amy's mother, named Georgina Mary Halliday but universally known as Jenny (pronounced Jinny), found married life something of a disappointment. Aged nineteen, she married Willy Leigh Smith for love. I have a scrapbook of Jenny's into which is pasted a

little sketch she made of her lover asleep. It is a tender image, ador-
ation in every line. It forms a poignant contrast to the restlessness, resentment, even bitterness, that came to characterize her long
marriage.

Willy was the least intellectual of the Leigh Smith children. A
school report survives from 1842, when Willy was nine. The school,
Bruce Castle in Tottenham, was an experimental one, favoured by
Dissenters. Despite receiving forty-eight lessons on ornithology,
learning 'the structure qualities and habits of . . . the turkey, partridge, passenger pigeon, house wren, marsh wren, fine warbler,
autumnal warbler, American partridge or quail, chimney swallow,
barn swallow, cliff swallow, ruby throated humming bird, golden
winged woodpecker and red headed woodpecker', Willy's success
at the subsequent examination was 'but very moderate'. He fared
little better at 'the making of wax fruit' and at furniture-making,
his success at orthography was 'very slight', and his study of the
lilac, the creeping snapdragon, the broad-leaved garlic, the rice
plant and the cashew nut also let him down, but his mental arith-
metic was 'satisfactory', his elocution 'very satisfactory', and his
'private perusal' of *Little Frank & Other Tales* also passed muster.
The overall impression is that Willy was not a high flyer. But as a
young man he was lively, good company, an energetic sportsman
and an excellent shot – perhaps taking revenge on the birds whose
'structure qualities and habits' he had been forced to study.

Jenny was proud of her well-bred and often intermarried family
of Hallidays, Noels, Wickhams, Dysarts and Tollemaches. (One
of the Tollemache cousins, a country rector, named his sixth son
Lyulph Ydwallo Odin Nestor Egbert Lyonel Toedmag Hugh
Erchenwyne Saxon Esa Cromwell Orma Nevill Dysart Planta-
ganet. The initials spell 'Lyonel the Second'. The luckless child
was known as Lyonel, which is better than Toedmag. His nine siblings were also extravagantly named.) Jenny's Noel relations were
reformers who had long been intimate with the Smiths and the
Ludlows, but Jenny herself found politics tiresome and tried to
prevent her guests from discussing current affairs. 'I shall be pleased

to have her,' she wrote of an outspoken female friend, 'if only she
& Papa [Willy] won't have rows over politics or other matters –
I must tell her that I cannot have Gladstone or women's rights or
anything irritating introduced.' Her sister-in-law Barbara was not
a kindred spirit.

Jenny was a striking girl, and far from stupid. Her letters are
observant and ingeniously catty; she had a reductive, satirical sense
of humour. Her strong visual sense showed in her painting and
drawing, in the way she furnished her house and the way she
dressed; she made the most of limited resources. In later life she
became an enthusiastic photographer. In her youth she had been a
member of Barbara's Portfolio Club – a group of artists and poets
of both sexes who met to discuss and display their work. But she
was anti-intellectual, and wholly out of sympathy with Barbara
and Nannie's views about the emancipation of women.

Jenny was only twenty-one when she gave birth to Amy, the
first of seven children. She was living at Glottenham Manor at
the time; Ben employed his brother Willy, who had trained at
Cirencester agricultural college, to manage his estates. When the
Pater died, the year after Amy's birth, Willy inherited Crowham
Manor. Jenny didn't want to live there, and Willy seems to have
been uncertain whether he wanted to embrace farming as his destiny. Crowham was advertised by a letting agent as:

> . . . a commodious family residence, with southern aspect, stand-
> ing in its own extensive grounds, and approached by a carriage
> drive of about a quarter of a mile, with lodge entrance, and com-
> prises four reception rooms, 10 bedrooms (including servants'),
> bathroom and dressing room, kitchen, servants' hall, pantry, scul-
> lery etc; conservatory and pleasure grounds of about two acres, to
> which meadow land to the extent of 50 acres could be added if
> required. There is also the rights of shooting over 270 acres. Good
> fishing. The house and premises, which are in thorough repair,
> are well supplied with good water. Coach house and stabling
> accommodation for six horses.

But no suitable tenant came forward. Willy and Jenny moved into Crowham and lived there for the next fifty years.

I know Crowham well. Hancox and Crowham are about six miles apart, and are old friends. Though it was sold in 1910 on Willy's death, my family have always been friends with the subsequent owners. For Amy, it became almost a prison, but for her daughter Ethne it was a rural idyll, the best part of her childhood. Ethne described her summer holidays there in her unpublished memoir:

Visits . . . began at Hastings with the sight of George* come to meet us, on the high driving seat of the wagonette, the silver buttons on his dark uniform shining and a smile on his neatly bearded face. I hear an echo of his Sussex drawl and can almost smell the horses and the leather harness and the stuffed seats of the wagonette.

Next comes the scrunching sound of thick gravel under the wheels as we reach the drive. There is bracken under the fir trees and when the drive turns, there, suddenly below us, lies the house.

George gets down to open the big gate into the garden, which has its own well-known squeak. We draw up at the door with a splutter of gravel, old Rover rushes out and, from the verandah come the Aunts with low cries of delight.

Looking back on those visits the curious thing is that it never seemed to rain. Often the wind roared among the forest-like thickness of the chestnut trees, but the lawn was always green and the sun always shone . . .

Aunt Jenny, (who did not like us to call her Grandmama) never seemed like an old person . . . Though her face was lined, the shape of its bones was beautiful. She had rather large eyes which I think were grey, a small straight nose, with particularly wide nostrils, a well-shaped, but fairly large mouth and a firm little chin. She had a deep voice and a way of emphasising her sentences that made anything she said seem original. She wore several rings and a gold

* George Dann, the coachman. His son, also George, became landlord of the Royal Oak at Whatlington, and a tenant of Milicent's.

bangle and she had a characteristic habit of shaking it back when it fell over her hand. Her quiet self-possessed manner was so full of dignity that it was obvious why her family nicknamed her 'the Duchess' . . .

Aunt Jenny had a big store-cupboard in the billiard room . . . In this cupboard, which Aunt Jenny kept carefully locked, were rows and rows of pots of jam, a good deal of it apple, or apple and quince, all neatly labelled by Aunt Jenny. She had a large bunch of keys and kept them in a little basket which she took up to her bedroom with her every night. There would be a spectacle case in it, some knitting, and other little things, and she would look through the contents carefully before going up to bed. There were only lamps and candles at Crowham and Curtis [the parlourmaid] bringing in the lamp was one of the events of the evening.

I used to think that the food at Crowham tasted more delicious than any I had elsewhere . . . The breakfast dishes, which were kept hot in front of the fire on cold days, were particularly good. They always included a dish of fried potatoes, the chunky oblong sort, and the scrambled eggs were very yellow and the bacon was thin and crisp.

For a London child like Ethne, Crowham was restful and comforting. For Amy, confined there almost all year round, it was stultifying. When the golden summer days gave way to the cold dark winters, the roads became impassable; the Sussex clay, which in summer bakes almost white, gives a brightness to the landscape and is firm under foot, becomes in winter a dark, sticky, gloomy brown. Willy and Jenny's tempers showed the same seasonal variability. Willy's obituary describes him as 'a highly successful breeder of Sussex stock'; it does not, of course, mention that he was a heavy drinker. Although he was genuinely interested in agriculture and in Sussex life, Willy's drinking, together with his insomnia – he often stayed awake until the early hours, which is no good for a farmer – meant the family was not as prosperous as it could have been. Alone amongst his siblings, Willy struggled financially. Childless Barbara supplemented the money the Pater left her by selling her

paintings and through her journalism; despite her endless generosity, she never ran out. Ben invested wisely, and became a rich
man. Bella combined her own fortune with that of the General
when she married. Nannie, also childless, lived abroad with Isa
Blythe, where living costs were lower; she was always more than
comfortable, and on occasion generous. But Willy had six children
to bring up (there was a seventh, a boy, who died in infancy) and
was farming at a time of national agricultural depression. Though
Jenny was regarded as socially a cut above, she brought little personal wealth to the marriage. Brought up to enjoy pretty clothes,
well-trained servants, an active social life and exciting excursions,
Jenny found herself stuck in an uncongenial rut of 'make do and
mend'. When the winter sun dipped early behind the hill, Jenny
faced long, gloomy evenings with the husband who had turned
from a charming, outgoing young man into a middle-aged drinker
who never wanted to go anywhere or do anything.

Crowham was also unhealthy. A lot of the farm was marshland;
the setting was damp and foggy. The children were fed untreated
milk, as was then normal practice; Amy and the youngest child,
Dolly, showed early signs of the tuberculosis that would kill them
both. Amy was a worry from an early age – beautiful, delicate and
wayward. It seems likely that Jenny was jealous of her eye-catching
daughter. There's a note of irritation in her letters to her. But then,
Jenny was irritated by most things. Roddy, aged eighteen, writes to
Amy that their mother has refused to allow her space in this large
house to set up her painting and carving equipment: 'Mama says
"She shant let me have the end room all to myself <u>at any future
period</u>." I know you are fond of these sorts of remarks.'

The girls' education, in Aunt Barbara's words, was 'frightfully
neglected'. Jenny was exasperated by Barbara's relentless desire to
'improve' Amy, but it was of some use to her – it was good to have
her rebellious daughter taken off her hands. From childhood, Amy
was carried off to meet Barbara's interesting friends. The first time
NM ever saw Amy was at a party in London, at Barbara's house in
Blandford Square on 9 May 1869, where he discussed 'the Hitchin

college' (the forerunner of Girton) and met 'a small niece' of Madame Bodichon's. When Amy was about this age Barbara painted a portrait of her with long, thick golden hair (it later turned a glossy chestnut) and large, dark eyes, holding a sheaf of reeds and rushes – a minor deity of my childhood.

Amy inherited the delicacy of her features from her mother, along with her visual sense. Jenny understood the significance of clothes; Ethne recalls her saying that she must have been the last woman in England to submit to wearing a crinoline – '*Horrid* things! I would not wear one until your Uncle Willy refused to go out with me without one, he said I looked indecent!' Despite their mutual hostility, the teenage Amy generously noted that her mother was the nicest-looking person at a local ball. In the many surviving photographs of Amy, she too looks elegant and well dressed, despite lack of funds. She had a knack of overcoming the restrictive ugliness of most late Victorian fashions. But she invariably wore a high collar, to hide the scars that were left when tubercular growths were cut out of her neck.

Aunt Barbara was a serious artist and had studied under Corot. Her many artist friends included Charles François Daubigny, Dante Gabriel Rossetti, whose signature can be found amongst those of Barbara's other visitors painted on the big brick fireplace at Scalands, and Hercules Brabazon Brabazon, the watercolourist who was regarded as Turner's natural successor. Barbara encouraged Amy's natural talent, by teaching her herself and arranging for 'Brabbie' and Miss Jekyll, the gardening expert who was also an artist, to give her advice. Barbara's letters to Amy about her painting are robustly critical, warning her against 'vulgar dash' at the expense of close observation. Barbara's speciality was wild landscapes in an impressionistic style; Amy painted flowers in pots more often than landscapes, but this may reflect her frail health rather than a true preference. Barbara as a vigorous and independent young woman had travelled widely, sketchbook in hand; such opportunities were not available to the sickly, overprotected Amy.

★

NM soon became a regular visitor to Scalands Gate. Barbara built the house herself, on Ben's Glottenham estate, on a ridge above a small river, surrounded by woodland but with a wonderful view of the blue Wealden landscape. She called it 'Dr Bodichon's cottage' because she hoped it would remind her husband of his childhood home in Brittany; it was an attempt to express her ideas about art and nature. It was supposed to be of Saxon design, with wide fireplaces, brick and timber walls and brick floors covered with matting, not carpet. Plain white shelves and solid wooden dressers supported books, pictures and Barbara's collection of Kabyle, Spanish and Breton pottery; bunches of wild flowers were the only other ornament. The latched front door opened straight into the living room. Cushions of Arab embroidery were scattered on the chairs. Upstairs, the room with the best views and the strongest light was Barbara's studio. Early-flowering pale yellow Banksia roses climbed the walls, to welcome the Bodichons when they returned from Algiers in May.

The interiors at Scalands formed the strongest possible contrast with conventional mid-Victorian taste, which favoured dark colours, heavy drapery, fussy, elaborate furniture and a plethora of curios and knick-knacks. Barbara's garden was also a departure from the norm. The typical mid-Victorian garden was a symmetrical arrangement of blocks of colour in lines and squares and circles, mostly provided by 'bedding plants' which would be removed by gardeners at the end of each season. Aunt Ju described this style of gardening as 'our useless meaningless vulgar imitations of vulgar carpets'. Gertrude Jekyll helped with the Scalands plan; there were informal lawns and paths, roses and clematis scrambling up trees and over walls, garden flowers mingling in drifts with the wild primroses, bluebells and Lent lilies under the trees, so that the division between the garden and its surrounding woodland were softened.

NM was very taken with Scalands. He wrote to his mother, 'This house is very tasteful. It is set on a hill and surrounded by woods. Round this room is a copy reduced and painted on paper of the Bayeux tapestry . . . I am going to see the field of battle [i.e. of Hastings] this afternoon. Dr Bodichon is tall, handsome and pleasant, but does not speak English.' Eugène Bodichon, seventeen years older than his wife, was a French physician and philosopher who had lived in Algiers for many years; after their marriage, he and Barbara spent the winter months in their house there, Campagne du Pavillon, named after the doctor's Breton home. Dr Bodichon was intelligent and philanthropic. He devoted himself to public health issues and, as a member of the Chamber of Deputies for Algeria, he was instrumental in bringing about the abolition of slavery in the colony. He was a strong republican, and the author of a mighty work called *De l'Humanité*, the first volume historical and the second ethnographical. These tomes sit on the library shelves at Hancox. They are not well thumbed, though NM read them all through.

The 'Docteur', as the family called him, was a deeply peculiar man. At Scalands, he often dressed in a burnous like an Arab, and sometimes he wore nothing at all. He could be a deterrent to casual callers. There is a family story that some relations said, 'We must go and call. It is so silly to believe the stories about Dr Bodichon.' So they set off and, as they entered the drive, a naked Docteur leapt out of the rhododendrons. He maintained that in this way he felt closer to his mother's spirit.

NM, who valued intelligence, adventurousness and sound moral principles above polish and social correctness, was in the minority of Barbara's friends who appreciated the Docteur. Barbara was generally regarded as courageous if foolhardy in taking on so unusual a husband. Some of the family, including the Pater and Ben, and Nannie, who couldn't stand him, had expressed their objections openly. But at least in the early years of the marriage, Barbara and Eugène's shared love of liberty and adventure kept them happy. In 1857, their extended honeymoon in America was more a fact-finding mission than a holiday. There were fifteen slave states and they visited all of these except Texas. They sailed up the Mississippi in a steamboat, walked for miles through alligator-infested swamps (the Docteur could walk for six hours without stopping), visited slave-owners on their plantations ('the Doctor's ideas of Universal Fusion and Universal Brotherhood to spring from it are not popular here at all'), took tea with freeborn negroes, and talked with every slave they met in the streets. Barbara kept a journal, and wrote articles about what she saw. She attended a slave market in New Orleans, and reported for *The Englishwoman's Journal*:

The auctioneer . . . showed me all the articles for sale – about thirty women and twenty men; also twelve or fourteen babies. He took me round and told me what each article could do. 'She can cook and iron; has worked in the field' etc . . . We descended into a dirty hall . . . the room was crowded with rough men, smoking and spitting. A bad-looking set they were . . . I pitied the slaves, for these were the slave-buyers . . .

A girl with two little children was on the block. 'Likely girl, Amy. And her two children. Good cook. Healthy girl, Amy. What! Only 700 dollars for the three? That's giving them away! . . . Healthy family. Good washer; house servant. 750!' etc . . .

Then a girl with a little baby got up, and the same sort of harangue went on until 800 dollars . . . were bid; and a blackguard-looking gentleman came up, opened her mouth, examined her teeth, felt her all over . . .

It is evident . . . planters in general only consider the slaves as a means of gaining money, and there is not the consideration for them which they pretend in drawing-room conversations.

Before I went, the young man who is in our house had said, 'Well, I don't think there is anything to see; they sell them like so many rocking chairs; there's no difference.' And that is the truest word that can be said about the affair.

In the spring the Bodichons left the southern states for the freedom of the north. They painted, birdwatched, stayed in a Quaker community, where the Docteur earned their keep by teaching, visited the Niagara Falls (Barbara's painting of the Falls hangs in Girton College), got as far north as Quebec, attended a

prayer meeting at Boston, where the preacher prayed to 'the Crea-
tor, the Infinite Mother of us all', which Barbara considered 'the
prayer of all I ever heard in my life which was the truest to my
individual soul'. In these early days, the marriage seems to have
been balanced and harmonious, each respecting the other's need to
work; domestic chores were shared. In later years, they spent more
time apart than together. Barbara never admitted to unhappiness
or disillusion, but it seems that a union based chiefly on shared
ideals became increasingly difficult to sustain. Once, when asked
why she had married the Docteur, Barbara replied, 'He was so like
Caractacus'; an answer, as my grandfather Alan put it, which put
an end to questioning but not to speculation.

Amy was not daunted by her aunt's peculiar black-browed husband. She spent much time at Scalands; in addition to the painting
lessons she received from Aunt Barbara, she had instruction from
the village schoolmaster. NM met her there often. Barbara, with
Willy and Jenny's knowledge, encouraged him to act as a kind of
informal tutor:

Scalands 28th July 1871.

[Amy] has driven away a 3rd governess & now there is an interreg-
num of doing nothing & I have not the least idea what her parents
will try next! But while she is here I like her to see my friends &
get out of that defiant state of mind. I think you can help me
because she likes you & I think you can give her an interest in the
country things among which she walks rather blindly at present.

NM often referred to Amy in his letters to his mother: 'Amy is
slightly ill and is at present lying on the sofa eating grapes.' He
describes in detail a weekend spent there when Amy's father drove
him, Barbara and the Leigh Smith children, including Amy, to
local places of interest – Bodiam Castle, Brede Place (a medieval
house largely destroyed by fire in the 1960s), and Ben's Glottenham
Manor, then housing the poet Christina Rossetti, who had lain

there very ill for several weeks. They finished the day at Crow-ham. This was NM's first visit to Amy's home.

Later in the same stay, NM rode out on an old pony to explore further. He called at Bateman's, near Burwash:

> The man of the house an old farmer in a smock frock was hospit-able and drew cider from a huge cask.
>
> He told us that he had twenty-one children. We saw one. It had the measles.
>
> The house had its ancient knocker, its original firedogs and fire irons.

Fifty years later NM was to visit Bateman's again, this time as the guest of Rudyard Kipling.

★

10th August 1875. Scalands Gate, Robertsbridge.

Dear Dr. Moore,
Aunt Barbara wants to know if you want to dissect the nervous system of a weasel we have a dead one here.
Yours sincerely Amy Leigh Smith.

This postcard was the first written communication NM had from Amy, and he treasured it all his life. His role as an informal, unpaid tutor meant that he was able to spend unchaperoned time with her. On 18 October 1875 they visited a sick shepherd together, after which 'I gave Amy a lesson in the rudiments of heraldry and then we had luncheon. After it Amy and I walked across the field to Firbank,* rooted among the books there and gathered a basketful

---

* Firbank is the same house as Brown's. It was renamed because the Pater planted five fir trees there, one for each of his children, who he hoped would grow up 'straight and true' like the firs. For a while the names were used interchangeably. It is now once again Brown's. The firs still exist, though some are leaning.

of grapes. I read to Amy Dryden's translation of Horace Book III Ode XXIX as we walked back.'

On the Sunday they went to Brightling church together, where Amy's aunt Bella had married the General sixteen years earlier. They returned to Scalands to dine off a roasted heron that had been accidentally shot. Amy did not like it, but 'the Doctor, Madame and I declared it game royal.' NM took the remains of the heron back to London and gave it to some of the Barts' students to finish. Apparently they were appreciative.

By this time, NM had realized that his feelings for Amy were serious. She was young – only sixteen – and he was hard up, with no prospect of inheriting wealth. He knew it would be unfair to approach her at this point. For almost a year he avoided going to Scalands if he knew she was likely to be there, but on 23 September 1876 he called at Firbank to take tea with Ben and found Amy there. 'We sat indoors while heavy rain fell, drank tea, ate grapes and read or repeated bits of verse from Andrew Marvell and from Crabbe BLS's [Ben's] favourite poets.' Potent emotions were roused. NM ends his letter with an outbreak of verse: 'I ventured forth, to Amy bade goodbye; And hastening up the hill: Outran the promise of the sky.'

After a year of abstention from her company, NM found his love for Amy not only still intact but stronger than ever. He decided to act. He told Aunt Barbara that he wanted to propose marriage. She gave him the green light: 'I cannot make out what she thinks and it may injure your chance, but she is so attractive that I am sure she will have more than one offer in the next six months so I leave it to your discretion to do as you please: I will give you an opportunity.'

The opportunity arose in November. A visit to the Elwins, NM's great supporters from Cambridge days, was arranged. Philip Elwin had recently died of typhoid; since his death, the Revd Whitwell Elwin had treated NM more than ever as a substitute son.

The Elwins lived deep in the Norfolk countryside, at Booton

Rectory. Whitwell Elwin, though a learned man with a wide circle of literary friends, had no worldly ambition beyond editing the *Quarterly Review* and carrying out the priestly offices for the family living. He was repeatedly offered bishoprics by Gladstone, which he steadfastly refused. Barbara had already made his acquaintance. She knew he was particularly good with young people and, sure enough, he and Amy took to each other at once.

Barbara sent a card:

> Dear Norman,
> We shall be at St Pancras on Sat. at 9.5. I suppose we shall find 2nd class carriages quite nice.
> Amy is in great glee at the idea of seeing somewhere new.
> Yours Affect'y
> BLSB.

NM had been at a dinner party until one the night before, but he joined them on the train. On the journey Amy lent him her drawing pencil. As an old man, he recalled how the look she gave him as she did so went straight to his heart.

They visited Cawston and Sall and Norwich Cathedral and received Holy Communion together at Booton – a moment of great significance for NM. He then had to dash back to his work at Bart's while Barbara and Amy stayed on in Norfolk. The following weekend NM rejoined them in Peterborough, though he only just made it. He was starting for the station when a message arrived: could he see a woman with a newborn baby, both very ill with smallpox? 'I never wished less to go anywhere. However I thought at so critical a moment if I deserved what I wished I ought not to hesitate in a point of duty so I took a cab to the place a shoemaker's shop a long way up in Islington.' In 1876 germs were still not understood; he showed no fear of catching or transmitting the disease. Despite the detour, he just caught the train. He changed his clothes en route; the train stopped at a station when he had nothing on and he was obliged to hang on to the door handle to prevent other passengers from getting in. He sent his pox-ridden clothes home by rail.

Aunt Barbara managed to contrive a time when NM could make his proposal. NM's diary entries usually consist only of the briefest listing of appointments, but on 30 November he more than filled the allotted space:

On this day in the north aisle of the choir of Peterborough Cathedral at a little after ten o'clock in the morning I told Amy Leigh Smith that I loved her with my whole heart and asked her to be my wife. Amy told me that she loved me with all her heart and promised to marry me.

We knelt in the choir just within the door from the north aisle and thanked God for having blessed us and we promised to help one another serve him.

Even at this moment of intense emotional solemnity, NM's antiquarian instincts could not be suppressed. 'Do not talk of architecture,' implored Amy as they left the Cathedral precinct arm in arm. Though only seventeen, Amy had a mature sense of the seriousness of the undertaking. 'You do not know,' she told her new fiancé, 'what you have got.'

They knew there would be objections to the match, but neither had guessed quite how strong family opposition would be. The stance Amy's parents took is not surprising. Amy was very young; she had led a sheltered life and had met few potential suitors. She was charming, talented and beautiful and could reasonably be expected to make a brilliant match. She was the eldest child and her parents had ambitions for her marriage, Jenny because she came from a semi-aristocratic family where such things were held in high esteem, Willy because, illegitimate himself, he had striven through his chosen role as lord of the manor to render himself more respectable in the eyes of the world. Willy always felt himself to be hard up; it did not suit him that Amy should engage herself to a man without capital.

Uncle Ben's antipathy seems less predictable. Since the death of the old Pater, Ben had taken his position as head of the family very seriously. It did not signify that Barbara was the oldest – Ben was male, and formidable, and his siblings were in awe of him. His devotion to his pretty niece might nowadays be seen as unwholesome, but at the time it was simply accepted as an established fact. As NM wrote to his mother when the storm broke, 'BLS is fonder of Amy than of anyone in the world therefore of course he is hurt and in fact sure to be an enduring opponent.' He was.

The day after the proposal, Amy wrote to her parents and uncle to break the news. She wrote from Cambridge, where she and Aunt Barbara were staying at an inn. She then wrote to NM. Despite having agreed to marry him, she still didn't use his Christian name:

> My dear Dr Moore,
>   I have written the letters. I can't say in them a bit what I want to say – but I hope they will make people understand.
>   Aunt B. is afraid that I don't know my own mind, but *you* trust me do you not?
>   The letter must go. Ever your
>   Amy.

Alas, the letters failed to 'make people understand', and those NM wrote fared no better. NM did not trust his to the post. He caught a train to Battle, walked the six miles to Crowham and delivered them in person. He had also prepared a statement of his income, outgoing and prospects, but Amy's father would not even look at this. 'Mr W.L.S. firmly refused to treat on the subject. He was not otherwise than very polite and sent me in a dogcart to the station.'

Though the root of Uncle Ben's objection may have been his possessive love for Amy, his proclaimed opinion was that NM was a gold-digger, a penniless Irishman only interested in marrying Amy to increase his fortune and improve his social standing. Ben may have believed that NM had his eye on his own fortune; as Ben was still childless, Amy would have been one of his natural heirs. In vain Aunt Barbara pleaded otherwise in a letter to her obdurate brother:

> I know Norman well and I think him a very fine character.
>
> He is upright, persevering and very affectionate. He has brain enough to take a good place in his profession.
>
> Thousands of English girls do marry struggling professional men and get on very well and are very happy.
>
> Whether Amy has the stuff to undertake this externally hard life I am not sure.

In NM's opinion, Ben had been corrupted by contact with 'sordid, mean, wealthy men . . . alas that so possible a hero should have been so far spoiled'. Ben denounced NM to his cousins the Shore Smiths as being 'only a house surgeon at St Bart's' on £300 a year, but this was hardly accurate. In fact, NM could offer Amy a respectable, though not lavish, standard of living. As Warden of St Bartholomew's Medical School – a post he had been awarded at the unusually young age of twenty-seven – he was given a rent-free house in Little Britain plus an allowance for coals – the only form of heating – and some domestic help. He was held in high regard by his fellow physicians, the medical school at Bart's was prospering under his care and he held several important posts at the hospital. With all the extras, he was worth about £800 a year. His professional prospects were good; he was a rising star in the worlds of literature and Irish scholarship as well as medicine. He had many eminent friends, as well as plenty of non-eminent ones. Uncle Ben himself had liked and respected NM before the entanglement with Amy. He had sought his advice about his last Arctic expedition; there had even been a suggestion that NM should accompany him. NM decided, with regret, that he could not afford to take so much time out of his career. In his refusal to countenance Amy's engagement, Ben was wilfully blinding himself.

The result of all the letters from NM, Amy and Barbara was a flat 'no'. Not only could the couple not marry, they were not to meet or even to correspond until Amy was twenty-one.

Just before the ban came into force, Barbara sent a telegram to NM from Cambridge, and he hastened there to join her and Amy. He later recalled their meeting:

> I think of your writing those notes at the 'Lamb' and Aunt Barbara sitting in the armchair and saying that you must write them without her help. And then I think of how anxious you looked when I arrived at the University Arms & of you & Aunt Barbara by the fire. And then of Sunday morning when you threw down what you were carrying & ran to the fire and took my hand & looked into my face & I hardly knew what to say but that I trusted you whatever happened & you answered with sweet, faithful, loving looks.

NM had to sustain himself on these memories for a long time.

The trio returned to London. On 3 December he wrote in his diary:

> This morning we parted Amy & I at the Liverpool St Station and it may be long before we are allowed to see one another again. Let it not O God be very long. It was at twenty minutes to one in the afternoon that Amy held out her hand and wished me a second goodbye.
>
> *A cœur valiant rien impossible.*

Aunt Barbara was in a difficult position. It was she who had introduced Norman to Amy, she who had enabled them to have time alone together. She wanted the marriage to happen; if anything, she wondered whether Amy was worthy of Norman, rather than the other way round. But she had also to respect the wishes of her brothers. She agreed to act as a go-between within the limits of honesty. NM described the discussion they had at Cambridge in a letter to his mother; '. . . Mme B promising to let me hear of Amy and she (her) of me but both agreeing if necessary ever to

follow her parents rules as to action until Amy is of age . . . in everything we agree not to act at all without consulting Madame B.'

And so the curtain fell on the first act of the drama. Amy
returned to Crowham, to spend the slow winter months cooped
up with her unsympathetic family. NM threw his energies into his
work, his reading and his social life. And though he was not
allowed to send letters to Amy, he wrote an unposted letter to her
every single day of their separation.

★

NM, well read in English and Irish literature of every age, liked
the eighteenth-century best. Jonathan Swift was a particular hero
of his. He entitled his series of unsent letters to Amy 'The New
Journal to Stella' in homage to the journal Swift kept for his 'Stella',
Esther Johnson. The eleven volumes of 'The New Journal to Stella'
are piled before me as I write. They are among the chief glories of
the Hancox archive, testimony to the value of my family's habit of
writing things down and never throwing them away.

'The New Journal to Stella' is valuable on several levels. It tells
the story of this very Victorian courtship. It eloquently expresses
NM's love for Amy and provides glimpses of her feelings for him.
It is a showcase in which NM set out his principles, his priorities,
his interests, as well as his emotions; it is the personal manifesto of
a gifted and unusual man. And it is also a record of daily events.
NM writes about his work at St Bartholomew's, his travels, his
researches, his friends. The enforced separation of the lovers resulted
in a detailed picture of a young doctor's life in Victorian London.

NM wrote in small bound notebooks, unruled, in ink that has
browned with time. They would have been written with a quill
pen, by candlelight or the light of a gas lamp. Judging by the few
deletions, I would guess that he copied them in from a rough draft.
He didn't miss a day – quite an achievement when one considers
that on top of his hospital workload he wrote almost daily to his
mother, corresponded with many friends, studied ancient Irish
manuscripts, wrote papers for the Pathological Society, and was

frequently sidetracked by projects such as the writing of a paper for the London and Middlesex Archaeological Society about the two Roman tombs in the foundations of St Bartholomew's – NM examined the skeletons and concluded that they had died in an epidemic shortly before the end of the Roman occupation. As well as all this, NM dined out often, went for long walks and paid visits to friends all over England, Scotland and Ireland. When he began, he had no idea for how long he would have to keep the journal. He had high hopes that the ban on communication with Amy would soon be lifted, but the couple had to endure several false dawns before at last, a year and four months after the proposal at Peterborough, the older generation relented and allowed them to correspond.

NM took comfort in the medieval chivalric ideal. He makes frequent references to poems and folk tales in which the constancy and courage of the beleaguered lovers is eventually rewarded. 'Look over the battlements of your castle, my fair imprisoned princess, into the far distant country & think you see comfort slowly coming. The dragons at the foot may cast forth fire & smoke but their days are diminishing & your release drawing nearer & nearer.' Several times he relates their situation to the old ballad 'The Nut Brown Mayd':

Last night I dined with your aunt Barbara & your great Aunt Julia. They asked me to read some ballad & I looked for Bird Helen but could not find it, so read Sir Patrick Spens but I longed to read The Nut Brown Mayd so I talked about it till your aunt Barbara who guessed the why of my wish asked me to read it. So, mine own heart true, I read it to them but my thoughts were directed to you all the time and I am afraid I read it stumblingly. The sweet constant Nut Brown Mayd is you in every thought and when I think of our conversation on the way from Cambridge . . . I seem to have done nothing but tire you with a long declamation on duty when I might have said fifty better things. What things Amy we have left unsaid when shall we say them, when, when, when, how, how, how is this dreary silent time to end . . . The consolation is that we have a great enduring happiness before us & that though we sigh

now the time is not very far off when we shall live happily ever
after as is truly said in fairy tales.

Often he draws on Irish myth and legend. Irishness was central
to NM's character. Though he never lived in Ireland for longer
than a few weeks at a time, he visited every year and explored the
country thoroughly on foot. In his lifetime he visited every county
except Kerry. He spoke and wrote the language and became an
authority on Irish history and literature – the historian J. R. Green
described him as, 'the only Irish person from whom I ever learnt
anything about Ireland'. It seems that, in the absence of his unsatisfactory father, NM found a sense of rootedness, of belonging, in
his intimate knowledge of his fatherland.

It was essential to NM that Amy should come to love Ireland
and all things Irish. Though she had never set foot there, her father
owned some land in Galway, which pleased NM; he could refer to
Amy as 'my Galway maid'. 'As your father is a Galway man you
ought to be a Connaught girl & must turn your tongue to a little
Irish. Connaught has produced many fair & famous women. Perhaps the greatest was the renowned Queen Medb [Maeve] whose
history I must some day tell you.'

He goes on to talk about how important his knowledge of his
own ancestry is to his sense of well-being. 'My mother's ancestor
Ceallachán was king of Cailsil and when I crossed the plain & saw
the grand old rock of Cashel before me three years ago I was
rejoiced to feel that it was no strange or foreign grandeur which
surrounded its old towers but a kindly family love.' This strain was
too fanciful for my grandfather Alan. Reading the NJS in 1949, he
pencilled in the margin, 'An example of NM's power, not quite of
self-deception, but of finding something he wants when he wished
to find it.' Certainly, describing Sussex-born-and-bred Willy
Leigh Smith as 'a Galway man' is stretching a point.

NM converted his own adventures in Ireland into a kind of
personal mythology. It was as if he lived two lives; his prosaic
London life was enriched and elevated by his Irish life, in which

high emotions could be experienced in a pure form. Praising Amy for her steadfastness, he writes:

One stormy day I rowed across Lough Derg from Drumineer to Tintrim in Galway. The boat was a leaky one & a bent old man rowed the stroke oar. The wind was high & the old man wanted to turn back: I said I must go on. So we went on & the whole way across the old man never ceased saying 'Row on my hayro [hero].' So I say now to you Row on dear heroine, row on and be the winds & waves never so fierce you shall yet reach a safe port.

Another letter depicts Ireland as a place of spiritual, as well as emotional significance. He wrote of Glen Columbcille:

It is a place of pilgrimage & I have seen the pilgrims in long lines at five in the morning winding through the glen and kneeling at the ancient stations of the cross . . . The last pagans in Ireland are said to have lived in [Glen Columbcille] . . . St Columbcille lived in it & made it holy & it has a sacred character to me myself for in it I first received the Holy Communion. Some day I hope, dear Amy, you & I will visit Glen Columbcille for I love it dearly know every rock in it, & as I think of it I can almost hear the great Atlantic dashing against the glen foot & see the waves sending white spray high in the air. Often & often on a sunny afternoon when the sea was high have I seen seals rising in the Glen bay looking round with their slow eyes & gracefully sinking straight down into the sea.

NM was a firm believer. Surprisingly for such an intellectual man, he disliked theological or philosophical discussions and investigations. For him, God was the force behind the natural world, behind the birds and animals and rocks and trees he loved so much. This attitude made him slow to accept Darwin's ideas. In 1871, NM, aged twenty-four, had been asked by John Murray to review *The Descent of Man* for *Fraser's Magazine*. 'My review will be so hostile that I doubt their inserting it,' he told a friend. His prediction was right. The review never appeared, which was just as well; if it had, the affectionate friendship that developed between NM and Darwin would hardly have got off the ground. NM became a regular visitor to the Darwins at Down House through his undergraduate friendship with Charles's son Frank, and he was soon won over by the gentle hospitality and fascinating talk of the 'head sage'. 'I wish you had been here,' NM wrote to Barbara from Down, 'for there can have been few more lively, interesting fireside conversations going on in England.' NM became Darwin's trusted medical adviser; he was summoned to his death bed, and wrote his death certificate.

For the fatherless NM, God was his personal protector and father-substitute. In 'The New Journal to Stella', he describes the way he spent the night of his unknown earthly father's death:

> The night my father died I slept on a wild mountain in the North-west of Ireland called Lough Salt. I was ignorant of his illness. I had lost my way & was very tired so I lay down in a hollow & covered myself with pieces of turf to keep off the wind which swept furiously across the mountain. Fierce driving rain followed but at last I fell asleep & when I woke it was a clear starlight morning. I walked on thinking of the protecting care of God. My father had been dying that night & I had walked on, as far as strong worldly protectors go, alone in the world. But God has always been my helper & to him I shall always look for help.

NM was delighted when Barbara told him that Amy had worn a locket containing a shamrock on St Patrick's Day; 'You are a true sweet love and a real maid of Erin.' He longed for the time when he could show her Ireland: 'In giving your heart to me, my dear one, you gave it to Ireland. You are all the world of people to me and Ireland is all the world of land. How happy that day will be when we land together on her lovely coast.' Though NM and Amy did indeed visit Ireland together, her deteriorating health meant that these journeys were less frequent and less adventurous than he had hoped. All too often, he had to travel alone.

NM was highly principled. He believed that the deepest satisfaction in life came from following sound codes of conduct. On
his thirtieth birthday, 8 January 1877, he wrote an account for Amy
of the vows he had taken on his twenty-first:

I went on the eighth to Glastonbury Abbey. . . Glastonbury had a
close connexion with Ireland, some relics of Saint Patrick were kept
there, & many Irishmen spent religious lives there. So as I could not
be in Ireland on that day I chose Glastonbury as a place of medita-
tion. I thought over my past life and tried to think in what ways I
could live in future a better life. The day was cold, with wind and
sleet & no one was in the ruins but myself. After I had thought a
long time I knelt before where the high altar, I thought, must have
stood & made three solemn vows as to my life from that day forth,
my free, uncontrolled life as a man. The monastic vows were three:
poverty, chastity and obedience . . . I thought of these vows when I
made mine, but as I had resolved to live a life of battle in the world &
not of contemplation in a cloister I formed different resolutions.
First then I resolved that I would always prefer duty & learning to
money & that the desire of growing rich should never lead my ways.
My next resolution was that I would live in faithful attachment to
someone whom I should marry and that though I then had no idea
who she would be or whence she would come or when, that I would
think of her as one to whom I had the duty of pure, unwavering,
unalterable love just as much now when she was unknown even to
my imagination as when she should be my wife. My third vow was
that regardless of consequences I would obey my conscience and
that if I could avoid temporal misfortune or ruin by altering my
opinion or changing my course I would not do so but come what
might would stand to the truth and the right . . . I have kept these
vows faithfully & I feel their full force still. I had not then seen you
but I may fairly ask you to count my love of you from that day. I
might have seriously considered marrying another than you without any breach of my second vow, but it so chanced that I never did;
so you may claim to have had my faithful devotion since ever I made

a resolution on the subject. In this I see most plainly the kind guiding hand of God. I have never during these nine years said one word of these vows, not even to my dearest friend, but you, Amy, are to share the life that is based upon them so you must know them. Life, mine own heart true, is a serious affair but if it is pursued with this knowledge . . . it is far more cheerful & it never palls.

Though there were many times of despondency and anxiety during the fourteen months of enforced silence, NM never gave way to doubt or despair. His was a temperament that rose to meet challenges. In April 1877, Amy managed to convey a posy of spring flowers to him via Aunt Barbara; he wrote the letter of thanks that he could not send:

Thankyou for both my Amy. The flowers are sweet & the love far sweeter. I do my best to be very cheerful but I must tell you truly that it is hard work. Burke [the political philosopher and orator] says that Nitor in adversum 'I strive against opposition' had been his motto through life. It is that of every man who tries to do his duty. I hope it is mine. I never found a struggle so hard to bear before. This is not wrong. The prize is the greatest.

Many years later, when NM was made a baronet, he adopted Burke's motto and incorporated it into his coat of arms.

His prodigious energy helped keep gloom at bay. On 23 February 1877 he describes a typical day:

In the morning I saw a hundred outpatients & received a call from a Mrs Lankester widow of a Dr Lankester a person of some note & little worth, then I made two post mortem examinations then took a class to which I demonstrated the anatomy of the lobster. Then a call from a naval official from Chatham about the best way of educating his son. I next taught medicine for an hour & then dined in hall. On my right sat a student named C.R. Smith from Magdalene Coll: Cambridge & we talked chiefly about Southey's Life of

Nelson which he is reading & about the glorious actions & wonderful intrepidity of the great naval hero.

　After dinner I taught physiology for an hour, & since that have
been looking through some French books on the construction of
hospitals.

And after that, of course, he wrote it all down for Amy.

　Though there was no direct communication, each received just
enough news of the other to be reassured that faith had not wavered.
Aunt Barbara showed Norman the letters Amy sent her. Amy's parents liked to believe that she was losing interest. In March, Jenny
sent a characteristically dismissive note to Barbara – 'Please do not
speak of Dr Moore to her. She has seemed quite happy and con-
tented lately & we do not like the idea that the subject should
be revived in her mind. You cant be surprised that on that account
we are sorry she should see you. I don't think I can go to Scalands it
is such a long tiring drive.' Amy's dwindling interest was wishful
thinking on Jenny's part. A couple of weeks later, Amy burst out to
Barbara, 'I believe they expect me to be made of stone or something with no feelings of any sort.'

　NM sometimes sent Amy presents without an accompanying
note or any indication as to the donor – a book of Norfolk landscapes by John Sell Cotman, a penwiper 'made like a bishop' for
Valentine's Day. Most thrillingly, he sent her a book of Irish airs
– Amy played the piano well – containing coded messages. 'I put a
mark thus under letters in the table of contents making "adieu my
own heart true reviens Amy trop long est ta demeure"* & in the
preface to N°1 "Let Aunt Barbara hear from you often we will not

---

* This is a line from a rondeau by the fourteenth-century French poet Jehan
Froissart:

>　　　Reviens, amy; trop longue est ta demeure;
>　　　Elle me fait avoir peîne et doulour.
>　　　Mon esperit te demande à toute heure.
>　　　Reviens, amy; trop longue est ta demeure

wait three years it is too long when you are nineteen at latest we must make them let us marry I will do anything you wish me to do let Aunt Barbara hear & ask her about me." ' He hardly dared hope that Amy would decipher the messages, or even notice that the book was marked at all, but she did, and let him know via Barbara. 'March 29 1877. My dearest Amy, so you saw the marks in the Irish tune book. That was clever of you with no hint at all. I could not say a word to Aunt Barbara of them as then she could not have sent the book & I hardly expected you would notice them but I am very glad you have.' The marked songbook is now at Hancox.

Aunt Barbara gave NM a photograph of Amy; he chose from her album:

Of the four pictures of you in Aunt Barbara's book I like the one with the curious cambric headdress the best because in it I see best your eyes & because in all the others there is a slight expression of sadness . . . The photograph does show your beautiful long hair but it gives me a faint and distant semblance of your eyes into which I have not looked in vain nor ever shall for love and kindness & sympathy & for every dear & tender sentiment . . . Now that I have your picture here I look at it very often & long to see your real face more & more. How, when, where shall we meet. The thought seems to check my breath & to quicken my heart & I hardly know that I should not burst into tears if I saw you suddenly.

Barbara was the prop and stay of both NM and Amy. For NM's birthday, the one on which he recalled his Glastonbury vows, she sent him a symbolic present of salt cellars. 'My father used to say to me, "Salt of the earth ye virtuous few" etc. as an encouragement to stand up against the crowd of worldlings the word salt is in consequence very pleasant to me as well as the taste. What signifies more than the words salt sea! It has such a wholesome tasting sound.' The 'worldlings' Barbara wanted to help NM resist were Ben, Willy and Jenny, who seemed to her to be opposed to the marriage on sordid mercenary grounds. She expressed her disgust with Amy's parents in a letter to her best friend, Bessie Belloc: 'They call me a fool to Amy! . . . It is too childish . . . the sort of latent quarrel is horrible for her character . . . Roddy is utterly neglected by both father & mother.'

Nannie, living in Algiers with Isa, expressed her opinions but refused to take sides. Nannie had a low opinion of men in general. She was not pleased that her niece had made her choice so young, but she was wise enough to see that young people in love were not likely to have their minds changed by a grumpy older generation. She wrote to Ben urging him not to blame Barbara for the affair – 'I don't see that anyone ought to think *she* got Amy into a scrape' – and trying to persuade him to soften up a little: 'If Amy has [her heart in it], it wont alter things in the end, that we wish Mr Norman Moore in the sea. People every day make stupid marriages, & are miserable, but the question is, would not they also have been miserable if they had been prevented?'

Her advice to Amy seems stern, but quite balanced and judicious:

I think if you try to put yourself in yr Uncle Ben's place, you <u>might</u> see that he is not meaning to be unkind to you.

You must start with remembering that he is convinced you will be very unhappy as Dr Moore's wife – & rightly or wrongly of this he has no doubt . . . The longer I live the more I see how few married people are happy – more especially those who make their choice very young . . . Life does not change by marrying in the way people seem to expect - & at all times you must find the only real part of happiness in your own self. I am not denying the intense happiness of true companionship – no one knows this better than I, for I possess it – but it rarely exists between men & women - & the sort of glamour girls feel before marriage – disappears very quickly if the real sources of union do not exist . . .

Nannie's feminist, unconventional instincts made her want to support Amy against her parents' oppression. In another letter, dated 28 March 1877, she writes, 'That you do it against the wishes of all your own people is not <u>wrong</u> to my mind – so long as you are as sure as you can be, that it is the one thing to make you happy.'

General Ludlow's opinion can only be inferred. His diaries breathe no word of criticism of NM, but the invitations to Yotes Court dried up. The General and Ben had immense respect for one another and had been through a great deal together in their attempts to deal with Bella's madness. To continue his patronage of NM after Ben's clear statement that he was *persona non grata* would have felt like treachery to the General. He seems to have decided that silence on the subject was the safest course. However, he maintained contact with Amy, sending her three of the Wellingtonia seedlings he had raised from the seed Ben sent back from the Yosemite Valley. His letter to Amy on the subject is characteristically pleasant, and avoids all reference to tricky matters: 'You know that they grow some 200 miles from San Francisco, in the Manitosa and Yosemite Valley (which is <u>8000 above the level of the sea</u>) 30 feet in circumference and 300 feet in height. So, *when* will you have your Conifers? – It is to be hoped *before* they attain full growth! – overtopping all creation of their kind.' The Wellingtonias were duly dispatched and planted; they still flourish at Crowham.

Barbara may have been disappointed by the General's unwillingness to support her cause. She did not say so directly, but a letter to Amy written at Blandford Square makes an oblique criticism of the General's cautiousness:

12 December '76. 12 o'clock.
    Dark as night, candles lighted, quite <u>black</u> outside.
    General Ludlow has refused to come to town because of smallpox of course it is bad as you see by the papers but no one here thinks about it, I am not the least afraid.

NM was deeply conscious of what he owed to Barbara's courage. Often in the Journal he reminds himself and Amy of their duty to cherish her and to include her in their future happiness:

'Often and often, my fair loved one, I hope that you and Aunt Barbara shall sit together by the fire & I shall look into your eloquent eyes and feel that the world does not hold a happier man. We shall join hands and feel that three more united, trusting, true, loving, joyful hearts are not on earth.' 'She is indeed our best friend and one part of our joint duty will be to love her & to cherish her all her days. We will meet her enemies in the gate, for every good person has enemies, & when she grows old we will make her every day gladder that she did so great a service to each of us.' 'I saw Aunt Barbara . . . the fire shone on her face & she seemed to me to look a goddess of kindness.' He could have no inkling that Barbara's support was to be suddenly and shockingly removed.

7. 'Aunt Barbara's Amy'

The Leigh Smiths' desire to thwart their daughter's romance caused them to shake off their habitual torpor. They decided to take her on a long European tour – her first trip abroad – from April to November 1877. On the eve of departure Amy wrote to Barbara with a message for Norman: 'I cannot say what I want to through a third person, even when that third person is you, but please tell Norman to be of good heart, if it is only because I cannot bear to think he is unhappy . . . I won't say anything about going abroad making no difference in me – For I am sure <u>he</u> knows that I shall always be his own true Amy.'

Uncle Ben joined them in Paris. This gave Barbara cause for hope: '<u>I am very glad</u> Ben is going to Paris. I hope you & he will get to be great friends & in time talk about your plans for I do believe Ben is only afraid you will not like poverty & he calls one servant poverty but there are many things worse than that in life! Ben really does value good things & I always hope he will see your plans of life as a good thing. God bless you my dear child – whatever you do & wherever you go.'

Ben was a far more experienced traveller than Willy or Jenny and he made sure Amy did some proper sightseeing. But Barbara was over-optimistic in her belief that he would relax his attitude to the engagement. Once the Leigh Smiths left Paris for Switzerland, Ben returned to England. Amy wrote to him from Montreux. The letter shows both her affection for her uncle and the seriousness of her feelings for Norman: 'Now look here – Uncle Ben – I had <u>lots</u> of things I wanted to talk to you about in Paris – but I did not because I kept on putting off for a better opportunity which never came – and because I thought it would worry you and I <u>hate</u> doing that – but it will come some day – and, Uncle Ben, I have <u>never</u>

changed my mind one bit <u>and</u> <u>never</u> <u>shall</u> – Do see I am not a child any more – I think you do see it really don't you?'

Willy Leigh Smith's boyhood sense of fun and adventure was reawakened by travel. Barbara urged Amy to make the most of it: 'I am very happy to hear you & your father are so happy together I do not think you have any idea how fond I am of him . . . Cannot you really make friends with him & talk of what is in your heart to him.' The letter continues in classic Barbara fashion; no opportunity for self-education should be lost: 'Find out how the babies are treated by the poor people & how the infants are taught . . . & what the great republic is doing to bring up its citizens . . . & what lectures are going on in the town hall & how they sing in singing societies . . . Do not come away & know nothing of any people in the country.'

However, this wasn't Amy's style. She was deeply appreciative of natural beauty. The following year, after the ban on correspondence had been lifted, Amy recalled her time at Montreux in a letter to NM: 'There was a fairy land I used to go to – a field made of forget-me-nots & cowslips & blue mountains & blue lake seen through apple trees covered with blossom . . . When I used to get all alone there it was the happiest time in all that year.' But she never shared her aunt's enthusiasm for fact-finding. Barbara was doomed to be disappointed in her niece. An ongoing theme was that Amy should study at Barbara's beloved Girton – 'my own Palace', as she called it in a letter to Amy of 12 April 1877, referring to Tennyson's poem, 'The Princess', about an academy of females. 'It is very delicious & our 35 students & their 35 little homes very jolly . . . I have just been to Dr M Foster's lecture with 3 students & seen them work after with their 3 microscopes in a dear little gallery all got ready for them with 3 little tables & lots of little bottles . . . I do wish you were here.' But Amy did not echo the wish. Well or ill, she never possessed a tenth of Barbara's physical or intellectual energy. It was her apathetic response as much as her parents' knee-jerk opposition that thwarted Barbara's dreams of higher education for her favourite niece.

These letters are among the last that show Barbara in her full vigour. She bought the Poor House, a granite cottage on the edge of moorland with fine views of the Atlantic, at Zennor in Cornwall. This was intended as a haven for herself and her artist friends. Always the egalitarian, Barbara recorded her servants' opinions of Zennor in her letters to Amy; I imagine not many Victorian employers would have treated their maids' opinions with such respect, but Barbara always involved herself with their concerns and, when travelling, sometimes shared beds with them. 'Henrietta & Margaret & the new Charlotte are here & like this <u>house</u> far better than Scalands but would not change the woods for the cliffs & rocks & sea.' '<u>Can you</u> send me by parcel post some of those dear gentian roots . . . address them to Henrietta. She & all are weeping at leaving this place they like it more & more. All well the 3 servants are going to see the grand fête of opening the rail at St Ives.' Henrietta, especially, was a very important person in Barbara's life. It was she who reported to NM that, when his name was mentioned to Amy, her face was 'full of love', which must have been a welcome snippet.

Barbara's other companion at Zennor was Jessie White Mario, who years before had been a helper at Barbara's Portman Hall School, the 'model day school on unconventional and advanced lines' which Barbara had set up in London in 1854. Jessie was an extraordinary character. She had tried to enrol in medical school, but had been barred on gender grounds. A fanatical advocate of Italian unity, she was arrested and imprisoned in Genoa for her involvement in Mazzini's republican plots. She married a fellow plotter, Alberto Mario, and became the Italian correspondent for *The Nation*. Aunt Ju described her in a letter to Amy as 'a fine energetic heroic kind of woman who attended the sick & wounded Italians in the Austro-Hungarian war . . . the . . . love of freedom especially Italian freedom possesses her still shining in her eyes & ringing in her voice & keeping her as young as when I first knew her fourteen years ago'. In 1877 Jessie was suffering from an injured

1. Marble bust of Bella Leigh Smith, made by Alexander Munro, a sculptor associated with the Pre-Raphaelites, before her marriage. This is a Victorian photograph; I don't know what became of the bust.

2. Major-General John Ludlow. Photograph taken in about 1880. Milicent kept this in her box of treasures with her father's letters.

3. Ben Leigh Smith on board the *Eira* in 1881. Ben is second from the left. The young man next to him with his hands in his pockets is, oddly enough, Arthur Conan Doyle, ship's surgeon on board Sir Allen Young's whaler, the *Hope*. He did not travel on the *Eira*; in this picture, he has come aboard just to have a look. The man on the far right smoking a pipe is Dr William Neale, the *Eira*'s surgeon, who recounted their adventures to Nannie and Isa.

4. Bob, the *Eira*'s dog, with a member of the crew, probably Captain Lofley. On the back of the photograph it says, 'This sagacious animal enticed the Bears from a distance, by going near to them, and then running away till he brought them within the range of the Guns of the Arctic Voyagers, and thus by his skilful manœvre, supplied them with food.'

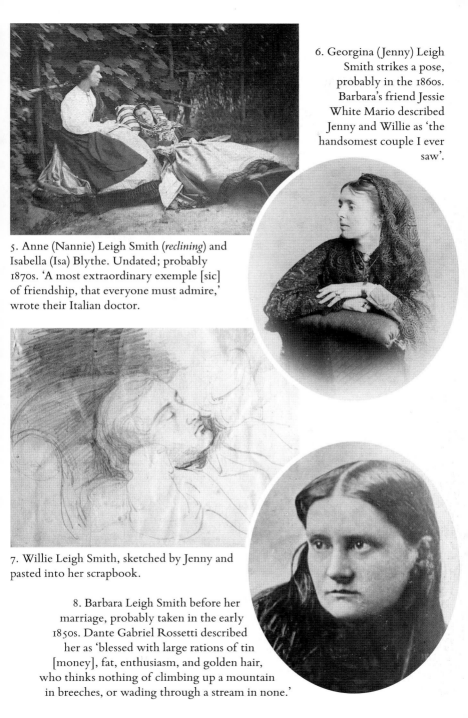

6. Georgina (Jenny) Leigh Smith strikes a pose, probably in the 1860s. Barbara's friend Jessie White Mario described Jenny and Willie as 'the handsomest couple I ever saw'.

5. Anne (Nannie) Leigh Smith (*reclining*) and Isabella (Isa) Blythe. Undated; probably 1870s. 'A most extraordinary exemple [sic] of friendship, that everyone must admire,' wrote their Italian doctor.

7. Willie Leigh Smith, sketched by Jenny and pasted into her scrapbook.

8. Barbara Leigh Smith before her marriage, probably taken in the early 1850s. Dante Gabriel Rossetti described her as 'blessed with large rations of tin [money], fat, enthusiasm, and golden hair, who thinks nothing of climbing up a mountain in breeches, or wading through a stream in none.'

(*above left*) 9. Milicent Ludlow, at about the time she moved into Hancox. 'She looks like a hop picker,' said her elegant cousin Amy.

(*above right*) 10. Mabel Ludlow, probably late 1880s. 'Quite the best mounted & set up lady in the ground,' said Aunt Jenny.

11. Ludlow Coape Smith at the time of his engagement to Mabel. 'A little bantam cock sort of fellow' was Aunt Jenny's verdict.

12. Scalands Gate, built to Barbara's specifications in 1863 and later enlarged. Barbara called it 'Dr Bodichon's cottage'.

13. Yotes Court, Milicent's childhood home. The figures in the foreground probably include Mabel and Milicent.

14. Glottenham Manor, extensively remodelled by Ben in the 1890s. A whale's jawbone, a souvenir of his Arctic travels, can be seen. Glottenham is now a nursing home.

15. Crowham Manor, Willie and Jenny's home from 1860 until 1910.

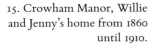

16. Amy Moore, née Leigh Smith, in her twenties. 'How superior anyone must feel with a nose such as hers!' said Emma Darwin, Charles's widow.

17. Amy aged 19, in costume for amateur theatricals. 'I hope you will enjoy the acting without one trace of thought that I do anything but approve,' wrote Norman Moore, her fiancé. However, he warned her that, once married, such an activity would be unacceptable.

(*above left*) 18. Robert Ross Rowan Moore; a daguerrotype from the 1840s. 'For God's sake keep Moore off our platforms,' wrote John Bright MP to Richard Cobden, his colleague in the Anti-Corn Law League. 'I do not think there is any man in either party he has not cuckolded.'

(*above right*) 19. Rebecca Moore with her son Norman (NM), *c.* 1864.

20. NM at about the time of his marriage to Amy.

21. Uncle Ben at Scalands in 1892 with his sons Valentine and Philip (the baby), in front of one of his 'big trees'.

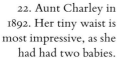

22. Aunt Charley in 1892. Her tiny waist is most impressive, as she had had two babies.

hand; Barbara invited her to Zennor with the intention of curing her. She bought a 'writing machine' with a 'manifold copier' (an early typewriter) so that Jessie could carry on with her journalism using her good hand. The machine was nicknamed 'Tryphena' after a Smith ancestress. After initial struggles the two women managed to persuade 'Tryphena' to do their bidding; Jessie's letters from this period are in jerky purple typescript. Twenty years later, when Amy travelled to Rome, Jessie was still using Tryphena. Her typed note to Amy urging her to pay her a visit – 'It is utterly out of the question that Aunt Barbara's Amy should be here in Rome and I not have a sight of her' – ends 'Tryphena sends her love.'

While Jessie worked on an article about ambulances, using material sent by Barbara's cousin Florence Nightingale, Barbara sketched the rocks which were '<u>green</u> stone & granite of many colours', walked to investigate local tin mines, and admired the wild flowers – 'bluebells, anemones, wood sorrel gorse milkwort & bilberry', she reported to Amy on 24 May, the last day of her fully active life.

Barbara was out sketching in a cold east wind when she suffered a stroke. Barbara had invited NM to Zennor for a holiday; he arrived, walking, of course, the eight miles from Penzance station, to find that the disaster had just happened. Though competent to treat Barbara himself, NM also telegraphed for Reginald Thompson, who was one of Barbara's trustees as well as being a doctor. (He was the son of the General Perronet Thompson, who had donated the African throne.) Even if she survived, which at first looked uncertain, NM knew that Barbara would never be the same again. Her speech and movement were much impaired; one of her main worries was whether she would ever again be able to paint. In 'The New Journal to Stella', NM wrote in pencil, 'Poor Aunt Barbara is I am sure very ill. God help us all.'

The stroke brought about an immediate shift in family allegiances. NM was no longer a welcome visitor; in her weakened state, Barbara could not cope with the anxiety about his engagement

to Amy. Instead she yearned for Ben, with whom she had not
been on speaking terms for months. Dr Thompson wrote to Ben
pleading with him to visit – 'Dear Sir, it would I am sure be a great
consolation to your sister if you could run down only for a day . . .
merely the sight of you would do much to relieve her mind.'
Ben obeyed; Barbara, who believed her death was near, was much
comforted. 'Aunt Bar has such a bright smile on her dear face,'
wrote Jessie White Mario to Amy about the prospect of Ben's
arrival. Tryphena's quirky violet typescript looks incongruously
jaunty, given the news Jessie had to impart.

Jessie had come to Zennor to rest her injured hand. Instead she
found herself turning into Barbara's nurse and secretary. NM was
concerned that the forthright and unconventional Jessie was not
the ideal companion for an invalid. But Dr Thompson's opinion
was that 'such a patient as Madame with her intellect fully awake
requires great acuteness in her attendants in order that the clue of
her thoughts may be caught at properly . . . Fortunately in Signora
Mario Madame has an old friend who remembers past events.'
Bessie Belloc, who longed to be by Barbara's side ('she loves me
better than anybody in the world except her singular Docteur'),
but who could not leave her two young children Marie and Hilaire
for long, also reassured NM about Jessie: 'I want to repeat to you
that my memory of her is of a perfectly kind & trustworthy nature,
who would never plot.'

Amy and her parents cut short their European tour, but the ban
on contact with NM was not lifted. By mid-July Barbara was able
to walk. On 22 August she returned to her house in Blandford
Square, but there was no chance that she could resume her former
role in the affair of NM and Amy. The eminent physician Sir William Jenner was consulted; he warned that excitement or agitation
might prove fatal. 'It is clear,' NM wrote in the Journal, 'that in
our contest Aunt Barbara must be neutral.' He sent a brace of partridge after a weekend's shooting in Kent, but resolved not to visit
Barbara until he was invited. On 10 October he was greatly cheered
when she called on him in person. She brought news of Amy, that

Oct 15
1884

Mrs Bodichon is
improving slowly but
for the improvement to
make progress it is
essential that she be
quiet in mind & body
She should see no one
who is not in attendance
on her — This exclusion
of all visitors should be
absolute for a least the
next fortnight

William Jenner

she was well and not unhappy, but explained that she could not
invite Norman to Blandford Square because Ben had said that if

Norman came there he would not. Barbara no longer felt able to stand up to her beloved but intractable brother.

Willy and Jenny continued their fierce opposition to the match. An entry in General Ludlow's diary indicates that they were encouraging another suitor, but Amy was not tempted. They re-iterated that Amy could not marry or even see Norman until she was twenty-one and not then if it could be prevented. She was barred initially from seeing Barbara, though this was relaxed after a few weeks. Madame Belloc acted as a kind of proxy for Barbara though, as she told NM, she had to tread carefully as the Leigh Smiths regarded her as Barbara's 'doppelganger'. NM consulted her about a letter he wanted to send Amy's father on 30 Novem-ber, the first anniversary of his proposal at Peterborough. Madame Belloc approved the letter and advised NM to write to Amy at the same time, and to send Amy a copy of the letter to her father. He transcribed his note into the Journal in case Amy was not allowed to receive it. 'Dearest Amy I send you a copy of a letter which will reach your father by this post. You will see that my wish to be your husband is unchanged and that I remain ever yours affectionately Norman Moore.'

In his letter to Willy Leigh Smith, NM sent an updated account of his income and financial and professional prospects. His hand-writing could scrawl to the point of illegibility but this letter was immaculately written:

My dear Sir,

It is now a year since I asked for your permission to marry your daughter Amy. You wrote, as you will recollect, to ask me not to correspond with your daughter. This request I have followed and I hope that this deference on my part will now incline you to a favourable answer to my request. Since I waited upon you in 1876 I have had the unexpected honour of being elected a fellow of the college of Physicians. I was before a Doctor of Medicine of the University of Cambridge and I am by this election placed in the highest possible degree as physician . . . I hold three offices at

St. Bartholomew's Hospital. I am Warden of the College, Medical Tutor, and lecturer on Comparative Anatomy. I hold in addition the honorary secretaryship of the Medical school which is the largest and richest in London . . . Since I was elected in 1873 the Medical School has steadily increased. The Warden of the college has a comfortable house which is furnished, kept in repair and lighted at the expense of the hospital. He receives in money £115 a year. The Office of Medical Tutor and that of Lecturer on Comparative Anatomy each yield a little over one hundred a year . . . I am in addition allowed to practise in private as a physician and as the Warden's house has a door in Duke Street as well as one towards the hospital, he has a fair chance of obtaining some practice . . . From all these sources . . . my actual receipts for this year have been £725. I shall probably receive about £40 more between this and Christmas . . . Since I became Warden I have saved the sum of £900 3 per cent consols . . . The Office of Warden . . . is as safe a step as it is possible to obtain to professional success and as I have had unusual success so far I may fairly hope to continue to prosper. My mother has a sufficient, though not large income, and she has been good enough to say that in the event of my death she will provide for my wife . . . My heart is entirely [Amy's] and I entreat you to give your consent to a marriage which I shall do my utmost to render a source of satisfaction to you and your wife as well as a blessing to your daughter who cannot be dearer to any parents, however fond, than she is to me.

    I remain, my dear Sir,
    Yours sincerely,
    Norman Moore.

Willy Leigh Smith did not even reply. He got Jenny to send a curt refusal: '. . . he has not at all changed his mind.' Amy was allowed to read Norman's letters but was forbidden to answer them. At last, after an interceding letter to the Leigh Smiths from Rebecca Moore, Amy received grudging permission to write once and once only: 'Mama says I may do that . . . but it is to be short and I am not to hold out any hopes to you . . . I am so disappointed . . . Am I to make up my mind not to see or hear anything of you for 2 years and 2 months? <u>They</u> say so . . . I don't see what is going to happen next but whatever does I am your Amy.'

Things seemed to be at a standstill. Then, quite suddenly, a thaw set in. In late February 1878, NM heard that a great Irish friend was dangerously ill. He arranged to go at once to see her. Then news reached him that Amy was coming to London to stay with Uncle Ben. He could not renege on his promise to go to Ireland but nor could he pass up the chance of catching a glimpse of Amy. He knew she would be coming up on a train from Hastings on either Thursday 28 February or Friday 1 March, so he joined every train at London Bridge until he found her. They travelled together to Charing Cross, two stops further on; there he parted from her and set out for Ireland and his dying friend. His entry in the Journal for 1 March is a pencilled scribble written at Chester railway station:

My dearest Amy,

The thought of having grasped your dear hand and kissed your fair cheek & talked ever so few words with you is the best event of my life this year & last year. But I thought you seemed heartsore my Amy & there was no time to console you. Be cheerful do all you can for Aunt Barbara & the good time will come. It was a very short glimpse was it not but far better than none at all & I like to think that our wedding day is fixed for April 1880 at latest.

Amy bravely told her mother and uncle about the meeting on the train, which had been a complete surprise to her. She was not quite courageous enough to tell Uncle Ben to his face, but she wrote to him after her stay in London:

I saw Dr Moore when I was in London. It was only for 5 minutes & you must not blame us because remember we had not seen each other for a year and three months.

It was in the train between the two stations before Charing X &
it wasn't arranged <u>at all</u>. He heard in a round about way [in fact,
from Barbara] that I was coming up to town & he met all the trains
of Thursday & Friday – till I came in hopes of seeing me . . . I can't
write more because I'm rather weak.

The weakness was part of a prolonged bout of ill health. It
seems to have been this that finally caused the Leigh Smiths to
lower their defences. It was planned that Amy should stay with
Aunt Barbara, but she was too ill to go. NM, hearing of this, was
seriously worried, his fears intensified by the time he had spent
with his dying friend. He wrote to Barbara and transcribed his letter into the Journal: 'The most dangerous condition in which to live
as regards health is that of a continuously distressed mind. Hardship
& exposure are safe to most people compared to anxiety. For a year
& a half this has been the state of Amy's tender and affectionate
mind.' He changed his mind about sending the letter, deciding not
to worry Barbara, whose own state of health was still precarious,
but he did write to Amy's mother: '. . . her illness . . . makes me wish
much more that you could see your way to lessening an opposition
which I know is a source of continued distress to her.'

Jenny did not reply at once. In the meantime, NM reached the
end of volume X of 'The New Journal to Stella'. 'Ten years was
Troy besieged & I no more thought this would reach ten volumes
than the Argive heroes that they would spend ten weary years on
that plain . . . but since it seems all I can do at present I will go on
if it is to volume ninety.' But hardly had he begun volume XI
when the breakthrough came. Worried by their daughter's physical decline, the Leigh Smith parents decided to let them write,
though not yet to meet. Amy wrote to NM with the happy news.
Her letter reached him on 25 March, and he made his last entry in
the Journal:

So at last I may write to you, & not to a dumb book only. Your
letter rejoiced me as the dove did old Noah . . . End, then, dull,

dreary unsent letters and if my Amy ever reads you try and show
her one thing, that I have never been without the thought of her . . .
Here then my Amy end the last, the shortest and the happiest of
these volumes of the New Journal to Stella begun in sorrow but
ending in joy is happily done with.

★

Life became much more bearable now that letters could be exchanged, and Amy's health improved. She told NM how she used
to wake crying in the night, but now when she woke, 'I take your
letter from under my pillow and kiss it and soon go to sleep with
it in my hand.' NM wrote every day, sometimes three times a day,
and he sent her the Journal to read as well. One long letter, written
on 23 April 1878 and sent from Killibegs in County Donegal,
reveals his views on marriage. Amy had gone to stay with family
friends in Edgbaston and was to take part in amateur theatricals.
She was anxious about the propriety of this, especially as a young
man also taking part seemed to be paying court to her. As always,
she wanted to take her lead from NM, who seemed to her stronger
and wiser in every way – 'I feel as if you were a large big beautiful
river – flowing over all obstacles to the sea – & I – a little stream
hardly strong enough to get on at all.' NM replied:

> My own darling I will do my best to guide you in everything &
> you will never find what I ask hard for it shall never be so. But
> what I said about the acting I exactly meant. Please always tell me
> if what I say as to a wife's duty is what you think for I never will
> try to force my opinion on you, only I will try to put it clearly
> before you & then you shall act. My view then is this. A wife
> should never appear publicly in a separate way . . . She may do
> many things which fall to her way of life but in which her husband
> has no part as painting, writing etc. but which do not require her
> personal appearance separately. Her mind should be free and work
> as it will in the directions it is suited for but her physical frame
> should never appear except associated with her husband. Her

frame, her grace so to speak, are his and his only. She cannot be too careful to avoid anything which goes the least contrary to this & I think acting in society does just reach the point of emerging from that seclusion into which a woman retires as far as admiration goes when she marries. With an unmarried girl, even if engaged, it is quite different. The two cases are not the least alike & I hope you will enjoy the acting without one trace of thought that I do anything but approve.

NM's outline of the mode of conduct desirable in a married woman may make the modern reader uncomfortable. He was no feminist, despite his high opinion of Aunt Barbara and his own mother. It seems odd that a man brought up single-handedly by the tough, adventurous, resourceful Rebecca should see women as inherently physically weak, but this does appear to have been NM's view. He believed that women should not be doctors, not because they lacked intellectual capacity but because they would not be able to stand the hard physical labour of the post-mortem room. However, he allowed that it was fair to let them try. Though he corresponded with several women whose behaviour contradicted his views, such as Florence Nightingale and the great gardener Ellen Willmott, he seems never to have examined the contradiction.

Part of the attraction of Amy – young, frail, ethereal-looking – was her aura of vulnerability. The chivalrous instincts she aroused in him would have contrasted strongly with anything he or any other man could have felt about Rebecca. And Amy, despite the liveliness of her character, was glad to be treated so. She described to him a conversation she had with her Aunt Dora, Jenny's younger sister: 'When Aunt Dora was married in December she asked me if I meant to say "obey" when I was married. She said "of course every one says it because it is there but I wonder who means it I don't". I told her my opinion & she told me she thought I was a weak thing well then if it is so then I am glad to be weak.' (Aunt Dora also asked Amy if she should tell Bill Wickham, her husband-to-be, about her false hair or just leave him to discover it for himself. Amy was vastly amused by the dilemma.)

Aunt Barbara, the architect of the Married Women's Property Act, would have argued vigorously against such views. Indeed, in a letter she wrote to NM several years later, when a coolness had arisen between them, partly because of his antipathy to her radical friends, she chided him for his conventional outlook:

> . . . I think you do not know I was nearly doing a great many things which would have made you *prevent* Amy from coming to see me. I asked George Eliot to come and live with Dr Bodichon & me, when Mr Lewes died for instance.
>
> You do not think of the truths of things but accept what religion your country has etc etc. I dare say as years go on you will become more & more catholic and Amy too.
>
> I shall have sympathy with your mother I think! You see I feel more & more since I have been ill the want of strong minded women.

Barbara's remark about becoming 'more & more catholic' was prescient. This was a difference between her and NM that could never be fully reconciled. In the long letter to Amy quoted above, NM goes on to deplore the Bodichons' version of marriage:

> I know that many people nowadays think a wife should remain a separate individual living in occasional association rather than in close, continuous, intimate relation with her husband but this is not my view and I can see it is not yours. Your wish, if I understand you & I think I do, is to come to my house without casting one look behind & without one wish for a separate course while we live. This is entirely my wish. I do not want part of my life to be gladdened by your fair presence! I want the whole of it to be altogether associated with you . . . Thankyou dearest for saying you would 'kiss me with all my whole heart'. True affection ought to be expressed as I felt when Madame Belloc told me this. She said

meat larder — Lea Hurst

May 28 /78

I have been writing a good
many letters for Aunt
you. & so now I am going
out. I have not told you
much. but I will not
bewilder you with any
more now.

Thank you for Mrs Moore's
letters, I wish it ~~was~~ they were
cleaner. Our affairs I mean

Ever yours

Amy —

that Aunt Barbara told her that Dr Bodichon never even took
her hand when he went to Zennor till she asked him to feel her

pulse & that Aunt Barbara told her this with tears in her eyes.
I could have shed tears myself to hear of it & to think that dear
beautiful Aunt Barbara should long, in her illness, for a caress from
her husband long to see him & that when he came he should not
even kiss her, & that her tender, longing heart should be disappointed. I do not believe Dr Bodichon is unloving or unkind,
whatever anyone says, but he is too much of a philosopher & did
not consider that a mere word or sentence does not satisfy the
longing loving heart of a true wife. We have bodies as well as souls
and love permeates & flows through & through both & kisses are
the language of the flesh just as words & looks are of the soul. I
always mean to do all I can for Dr Bodichon & to think well of him
for he is part of Aunt Barbara. But even Aunt Barbara would have
been happier I think if they had not been so much separated, if
they had been more constantly associated.

Though Barbara never openly expressed dissatisfaction with her
marital arrangements, NM clearly has a point. My own twenty-
first-century view is that Dr Bodichon was at the highest-functioning
end of the autistic spectrum and completely lacked the empathetic
qualities that his wife possessed in such abundance.

It is not surprising that Amy entrusted herself so willingly to
NM's care. All her short life she had been yearning for affection
and attention from her parents and had never received much of
either. 'Did you really like me when I was a little girl?' she asked
him. 'I thought nobody did except Aunt Barbara. I believe one
reason why I was such a dreadfully naughty child was because I
had a sort of reckless feeling that nobody cared for me much & it
did not matter what I did.' 'I don't know why Mama never cared
for me very much. It has been so ever since I can remember she
always calls the others Roddy, dear – Willy dear & speaks to them
like that & I can <u>never</u> remember her having done so to me – or
kiss me except just in the morning & evening, bye the bye Papa
has left off that, since Dec. 1876.' When they were in Switzerland,
Amy's attempts to broach the subject of her engagement with her

father were blocked with a lament 'that he couldn't send me to a convent'.

Having had affection withheld for so long, Amy immersed herself completely in NM's love – 'I would give up everything for you.' For a young, overprotected Victorian girl, she expresses her passion with surprising freedom:

> Every night as I put out my candle & lie down I turn to the side I think looks towards you and think of nothing else but you my own Norman until I fall asleep . . . if you could only know the wonderfully happy feeling it gives me to feel your hand caressing me . . . I like to think now where your dear lips have been – and that you really love me enough to kiss me so.

This was written after the pair had been able to meet as well as write. The parental rules slowly relaxed. NM was not allowed to visit Amy at home, but when she stayed with relations he was often invited too, and the Leigh Smiths do not seem to have attempted to prevent this. Soon after the theatricals at Edgbaston, Amy set off for Lea Hurst in Derbyshire, the childhood home of Florence Nightingale. She went as companion to Aunt Ju, now seventy-eight but still a vigorous participant in the family affairs of both the Nightingales and the Leigh Smiths. Her niece Florence Nightingale, who was very fond of her, nicknamed her 'Stormy Ju', and old age had not destroyed her passionate advocacy of causes in which she believed. One of these causes was NM and Amy's romance; with Barbara incapacitated, she took up the role of facilitator. 'Aunt Bar has told me the embargo is taken off & now may justice & good sense reign & may the blessed truth shine forth & lead all right! & God bless us all,' she had written to Amy in March. Aunt Ju was tiny; Barbara had the legs of valuable Sheraton chairs cut down for her benefit. She once absent-mindedly walked out of a first-floor window, but she was so light, and her crinoline so voluminous, that she sailed to the ground unhurt.

Amy loved her time with Aunt Ju at Lea Hurst. 'Aunt Julia . . .

calls me her "playfellow" now don't you think she is a dear old lady,' she wrote to NM. She described the place to him, ornamenting her letters with pretty little sketches of flowers, views, pieces of furniture. 'The house is ramshackle all windows & staircases so that I do not know my way over it yet . . . There are grass walks between high hedges expressly constructed for old Mrs Nightingale who did not like being looked at.' (Old Mrs Nightingale, née Fanny Smith, mother of Florence and sister of Aunt Ju, was still alive, but was senile and virtually blind.) Amy told NM about local customs, such as the villagers painting their houses in readiness for the Wakes, and about the mill girls she passed on her walks who called out rude remarks about her appearance. On 7 June, the eve of NM's visit, she wrote in high spirits, 'Here is Friday at last and it is fine and the glass is going up and Aunt Julia is as well as can be expected and has not changed her mind! And I am just going to make you a loaf of bread & the gooseberries are bigger (& rosier) & Mrs Turner is "chary" of her bloater paste & there is no pig & no cheese -.' NM arrived, and all was blissful. 'Miss Julia Smith runs upstairs & down with the airy vivacity of a water wagtail,' he reported to Barbara, 'Martha her maid is heard singing in one corner of the house & at the moment Amy is singing in another so Lea Hurst you see is lively & cheery.'

But their difficulties were by no means over. Uncle Ben remained implacable in his view of Amy as 'a child still in body & in mind'. In September he wrote coldly to her:

You seem to recollect our conversations at Brown's I told you then what I thought calmly & kindly it might not be agreeable to you but you have no right to complain as you asked me to do so.

As you wish it I will not discuss your affairs with you any more.

I am very glad I am not your father.

Please do not write again or think of coming here as I cannot stand any worry or excitement. [Ben had lost a lot of blood in a cab accident earlier in the year. The accident had been followed by a bout of typhoid and he was still semi-convalescent.]

Amy also suspected Ben of stirring up trouble at Yotes Court. When the news of the engagement first broke, the General withheld it from Amy's cousins, Mabel, Harry and Milicent, in deference to Ben's wishes. When Harry and Mabel came to Hastings and spent a lot of time with Amy, she was startled to discover that they did not know her story. She decided to enlighten them:

> I said I should tell Mabel & I did & she was a proper goose . . . she was sitting on my knee & she got up & looked – stared at me in astonishment & said – 'why he will be my brother, won't he?' When I had explained that you would *not* be her brother & she had a little recovered from her astonishment she talked about it . . . [Harry] was so funny when I told him – he nearly cried. I don't know whether he thought that because I married him 10 years ago nearly I suppose under the Sycamore tree on the lawn with a ring cut out of a leaf – I was behaving very badly.

Mabel's snobbish instincts, fuelled by Uncle Ben, caused her to disparage NM, whom she regarded as a tutor, therefore almost an upper servant. Perhaps she was also jealous that Amy, the closest cousin to her in age, was embroiled in a romantic drama when she, Mabel, was not. Her former girlish chumminess with Amy evaporated and her letters became prim and inscrutable, so much so that Amy wondered whether the General read them. Roddy was now pointedly invited to stay at Yotes without Amy; she reported that Mabel considered Amy was 'throwing herself away'. At Yotes, the shy Roddy was whisked into a whirl of balls, dinners and expeditions while the more social Amy was stuck at home with her petulant mother, irascible father and two teasing brothers. Barbara offered to pay for Amy to study art at the Slade, but Amy's parents refused the offer. Uncle Ben installed Mabel as favourite niece in place of Amy. In November he took Mabel and Roddy to Paris for a few days of pure indulgence. Amy couldn't help minding. 'Well, I think perhaps I do have a little bit of regret about Uncle Ben . . . I don't regret that he has taken up Roddy but that he should be so unkind to me . . . its when I think how very fond of him I used to be when I was a little girl that it feels the worst.'

Ben treated his two compliant nieces royally in Paris. Roddy wrote to Amy from the Hotel Continental:

This is the most gorgeous hotel I ever saw – Our bedrooms are wonderfully furnished, Mabel's with red velvet & mine with green & each with gold clocks of course . . . Mabel is having a ball dress made . . . There is going to be a concert here this evening, we went into the concert room just now & Mabel coolly went & played on the piano which is up on a platform, the waiters came and staired in horror but she did not care a button.

The difference between being a Ludlow daughter from Yotes Court and a Leigh Smith daughter from Crowham was highlighted by the fact that Mabel had £30 spending money, Roddy £3. Amy reported to NM that Mabel spent half her money on the ball dress, the rest on 'silver chains & bracelets for her friends and the <u>servants</u>! at Yotes.' I find it attractive that Mabel bought presents for the servants, who were numerous, but Amy seems to have been shocked. I found the pink silk flowers that decorated the ballgown, preserved by Milicent in a box of mementoes.

Mabel wrote to Aunt Barbara from Paris:

Roddy & I are enjoying ourselves more than you can imagine . . . We saw Sarah Bernhardt the actress Aunt Nanny spoke so highly of . . . we are on the troisième [floor of the hotel] and I always go up & down in the lift. The man who works it has become a friend of mine and I always air my French in mid air.

Bold, dressy Mabel, who loved dancing, singing, tennis and hunting, could hardly have been more different from gawky, put-upon Roddy, who always lacked partners at balls, but they developed a rapport. 'I think Mabel fascinates her,' said Amy. As well as mourning her loss of status in Uncle Ben's affections, Amy became jealous of the new bond between her sister and her cousin. 'Roddy says Uncle Ben says he will take "us" to America some time. I was surprised, but it seems "us" now means Roddy & Mabel!!'

A new relationship came into Amy's life, which did much to relieve the gloom and tedium of life at Crowham. On 11 November Jenny gave birth to a baby girl – named Bella, to General Ludlow's delight. The child was not greeted with universal rapture – 'Mama did not care for it and only said "keep it away" & Papa called it "a crying brat" & that sort of thing so I was obliged to like it & now I like it very <u>much</u> indeed.' Baby Bella was so pretty and charming that, Amy declared, she could 'tame a narwhale'. Five-year-old Lionel took a scientific interest, because he was that kind of child. When Amy read him fairy stories he said 'that's enough of <u>that</u> lets have something <u>really</u> nice now about ants or some sort of insects you know.' Looking at his newborn sister, he asked 'Take her altogether, how <u>long</u> should you think she was when she stands up?'

Jenny's confinement meant that Amy had to take over the running of the household, which she found difficult. 'We have got the most dreadful lot of servants,' she wrote on 14 November, 'and the cook is a sort of fiend – "Well Miss, I cant make *that*, there aint no heggs nor butter nor nothing" – "Buy some eggs! Why all the hens in the village have left off laying." "There aint no meat at the shop . . . and the cows is 'orrid we don't get 'alf as much butter as we did . . . so your Ma coudnt eat 'er breakfast, that 'er coachman were so in the way and I were <u>that</u> muddled".' Amy's second cousin Alice Bonham Carter, who in September had had Amy to stay with her at Ravensbourne in Kent and had invited NM there at the same time, sent well-meant advice: 'I think that each of us has to find out for ourselves how we can best influence and gain authority over our servants – You will conquer them if you try – Make them feel that you want them, for their own sakes – to be good servants who will take a real pride in their work & their duty.' But Amy wrote sadly to NM, 'I suppose it is natural they should be rude to me and not do what they are told after – everything.'

It was a hard winter. There was skating in the Brede Valley, which Amy loved, but the roads were often impassable. The mid-afternoon darkness at Crowham got on Amy's nerves, and she asked NM about electricity: 'I am very ignorant about this electric light – is it hot? Can you light a piece of paper at it?! Have you ever seen any and do you think people will use it?' The lamps and candles that were the only source of light at Crowham were dangerous with Amy's drunken father about. 'The consequences after dinner are not pleasant . . . [Mama] cries half the day upstairs'; 'I prevented Papa from upsetting a paraffin lamp . . . I sometimes think there never was such a dreadful house as this'; 'I am always expecting Papa will shoot himself . . . once he shot his gun off in his room by mistake you know.' And Norman was a long way off. On Christmas Eve, while Amy was skating on the frozen fields, he and his friend John Fitzgerald were in Galway, walking across the bare land that belonged to her father. They lost each other in the snow. Though he carried a bunch of heather in front of his face, NM's hair and beard gathered a mass of frozen snow. He crossed six lakes, arrived at a police barracks at 1 a.m., and, revived by cold tea and cake, he set out again at sunrise. When he reached the inn he had started from he found a board laid for his body and preparations in progress for his wake and funeral.

At Yotes Court, with its huge high-ceilinged rooms and exposed position, the cold was even more intense than it was at Crowham. Despite his sociable, hospitable nature, General Ludlow was austere in his personal habits, and Yotes was notorious in the family for being underheated and underlit. ' "As cheery as Yotes" will never grow a proverb,' wrote NM to Amy. Barbara, whose mobility had been reduced since her stroke, felt the cold badly, and worried about Milicent's health. Mabel and Harry were energetic teenagers who tore about the country on horseback or skated with their friends on the frozen castle lake – when the daylight faded they carried on by starlight, with lanterns made of mustard tins – before returning home to eat ravenously of 'brawn and pressed beef beside drinking a bottle of Madeira . . . and all the wine . . . that was left for them'. But skinny ten-year-old Milicent was prone to chest infections, and both Barbara and Nannie remonstrated with the General, to his annoyance. '[Barbara] cannot get warm – from no doubt some abnormal condition of body,' he wrote in his diary, but as other entries reveal that 'the sponge in the bathing room was frozen' and that the thermometer in the hall stood at freezing point despite the presence of a fire there, Barbara's problem does not seem so very abnormal. Roddy, overawed by sleeping in the State Room at Yotes, which had a fireplace in it large enough 'to roast an ox', nonetheless told Amy that 'the cold in this house is awful or else I feel it more than anyone else.' But, Amy told NM, she was 'too much enchanted with parties & hockey on the ice to come away', despite the horrible discovery of a murdered baby in a brown paper parcel on the pond on which they were about to skate.

In the New Year, 1879, Amy was allowed a little gaiety herself. Perhaps hoping she would meet a more acceptable suitor, Jenny and Willy allowed her to stay with the Combes at Oaklands Park in Sedlescombe. Mrs Combe was the sister of the artist Hercules Brabazon Brabazon; a bachelor, 'Brabbie', loyal and cheerful friend to all the Leigh Smiths, spent a lot of his time with his sister's family at Oaklands. He gave Amy a taste of the cultured life which suited her better than the cattle-breeding and rat-catching world of Crowham: 'Willy Combe . . . took me up to Mr Brabazon's room (decorated by Miss Jekyll) . . . Mr Brabazon played to me – Scarlatti, Handel, Bach, Mozart.' The house party went to a ball and Brabbie danced with Amy a great deal – 'I didn't mind as he was the nicest man there and old, you know & good natured.' Amy sometimes laughed at Brabbie's pretentiousness, as when he went into raptures over a 'gigantic' bunch of flowers Miss Jekyll gathered at Scalands for Aunt Bar – ' "What is more exquisite than pink in shadow!!!" and the greys "oh those greys how lovely etc etc etc . . . now really I must go I cannot stand them any longer" - & off he went his feelings over "the greys" being too much for him. Perhaps you will believe that even Aunt Bar indulged in a little laugh.' But the quality of the attention he paid to Amy made him a lifeline at this drab time in her life.

On the rare occasions when she was allowed out, Amy was a great success, always asked to dance every dance. But often Jenny barred her way, claiming that she could not afford a suitable dress, or that the horses could not be spared. Amy was furious at having to turn down an invitation to stay with the immensely rich Brassey family at Normanhurst, their extravagant copy of a French château near Battle. Jenny said getting Amy ready for the visit would be 'too much bother'. 'There always is a fuss if I want to do anything but stop in this room,' Amy lamented. She dragged herself through the icy days playing the <u>Dead March</u> in Saul to little Bella – 'to enliven her you understand' – while 'Mama goes about like Mrs Wilfer* in black kid gloves & a shawl – Bella peeps out of a roll of flannel & Lionel is chiefly pocket handkerchief. Papa wears a large woollen comforter & a black skull cap always. We're a lovely family take us altogether.' But she was amused and encouraged to catch her father 'trying the Irish airs on the piano with one finger'.

She was very conscious of the disparity between her life and NM's – hers, monotonous and apparently devoid of direction or purpose, his a ceaseless round of difficult, valuable, interesting work and lively socializing. She expressed jealousy of the sophisticated women NM met at dinner parties: '. . . when you are surrounded by that galaxy with not one thought to waste on the rustic maiden who is pining away on the dreary hillside in the farmhouse – damp – and where the grass grows up between the stones – the bats fly & the winds howl in the chimnies . . .' But at the end of February she was at last able to see him again when she went to stay in London with the Shore Smiths, at 30 York Place.

The York Place household consisted of Shore, his wife, Louisa, their four children, Rosy, Sam, Louis and Barbara, all quite close to Amy in age, and old Mrs Nightingale – Aunt Fanny. Shore was heir to his uncle Nightingale's estate (in the absence of a

---

* Mrs Wilfer is the autocratic character in Dickens's *Our Mutual Friend* who feels that her marriage has brought her down in the world.

Nightingale son) and he took the name of Nightingale, though the family never got out of the habit of referring to 'the Shore Smiths'. When Shore was a boy, Florence Nightingale called him 'the son of my heart' and made him her special project. He had been a sickly baby; when the husband of his wet nurse died, the poor woman was not told, in case the shock interrupted her flow of milk. Florence nursed Shore through his childhood illnesses, often taking him into her bed, where his 'extraordinary snortings, groanings & grumblings à la walrus mingle agreeably with my dreams,' as she wrote to her sister Parthenope.

Shore and Louisa were a happy couple – Amy described how Shore would pick up Louisa's hand at the dinner table and kiss it with the words, 'Lou dear – I really <u>must</u>,' at which Louisa would murmur indulgently, 'Don't be foolish Shorey.' They had a strong sense of family duty and did a good job of looking after old Aunt Fanny Nightingale. Aunt Fanny, noticing Amy and asking who she was, said 'Oh – a niece of mine – indeed,' and then 'is she a <u>nice</u> sort of person?' Cousin Louisa, who also played a big part in the lives of Mabel and Milicent, was sensitive to Amy's romantic predicament and allowed NM to pay her several visits at York Place, though even this was not enough for Amy: 'Why can't one's relations be nice and say "I hope, Dr Moore, you will come <u>every</u> moment you have time and the back drawing room is at your service always."' Seeing her beloved in company was both a thrill and a strain – 'You had got twinkling eyes do you know when your eyes twinkle? It makes you look as if you ought to be kissed straight off so don't let them do it in drawing rooms.' A visit to the theatre to see *Hamlet* led to a vivid dream: 'in my dreams you arrived with a large black cloak . . . and said the convent doors were open . . . you see the effect of excitement on a country girl.'

She was deeply upset by being 'cut' by Uncle Ben in a chance encounter: 'He was quite near & stared in a queer sort of way & then looked away. It wasn't pleasant. I always think I don't mind before hand but when it comes to the point I do. Cousin Louisa was rather angry with him.' She was also horrified by Louisa's hint that one reason for family opposition to the engagement was that it spoiled her chances of inheriting Ben's fortune. 'It made me quite wild when she said it. Why do people spoil everything by always thinking about money.'

In April, Amy went to Booton Rectory to stay with the Elwins for three weeks. NM joined them at weekends and they had blissful breakfasts and walks together. Mr Elwin gave her sound advice – '[he] said I must put myself right before I could hope to put things around me right.' 'I feel I might be his own daughter at least you see I don't know how fathers talk to their daughters.'

Now, for the first time, Amy was able to see how her own attitude might be contributing to the poisonous atmosphere at Crowham – 'I didn't know what a horrid minx I had got into till I found it out at Booton.' Under Mr Elwin's guidance she wrote a letter to her father which at last seems to have softened his heart. Both parents accepted that the wedding would take place the following March, soon after Amy's twenty-first birthday. It became possible to mention Norman's name in the house, though fourteen-year-old Willy got the wrong end of the stick as usual – 'Willy asked Roddy . . . in a confidential way, "I say, is it Sir Thomas More Amy is engaged to?"'

Summer weather raised everyone's spirits. Amy had 'what may be called a game of romps with Papa and Uncle Lionel [Halliday; Jenny's brother] out of this window with Roddy during which tennis balls, red roses and wet sponges changed hands rapidly as they would say in the paper'. Amy visited Aunt Barbara at Scalands and showed her drawings, played the piano for her, wrote dictated letters, learned how to make an omelette, picked strawberries and blackcurrants. Barbara's latest plan for Amy was to send her to France for several months to learn the language; though she still supported the engagement, it grieved her feminist soul to think of her niece moving straight from childhood to wifehood without any time for independent intellectual growth. Amy was receptive to the French plan, but as usual it was shipwrecked on the rocks of Willy and Jenny's inertia.

On one of Amy's visits to Scalands, Mabel and Harry were there. Amy was amused and irritated that Mabel treated her as if she had been 'Sukey the kitchen maid', and even though Harry greeted her warmly, he was soon 'awed by Mabel into a distant sort of coolness'. Mabel was fresh from another round of picnics, tennis parties and sightseeing with Uncle Ben; she had completely usurped Amy's position in his affections and seemed rather proud of this. Barbara thought Ben's treatment of Amy was 'shameful' and became extremely agitated by the subject, but was a little mollified by the good news that NM was at last to be allowed to visit Crowham. Amy was in great glee at the prospect, and wrote him a teasing letter in anticipation:

> Sunday might be very nice if we were let alone – and Willy lost himself with his butterfly net in a distant wood and did not get out till the evening . . . You will of course have to give me French lessons most of the time. You like to do what Aunt Bar tells you don't you. I'll get the books ready and you can begin directly. The rest of the time you can read the Waverley novels out loud when Mama is not there. When she is you must talk about Bella's pink sash etc. Out of doors you may be allowed one game of Tennis with Roddy & the rest of the time you must hunt for Azure blues & Emerald moths etc etc.'

In celebratory mood, she included a glowing sketch of a spray of raspberries in her letter.

NM's first visit seemed quite successful, but after the second the coachman George Dann drove NM back to Hastings to catch the London train and somehow managed to upset the dogcart. Neither man was much hurt, but when the news reached Crowham, 'Willy . . . took good care to bring me the first tidings by rushing in and saying "They were upset & Dr Moore is killed" he then changed it to "dangerously hurt!" Roddy followed shouting "He is telling stories."' On this and on subsequent visits, Amy felt ashamed of her parents' behaviour – 'I was thinking all the time to myself that Papa & Mama were behaving horribly to you – and that if you had not got the sweetest temper you would never enter the house again . . . It is my fate to bring worries & unhappyness to everyone who has to do with me.'

Unsurprisingly, it turned out to be Uncle Ben who was trying to spoil things. He told Willy that Amy only wanted to marry to get away from home. Money was also an issue. NM was naturally appalled to find that Amy had been left a legacy by Aunt Dolly Longden, but that Willy had spent it 'on cows & sheep' and had no intention of repaying it. 'I had better perhaps not be married at all as I have no money of my own,' mourned Amy. NM negotiated his way as tactfully as he could through the financial wrangles and undertook to insure his life for £1,000. Barbara, whose condition deteriorated with the approach of winter, rented a house in Brighton and asked Amy to join her. The visit was not a cheerful one, as Amy was unable to prevent Barbara from bewailing the rift with Ben – 'When she said Uncle Ben was coming here I said, let him come I am not afraid of him – but I am, said Aunt Barbara with tears in her eyes.'

It seemed that, following her stroke, some of Barbara's clarity of thought had gone. She implied to Amy that NM was selfish in wanting to marry her, as he would be taking her to live in unhealthy London in a narrow street – 'even your carpet has too big a pattern to please her.' Amy was most hurt by the suggestion that her engagement had caused Barbara's illness – 'if it had not been for this affair I should have never been ill that is most people's opinion,' said Barbara. Amy tried to escape the doom-laden atmosphere by walking alone through the streets of Brighton, but was accosted by an 'odious' man, and rescued from him by a 'gentleman' – 'I was right not to say anything to Aunt Bar was I not.'

NM told his mother about Barbara's state of mind. Rebecca wisely remarked, 'Poor Barbara, it is only the nervous way of invalids she is all right at heart.' No longer looking to her aunt for support, Amy cared for her as best she could. 'I am to be her night nurse for Sanderson is completely done up and must have a rest.

Very often A. Bar is read to for two hours in the night and there are two fires to be kept up.'

Soon after her return to Crowham, scarlet fever broke out among the cottagers and the Leigh Smiths decamped to a hired house in Hastings, 39 Marina. Here Amy spent most of the last few weeks of her single life. Being forced into even closer proximity with Jenny was not elevating to the spirits – '[Mama] says she knows <u>she</u> would cut her throat in six months if she tried to live in St Bartholomews.' But at least Jenny had accepted the wedding as an inevitability. 'I walked down to Hastings with Mama ostensibly to pay a bill – however she said when we were in a shop "I think you had better look at some things" so we went upstairs and spent some time examining garments a large parcel was sent home and she evidently thinks we are in for it & had better make the best of it. Mama's ideas are much grander than mine I find. I think there is no fear of my not having a <u>proper trousseau</u>!' Barbara's beloved maid Henrietta, always a great supporter of Amy's, was an excellent needlewoman, and she contributed garments to the trousseau which pleased Amy very much.

Cousin Alice Bonham Carter wrote offering a 'Dark Green Cashmere Gown trimmed with quilted Green Satin & turned up with dull red', but Amy feared this would be too 'artistic' for her fiancé's taste, and besides 'the whole family will die on the spot unless I consent to be married in a white dress.' Aunt Barbara lent the veil she had worn at her own wedding. Amy wrote to Aunt Nannie in Algiers and asked her to send some real orange blossoms: 'Dr Bodichon will be so pleased, said the Aunt if you wear my vail and Algerian orange flowers.' In the run-up to the wedding Barbara became happier about it all, took trouble over choosing her gift of brass candlesticks (she also, eccentrically, gave them a great deal of much-mended china), and praised NM to Amy: 'She said suddenly this evening How well you talked & that you had a gift that so few people have, that besides being one of the cleverest people she knew you had the greatest & most accurate memory of any one she had known.' Amy, who really loved her aunt, was overjoyed by the change in her; 'there is Scalands Gate <u>wide</u> open you see which is a great blessing.'

Rows with Willy and Jenny still flared up, and they still could not bring themselves to say a civil word about NM, but Amy was optimistic: 'I think as they call themselves civilised Unitarians they will behave like decent people.' She also hoped that her father's concern about keeping up appearances would prevent last-minute dramas. On 11 February 1880 she wrote, 'Papa is so much afraid of any of us doing anything remarkable in any way that you will, I fancy, see that he will, within the next two months give me, dressed in white silk, to you: in Westfield Church.'

The date was fixed for 30 March. On the twenty-fifth, NM wrote that he had made all the necessary arrangements, 'everything but a necktie which I now go to get'. Amy was embarrassed at her parents' failure to offer hospitality to NM's mother, but Barbara put her old friend up at Scalands, along with the Revd Whitwell Elwin, who was to conduct the service. Triumphal arches were erected over the Westfield road. NM's best man was his Irish friend J. D. Fitzgerald; Amy's bridesmaids were Roddy and her close friend Kathleen Orr. After the ceremony a grand wedding breakfast was served at Crowham. Amy folded up the ornate printed menu and stored it with her love letters:

Mayonnaise of Salmon
Roast Chicken   Chicken à la Reine
Quarter of lamb
Aspic of lobster   York Ham
Raised pie of pigeons   Galantine of Veal
Tongues with Aspic   Lobster Salad

* * *

Trifles
Golden jelly . Strawberry Cream . Charlotte Russe
Gelées à la Macedoine

Swiss Tartlets Cheese cakes
Fruits Bon Bons

* * *

Ices
Strawberry Vanilla

This banquet was quite an achievement, considering the difficulty of obtaining even everyday ingredients in the depths of the country at that time.

NM and Amy spent one night at the Warden's House at St Bartholomew's, before setting off on honeymoon to Paris, Turin, Rome, Bologna and Venice, where their gondolier kissed Amy's hand in homage to her beauty. But the carefree time was short. In mid-July Amy had a swollen gland in her neck. A planned visit to Ireland had to be postponed. Just four months into her marriage, Amy was showing symptoms of the tuberculosis that would dominate and eventually claim her life.

8. '*Eira* is awa''

Yotes Court
June 13th
1880

My dear Uncle Ben,

The beautiful foxes that you sent me came yesterday. Thank you very much indeed for them, they are lovely and it was very kind of you to send them to me.

I hope you will find the north pole, if there is such a place, for I don't quite see how anybody can know as nobody ever seems to have been there; and bring back the old man with his lantern who sits upon it for us to see.

Goodbye,

Your loving niece

Milicent

A terracotta bust of Uncle Ben sits brooding on the landing at Hancox. It was made in 1884, four years after Amy's marriage and two years after Ben's final dramatic return from the Arctic, at a time when his (to him unwelcome) fame and popularity were at their height. It's the portrait of a strong, handsome, heavy-browed man with a luxuriant beard, a dignified profile, and the same bony nose as my father and elder brother. Ben looks every inch the heroic Victorian gentleman-explorer. However one judges his behaviour towards his nieces, in his Arctic exploits Ben Leigh Smith was indeed a hero.

The Pater had pushed his son into the legal profession, but Ben was only really happy out of doors. After the Pater's death, the revenue Ben received from the Glottenham estates which he inherited enabled him to indulge his passion for sailing and exploring. He took

the Board of Trade 'ticket' to command his own ships and invented
an instrument for computing time at sea. Between 1871 and 1882 he
made five Arctic voyages, on which he collected plants, fossils, birds'
eggs and even live animals, took soundings, and charted previously
unexplored stretches of coast. His findings were scientifically and
geographically important, and he demonstrated that it was possible
to get to within 500 miles of the North Pole solely by ship. In 1873
his relief of the stranded Swedish expedition led by Adolf Erik Nordenskiöld made him something of a celebrity.

For his last two voyages Ben used a 300-ton steam vessel, the
Eira, which he had built to his own specifications. The *Eira*'s maiden
voyage went well; Ben surveyed 110 miles of unknown coastline
and showed that a ship could safely reach Franz Josefland and
return, something the Austro-Hungarian expedition that discovered the islands in 1873 had been unable to do. On 28 September
1880, while Amy was recovering from an operation on the tubercular swellings on her neck, he sent a telegram from Hammerfest to
the Ludlows at Yotes: 'Reached Franz Josephland on Aug 14th.
Explored land to west as far as 45 and 80.20 and sighted land from
that point about 40 miles at W.' He returned to Aberdeen on 12
October with two young polar bears on board, which he presented
to London Zoo. (On an earlier expedition, he had brought back
another white bear, Sampson. On board ship, Sampson had escaped
and had been about to plunge overboard; Ben recaptured him with
a kind of rugby tackle.) He had a tippet and muff made up of wol-
verine skins and sent them to twelve-year-old Milicent; these can't
be the foxes she mentions in the letter quoted above, because the
dates don't fit. The foxes must have been another furry present.

The following year, the *Eira* set off again. She left Peterhead on 13
June with a crew of twenty-five (mainly hardy Scotsmen), a kitten,
a canary, and a black retriever named Bob. On 30 June she reached
Matotchkin Straits. 'In ordinary years,' *The Times* explained:

the main pack of ice in the months of June and July is open, but this
year the coast of Spitzbergen was encumbered with ice. Along the

west side of Spitzbergen the surface temperature, usually 40deg
[Fahrenheit], . . . was standing as low as 34deg. The ice this year was
met by whalers more than 300 miles further east and south than in
ordinary years . . . It was necessary, therefore, before Mr. Leigh
Smith could reach Franz Josef's Land, that he should make his way
through an immense barrier of ice, and his success in penetrating this
field depends wholly upon the condition in which he found the ice.

This report appeared on 7 December 1881, at a time when concern
about the fate of the *Eira* was growing. Ben had expressed his intention of returning before the beginning of the British winter; as early
as 1 October, General Ludlow noted in his diary 'No news of the
Eira yet – I am beginning to get anxious.' In November, Sir Henry
Gore-Booth offered to mount a search party – he had hoped to go
with Ben on the expedition but, failing that, he had built an ice-going
ship of his own. William Baxter, Ben's agent at Peterhead, wrote to
Ben's brother Willy. His opinion was that a provisioned relief vessel
should be sent in the spring. The General made many laborious copies of this long letter and sent them to friends and relations.

Willy and his cousin Valentine Smith lobbied the government
and the Royal Geographical Society to organize the rescue mission. Valentine offered to advance £8,000 of his own money if
necessary. On 1 December, Mabel's twenty-first birthday was
celebrated at Yotes with a grand dinner party and a bonfire in the
garden, but the undercurrent of anxiety about her uncle was
strong. The General 'wrote to Valentine and said that shd the Govt
fail to rescue Ben & his crew of the Eira the result of Ben's exploration in 1881 might be lost altogether – and some other nationality
might at some future day gain the credit for what Ben has
already achieved!' This does not reflect the General's own sense of
priorities – he put the personal safety of Ben and his men above all
else – but it was probably a shrewd guess at what might most moti-
vate the government to act in those Empire-building times.

Troubles crowded in on Barbara: the retirement of her beloved
maid Henrietta, the death of George Eliot late in 1880, the poor

health that had blighted the first year of Amy's married life, and now the worry about her missing brother. She still managed to find the energy to set up a Night School at Scalands for working-class men – 'Aunt Ju takes the big men who can't read.' Tiny Aunt Ju was now deaf and eighty-two years old, but she threw herself into the work. She wrote to Amy, 'The excitement of teaching . . . is mingled & lightened up to me by fits of indignation against church & state, & education board, that have left them in this condition. But I have unlimited faith in Aunt Bar's success in whatever she undertakes & accordingly I look for great things to come amongst these specimens of South Saxonry.' Her faith was justified. 'We have such a school! It is quite a rage to go to school & learn, poor fellows like it so much. One walked 22 miles one night & came to Scalands School after,' Barbara told Amy. After Barbara's death, one ex-pupil who had emigrated to Connecticut wrote:

It was . . . about a week ago, that I received the paper, and I had occasion to go down into a lot, or field, to see if some calves there had enough water . . . As I walked along, I was startled and pained when I saw the announcement of Madame's death; and there I stood, in the middle of the lot, until I could not see the print very clearly . . . to her night school do I owe what education I have received.

Barbara was also anxious about her husband, who was showing the first signs of dementia. She was too ill to travel back to Algiers with him for the winter; despite NM's vast workload, he agreed to escort the old Docteur, to set Barbara's mind at rest. Barbara wrote to Amy, 'Give Norman an enormous mass of food for the journey *50 sandwiches* & big ones . . . I do not think you can eat too much going to Alger . . . Norman will want all his thickest things . . . Has he a pocket glass to see distances? . . . My love to Norman & say Take food Take food Take food.' The unhinged fussiness of her tone reflects her level of anxiety.

One good result of this trip was that NM found a secure place in the esteem of Nannie and Isa. Nannie, notoriously critical, even wrote her approval of him to the General, which boosted his standing in the extended family. For his part, NM was only too glad to escape from the privations of Campagne du Pavillon, the Bodichons' house, to the warmth and beauty of Nannie and Isa's Campagne Montfeld. Though Barbara had been confident that NM would like the Docteur's way of living, even he, who in earlier years had slept on bare floorboards with a block of oak for a pillow, found it challenging. Amy passed on his comments to Rebecca:

> The house is absolutely bare and nothing to eat it seems the Dr lives on about 2d a day he walks about the house at night with a loaded double barrel gun and has a ferocious dog to guard him who makes a point of biting everyone. N. managed by judicious kicks to escape and he had all his meals with Aunt Nanny.

Yet another cause of family concern was Mabel's mental state. It seems likely that she was showing signs of manic depression. She was an intensely social creature. Her father's diaries are full of references to the balls from which she came back fresh as a daisy at five in the morning, the dinner parties at which she sang without a trace of shyness, the tennis parties at which she triumphed against male and female opponents. On the hunting field, she sailed over five barred gates and was often the only woman in at the kill. She painted portraits of many of her friends and relations. She kept many animals – the General mentions her bathing her dog in front of the stables, a job which she could easily have handed over to a servant. She wrote letters for her aging father, taught at the local Sunday school and visited the poor and sick of the parish. She liked to spend her time in a throng of young people, of both sexes; though very close to Harry, she was clearly the dominant sibling. She loved spending money and dressed as flamboyantly as she dared.

But without warning her energy would desert her, and she would collapse. '[Mabel's] nervous system became unstrung – she has to take tonic and give up her morning cold water bath,' wrote her father on 2 June 1881. He must have felt sick at heart as he observed the emergence of symptoms similar to her mother Bella's, most particularly, insomnia. Mabel's breakdown in the summer of 1881 lasted several weeks. She was sent to convalesce, first at Scalands with Barbara, then at Crowham with Jenny. Neither aunt seems the ideal of restful companionship.

NM saw Mabel in September, and wrote to Aunt Barbara, hoping to set her mind at rest, 'Mabel has . . . been playing lawn tennis with us, with a good deal of activity & looks much better . . . & in as good spirits as most young ladies whose occupation is amusement . . . Yesterday after dinner we talked and played the word game. Mabel & Milicent both played with interest and Mabel made puns & seemed to enjoy herself a good deal. There seems nothing unusual in her manner.' But when Mabel returned to Yotes the General's diary shows that he still was not satisfied that she was well, despite her attempts to reassure him. 'Mabel . . . said that by making an effort she should be quite well she felt assured.'

Concern for Mabel together with his habitual stoicism led the General to play down his own health problems. For some years he had suffered from attacks of 'irritability' from stones in the bladder; riding, once such a pleasure, became agonizingly uncomfortable, and even a carriage drive was difficult. In January 1882, at the age of eighty, he went to London for an operation performed by Sir Henry Thompson at 33 Wimpole Street. 'Mr Moss Sir Hy's man who "etherised me" asked if I had any false teeth! The operation was performed and a great amount of stone was removed . . . The doctors speak in terms of admiration at the wonderful soundness of my constitution.' I'm glad to read that he had 'troops of visitors', including Florence Nightingale's sister Lady Verney, and Mabel bearing tulips. Harry had not yet returned to Oxford for the new term, where he was at Exeter College and struggling rather. He and Mabel lodged with the Shore Smiths for the duration, and Mrs MacCreath stayed in the nursing home with the General. Milicent remained at Yotes with the governess and cousin Fanny Walton. The General would not let her come to visit him.

His instinct was always to shield his children from anything that might distress them.

One cheerful piece of family news that the General received at Wimpole Street was that his niece Amy had safely given birth to her first child, my grandfather Alan, on 23 January 1882. Amy began by breastfeeding Alan. Her mother wrote, 'What a good thing not to have to bottle the baby – but don't you hate the little wretch at night when it wakes you up?' To NM she wrote, 'tell Amy I am glad it is a boy – I shant be a great grandmother quite so soon.' The emphasized I is to point a contrast between herself and Aunt Nannie, who made no secret of the fact that she regarded boy babies as a waste of time. Roddy wrote describing nine-year-old Lionel's reaction: 'He said, "Of course if he is my nephew he must belong to me. I shall call him 'Lionel' & I shall be able to try experiments on him, I'll bring him up on sawdust." ' Jenny herself, at the age of forty-four, was pregnant for what was to be the final time. This might have brought her closer to Amy, had their attitudes to babies and pregnancy not been so very different. In February, Jenny wrote, 'If you are half as bored as I am you are a good deal bored. I am going to have a tremendous piece of dissipation this afternoon I am going for a short drive to nowhere in particular in the wagonette.' She didn't want Willy-boy to come home for his exeat from school because she had concealed her pregnancy from him; Willy had asked his mother why she looked so like Aunt Barbara (i.e. fat) but she had sidestepped the enquiry. Jenny, it is alleged in the family, said that she 'liked to think people were full of pink cotton wool', though her seven pregnancies must have supplied conclusive evidence to the contrary. She refused to be called 'Grandmamma', but tried to hold back the march of time by making her grandchildren call her 'Aunt Jenny' and her husband 'Uncle Willy'.

Alan's little aunt was born on 5 March. 'I was born an aunt,' she would later declare, with pride. On the tenth, Roddy told Amy that 'Mama & Sophia Dorothea Hilary Alice Eira Julia are very well. Mama says she is ugly and like a pug dog.' Barbara was

delighted when the baby's name settled down to Dorothy, short-
ened to Dolly, in memory of Aunt Dolly Longden.

Meanwhile, plans for the relief of the *Eira* continued. In January,
The Times announced that the Admiralty would contribute £5,000,
but at least £14,000 was needed. The Lord Mayor of London called
a meeting at the Mansion House to discuss the subject. Nannie
wrote to General Ludlow saying she would give £1,000 and she
believed Barbara would do the same; the General pledged his own
£1,000. In April, Sir Allen Young was named as commander of the
search vessel, the SS *Hope*. 'Sir Allen Young is a rich man and has an
ice-going vessel of his own,' the General wrote in his diary. 'He too
is a personal friend of Ben's and he has a passion for Arctic exploration.' He and Harry wrote letters to Ben, care of Sir Allen Young.
'Lilybel [Milicent] gave the letters a kiss for good luck.' Valentine
Smith and Willy Leigh Smith planned to travel some way up the
coast with the *Hope*, and Mabel went to see it set sail on 17 June.

I found a little diary for 1882 kept intermittently by Milicent.
It's prefaced with a stern warning to snoopers –

> This Book is mine
> Whoe'er doth find
> It open must not look
> Into this book . . .
> Let me but find him at it –
> And oh my! won't he catch it!

Anyone disobeying this order, as I have done, would find a disappointing lack of revelatory material. The entries are mostly
concerned with the diurnal round – church, walks, tennis, shopping, picnics. But on Monday 21 August there is an explosively
exciting entry. 'What do you think? We got a telegram from Uncle
Ben! He is all right, he says I think "Got back all safe but Eira is
awa'" or something like that.' On 11 September she adds detail:

One man had a canser (I think) on his lip, and died afterwards.

Another had something the matter with his arm. They spent the
winter in a hut which they called 'Flora Cottage' or Flora Something; it was at Cape Flora I think, in Franz Joseph Land. The Eira
went down and they had only about two hours to save things, if as
much, I don't know exactly. The men said 'She's awa', 'she was our
home', 'she was a bonnie ship'. Pretty, is'ent it? They had a dog and
a cat. They lived on bear and walrus besides what they had saved,
which was I think about a fortnight's provisions. In the spring or
summer they started in their boats on a 800* miles journey or
something. They rowed or sailed part of the way and I should
think they must have been carried along on ice the rest of the
way . . . When they started from Flora Cottage they were obliged
to drown the cat, because the sailors said they would never get
home (I suppose) safely if they had a cat on board.

Flora Cottage was named after Cousin Flora Smith, Valentine's
sister. Ben was in the habit of naming his discoveries after his
relations – Cape Ludlow, Cape Leigh Smith, Mabel Island.

Nannie and Isabella Blythe were in England for the summer.
Knowing that Ben would refuse to supply them with details, they
captured Dr Neale, the *Eira*'s doctor, and plied him with questions. Isa then wrote a full account for Aunt Ju. This was copied
and circulated within the family:

One scene he told very simply is the wreck of the poor Eira –
when she was pitched between the ice and land-floes they had no
idea that any vital mischief was done, she had however a great hole
somewhere, where, they never knew. Mr Smith [Ben] was on the
ice with others storing the things the men were getting from the
hold as a precautionary measure only, then the boats were taken
from one side and the Eira righted herself but the doctor & those
working on board saw that the water rose & rose & the sailors
began to break the windows and send things up through them

---

* Actually about 470 miles.

from the cabin, when Mr Smith called 'Stop that.' Then the Doctor said 'She is going fast'. Mr Smith was on board in a moment, saw how it was & they all worked saving what they could, the water fast rising then they all leaped on to the ice & then she went slowly down & two great ice floes closed over her and only the tops of the masts were above the water. Your nephew looked very grave & only said 'Poor old Eira'. Then the men hacked down the masts to add to the firewood and then the men who were 'dazed like' when the Captain gave them an order said 'There's no ship now & we are all alike' grumbling. [When a ship is wrecked the sailors are released from their duty to obey the captain.] Mr Smith stood forward & said 'what is all this grumbling about I can do better without you than you without me; will you act just as if you were on board ship and I will do my best for you all'. – They cheered and said they would do anything for him; but he said they must obey him through the Captain to whom he would give his orders and so it was agreed . . . They tried to blow up the Eira or rather make her rise with gun cotton* as the floes of ice parted again and then they saw her in the clear water far below. . .

They saved guns, powder, flour, curry powder, rum sherry & tobacco and the boy saved a few currants so at Christmas time they had a little dough pudding the size of a penny bun with a few currants in it! They saved a few clothes and a few books but all the precious collection for Kew & the really valuable fossils . . . account of observations . . . notes & maps . . . went down. They saved the cat & dog. They built a house 30ft long by 12 wide.

Going through Hancox photographs, I was very pleased to find an official portrait of the *Eira*'s dog, posing with an unidentified member of the crew. The photograph is captioned ' "BOB" the celebrated dog of the "Eira" boat', and on the back it says 'This sagacious animal enticed the Bears from a distance, by going near to them, and then running away till he brought them within the

---

* An explosive made by steeping cotton in nitric and sulphuric acids.

range of the Guns of the Arctic Voyagers, and thus by his skilful
manœuvre, supplied them with food.' Bob is a black retriever with
a white bib and white paws; he looks stout and very woolly. He
was vital to the survival of Ben and the crew. Their supplies of
tinned food they decided to save for the return journey they knew
they would eventually have to attempt. They were not to reach
home for ten months. Their diet mainly consisted of walrus, polar
bear and 'loom' (as the sailors called guillemot), which laid its eggs
on the rocks. Whenever possible the blood was saved when a bear
was shot, as, said Dr Neale, 'a pint of it put into the dinner pan
made the soup beautifully rich.' The contents of the bears' stom-
achs were also saved. If the bear had been eating seals, 'more than
once we obtained a good bucketful of oil for cooking purposes.'
Dr Neale was very worried about the loss of all their stocks of
lime juice, but in fact none of the men developed scurvy; this
demonstrated that fresh meat contains sufficient vitamin C to protect against it.

They all survived the long dark winter months, when the temperature was sometimes 40° below freezing point, the sailor with
mouth cancer taking his turn at every task despite the great pain he
was in. The following June, when the ice started to break up, the
men began their homeward journey in the longboats they had
saved from the wreck. They hoist their large damask tablecloths
for sails – such tablecloths were clearly regarded as an essential
piece of Arctic expeditionary kit, and these had fortunately been
salvaged. Isa's narrative resumes:

On June 21 they started at 10 at night leaving in the house six bottles of Champagne! . . . then they all rowed away, six men in each
boat in Mr Smith's boat seven, for he had the poor cancer man with
him – Think of the brave fellows & so for many a long long day (45
I think) thro' <u>fearful</u> storms often, & weary watching & sometimes
for days beset in the thick ice, they sailed & rowed 1000 miles and
more! One day the waves rose mountains high; it seemed as if the
boats could not live a moment in such a fearful sea but the men at

the helms knew the lives of all depended on them & they were splendid men – one had but one arm, poor fellow. So at last they got into the straits & if they had gone on another mile they would have seen the Hope at once. After 43 days, they met the Hope at Novaya Zemlya. They were queer objects – their faces nearly black their clothing strange 'and with a strange smell of fish about them'. Sir Henry Gore Booth was in such a state of violent excitement & delight that he could not see them for a whole day but paced his cabin all alone!

In another letter Isa adds:

I don't think I told you about the Hope passing Peterhead on its return. Capt Grey saw the Hope steaming past & put off in a steam tug after her & the moment he was near enough he shouted 'What news of the Eira?' Sir Allen Young 'Gone to the bottom' – Capt Grey 'And the Crew?' Sir A Young 'Here on board' Capt Grey 'and Mr Smith?' Sir A Young 'Safe on board' Capt Grey 'Stop, let me up; I <u>must</u> see him I <u>must</u> hear his voice etc etc.' Somehow or other Capt Grey did get on board & then followed such a scene of rejoicing & cheering!! Capt Grey said 'Little Peterhead shall have the honour of telling the news I'll go off and Telegraph' & away he went in his tug utterly beside himself with joy Dr Neale said. The Hope could not put in to Peterhead as she would have done (most of the men's wives being there) because being out of repair and owing to some insurance formality she had to go right on to Aberdeen.

Ben returned to find himself a national hero though, as he told General Ludlow, he dreaded public acclaim 'worse than ice'. He received the gold medal of the Royal Geographical Society and was made an honorary fellow of Jesus College, Cambridge, where he had been a student. (As a Dissenter, he had been barred from taking his degree.) Ben shrank from such honours – asked to give a lecture to the Royal Geographical Society, he pulled out at the last minute, leaving someone else to read his script. However, they were richly deserved. As his obituary in *The Times* was eventually to put it, 'Mr Smith and his companion, Dr William Neale, deserved great credit for the way in which they managed to maintain discipline and good feeling among their men under very trying circumstances.'

His family and friends were, of course, overjoyed by his return and by his heroism. Nannie told Barbara that Ben 'looks very well & was very pleasant indeed . . . it is certain he feels we have all been feeling for him & his men. He was very nice indeed.' However, Nannie felt obliged to warn Amy that as far as her marriage was concerned Ben had 'come home in just the same mood that he went away . . . I had hoped so much he would come back with the past over & done with . . . but it is not so.' Mabel still held sway as Ben's favourite niece. On 21 September, Milicent wrote in her diary, 'Mabel has gone to Scotland! With Cousin Val [Valentine Smith] and Uncle Ben!' They had gone, amongst other places, to Ardtornish, Cousin Val's imposing and luxurious mansion in Argyllshire. Milicent had to content herself with a November visit to Eastbourne with Mrs MacCreath and the governess:

Waiting Room. Tunbridge Station. November 22nd 1882.

Creathy, Miss Kahn and I are going to Eastbourne. Hope its alright . . . Groombridge – Mayfield – Jolly high-art station – Shoreham Road ditto – Hellingly ditto. Hailesham. ther's the backbone of Beachy Hd!!!! Polegate!!

This may be the only time in history that the dull town of Polegate has merited two exclamation marks.

Milicent's spirits would not have been so buoyant had she known that she was never to see her father again. The General was eighty-one, but had shown no signs of decline, and had made an excellent recovery from his operation in January. The letters he wrote to Milicent while she was at Eastbourne she kept in a lockable box along with a small packet of photographs of him, and other pre-

cious or important documents. His handwriting is as steady and
even as ever; he tells his 'Darling Lilybel' that he is going to London
for the day, that he has just 'bottled up the contents of the whiskey
jar . . . and find that it filled 12 bottles & a little more than ½ a bottle! I have tasted it, although it is early in the day for such potent
imbibing, and the whiskey is <u>delectable</u> – such as I have no doubt
as the Queen drinks in her Highland Home at Balmoral.' On
25 November, five days before his death, he writes, 'Our dinner
party went off pleasantly . . . and the moon shone bright to light
the diners out' though he bemoans the '<u>impossibility</u> of getting a
good <u>sober</u> Cook to take service in the Country'. Milicent's young
tom cat, he tells her, 'followed me up yesterday into the morning
room and behaved very badly – getting repeatedly upon my shoulders – upon the table & upon the writing paper'. The very last
letter, mainly concerned with travel arrangements for Milicent's
return, is dated 30 November, the day before Mabel's twenty-
second birthday. The unaltered handwriting gives no indication
that by the end of that day General Ludlow would be dead.

He was buried in the tomb at Fordcombe beside his wife Bella
and little Edmund; they would later be joined by Harry, Mabel,
and Mabel's cousin-husband Ludlow Coape Ludlow. Bella's friend
Miss Greatorex sent a wreath, as she had for Bella; Milicent dried
and kept a flower from it, in her box of treasures. The inscription
for the General reads:

NOW THE END OF THE COMMANDMENT IS CHARITY
OUT OF A PURE HEART, AND OF A GOOD CONSCIENCE,
AND OF FAITH UNFEIGNED (I. TIM. I.5).

which seems extremely apt. I read my way through all twenty-
three years of the General's diaries, and found myself marvelling
at the consistency of the man. He could be a little pedantic, a little
old-fashioned, perhaps too much of a stickler for etiquette at
times, but his courage and kindness, his devotion to his friends
and family, his non-judgemental fair-mindedness, and the lively

interest he took in every aspect of the world around him, were un-wavering even in the face of great trial and sorrow.

Milicent's diary is empty for the fortnight after her father's death. When she resumes it on 14 December, it is clear that Uncle Ben had taken over the management of the three orphans. He installed them in his London house, 64 Gower Street, and took them on a round of sightseeing – Madame Tussaud's, the National Gallery ('We saw a picture of two dear little King Charles spaniels, by Sir Edwin Lanseer'), the Albert Memorial, Cleopatra's Needle. There was also a great deal of social activity – teas and dinners with the Shore Smiths in York Place, with Cousin Flora Smith (Cousin Val-entine's sister) in the Cromwell Road, and with the General's old friends and relations in Wimbledon. Ben kitted Milicent out with an evening dress and gave her 'two little cameos'. His vigorous attempts to distract her from her grief were perhaps almost too successful. On New Year's Eve she wrote, 'The year has nearly gone. I think the greatest event of my life has happened in it and I do not mind one quarter enough. I must have a very hard heart. I must pray to have it made softer. Oh dear.'

Family meetings were held to discuss the Ludlows' future. Mabel regarded herself as fully capable of managing on her own as mistress of Yotes Court and was longing to return there to com-mence her reign. Harry, not quite twenty-one, had not yet finished his degree or chosen a career, though Milicent's diary mentions that he is to be an 'enginer'. Milicent's upbringing was largely in the hands of Mrs MacCreath, to whom she was devoted, and Miss Kahn, who was turning out to be one of the most satisfactory of a long line of governesses. Cousin Flora Smith, who was childless, and Louisa Shore Smith, whose children were old enough to allow her to direct some of her attention elsewhere, were to play an inter-mittent supervisory role. But the person who was placed most firmly *in loco parentis* was of course Uncle Ben.

The question was, what was to become of Cousin Fanny Wal-ton, who had lived with the Ludlows since before Milicent's birth? She was a middle-aged spinster who regarded herself as a semi-invalid (though, as she lived at least into her eighties, her alarm on her own account may have been misplaced). She had made herself fairly useful to the General, answering letters, returning neighbours' calls when Bella had been too ill to do so, and generally superintending the running of the household. She now assumed that the General's death would make no difference to this arrangement, but Mabel and Milicent disagreed. 'There was a real old Parliament. We "sat" on Fanny. You see we don't, I suppose, want her to go on living with us now . . . if she once comes back to Yotes without anything being said it will be rather difficult to make her move, poor old thing.' Milicent, that 'persevering little person', got her way. Fanny did not come back to Yotes, except on visits.

Aunt Barbara, still partly incapacitated, fretted about the fate of the Ludlows and was grieved that she was unable to take a more active role in their lives. NM gently satirized her attitude in a letter to Amy: '21.12.82. I should like to know as you are writing 1. Does Mabel practice the castanets regularly every day? 2. Does Harry read a whole chapter in Thucydides every day. 3. Does Milicent stitch her sampler every evening.'

In January, Uncle Ben took a house in Hastings, 60 Eversfield Place, and installed Mabel and Milicent. The Crowham Leigh Smiths were bidden to join them, to make a jolly family party. Aunt Jenny wrote to Amy in her usual sardonic vein:

> It was certainly unnecessary for us to go to keep up the spirits of the Ludlows. I think all they want is a little keeping down. I cannot understand Mabel – something seems to have been left out of her composition could it have been her heart – is she a mermaid or what – it doesn't seem quite as if she could be judged by ordinary rules - & in spite of it all I like her better than Milicent – though the latter is somewhat quieter - & might be supposed to give a passing thought to her father say once a week (Don't tell what I say about them to Aunt Barbara).

It seems to me likely that the legacy of living with their mother's

insanity was that Mabel and Milicent were inclined to compartmen-
talize their lives, and to shut the lid firmly on all that was distressing.
For Milicent, this habit kept her strong through extremely difficult
times, though it may have blunted her ability to explore her feelings fully. Norman, my uncle, who remembers Milicent well (he
was twenty-four when she died), wrote to me à propos Bella's illness, 'It all explains, how despite much goodness and kindness she
[Milicent] had a perplexing lack of warmth. No wonder poor
dear.' In Mabel's case, the refusal to confront painful emotions was
soon to have disastrous consequences.

At the family gathering in Eversfield Place all was manically
jolly. 'Can you fancy a household,' Jenny asked Amy:

> with Uncle Ben for President Mabel for Vice President and
> Mrs MaCreath what shall we say Archbishop of Canterbury – I
> don't know that it is altogether an agreeable combination . . . the
> meals are wonderful affairs a very long table a very dirty tablecloth
> and all kinds of queer dishes – Uncle Ben's idea of bringing up his
> young family is to go & buy them endless quantities of goodies –
> so that at teatime chocolate creams – candied fruits – and all sorts
> of incongruous things appear.

Despite Jenny's sniping, the cousins enjoyed their time together.
Milicent's diary records scrambling on the rocks with Roddy, Willy-
boy and Lionel, and going to the swimming baths and fishmarket.

Back at Yotes, Mabel was more or less in charge of managing
the servants, the household finances and the family's social life.
But it was still considered impossible for her to see young men
unaccompanied by a chaperone. When Harry was at home she
consorted freely with his friends, but in his absence she was sometimes stuck. Creathy would do at a pinch, but she had plenty of
household duties to attend to, and her status some way between
the family and the servants meant that she could not accompany
Mabel to balls and dinner parties.

One of Harry's friends, Arthur Glover, became especially attentive. Arthur Glover had been a familiar figure at Yotes for several years. His courage on the hunting field had won him the approbation of the General, who had also noted how helpful he had been in guiding Harry through the Oxford entrance procedure – Glover was already 'up'. I'm not sure whether his courtship of Mabel had become obvious before the General's death. The last volume of the General's diary is the only one to have been partly destroyed; all the entries from August to November 1882 have been torn out. This leaves me wondering whether there were references to the romance which Milicent, in the light of what was to happen to Mabel, thought it prudent to remove. If so, it's odd that she made no attempt to censor anything else. Perhaps the explanation is quite different, and a careless maid used the diary to light the fire. I don't suppose I'll ever know.

Milicent's own diary indicates that, by the summer of 1883, young Glover was a household fixture. The catalogue of picnics and tennis and cricket matches is interrupted in June, when Milicent developed a bad sore throat, which she attributed to eating 'mellon strawberries and cream etc' and drew a sketch of herself pulling a long face. It turned out to be diphtheria. Several friends and neighbours also caught it, including 'little Jenny Nichols', who died. Mabel would have remembered the death of her little brother Edmund from the same illness; her anxiety for Milicent must have been acute.

Aunt Nannie was much alarmed, and decided to act. 'Aunt Nanny has sent me such heaps & heaps of things since I have been ill,' wrote Milicent on 19 July, when she was beginning to recover. On the twenty-fourth, Creathy took Milicent to stay with Ben at Gower Street, where they enjoyed meeting the sagacious 'Bob', who had quite a following: 'Today 2 ladies came and brought him a collar worked by hand. It had I.M. (In Memoriam) EIRA. It was done in silks.' Aunt Nannie came, bearing flowers, and, mysteriously, 'an elephant'.

Ben took Mabel and Milicent to Southsea. After a few days they were joined by Nannie, Isa and their faithful French maid Emilie,

also by Harry and Arthur Glover. They looked over the *Victory* –
'We saw the places where Admiral Nelson fell and died. "Honor
the brave"' – crossed to the Isle of Wight, where they went over
Carisbrook Castle, a momentous event for Milicent, who had a
romantic passion for King Charles I despite the fact that her ancestor Edmund Ludlow had signed his death warrant. She picked
leaves and flowers from Carisbrook, and pressed them in her diary.
'Delightful place, and a delightful day we spent there. I wonder if
I shall enjoy things so much when I get older.'

On the island Milicent took warm salt baths. Though she was
allowed to swim in the sea and go for walks and boat trips, Aunt
Nannie decreed that Milicent was to be carried upstairs at night.
There is an inevitability about the fact that Nannie decided Arthur
Glover was a poor creature, and told Mabel so. Mabel took offence.
When they all returned to Yotes at the end of August, Nannie also
succeeded in putting Milicent's back up by continuing to treat her
as an invalid. 'We had a party here. [Nannie] wanted to go into the
garden and watch the tennis, but I was to lie down part of the time!!
Quel idée! I would not do it. If I thought I should be an invalid all
my life it might be different but I hope I shall get strong again.'

Undeterred by Nannie, Mabel and Arthur saw each other as
often as they could. 'Arthur Glover dug a ditch bigger by the wood &
watercress beds to jump over'; 'Mr Glover is doing a coat of arms
for Mabel in oils'; 'Mabel and AG . . . sailed a boat on the pond.'
Nannie and Isa returned to Algiers for the winter, Nannie disgrun-
tled that her attempts at mothering her nieces had been rebuffed.

As Mabel took more and more control at Yotes, the chaperoning rules relaxed. There was a large group of young people in the
house at Christmastime; they enacted a charade of *Hamlet* which
must have given rise to some outré behaviour, because Milicent
commented, 'Poor Mr Glover! Harry is a very defective chaperone.' The next day she exclaimed, 'Harry badder than ever! What
do you think? He went to London! Leaving . . . me the only
approach to "a Chap".' She later adds, 'It was exciting without a
Chap . . . In the aft. we played cricket in the attic, great fun.' (This

gives an idea of the size of the attic at Yotes.) For Milicent, joining in the activities of the young adults was rather thrilling – 'I fear it was not a Sunday-y Sunday. We mesmerised, & tried lifting people up with fingers holding their breath.' But her presence was not always welcome. When she went with Mabel and Arthur to Tonbridge in the Phaeton, 'Mabel (curious to say) evinced a sudden desire for me to have my hair cut! Why, oh why? She used to hate it, more or less!'

No diary of Milicent's survives for 1884, and references to her or Mabel in family letters are few. My guess is that they carried on enjoying themselves at Yotes, their time punctuated by visits from Uncle Ben and Louisa Shore Smith. Milicent continued her lessons, her painting and her writing; her ambition was to be an author.

Harry's movements are also unclear. By the end of 1883 he seems to have started some kind of engineering or architectural training, which sounds like the sort of career towards which Uncle Ben would have steered him. In the summer he set off for India. He wanted to explore the places where his father had lived and worked, and make the acquaintance of the General's old friends. He may also have gone to visit his cousins the Coape Smiths, several of whom were in India. A few years before, Marianne Coape Smith had written to General Ludlow inviting Mabel to come out to India with them. The General had asked Cousin Fanny Walton to pen his letter of refusal, as the thought of exposing his child to the dangers of India made him feel physically sick. Such fear did not prove groundless.

On 25 August, Harry wrote to Milicent from 'Jeypore':

We are guests to the Rajah . . . They are very full of the remembrance of my Father here. I shall have lots to tell you when I come back . . . The Rajah is a very fine looking fellow . . . The flying ants are horrid.

One man who is <u>very</u> civil to me here is Seith Moolchand Goleta . . . our Father 'made' him – did a great deal for him – Seith showed me a ring that our Father sent out to him . . . At his house he has a garden which was laid out to the order of our Father and upon which was spent 200,000 rupees – I enclose some rose leaves from the garden –

The brown petals are still in the envelope.

Meanwhile, Mabel and Arthur fixed their wedding for September. Jenny and Willy offered to host it from Crowham, apparently because Uncle Ben was unhappy about it. Amy told NM, 'Money seems tight indeed, and they [Jenny and Willy] are lamenting a good deal over the wedding which they say they can't afford a bit. U.B [Ben] seems very anxious to get out of it altogether and told Roddy Mabel only cares for <u>presents</u> & was thinking always of what present he was going to give her!' Ben was concerned about the financial disparity between Mabel, who had inherited a comfortable fortune, and Arthur Glover, who, as far as can be ascertained, had no such prospects, but talked of taking up farming.

In September fate struck Mabel two cruel blows. Arthur Glover became very ill, and the wedding was postponed. I don't know what the illness was, but it was thought to have long-term consequences – Aunt Nannie lamented at the thought of the sickly children such a union would produce. Even worse followed. Harry, returning from India, perhaps planning to be back in time to give his sister away, died on board ship in the Red Sea. On the back of the letter quoted above, Milicent has written, 'Received at York Place after the news had come to us.' Again, information is scarce; I imagine Harry caught a tropical disease. Mabel and Harry had been close, devoted siblings from the earliest age. Only fourteen months apart, they had shared friends and interests, and had clung together through the tragedies that had befallen the family. Now, Mabel had lost both parents and both brothers, and her marital prospects were blighted, if not ruined.

There seems to have been another attempt to hold the wedding in December, but this time it was Mabel's health that broke down. Jenny wrote to Amy, 'We heard . . . from Flora Smith yesterday that Mabel had arrived there [at Flora's house in the Cromwell

Road] quite ill & unfit for anything & all idea of the wedding is given up for the present, it is a great relief to me that she is not coming here this week it seemed such a dangerous thing to do just after she had been ill because of the cold. I wonder if that wedding will ever come off now.' From Algiers, Nannie ranted to Amy about the thoughtlessness of her family:

I hear <u>nothing</u> not even a Xmas card from Mabel or Milicent – of course I am deeply hurt – v. anxious too – why is Mabel not married? Where are they? Is Milicent ill? & where is she? I know <u>nothing</u> but yr phrase that implies that Mabel's marriage is deferred – it does seem hard when I am so bothered here that I am let to be anxious about the girls at home – but they have no hearts & no imaginations.

Poor Mabel was not in a fit state to send anyone a Christmas card. While staying with her fiancé's parents at Edenbridge in Kent, she fell into 'an excited condition', as NM put it in a letter to Nannie. She attempted suicide by throwing herself down stairs. The Glovers attributed this simply to her despair at finding her marriage yet again postponed, but NM considered that her mental instability had been 'of more gradual growth'.

Uncle Ben took charge. Yotes was given up, Milicent was placed in a small boarding school, Hamilton House in Tunbridge Wells, and Mabel was incarcerated with Ben in Gower Street. Now Ben had what he had perhaps always longed for, a captive niece. NM had conversations deep into the night with one of Mabel's doctors, the humane and sympathetic Dr Barlow. On 6 January 1885 he noted in his medical casebook: 'Walked back [from the Pathological Society] with Dr Barlow. His account of the case of Mabel Ludlow [NM wrote her name in Irish, to preserve privacy] Jaundice. Extreme agitation. Attempt to throw herself over stairs. Sense of contrition also belief that she has signed cheques fraudulently & will be imprisoned.' On 14 January he wrote Amy a fuller account, based on what Dr Barlow had told him about Ben's ménage. NM was still, of course, barred from Gower Street.

. . . Mabel makes scrapbooks & knits and sews for the children's hospital. Dr Tuke [presumably the same Dr Tuke who saw her mother Bella] said that it seems advised that she should not go out to drive & thought the danger of suicide not over. The polar bear [Ben], however, now chaffs her about suicide for she now & then talks of it. Dr. Barlow thinks it necessary to be careful with him: says he is much too arbitrary. He (B) did put off the wedding of his own motion before Arthur Glover had been seen by Barlow & without telling Mabel at all. Mabel wrote to A Gr saying that she wishes for the present to make him an allowance. This letter U. Ben retained. He told Barlow of this. I thought it was not right, said Barlow, & I told him I thought it was not right to have kept it, especially as he had given Miss Ludlow to understand that it was posted. 'I will take the responsibility' said U.B. 'You will have to' said Barlow.

Barlow says there is an evident desire on the part of U.B. to make him a tool for breaking off the marriage which said Barlow I do not mean to be made. Dr Barlow is a fine straight forward excellent fellow who will not flex one inch for anybody . . . Barlow's opinion is that U.B. thinks too much of the money aspect of the question. Mabel plays a little on the piano & paints a little. She has not been out at all yet.

I think it would be a kind & useful thing to write (for you) to Mabel, quite a general letter as if nothing at all had happened but probably you will not think so.

Meantime A. Gr makes poor Dr Barlow's life a burden by calling on him. U.B. will not see A. Gr. A Gr sends Mabel flowers but not notes at all.

Mabel remained under Ben's total control for several months, at Gower Street and at Eastbourne, where she was taken for a change of air. Nannie was not slow to pronounce on the case. 'I have no doubt,' she wrote to Amy on 17 January:

that this attack might have been prevented, if there had been any-

one in authority over her, but as you know, she is now 24 years
old, & entirely her own mistress - & she turned against me directly
she engaged herself to Arthur Glover – knowing beforehand (as
I told you) what my opinion was about him . . . As you know
Dr Barlow will you tell him from me that under no circumstances
must they send Mabel out to me – It would be useless for her - &
it would kill me . . . I trust Arthur Glover will be sent off on a voyage - & that wd give Mabel a tranquil time to recover.

When she wrote to NM a few days later her tone was more
sympathetic: 'I have good hopes of Mabel because I think she has
so much of her father in her . . . I think she will get well – but her
future is the sad part – with her heart set on a man who cannot live
long.'
A month later, Mabel's condition had not improved – Nannie
was worried that Mabel had inherited 'the family taint', but as usual
was only able to discuss the problem insofar as it affected herself:

My dear [Amy], the news of poor Mabel is horrid – but I am quite
sure the best chance for her is not to have any one of her family
with her. You see no one knows by sadder experience what it is –
for I was months & months with my beloved sister Bella - & God
only knows what I suffered - & now looking back I see that it
destroyed my health without saving her.

How much did Milicent know? She knew that her sister was ill,
and that for the first few weeks she was not allowed to write to
her. She knew that Yotes Court, the only home she could remember, had been hastily given up, and that it was unlikely she would
ever return. She knew that Miss Kahn, of whom she was very fond,
had been dismissed – not because of any ill conduct, but because
Milicent, aged sixteen, had been sent to school for the first time in
her life and no longer required a governess. She knew that the
faithful Mrs MacCreath was temporarily lodged at Crowham –
though whether she knew how irksome Aunt Jenny found this

arrangement is not clear. Milicent's world had, indeed, been turned upside down. But her tenacity and powers of self-control enabled her to cope, and besides, she rather enjoyed boarding school. Serious-minded and fairly clever, Milicent applied herself to her studies in earnest; she was particularly keen on learning languages. She had been torn away from the network of friends in which she had grown up, but she had no difficulty in making friends with the girls at school, and she found the principal, Miss Goldie, 'delightful'. At Hancox there's a photograph of Milicent at the school in a group of five girls. They're neatly but quite ornately dressed – Milicent is wearing a pale muslin gown printed with a pattern of diamonds, ornamented with dark velvet ribbons and topped with an overladen straw hat. At least two of the girls in the picture were special friends of hers. All her life, Milicent valued her female friendships and was good at maintaining them.

Aunt Jenny, making more than her usual effort, visited Milicent at school and reported to Amy that she was:

> greatly improved, school seemed to have had a most humanizing effect on her. I always thought her such a dried up little thing but now I'm not at all sure she isn't going to turn out quite pretty . . . Uncle Ben writes that Mabel is no better & thinks some change will have to be made. Of course I avoided the topic with Milicent as I didn't know how much she knew about it. She asked me eagerly if I had heard lately how Mabel was & said she was now allowed to write to her under cover to Uncle Ben – I think she must guess what is the matter with her – but we did not let on at all to one another – She said how dull it must be for Mabel in Gower St & I agreed.

Just as she kept her exercise books from the schoolroom at Yotes, so Milicent preserved some of her work books from Hamilton House. In amongst the German exercises and the essays on topics such as 'The Sun And His Work' are poems, scribbled in pencil, not intended for the eye of Miss Goldie. Milicent seems to have had a crush on one of the other girls, May Rutherford:

Once more once more in my heart you'll rest
Once more on my shoulder your fair head nest
Once more to each other our lips be prest,
Once more I'll see you May.

And, poignantly, there's a poem addressed to Harry:

Something in my life is missing,
Missing, dear, because of thee,
Something in me still is wishing
For the days that used to be.

Never never can thy place
Filled by another be
Never never will this world
Be quite the same to me
Never never will my life
From this desire be free
Never, for never canst thou come
In this life back to me.

For our love to one another
Was not to aught else akin
None else here is like a brother
Or the feeling borne to him —
So the life's sad vacancy
Filled by no one else can be.

★

1884 had not been a good year for the Leigh Smith aunts. Dear old Aunt Ju died in December 1883. Harry's death and Mabel's break-down soon followed, and there was also the degeneration of Dr Bodichon to contend with. The old pattern of the Bodichons' married life, whereby they spent the winter months together in Algiers and returned to England in spring, had collapsed since

Barbara's first stroke. The Docteur had taken to spending some of the summer in England, returning without Barbara to Algiers in the late autumn. In Algiers, he was a near neighbour of Nannie and Isa, and he drove them – or at least Nannie – wild with irritation.

Nannie was a tempestuous character. She could be extraordinarily charming and charismatic, or devastatingly cutting, even malicious. When somebody was in her favour, she fêted them royally. NM, staying at Campagne Montfeld in December 1886, wrote to Amy in fog-bound London, describing his welcome:

> I wish you were here now, dearest, to enjoy the sun streaming in at the window & the fire radiating out of the grate, the best of tea & fresh eggs & toast brought up by the cheerful Emilie & all the other delights of this happy clime. Our aunt looks exceedingly handsome; indeed I doubt if a [more] handsome person is to be found on this continent . . . Aunt Nannie then & Miss Blyth came out on the stairs gorgeous in dressing gowns & welcomed me most cordially & having been petted & kissed I retired to my room & now await the announcement of a hot bath.

Nannie had bought Campagne Montfeld for several reasons. She believed that she had inherited her maternal family's propensity for lung disease, and that only wintering in a warm, dry climate could keep her alive. Had she been able to foresee that she would die at the age of eighty-seven having outlived all her siblings, she would have considered that the point had been proved. Nannie was an artist and an aesthete – 'I think [her sketches] are as nearly perfect as any sketches I ever saw – so poetic & yet so true,' wrote Aunt Ju to Amy. She wanted to live surrounded by beauty. The quality of light and the wide, mountain-framed views made Algeria a watercolourist's delight. Campagne Montfeld was exquisitely decorated, its white walls relieved by the rich colours of the Arab pottery, metalwork and textiles she collected, its courtyard planted with citrus trees, bougainvillea and palms. It was a fit setting for Nannie and Isa to entertain their friends, many of whom

were writers, painters and musicians. The poet Robert Browning,
for instance, was a close friend. I have a couple of splendid photographs, probably taken in the 1870s, of a large group of visitors
of every age and both sexes clustered round Aunt Nannie as if in
homage to her. Nannie, bony and regal, takes centre stage; Isa,
bosomy and smiling, stands protectively behind her.

When times were good, Campagne Montfeld was a place where
Nannie and Isa could celebrate their love for one another more
freely than they could have done in England. A letter written in
1872 from Nannie to the schoolgirl Amy gives a pleasing picture
of their way of life: 'I have drawn an oasis in the desert – the sun
rising – & Arabs just starting off . . . Isabella is working hard at the
sewing machine making curtains . . . they are white Arab stuff
lined with red – & hung on black poles with the crescent & star in
silverd metal at the ends of the pole.' A series of letters survives,
written by Isa to Nannie throughout the winter and spring of
1860–61, the time of Bella's crisis after the birth of Mabel. At this
stage, Isa was stuck in Hampstead giving piano lessons and looking after her ailing mother while Nannie was in Algiers with Barbara. Their relationship was a couple of years old; Nannie had not
yet decided to buy a house in Algiers. The letters are full of love and
passion. Isa calls Nannie 'Doody' and 'my red dabchick'; she recalls
their joint visit to Algeria the previous winter: 'My dearest dear I
should like to be with you at this moment on a hill top in a great
high wind & to chase you & see you laugh'; 'Nannie I want to see
you in black velvet my beautiful dear'; 'I like to think of that little
rock you landed on, and your singing away "all alone by yourself"
out there at sea . . . oh the glory of the sunrise over the Atlas! . . .
I hope you are fast asleep; the beautiful old sleeping face!'; 'How
does the old Heaven look? . . . and the big orange tree in the field,
and the little rocky land where you were a wild beast and ate me all
up, and the pretty road where you <u>killed</u> me as the man did his
wife'; 'I shall always see you get on your horse and look out for me
my beautiful old dear in the tight fitting habit; you know you think
you look well in a habit, so don't deny it!'; 'Oh my dear let us be

faithful & endure to the end & this "longing for happiness" you speak of will be fulfilled.' It is a pleasant fact that, though Nannie quarrelled with almost everyone else in her life, her love for Isa, her 'own particular One', did indeed 'endure to the end'.

The Leigh Smiths all liked Isa, and seem to have treated her as an honorary in-law. NM described her as Nannie's 'fetch', or double; Aunt Ju, interestingly, wrote about the pair in a letter to Amy in words that echo the marriage service: 'Miss Blythe as you know sticks to her in sickness & in health I can't imagine her without Miss Blythe.' It is impossible to determine whether the family recognized the relationship as a sexual one. It is said that lesbianism (unlike male homosexuality) escaped punitive legislation because Queen Victoria refused to believe in its existence; perhaps the majority of Nannie's relations took this view, or simply didn't, in the modern phrase, 'go there'.

When Nannie bought Campagne Montfeld it was because she wanted to be near her beloved sister Barbara. She never got on with Dr Bodichon, though Isa tried to get her to see his good points, partly because Isa was by nature a peacemaker and partly because she had some real affection for the Docteur, who told her funny anecdotes and always declared, with autistic want of tact, that if he weren't married to Barbara he'd quite happily marry her. But Nannie simply abhorred him, and saw part of her role as protecting Barbara from his worst excesses.

Dr Bodichon had several obsessions, and one was with the eucalyptus globulus. As his obituary in *The Times* (probably written by Barbara) was to put it, 'Dr Bodichon was one of the first to draw attention to the valuable febrifugal [fever-reducing] qualities of the eucalyptus globulus, and of late years entirely devoted himself to its dissemination throughout the colony.' The eucalyptus plantations were also intended to encroach on the desert, in effect 'greening' the arid country. Their hard, fast-growing wood was valuable for making vessels. But Nannie was unmoved by the eucalyptus's special qualities; what she cared about was that the Docteur's plantations spoiled her view of the bay. The feud rumbled on for years.

By 1883, Barbara was worried about her husband's mental health, which was why she asked NM to travel back with him to Algiers, armed with fifty sandwiches. In January 1884, Nannie rebutted any notion that the Docteur needed taking care of: 'Dr Bodichon is perfectly well – he has been cutting down the olives and other beautiful native trees . . . I think when he is mischievous his health is always excellent. It is one of the mysteries of life that such beings should live so long – being neither a pleasure to themselves nor use to others.' In September one of Dr Bodichon's relatives, a physician called Louis le Grand, was sufficiently alarmed as to conclude that the Docteur needed someone to look after his financial affairs (he had a habit of storing large sums of cash in bags or jars in his house), a medical supervisor and a male nurse to accompany him at all times. Nannie told NM and Amy that:

Dr Louis of course thinks as I do – that Dr Bodichon has never been sane! . . . I think [Barbara] imagines him perfect when she is not with him! . . . & somehow no one ever seems able to tell Barbara the truth about things . . .

Twenty seven years of trouble in a family - & this is the end! . . . no Frenchwoman wd have been allowed to marry the Doctor! He had neither money nor sense!

. . . I do wish my house were not so near – one cant get the poor old creature out of one's mind.

The ultimate proof, for Nannie, that the Docteur's condition was deteriorating was that he now allowed people to cut down his precious eucalyptus trees and cart the spoils away for their own use.

Barbara, desperate with anxiety, wanted NM to go again to Algiers on her behalf. On 5 October she visited NM and Amy at the Warden's House to discuss the situation and to visit Henrietta Blackadder, her former maid, who was dying in St Bartholomew's. Out of the blue, Barbara suffered another stroke. NM made an entry in his medical casebook:

I went to get beadles to carry B.L.S.B. to the ward [to visit Henri-etta]. On coming into my drawing room to announce that they were ready I found B.L.S.B. on the sofa opening & shutting her eyes and holding Amy's hand with her right hand. Her pupils were equal & natural. Pulse somewhat irregular & bounding. Tongue slightly furred all over. She had completely lost power of motion in her left hand & sensation seemed also gone. She had some loss of power, but not complete loss of power in the left leg. The beadles carried her to bed.

Three days later he noted: 'In a very excitable crying condition at about 8 a.m. Much better after some bromide of potassium gr X.' She talked incessantly, but the flow was not always consequen-tial: 'Oct. 14. Saw her at 5.45 a.m. . . . [she] talked of beryl & pre-cious stones.' She rubbed continually at the left side of her face.

NM and Amy looked after her in their house for a month, which cannot have been easy since, as well as being emotionally labile and calling for NM at all hours of the night, Barbara had lost control of her bowels. The Shore Smiths took two-year-old Alan to Embley (another Nightingale family house) with them to keep him out of the way. Nannie and Isa came to England to see Bar-bara, a major concession given Nannie's dread of cold weather. On 7 November, Barbara was moved to the house of her friend and doctor Reginald Thompson, 48 Cheyne Walk, Chelsea. She had made some physical progress but, NM noted, 'Her mental condi-tion is one of extreme feebleness. The least excitement causes her to throw off all self restraint. She seems to have no regard to truth and no settled honour. Her only aim & consideration seem to be herself & this she professes without hesitation.' The contrast with the scenes NM envisaged in 'The New Journal to Stella', with Bar-bara, an 'angel of kindness', sitting in perfect harmony with him-self and Amy by their fireside, is indeed painful.

Poor old Dr Bodichon in his lucid moments was as worried about his wife as she was about him; he expressed a desire to come to England to be with her. 'It is really grotesque – only it is so pitiful . . . the idea of his being with Barbara at Scalands, as he now proposes,' wrote Nannie in late November. Thereafter his decline was rapid. He became violent, though too weak to do much harm; on 5 December, Nannie told Amy that he 'walked about in his house (oh so cold that house is) naked all night & in & out of his garden in the morning - & over here, with only a cover Emilie threw over him . . . I write to Norman about it, because I know he wont allow me to be left here with this upon me – you know I don't talk of my body – it is not my way – but I guess he knows what a bad heart I have got . . . If only you knew all I have gone through for Barbara's sake, with this man!' As Nannie's letters are full of descriptions of her ailments, her claim to reticence on this point is comical but, nevertheless, dealing with her naked, aggressive old enemy can't have been pleasant. 'He is not a man – but an unintelligent semblance of humanity . . . [Barbara] had better know that he is imbecile - & happy - & that he gets everything he can possibly need.'

NM was ready to go out to help again, but Dr Bodichon contracted pneumonia, and on 28 January 1885 he died, recognizing nobody. One of Nannie's more amiable characteristics was a habit of praising her servants. Writing to tell Amy about the death of the Docteur, she told her that 'the kindness of Emilie & Laurent was beyond all praise.' In the last weeks of Dr Bodichon's life it had been Nannie's household, if not Nannie herself, who had fed him, cleaned him and made him as comfortable as possible. And Nannie was no hypocrite. Aunt Jenny, at Barbara's request, kitted herself and Roddy out in black cashmere, but Nannie told Amy, 'I really could not have put on black for the Doctor.'

★

Mabel made a gradual recovery from her crisis. From the spring of 1885 onwards, Arthur Glover no longer seems to have been considered as a future husband. Aunt Jenny invited Mabel and Milicent to Crowham for the summer, though her attitude was somewhat grudging ('Milicent is here . . . I could do so very well without

her'). Mabel had recovered some of her old buoyancy and enjoyed
sketching out of doors and spending time with her cousins and
sister. Jenny found Mabel overbearing at times, but preferred her
to Milicent, 'who is too virtuous for my depraved taste'.

Mabel divided her time between Uncle Ben, Flora Smith, Louisa Shore Smith, Aunt Barbara at Scalands, and Crowham. She
spent a lot of the winter of 1886–7 at Crowham, hunting as often
as she could. Roddy told Amy of a 'horrid accident' that befell
Mabel's horse 'Football': 'She was jumping a hedge & a spike ran
ten inches into its body . . . perhaps a good thing as she wont be
able to hunt so much.'

In January 1886, Amy had given birth to her second child, a girl
named Ethne Philippa. Ethne (pronounced Enna) was the name of
the mother of St Columba; Philippa was added in memory of
NM's friend Philip Elwin. The baby was born just before Alan's
fourth birthday, and he remembered being told that he had a special birthday present. ' "A little sister" said an ingratiating voice.
The vision of a toy train faded.'

Amy and Roddy were only two years apart in age, and they
were very fond of one another, but the gulf between their lives
was wide. Amy was happily married, the mother of two, mistress
of the Warden's House and, when well, a charming hostess to her
own and her husband's many friends; she also, when able, did
'good works' in the East End, including running a wood-carving
course for poor boys. Roddy had made an unsuccessful attempt to
get into Girton, but since then she had been stuck at Crowham,
single and with no recorded suitors. When Amy invited her to go
with her to a ball the Bonham Carters were holding, Roddy
declined: 'A little while ago I should have jumped at it but now
after that Battle Ball I don't feel as if I <u>ever</u> wanted to go to
another . . . it will take me a very long while to recover from the
<u>17</u> dances that I sat out at that deadly place.' At home, Roddy was
at her mother's beck and call. She was teased by her father, who
was always 'jibing & jeering' at her artistic efforts, and Willy-boy,
loafing around at home, got on her nerves. His habit of catching

insects and small animals and trying to preserve them made the drawing room 'smell like a killing-bottle'.

Suddenly, Roddy had a piece of luck. Cousin Valentine Smith made her a handsome cash present. She wanted to explore her talent for wood-carving, which she was unable to practise at Crowham due to Jenny's refusal to let her occupy a suitable space, so at the end of 1886 she went to live with a Miss Kinslingby, who planned to set up a day school at 17 Gordon Place, off Kensington Church Street. When Milicent left Hamilton House she joined Roddy at Gordon Place. Roddy went to an art college in South Kensington; Milicent studied for the Cambridge Higher Local Examination.

Miss Kinslingby had a very able assistant teacher, Eugénie Sellers. Eugénie was a former Girton girl, an orphan with no money of her own. She eventually became an eminent archaeologist and assistant director of the British School in Rome, but in the 1880s she supported herself and her sister Charlotte by preparing girls for the London University matriculation and the Cambridge Higher Local Examination.

Charlotte Sellers, known as Charley, was younger than Eugénie – the same age as Milicent. She kept house for her sister in the flat they shared in Regent's Park. Charley was extremely attractive, stylish and penniless. She was the woman who gave me my name.

9. 'Free-minded Albion's daughters'

Charley and Eugénie Sellers were the daughters of a peripatetic English wine merchant; the family spent long periods in London, the Dordogne, Paris, Valladolid, Rome, Greece, Sicily and Germany. The girls' mother was half French; though she died when Charley was only three, the extended French family remained a strong influence, and Charley spoke with a strong French accent all her life. She was also, like her mother, a Roman Catholic.

Both girls were cultured, intelligent and beautiful. When Eugénie gave her archaeological lectures she was concealed behind a screen lest her dazzling appearance distract the students. Eugénie was one of several former Girton girls who took it upon themselves to visit Barbara, now almost housebound at Scalands. Sometimes she took her younger sister with her; it was probably at Scalands that Uncle Ben first encountered the ravishing and vivacious Charley.

To everyone's amazement and most people's dismay, fifty-nine-year-old Ben began to pay court to the nineteen-year-old orphan. He proposed, and was accepted, in June 1887, just at the time of Queen Victoria's Golden Jubilee – 'so thoughtful of them', was Aunt Jenny's sarcastic response to having her celebrations overshadowed. Ben visited Charley at Gordon Place, where Milicent and Roddy lodged, and where Eugénie (and possibly Charley too) was employed. 'I am writing while they are spooning in the drawing room,' Roddy told Amy with amusement.

Aunt Nannie could be relied upon not to mince her words: 'It seems to me simple madness . . . Mabel says that her uncle wished me to be told, but she makes no comments – only tells me the girl is 19 years old & a R. Catholic!!!! Words fail me . . . Men certainly about yr Uncle Ben's age, seem to go crazy & I am sure it ought to be illegal . . . Mabel says Roddy likes her. I feel that she must be doing it for money – don't you?'

No record of Barbara's reaction survives, but Charley was very fond of her, so I hope the news brightened her increasingly gloomy life. Years and years later, in 1916, the widowed Charley wrote to NM, 'I am at Scalands living in these two rooms you know, upstairs - & I find the thought & memory of Barbara helpful & soothing.'

Aunt Jenny expressed her feelings honestly and with less than her usual cattiness in a letter to Amy:

Papa is pretty well thankyou & consoles himself with making irreverent remarks upon disparity of years – I don't feel that side of the question so much, in these days I don't think anything is remarkable – but to pretend that I don't feel the loss of Uncle Ben would be ridiculous I have relied upon him so much, too much I suppose - & he is gone & I feel lost . . . I want to like her . . . I do want to believe in her & think she is a thoroughly nice girl. The fact of her marrying Uncle Ben is not to me a sign that she is necessarily mercenary or unworthy in any way of course it's a pity she's not older – but she cant help that. I have invited her & am going to make much of her. I do not fancy she will be much in Papa's style but he can't help admiring her at any rate.

When kind General Ludlow had taken Bella off the family's hands twenty-eight years before, nobody had made 'irreverent remarks upon disparity of years'.

The wedding was a quiet affair at Christ Church, Marylebone – so Charley seems to have been willing to accept a Protestant ceremony. 'I've got a new dress for it,' Roddy told Amy, 'its only cream coloured flannel. Its got silver braid on the body . . . I'm not sure if I don't hate it.' Amy, of course, was not invited, though Eugénie made friendly noises, as Roddy reported: 'Some great friends of [Eugénie's] who you know I forget the name told her that you were the loveliest person they had ever seen much more so than Charlie & <u>so sympathetic</u>! is not that sweet. I hope you like butter laid on thick.'

The ceremony seems to have been largely boycotted by the family. Jenny's good resolution 'to make much of Charley' did not last long, and she stayed at home. Roddy found herself at a very select gathering. She gave Amy a full account:

> Well to begin with I will tell you that they <u>are</u> married it went off all right the earthquake Mama has been hoping for did not occur . . . I had dinner with [Charley and Eugénie, the night before] she shewed me all the presents which were not packed. Two lovely diamond stars two diamond brooches & a diamond bracelet from U[ncle] B[en]. The next morning I went in and saw her whilst she was dressing her dress was <u>lovely</u> old lace & silk & a kind of thin muslin & she looked awfully pretty. Tulle veil fastened with diamond stars & real orange blossom. Then I went to the church all alone in a hansom. I saw U.B. & Mrs Shore Smith in a pew alone in front of everyone else & made a dash at them. U.B. looked rather pale & ill but cheerful he was very glad to see me & I told him she would soon arrive which encouraged him we waited about ¼ hour more & then she came with Eugénie who was bridesmaid & young Lancaster [a cousin of Charley's] who gave her away. They got through the ceremony without any accident U.B. said he got the ring on after two or three tries & it was not on the whole quite so bad as he expected! Then we went back to a sort of stand up breakfast . . . After which they went away in a hansom without any shoes or rice in vain hopes that they would not be known as a B & B [bride and bridegroom].
>
> She wore a grey cotton & grey straw bonnet to go away in & looked sweet. I wonder when I shall hear anything more of them.

Aunt Nannie's pronouncement on Charley's Lancaster cousins was, 'I have the greatest prejudice against them . . . for reasons that I can no longer remember.'

Ben and Charley set off for the Continent on a long honeymoon

tour. Nannie soon had plenty of opportunity to confirm her preju-
dices at first hand. She and Isa had decided to leave Algiers.
Campagne Montfeld was let, or loaned, to friends and family.
Nannie and Isa now divided their time between Venice and Rome.
To Nannie's disgust, Ben and Charley intended to make prolonged
stays in both cities. 'Is it not hard upon me that they are going to
Rome,' she wailed to Amy; 'I can't bear their being here – in this
beloved place [Venice] – quite free of all family associations – but
it is my usual luck . . . I have been out painting on the lagunes,
where I always recover my temper – which has a habit of deserting
me when I see Ben & his wife!'

Charley, it seems, did her best to be pleasant to her ferocious
new sister-in-law, but Nannie was determined to take offence. Even
her beauty was an affront, as Nannie seemed to think it threatened
Amy's position as the acknowledged belle of the family: 'God bless
you, my dear, - you are 20 times nicer to look at than this young
person.' Charley's spending habits came under scrutiny:

> They are paying 50 francs a day <u>for their rooms alone</u> at Daniele's –
> such a hideous sitting room! & she does not a bit know how to make
> it pretty . . . my impression of Mrs Ben is that <u>she</u> is foolish - &
> spoiled - & means to be waited on & to get all she can out of her
> new position . . .
>
>   Meantime everyone here, holds up their hands & cries, what
> that lovely creature the wife of that old man!!! And he does look
> old by her side of course.

Ben and Charley bought matching pairs of yellow boots, which
afforded Nannie and Isa much entertainment. Even the good-
natured Isa gave vent to some bitchiness: 'No Uncle Ben not to
mention Aunt Ditto! to bother us with a sight of their yellow
boots . . . She has been buying some gorgeous furs . . . which seem
to yield her no little content.'

Was Charley a gold-digger? It was hardly astonishing that,
offered an escape from her life with no cash, no financial prospects

and a very scanty family network, she jumped at it. Eugénie had
supported her for years, and Charley would have known that her
marriage would remove a burden from her hard-working sister.
Nor is it surprising that such a marriage should soon run into difficulties. It wasn't long before Ben became restless; the couple
began to spend considerable periods apart, and when they were
based at Glottenham in the 1890s local gossip had it that Charley was
'carrying on' with Squire Egerton, of neighbouring Mountfield
Court. In the 1960s my mother knew an old woman who could
point out the hunting-gate between the two estates where the lovers
were supposed to have their rendezvous. What caused the most
scandal, apparently, was the length of time the horses were left
standing in the cold when Mr Egerton called on Charley. Whether
this is true or not – and it doesn't sound unlikely – Charley's marriage to Ben was not entirely cynical. She took him and his family
very seriously. She survived the initial hostile scrutiny to establish
herself firmly in the affections of several of them. She became a
popular and respected figure in the area, and carried on Barbara's
tradition of hospitality at Scalands. When NM was on his deathbed
in 1922, she was one of the very few people he asked to see.

Charley was a devout Roman Catholic, becoming increasingly
religious as she grew older. Ben was a free-thinker. My aunt Meriel
remembers Charley, as a very old lady, telling her how in March
1882, towards the end of the long Arctic winter, the bears, walruses and seabirds essential to the survival of the stranded *Eira* crew
were becoming very scarce. Ben, realizing that they would soon
have to break into the precious store of tinned food they needed
for the attempted journey home, had lain down in his berth in
Flora Cottage, turned his face to the wall and recited the Lord's
Prayer, then got up, went out and shot a bear. 'So you see,' Charley told Meriel, 'he was a religious man in his way, my Ben.'

*

After a summer holiday with Alan and Ethne at Southwold, Amy
left the children with their father in London and travelled with

friends to the Italian Alps for the sake of her health. While there, she made a snap decision to go on to Venice to see Aunt Nannie. (This was, as she pointed out to him, the first decision she had made since her marriage without consulting NM.) She arrived in Venice on 8 October to one of Nannie and Isa's famous welcomes, and wrote to NM in a state of jubilation:

> There was one particular thing I used to think would be ragingly nice; to stay in Venice with At. N & bathe on the Lido with Isabella well! I am doing & have done it!! & its (strange to say, as we live in this world) quite as nice as I imagined! . . . I arrived in Venice last night . . . in the dark & was struggling with Italian porters & bags when I saw an Isabella holding out her arms & before I knew where I was I was in a gondola – Aunt Nanny had been waiting for me in it for nearly an hour & I was carried off 'of course' said Isabella – 'Grand Hotel indeed! Why your room is ready & the Nan is just wild to have you. The minute she got your letter she wrote to yr Uncle Ben & said she was going to have her niece (who she loves as a daughter) to stay with her & if he didn't like it all he had to do was keep away & so come along' . . . Its just lovely such a delightful little flat so pretty . . . I went off in a steamer to the Lido . . . to bathe & had screaming fun. Isa is too splendid in a bathing dress.

Amy had not had any contact with Uncle Ben for eight years, but on her first day in Venice she caught sight of him standing outside a shop, 'Charlie being inside buying. He did not see me. He had on yellow boots & looked very fat!! I did not experience any emotion! The arrangement is that if we meet I am to bow & he can do what he likes then!'

Amy was ecstatic about Venice, last visited on her honeymoon. She admired Nannie's flat, 788b Zattere, in the same waterfront street as that of Robert Browning – 'its all white & that shows off the pots & things so well we will have our drawing room white next time I like it very much.' She also admired Nannie's 'most handsome gondolier Beppo . . . he is a beauty,' and she loved hearing Nannie and Isa 'sing [NM's] praises from morning to night'. Despite their enforced periods of separation, Amy and NM had a happy, mutually supportive marriage. A few days before her arrival in Venice, Amy had written to him in a half-teasing style, 'I must say the more I see of other people's husbands the more I admire Mrs Moore's husband he is the only man who is really clever all round that I have ever met in fact he is quite a different kind of creature I think it shows what an intelligent person ALS [Amy Leigh Smith] was to discover this fact about ten years ago.'

Nannie's attitude towards Charley softened slightly as she began to notice cracks in her happiness – cracks which she, triumphantly, was the first to detect because she had been on the lookout for them from the start. After Amy left Venice she wrote to her, 'Oh dear, - what a consummate goose she is! . . . Ben looks bored & I don't wonder. She actually said to me . . . "Do you sketch – I didn't know you could draw"! . . . I cannot help feeling that Ben will end by being rough with her - & finding out she is just idiotic.'

Ben never did find out that Charley was 'just idiotic', because she wasn't. She was intelligent, tough, amusing company, well read, very much a survivor. She could be 'managing', but Ben himself was, of course, 'managing' to the nth degree; in twenty-first-century parlance, he was a control freak. In Charley he may have met his match, and found it disconcerting. But Charley managed to create a rich and interesting life for herself around and after Ben. Norman, my uncle, writes that 'Aunt Charlie' 'was always very special. She was always very good to me as a boy, encouraging my interest in birds. She must have noticed that I had no contact with London except visits to the zoo . . . I had never been to the theatre. So, when I was 15 she took me to a play about the hero's individual stand against totalitarianism. I was enthralled.' My father, Richard, was also very fond of her. She died just before he married my mother; they told her that if they ever had a daughter they would call her Charlotte.

Before long, Charley was pregnant. Nannie was quick to spot the signs. 'I <u>suspect</u> Mrs Charlotte is beginning to feel uncomfortable, & that there is a reason for it . . . Ben of course knows nothing & has not ever had the habit of care for those around him. However here her determination to be waited on will help her - & I wd not wonder if she succeeded in training him into being a most attentive husband – it is a curious spectacle.' A few weeks later she wrote, somewhat gloatingly, 'The fair Mrs Ben has been very poorly – she is already 3 months enceinte, poor girl, & very sick – I do feel sorry for her – life is not going to be at all what she expected & the lovely gown from Worths in wh[ich] to be presented will vanish into thin air.'

Mr and Mrs Ben returned to Sussex in good time for the birth of the baby, a son named Benjamin Valentine. He was reported to be 'a splendid child – he weighed 10½ lbs! and is 23 inches in length.' Aunt Jenny told Amy of her first sight of this substantial new nephew: 'It was such a hot dusty journey . . . thank goodness that's over - & I needn't go & see them again for a year . . . just a fat chubby baby . . . not anything out of the way in prettiness . . . I could not see a trace of Uncle Ben . . . I think she'll kill him she tosses him about so roughly but that's her affair not mine.' Benjamin Valentine came to be known as Val. He turned out to be an unusual child – solitary, eccentric, wrapped up in his music; a misfit at school, from which he had to be removed; and, in my not unbiased opinion, another candidate for a diagnosis of autistic spectrum disorder. Oblique references in letters imply that he was sent down from Cambridge and underwent some kind of mental breakdown for which he received psychiatric treatment. My grandfather Alan, describing calling at Scalands in 1922, says that Val was playing the spinet and 'characteristically' did not look up or stop playing when he came in. On another occasion Val invited Alan and a friend, Joan Whistler, to lunch. A dish of chicken was placed on the table. Val helped himself to all of it without offering any to his guests. He also believed that the fine trees at Scalands had souls.

Val eventually went to live in Switzerland, where in old age he married for the first (and only) time. His bride was his housekeeper-cum-nurse. His younger brother Phil, with whom he was at daggers drawn, called her 'the Minx', so when we went to visit them my mother was amused to find that the Minx was a stout, sensible Swiss

female of mature years. I was four years old at the time of this visit.
I retain a dim memory of Val, a thin-faced old man with a lot of
iron-grey hair wearing a buttoned-up jacket of purplish-blue cloth,
advancing towards me on crooked legs. I'm glad that I have this
faint memory link with the vanished world of Uncle Ben.

*

In the summer of 1887, the time of Ben and Charley's wedding,
the future of Mabel and Milicent was still unclear. In August they
travelled with Aunt Jenny to Scotland – to Ardtornish, the home
of their very rich cousin Valentine Smith. Mabel and Milicent
insisted on third-class train travel, to Aunt Nannie's disgust –
'Think of them with all their money & no expenses – it is dreadful
to be so mean.' On her return from Scotland Mabel went to
Scalands; she was sufficiently her old self to be able to take her
turn in looking after Aunt Barbara.

This was not easy. Barbara's second stroke had brought about a
distressing change in her personality as well as complicated physical problems. Aunt Jenny gave Amy an account of an unsatisfactory visit to Scalands. 'She glared at me till my heart was in my
boots but I stood my ground for she is so helpless I knew she
couldn't do me any real injury . . . there is really very little of the
old Aunt B. left all the pleasantness is gone out of her & left a painful wreck.' Barbara, who had always been such an affectionate and
considerate employer, now told Mabel that she wanted to throw
her maid out of the window. 'I hope that no one else we love may
end in this sad way,' wrote NM to Amy.

Barbara was still bent on helping other people, however; when
she went to the Marina, Hastings, for a change of air in the autumn
of 1887 she lent Scalands to the otherwise homeless Mabel. I don't
know why, but Miss Kinslingby's ménage at Gordon Place seems
to have come to an end; Roddy returned to Crowham, and Milicent and Mabel decided to set up home together. In the winter of
1887–8 they rented a house in St Leonards, 1 White Rock Gardens,
to use as a base while they explored possibilities.

In the spring they began their house-hunting in earnest. They had evolved a clear idea of what they wanted: a house within easy reach of their Sussex relations, with enough space without for Mabel to keep her hunters, and enough within to house themselves, Mrs MacCreath, several servants and plenty of visitors. In the early summer they settled on Hancox. It was midway between Scalands, Browns and Glottenham in one direction and Crowham in the other, and it was only a longish walk or short ride away from their kind friend and mentor Hercules Brabazon Brabazon at Oaklands Park in Sedlescombe. The main road to London, now the A21, went straight past Hancox; in those days, before motor traffic, this meant ease of access to shops, friends and railways stations – unlike at Crowham, the roads to Hancox would never be impassable, whatever the weather – but without the noise and danger of heavy traffic which was to become a problem in the years to come.

The Ludlows wasted no time in establishing themselves at Hancox. On 12 July 1888, Amy told NM, 'Mabel has just bought at Shoolbreds [a London department store] five hundred pounds [worth] of furniture for her new house called Hancox near Sedlescombe but the lease is not signed yet.' In 1888, £500 was a great deal of money. It sits oddly with Mabel's insistence on third-class railway tickets.

Milicent was deeply interested in the antiquity of the place. When she met an old woman, a Mrs Jempson, who had been in service at Hancox in about 1830, she showed her round the house and recorded her memories: 'Recollects panelling in hall, but not carving over the mantelpiece . . . Dining room & windows in front of house seem to her unchanged . . . kitchen seems to her much the same . . . Remembers the Bowling Green [later the Tennis Lawn, now, more properly, Jake's football pitch] as a "field". There was no door on that side of the house . . . The small attick was a "rough little room" where the men slept.' At last, Milicent's life felt more settled and purposeful. Between arranging things at Hancox, keeping an eye on Aunt Barbara, continuing her study of languages and travelling to Brittany with old friends from Yotes days, 1888 flew by. Mabel built her loosebox, to add to the old stable already in the yard at Hancox.

The Ludlows entered wholeheartedly into the social life of the local gentry, much as they had done when they lived at Yotes. Mabel sang at some public '*tableaux vivants*' to which 'all the county' came. They both joined all-female cricket and bicycling clubs. In December, Jenny, writing to Amy about a forthcoming party at Oaklands Park, said, 'I hope we shant have any very disparaging remarks about Mabel's costumes. She means to go in the identical loud & unbecoming dress which she wore at the Steeple-chase in the spring – what a pity she can't always go about in a [riding] habit. We went to the meet at Westfield & there she really did come out in first rate style quite the best mounted & set up lady in the ground but all alone of course.' Arthur Glover had completely faded from view, and had yet to be replaced.

Hancox soon established itself as a meeting place for the extended family. Scalands had long been an 'open house' for the Smith clan, thanks to Barbara's bottomless generosity, but her invalid state had changed all that. Now, Hancox provided a useful base for people who wanted to visit Barbara but worried about imposing on her. Mabel and Milicent enjoyed being hostesses. 'Brabbie' often rode over from Oaklands to sketch with Mabel and Milicent, or to play the piano for them and their guests. Cousin Flora Smith wrote to Amy from Hancox in June 1889, 'I am very glad to be here with these girls & they are pleased to have me I flatter myself . . . I think this is a delightful air & how prettily Mabel has furnished the house.' Amy herself, when she stayed at Crow-ham, enjoyed bringing Ethne and Alan to explore the Hancox garden and breathe the 'delightful air'.

Their cousin Willy junior, now twenty-three, spent a lot of time at Hancox. He was still regarded by Mabel and Milicent as an amusing playmate, a boy who seemed to have no desire to grow up. Earlier in 1889 an attempt had been made to find gainful employment for him, but the experiment had not lasted long. As Jenny explained to Amy, 'Willy has come back & gone to play again with all his little friends. The lawn tennis & cricket seasons are just beginning which he thinks of as far more important than a little trifle like a profession.' Willy never made another attempt to earn his living but lived the rest of his life in perpetual boyhood, playing games, birdwatching and collecting butterflies. As Uncle Ben put it, 'Willy minor sticks to Crowham like a limpet and will till he is scraped off.'

Both Ludlow girls were full of enterprise and energy in 1889. On 30 July they set off on an expedition to Norway, together with Roddy and a female friend. They travelled by train to Hull, where they bought mackintoshes and boarded the SS *Eldorado*. Milicent kept a holiday journal: 'The Eldorado is practically commanded by a truculent stewardess, by name Mrs. Cox, a woman of the masterful type.' Milicent was rather smug about the fact that she did not suffer from seasickness: 'nearly every cheek was blanched: "yet a few hearts of chivalry rose high to breast the storm" and I enjoyed myself very much.'

The Norwegian holiday was strenuous, even dangerous. The girls walked, rode or drove in carioles (small one-pony conveyances) through precipitous country, feeding themselves on the bread, tinned beef and whisky they carried with them, supplemented by handfuls of wild bilberries and 'cow berries' and by bowls of 'sour and dirty' goats' milk from 'saeters' (mountain dairies). In the 1890s, Norway boomed as a tourist destination and many hotels were built, but in 1889 inns were still few and primitive. At one, the girls were served by 'a poor maniac, who . . . sat down on the bench by Roddy's side, and polished off some pudding she had left on her plate'. When they asked for a bath, four wooden buckets of water were planted 'in a neat little group in the middle of the big room!' Sometimes they slept on benches in simple climbers' huts in the mountains, wrapped in their ulsters (belted waterproof coats). At one such hut they found themselves breakfasting with the composer Edvard Grieg, 'who, curiously enough, had also passed the night in the hut . . . He . . . is very like his portrait at the beginning of a certain book of his songs. He is small, and insignificant looking.'

The four young women braved extremes of terrain and weather and covered great distances along perilous roads – 'as a rule there was nothing to prevent you going over the side where the ground fell away.' It is extraordinary to think of them struggling over the mountains in their heavy Victorian costumes, sketching as they went. Had General Ludlow been alive he would have been shocked that his daughters were travelling with no male escort but, I hope, proud of their spirit. Milicent allowed herself a little modest self-congratulation: 'I think the expedition had very seldom been made by any lady, never, I should think, by ladies alone.'

I imagine Aunt Barbara would have been pleased and impressed by her nieces' exploits, and would have recalled her own travels with Bessie Parkes. As young women, Barbara and Bessie had explored Belgium, Germany, Austria and Switzerland wearing short black boots with coloured laces and skirts cut, daringly, four inches above the ankle to make walking easier. Barbara had written a little ode –

> Oh! Isn't it jolly
> To cast away folly
> And cut all one's clothes a peg shorter
> (a good many pegs)
> And rejoice in one's legs
> Like a free-minded Albion's daughter.

Mabel, Milicent and Roddy had certainly shown themselves to be free-minded Albion's daughters and worthy nieces of Aunt Barbara.

*

1890 was to be a momentous year for Mabel and therefore by extension for Milicent. In the spring they visited Aunt Nannie and Isa in Rome and Venice. The visit was a success; Nannie overlooked past slights, real or imagined, and praised the girls to Amy as warmly as she ever praised anyone except Isa: 'I find them both much improved – or very much more considerate than they used to be . . . most days we go out in the afternoon & take tea with us - & sketch – this they enjoy more than anything'; 'Both Mabel and Milicent are growing generous – I cannot tell you how much this pleases me – for generosity was not activated in their early years – so all the more credit to them.' I believe the remark about 'their early years' to be a misjudgement. Though frugal in his personal habits, General Ludlow's diaries reveal an endless round of charitable donations and gifts. His children were sent from an early age to visit the poor and sick of the parish, equipped with food, wine, clothes and toys for the children. It seems that Nannie found it hard to overlook the third-class train journey to Scotland that Jenny had been obliged to endure.

The 'improvement' of Mabel and Milicent afforded Nannie great satisfaction. Having chosen to distance herself from her family, she nevertheless pined for a role within it, and the new malleability of the Ludlows seemed to provide an opportunity: 'they feel now that I am an Aunt – & one they like – & are not in opposition as before . . . [they] are dear good girls – ready to learn & find out – ready even to believe that other people may be right about some things . . . It is such a joy to me to be truly fond of them.'

The Ludlows returned to England in June. NM met them at a dinner party given by Flora Smith at 61 Cromwell Road. He had seen very little of them in recent years; usually, Amy saw them in Sussex while he stayed in London, detained by his work. He wrote a perceptive account to Amy, who was at Divonne les Bains, recovering from yet another bout of illness. His impression of the woman who was to become his second wife was not entirely favourable:

Mabel talked of the licensing bill compensation & so on like a veteran politician. They are staying at the South K[ensington] Hotel. Mabel I liked, Milicent I did not care for . . . Milicent talked as if the world was hers. Mabel was joky, lively but her face when you looked at it was very curious, such a thin upper lip hardly any. I did not think her well though quiet enough . . . They want to buy a brougham.

NM was the only person to suspect, rightly, that Mabel's recovery from her mental breakdown was not complete.

NM's own status within the family was now secure. His unalterable good nature, his refusal to bear grudges, his devotion to Amy and her obvious happiness with him meant that he was now held in high esteem by everyone except Ben, who would still have nothing to do with him. Though it was no longer possible to communicate with Barbara as they had in times past, she enjoyed seeing them with four-year-old Ethne, who, with her cloud of fluffy flaxen hair, immense green eyes and independent spirit, was known as a 'fascinating little person'. The Smiths en masse had found it useful to have an increasingly eminent doctor at their beck and call. On 1 July 1890 NM told Amy: 'I am getting quite a practice among the retinue of the clan Smith.

1. Flora's Butler's niece
2. Gertrude's housemaid
3. Beatrice's cobbler
4. Blanche's undergardener
5. Bertha's farm labourer's son
6. Beatrice's knife cleaner
7. Dear Willy's game-keeper
8. Madame Bodichon's housemaid
9. W. Leigh Smith's Lodgekeeper's wife
10. Madam Bodichon's maid
11. B. Smith's late attendant
12. A. Clough's courier.'*

His career was prospering, as were his outside interests. He was collaborating with Leslie Stephen on the creation of the *Dictionary of National Biography* – NM was to contribute accounts of no fewer than 459 lives to this great work of reference. He was

* All those named are descendants, or the spouses of descendants, of William Smith MP. 'A. Clough' is Arthur Clough, son of the poet, who married Blanche Smith.

in communication with Florence Nightingale about the British
Nurses' Association; he had become involved with the establishment of a medical teaching university for London and with nurses'
training. He called on Miss Nightingale at her home in South
Street, near Park Lane: 'Her face pleasant, smithy [i.e. a family
likeness to other Smiths] with fine eyes, some likeness to Anne L.S.
[Nannie], a pleasant voice and excellent sense in all she said.'

NM published a book entitled *The Pathological Anatomy of Diseases*, part of a Students' Guide Series. (In the preface he mentions
that he had made 2,360 post-mortem examinations.) He sent a
copy to Aunt Nannie, on the assumption that it would be welcome
to someone so deeply interested in her own diseases, but the gift
called forth a gem of a thankyou letter: 'Dear Norman, I have to
thank you for your book. It is very daunting - horrors always make
me ill. How well it is that there are minds that can find interest in
disease.'

Though Amy's illnesses, and the convalescent holidays that followed them, cost a good deal, NM was feeling prosperous enough
to plan to send Alan to Eton and, more imminently, to move out
of the cramped and dingy Warden's House. He rented 94 Gloucester
Place in Marylebone, a tall, airy house with five storeys and a
basement. Gloucester Place was a wide, elegant street; most of the
households kept their own carriage. NM did not feel he could
afford this, so Cousin Flora often sent hers round to take Amy for
drives in Hyde Park. Aunt Nannie, who was never mean with
money, however niggardly she was with her good opinion, sent a
cheque for £100 to pay for new furnishings.

NM's letters from the summer of 1890 show that the Coape
Smith family were in town. Frederic Coape Smith, nicknamed
Fritz, was the youngest son of the ten children of William Smith
MP, the sibling closest in age to Aunt Ju. His son, Henry Coape
Smith, joined the Indian Army and became a Major General.
Henry married Marianne Milward – 'Cousin Marianne, one of
the most delightful & valiant of women', Aunt Nannie called her.
They had five children, and divided their lives between Australia,

India and England. When they were old enough, Cousin Marianne brought the children to be educated in England, and to pay long visits to their many cousins.

May, Mona, Ludlow, Ida and Henry, who was nicknamed Bhaccia or Bhiah for reasons I cannot fathom, were regarded as a pleasant and exceptionally good-looking brood. They were, on the whole, welcome guests at the family houses, including Yotes Court. Mona embroidered a black velvet smoking cap for the General; she was close in age to Mabel and made friends with her; Ludlow went shooting and canoeing with Harry; Bhaccia and Milicent, the little ones, enjoyed being the 'hares' in the long cross-country chasing game 'Hare and Hounds'. The General always put Yotes at the service of the Coape Smiths. At the end of one stay, little Bhaccia announced that he was 'beastly sorry to get back to London'. Young Ludlow's vagueness and lack of organization irritated the General: '1st May 1878: Ludlow was late in starting [for dinner at the Rectory] – 7 o'clock had struck while he was bewildered in an ineffectual search for a white tie. He is too calm and careless – our breakfast is at eight & everyone has left the table before he makes his appearance of which bad habit I have become <u>tired</u>.'

Ludlow was something of a worry to his parents. A low achiever at school, he too was destined for the Indian Army, but his health was regarded as fragile, and he lacked application. Though there is nothing to suggest that he was anything other than kind and affectionate, he does seem to have been a feeble and vacillating fellow. 'Bewildered in an ineffectual search for a white tie' is a pretty accurate metaphor for his whole life.

By the time Ludlow resumed his acquaintance with Mabel on a more than cousinly footing in 1890, he seems to have been on sick leave from the 9th Bengal Lancers. Regular military drill being uncongenial, he was hoping to restart his career in the diplomatic corps. He spent a lot of time with Mabel during July and August, both at Hancox and at the London houses of various relatives. Nannie and Isa had made Hancox their base during their summer visit to England, so they had plenty of opportunity for assessing

Ludlow in his new role as Mabel's suitor. Remarkably, Nannie seems to have refrained from making any sweeping pronouncement on Ludlow's character, and she could detect little amiss with his health. The fears she had expressed over Mabel's engagement to the unhealthy Arthur Glover – 'if she marries a man like Arthur Glover – she has nothing to keep her well' – did not resurface. It seems to me quite likely that Ludlow, overawed by his father's successful military career, was counting on prolonging his mysterious ailments to delay the need to return to India and make an effort. A portrait photograph of Ludlow shows him looking handsome in uniform, with pointy ends to his luxuriant moustache, but though he looked the part, he was unsuited to military life. The things he really enjoyed were sketching, flowers and parties.

Aunt Jenny saw a lot of the Hancox party over the summer. Isa's increasing bulk did not pass without comment: '[the Crowhamites were] hoping that Isabella would come over somehow this morning but I don't expect her a bit. She & Aunt N. are doing each others hairs or putting hot water bottles to each others feet or something in that line no doubt. I shall propose to bring Isabella back here tonight . . . shant I catch it fr. Papa if she does [come] – loading Bobby [a horse] up with an extra ton!' Neither did Charley escape Jenny's barbs. Jenny's resolution to 'make much of' Charley seems to have been forgotten:

> Whilst we were at Hancox Mrs. B. [Charley] drove up in state. Victoria* - coachman & footman & all complete – an elegant toilette & her best feather boa . . . she gave Mabel such a bad account of Aunt B. that she quite upset her . . . She also took a gloomy view of Uncle Ben's health . . . Mabel has got some lovely sketches of At Nanny's she has had framed . . . R[oddy] has been presented a new dress by Milicent . . . it is at Mme Burnett's to be made up . . . not without misgivings on the subject as we hear it is

* A low light four-wheeled carriage with a seat for two & a raised driver's seat & a falling top – regarded as smart and dashing, the convertible of its day.

flimsy & flowry. Mabel had really the most terrible old clothes on
yesterday things that ought to have been given away long ago – she
really could afford to be plainly decent & in the fashion of today.

(The 'gloomy view of Uncle Ben's health' probably refers to his
slow recovery from another serious cab accident in which both his
arms had been badly damaged. This accident put paid to any further plans for Arctic travel and left Ben frustrated and restless.)
Ludlow Coape Smith was undeterred by Mabel's terrible old
clothes, and at the end of August the couple made their engagement public. Aunt Jenny's verdict was predictable:

> I do not take very much to those Coape Smiths. I think Ludlow is
> a little bantam cock sort of fellow not enough in him somehow to
> make him at all interesting - & Mabel is not at all her pleasantest
> self in the present state of affairs. She really seems as if she would
> burst with self-importance & of course the stupid people who are
> <u>not</u> in love with Ludlow don't see much cause for it all.

Poor Mabel. She was nearly thirty, alone in the world save for
Milicent; with her history of mental illness, she might well have
felt grateful that any man would have her, even if he was only 'a
little bantam cock sort of fellow'. Ludlow was familiar to her from
girlhood. He was a link with her much-mourned brother Harry;
he knew all about her and understood and accepted her circumstances. It is not surprising that she accepted his proposal with
alacrity, though the disparity in their energy levels – Mabel's
supercharged, Ludlow's rather faint – was to make for difficulties
later on. But for the present she thoroughly enjoyed her new
status. Notions of chaperonage had relaxed considerably, and
Ludlow spent a great part of the autumn at Hancox. Nannie took
an old-fashioned view, and wrote to Amy, 'I hear from Hancox
that Ludlow is there all the time – wh I think a pity. Could
yr mama not say a word?' Ludlow managed to get his doctors to
concur that he was still in a delicate state, and he was ordered to

winter on the Riviera. At first the plan was that Mabel would accompany Cousin Marianne to join him, but this altered, and Mabel decided to go out alone. Aunt Jenny disapproved. 'I do not like the appearance of Mabel rushing over the sea after Ludlow – it did not seem so bad when she was going with his mother. I suppose Marianne has backed out on a more intimate acquaintance with her future daughter-in-law.'

The wedding was to be held on 31 March 1891, at Cannes, so that the bridegroom's course of treatments would be as little disturbed as possible. Back at Hancox in the early spring, Mabel enjoyed the preparations. 'The Ludlows [Mabel and Milicent] came to lunch last Saturday,' Jenny told Amy. 'Mabel is quite absorbed in her wedding presents she thinks of nothing else just now. We gave her a small one – a pearl brooch – for evening wear that's the sort of thing she likes – only of course she would prefer a diamond necklace or tiara but I thought I would leave that to you.' It was at this time that the decision was made to change Ludlow's name from Ludlow Coape Smith to Ludlow Coape Ludlow. Alan, my grandfather, told my mother that the change was made for snobbish reasons, because 'Smith' sounded common. Perhaps it is also evidence of a desire on Mabel's part to perpetuate her father's name; since Harry's death, there was no direct male heir. Roddy wrote to Amy on 5 March 1891, 'Mabel is to be Mrs L. C. Ludlow on her cards she says. The Coape is to be treated quite as a Christian name.' In other words, Mabel Ludlow would remain Mabel Ludlow. I don't know what her new parents-in-law thought of the change.

Roddy was taking art classes in Paris at this time, arranged for her by Aunt Nannie. She accompanied Charley to a grand Parisian milliner's, where Charley chose a hat to wear to Mabel's wedding – 'enormous black lace & pink roses'. The dowdy and necessarily frugal Roddy was amused and astonished by Charley's clothes; 'I'm glad I have not got eight wardrobes full of dresses like Aunt C. to move,' she told Amy. The fact that Ben and Charley were to attend the wedding made Nannie and Isa decide to stay away.

Mabel and Ludlow both wrote to Milicent often while they were on their honeymoon; Milicent pinned the letters together in sequence. They started at Corsica, then moved on to Aix les Bains via Genoa, and ended up at Venice with Nannie and Isa. The letters describe an odd mixture of fairly strenuous sightseeing and the taking of 'cures', even more strenuous in a different way. In Corsica, the Ludlows were dismayed by their drivers' harsh treatment of the horses, but charmed by drinking milk at a farmhouse – 'such good milk – milked into our bowls'. At Aix, a Dr Bracket 'ordered Ludlow a very severe course of sulphur baths . . . the Hotel is not far from the Baths but on account of their intense heat Ludlow has to be packed in blankets & carried there by two porters in a covered chair like a sedan chair – he then is put to bed for 20 minutes (in a boiling hot condition) & then rubbed down - & stays in bed again at discretion before dressing – all this takes from 9.30 till nearly 12 o'c – when we lunch.' Dr Bracket 'says that Ludlow has a beautiful constitution, but that he is suffering from blood poisoning, the result of the illness he had in India'.

Ludlow's letters to Milicent are chatty and affectionate, not controversial or profound but full of reasonably well-observed detail. He obviously set out to be a concerned and considerate brother-in-law. He tells her of future plans. He has abandoned the idea of joining the diplomatic service in India, for fear of being posted to an unhealthy station:

> As the regimental routine does not satisfy me the only other alternative is the Staff College. Mathematics is the big obstacle in front of me and the one that requires most assistance to get over so as I shall have no other opportunity I mean to pass a deal of time with a coach in London. Saturday to Monday I shall spend at Hancox, and also a fortnight in August and the last month of my leave (septr) . . . It is sad because I was looking forward to Hancox like anything and to being with you and Mabel there but I know that you are 'just the fellow' to understand completely how much that coaching might do for me.

Milicent seems to have written back suggesting that a maths coach might be found to work with Ludlow at Hancox; the enthusiasm for setting up home together seems to have been strong on all sides. Mabel wrote, 'Yes dear, I do think that both you and Ludlow <u>are fortunate</u> in having each other for brother and sister – and what I am so thoroughly glad of is that you are both so fond of each other. Dearest Milicent you have always been the best little sister to me.'

Mabel's next letter shows clearly that she still regarded Milicent as very much the 'little' sister. It seems that the terms on which they had rented Hancox were coming to an end and that, as a result of Mabel's marriage, the lease was to be renewed in Milicent's name only. The 1891 census describes Milicent as the 'head of the household'. The Staff College for which Ludlow was applying would mean three years in England, but after that he expected to return to India. The idea was that Milicent would join them there, at least for a long visit. Mabel also mentions the possibility of Milicent's going up to Newnham College, Cambridge. While Mabel was on honeymoon, Milicent was at Hancox being coached by an 'aesthetic' lady called Miss Jebb for the University of Cambridge Higher Local Examination – the equivalent, roughly, of A level. She took French, Greek, German, Italian and Latin, and was placed in Class II. Was the Newnham plan dependent on achieving Class I? Milicent never did go up.

Mabel covered several sheets of notepaper with big-sisterly advice about renewing the lease on Hancox. She did not seem to think Milicent capable of making major decisions – 'Of course you will put the matter into the hands of a good lawyer . . . if I were you I should ask Uncle Ben's advice about it.' But Milicent preferred snap decisions. She decided to buy Hancox. By the end of the year it was hers.

Mabel and Ludlow moved on to Venice ('Aunt Nanny & Isabella are both full of kindness'), but they were no longer enjoying being away from home; Mabel, in particular, was increasingly anxious about the news from Scalands. Aunt Barbara was entering what was to be the final phase of her illness. 'Venice would be perfect with happiness in one's heart,' wrote Ludlow, but Mabel was not happy. 'I have been dreadfully grieved about poor Aunt Barbara and I do want to see her before she gets worse, for then she would not, perhaps be able to see one at all. How sad it is to think we will see her perhaps only once or twice more.' Milicent, the nearest available niece (for Roddy was still in Paris), took on the role of making frequent visits to Scalands and sending bulletins to the family. This can't have helped her exam preparation.

Mabel and Ludlow cut their honeymoon short, but even so they were only just in time. Barbara knew she was dying. In 1875, one of her maids, Esther Grealy, had given birth to an illegitimate baby called Alfred; Barbara rescued the baby from the foundling hospital where Esther had placed him and paid for him to be nursed by a Mrs Haselden in Robertsbridge. She hoped to persuade Esther to have him back. When this failed, she asked Willy and Jenny if they would adopt him; their response can be imagined. Barbara established herself as Alfred's legal guardian and paid for him to be fostered by a boatman's wife at Eastbourne. Now, sixteen years later, Alfred was employed by a grocer. Barbara summoned him to Scalands to tell him that she had put £200 into his trust fund so that he could buy his own business. He was still at Scalands when Barbara died on 11 June. Reginald Thompson, the doctor, was also there. He told Amy, 'She died quite quietly & without pain this morning at half past twelve. She had been in much the same condition as when I last wrote until yesterday morning, when she became unconscious.' 'Once how bright & delightful,' NM wrote in his casebook.

On 15 June, Barbara was buried in Brightling churchyard. A long procession of students from her night school followed the coffin. 'It may without exaggeration be affirmed,' said her obituary in the *Daily News*:

> that she has educated a generation of agricultural labourers in the principles of liberalism and Home Rule★ . . . the free libraries,

★ For Ireland; a cornerstone of Liberal policy in the late nineteenth century.

lectures, social evenings, excursions and Non-conformist religious services connected with these classes brought a wholly new element into the lives of the country people she loved so well . . . to her dearest friends she was ever 'Barbara', the Barbara whom, in Browning's words addressed to herself, 'it was a benediction to see.'

Aunt Nannie wrote to Amy as soon as she received the telegram. 'Now we can both think of all the troubles as part of her sad illness & know that it will all have dropped away - & left the noble & better part - the part that loved both you & Norman dearly.' The fact that Barbara left legacies to both Amy and NM bears this out. Scalands was left to Ben. There were bequests to friends, and Bedford College received £1,000, but the largest bequest was to Girton – £10,000 plus the paintings of Barbara's that hung on its walls. Shortly before Barbara's death, Cousin Alice Bonham Carter had written to the Girton Executive Committee at her request: 'Her hope indeed is always to impart to others through her paintings some of the strength and happiness that her intense study of nature has brought into her own life.'

*

It seems that Ludlow failed his maths exam, or perhaps simply changed his plans yet again, for the idea of the Staff College was dropped, and in early October he and Mabel left Hancox to rejoin his regiment in India, apparently with the intention of staying there for some years. The long sea journey was a little tedious. In Ludlow's opinion 'rational conversation' was 'unknown' to their dinner companions and, according to Mabel, the doctor who 'got up' the amusements was 'rather a feeble little man so the concert & the dance were not great successes – dancing on a deck is not much fun'. Mabel found the heat of the Red Sea difficult to bear; she must also have been oppressed by memories of Harry's death there. But they enjoyed seeing the desert by moonlight, shoals of flying fish like little white birds, and donkeys at Port Said named 'Gladstone' and 'Mrs Langtry'.

They reached Bombay on 25 October. Mabel found the brilliance
of the colours overwhelming, and felt the want of print dresses in
the blinding heat. 'I wish I could get a peep at Hancox & see what
you are doing,' she wrote wistfully. They moved on to Peshawar
– 'the prettiest place I have ever seen'. The military station was separate from the romantic old town. They stayed with friends in a
windowless room 'like a vault' while their own bungalow was made
ready. 'Each person has a bathroom in India as there is no drainage
– everything being taken away and buried.' Mabel occupied herself with buying china, ordering settees to be covered in Liberty
chintz and, of course, riding; she lost no time in procuring an Arab
mount.

Mabel suffered from homesickness, and soon began to show the
old symptoms of mental disturbance. She must also have been in
the very early stages of pregnancy, though this was not yet
announced. Ludlow, who had hardly begun work and whose
duties in any case did not seem onerous, at once took leave and
carried Mabel off to a hill station in the Punjab in the hope that the
bracing air would revive her. He was anxious to reassure Milicent
that Mabel's problems were being nipped in the bud: 'You must
not feel upset by this news as her attack was slight & I will always
look after her well as you know.'

They had only been in India a month when they began to talk
of retiring before the next hot season. Mabel had not even unpacked
her dresses – 'I am almost afraid to face the white satin!' – when
their plans changed. Mabel wrote, 'I don't influence him either
way, it is for him to decide in which way he will be happiest,' but
this may have been self-deluding:

> It turns out that if Ludlow were to try & get a billet in the Hills for
> the hot weather that his brother officers would think it very bad of
> him – some one of course would have to frizzle in his place . . .
> Now that we have settled to go home, I feel quite jolly – I have
> only just found out that Ludlow hates India . . . We are both look-
> ing forward to Hancox with joy. I know we 3 will have good times

Ludlow is most anxious to be useful there, in fact he wont be happy unless he feels that he is – I am sure that he will be – I know you will be very glad at this decision.

Mabel sold off the Liberty chintz. She indulged in some souvenir shopping – baby camel skins, a white astrakhan skin, an antique purdah with fine silk embroidery. And by the spring of 1892, she and Ludlow were back at Hancox, ready to start their new life with Milicent.

10. 'Looking after the farming business'

Even with Mabel and Ludlow away in India, Milicent kept house on a generous scale. Amy described Milicent as 'penuriously extravagant . . . It comes of always having more money than you know what to do with.' This wasn't strictly true; Amy's slightly bitter tone arose from awareness that her frequent bouts of illness made great inroads into NM's resources. Milicent was a great deal better off than Amy, but her funds were not bottomless. Her inheritance from her father came in the form of stocks and shares rather than property – the General had only ever rented Yotes Court. In order to buy Hancox and the farm she sold £5,000 worth of Consols, in the autumn of 1891. Her odd habit of scrimping on details – to Amy's annoyance, she always opted for the cheapest hotel rooms when travelling, sacrificing beautiful views, sunlight and creature comforts for the sake of a few francs or lire – was perhaps the result of coming into her money so young, without much guidance as to how to manage it.

A bundle of bills for housekeeping at Hancox in 1891 indicates that, at home, there was plenty of everything. An invoice from Mitchell and Co., Wine Merchants, details a surprisingly large order for a 23-year-old single woman. Six dozen bottles of superior claret at £6.6/–, half a dozen pints of Goulet's choice Champagne at 19/–, and two bottles of 'choice three grapes brandy' at 11/–; this is dated late October, soon after the departure of Mabel and Ludlow. It is an order worthy of Milicent's father; the General loved wine and was fairly knowledgeable about it. The brandy may have been for Mrs MacCreath, who was ill; 'dropsy' was one of her symptoms. But it seems that Milicent was also allowing for a great many visitors. She always did enjoy parties. Norman, my uncle, remembers visiting her in St Augustine's Nursing Home in

St Leonards in 1947 when he was twenty-four and she was dying; 'Despite being semi-delirious she described in great detail a grand dinner party she planned to give me.'

Most of the household groceries came from Amoore & Son, of Robertson Street in Hastings – 'Tea, Coffee, Provisions and Colonial Produce'. The list includes four kinds of sugar, tapioca, sago, blacking, mustard, candles, saddle soap, honey soap, oatcake (ordered by the drum), caraway seeds, kitchen 'sorrder' (soda), bacon, marmalade and a carriage sponge. The total for thirty-seven items is £6.2/3. Milicent's monthly order from Ticehurst & Co., stationers and newsagents of Battle, reads like the requirement of a small hotel: one daily newspaper – unspecified, but probably *The Times*, as she regularly posted this on to Mabel – plus the *Graphic*, *Punch*, the *Overland Mail*, the *Athenaeum*, the *Sussex Express*, *Gardening Illustrated*, the *Queen*, and two railway timetables. Ticehurst's also provided Milicent with her art materials as well as kitchen paper and something which seems to say '2 pkts useful paper', as if all the other paper was of no use. These bills are all handwritten; a fanciful script with plenty of flourishes seems to have been regarded as a mark of quality, but it's a nuisance to decipher.

Coal was delivered from London to Battle station, where it was collected in a cart by one of the farmhands. It cost 22/– per ton. This was 'kitchen coal' for the range and to heat the greenhouse; the fires in the rest of the house, then as now, burned wood, which was and is easily obtained from the surrounding gardens and farmland. The pervading smell at Hancox has always been woodsmoke.

Wightwicks of Robertsbridge provided materials for the repairing and redecorating that Milicent got under way as soon as she bought the house – 'distemper, pipes, mortar, doorhandles, plaster of Paris, pink paint, glass'. The bill I'm most intrigued and most frustrated by is from Bunyard's Old Nurseries at Maidstone, one of the leading Victorian fruit nurseries. Embarking on a major planting scheme at Hancox, Milicent turned to the nursery that had supplied Yotes Court. I'm intrigued because this large order indicates the scale of Milicent's plans, and because several of the listed items still survive, a hundred and seventeen years later. I'm frustrated because, try as I may, I cannot decipher all of the Bunyards' clerk's curly script. '4 Clematis' – there's one left, the knotty old montana clinging with increasing difficulty to the west-facing side of the house. It blew right off the wall in the great gale of 1987. I inexpertly hoicked it back up inside out; it's never flowered as profusely since then, but its almondy smell is still sweet in late April, and its arthritic twists and turns make good hiding places for an Easter egg hunt.

'One fig' – that might be the one leaning through a gap in the wall between the orchard and the kitchen garden. 'One walnut' – that's gone. I planted a new walnut on the tennis lawn in 2006, and proudly harvested a crop of four nuts last year. 'One mulberry' – that's in the orchard. Its knobbly rust-coloured trunk is horizontal now. It's the last tree to come into leaf and almost the last to bear fruit. But a ripe mulberry is worth waiting for. One reason mulberries are so special is that you never see them on sale. Their thin-membraned delicacy, and the fact that they're at their most explosively delicious at the point of decay, make packing and transporting them impossible.

Bunyard's sent a cherry, too, and I want that to be the cherry on the tennis lawn. Its weight now eats into the top of the wall, but its pom-poms of pure white blossom in April are as bountiful as ever. It's a 'white' cherry – possibly a Frogmore Early – the fruit is yellow with a rosy flush, less sweet and more winey than its black cousin, but we rarely eat our fill of it because the squirrels and blackbirds strip the tree just a day or two before the cherries are fully ripe. The cherries attract all comers; our husky dog used to jump up and snatch them off with her teeth.

Milicent created an orchard-come-nuttery out of a patch of ancient woodland between the garden and the Little Warren. Rows of fruit trees were interspersed with rows of filberts, which were kept to a height of five feet for easy picking. In spring, the white blossoms of the fruit trees overhead and the primroses, wood anemones, cuckoo flowers and bluebells (all wild) mingling with the drifts of (planted) daffodils made the orchard a glorious place. The lime trees Milicent planted in a row between orchard and farmland are now very tall, and in early July they pour their elusive honey scent into the air. The walled kitchen garden at Hancox is an approximate square enclosing about an acre, bordered to the north by the brewhouse, pigsties and dairy, to the west by the tennis lawn, to the south by the orchard and to the east – its most open aspect – by the farm. The brick walls are probably Tudor. I don't think Milicent started it from scratch, I think she just reorganized what was there. It was laid out to a traditional plan of six large rectangular plots, divided by cinder paths, with narrower beds, mainly for fruit, against the walls. Milicent framed each plot with espaliered apples and pears. The gateways were surrounded by clipped box. She installed water tanks, and put a greenhouse the other side of the wall, in the orchard – a bad place for it, because it quickly became too shady; there's nothing left now but a few rusty pipes. There was a coal-fired furnace to heat the greenhouse; the cinders from the furnace were spread on the paths. Strawberries were grown under glass cloches along the south-facing wall.

The main plots were planted with cabbages, Brussels sprouts, potatoes, carrots, onions, peas and beans, and there was an asparagus bed. Rhubarb was forced through terracotta chimneys, and there were big fruit cages for raspberries and currants. In amongst the vegetables were clumps of chives, horseradish and saffron – autumn crocus – which still survives. All the paths were lined with columbines except for two rows of daffodils, snowflakes, Japanese anemones and peonies. Along the walls were masses of primroses, Milicent's favourite flower – crimson, pale pink, tawny and white, as well as the usual yellow. Many of these flowers have survived the dereliction of the kitchen garden.

'Kitchen roses' grew everywhere. There are still eight or nine bushes left, bearing heavy-headed deep pink flowers of the Centifolia type, scrolled like cabbages, powerfully scented, in late May. In the nineteenth century the roses would have been used to make rosewater for cooking and for perfume, syrups and conserves, and pot-pourri. In earlier times, rose preparations were used medically, as an antidote to fever, but the Victorians had rather grown out of making their own medicines.

The handwriting on the Bunyard's order is particularly ornate, and I cannot work out what the 'seven dwarf poacs' are. They might equally be greocs or raaces. I'm going to settle for peaches, because in the nineteenth century it was common practice to plant dwarf fan-trained peaches twelve feet apart against a kitchen garden wall. I can just remember a couple of peaches, on the wall that catches the early morning sun. They didn't do well, perhaps because the early warmth gives way to deep gloom for a large part of the day.

Milicent sought her uncle Willy Leigh Smith's advice about the espaliered trees to frame the vegetable plots; he recommended the Celline Pippin, the Blenheim Orange, the Wellington and a cooker called the Lord Suffield. I also remember russets, Beauty of Bath, Worcester Pearmain, and nameless hard brown cooking pears. The trees were planted so that the fruit would come to ripeness at different times to prolong the supply. Half a dozen of these trees remain, reverted to crabs. They've long since cast off their trained espaliered shape; now they throw their twisted arms unfettered to the sky; our pigs rootle beneath them, gobbling the hard, unusable fruit, turning over the soil, fertilizing as they go, preparing for the time when we will restore the kitchen garden to the haven of abundance it once was.

There's a bill from Thomas Dun, Tailor, for a footman's livery coated vest and trousers – expensive at £4.17/6, when you consider that the total annual wage for a cook was £28. A tweed suit is also mentioned, I think for the footman when not on waiting duty. There's a 'licence for Male Servants, Carriages and Armorial Bearings' in the name of Amabel Ludlow, so perhaps it was Mabel rather than Milicent who had grand ideas about footmen.

It seems that Milicent involved herself in every detail of work on the house, garden and farm. A neatly written letter from a builder, James Adams, reads like the upshot of a careful conversation: 'I will agree to tile the Cart Shed at Hancox Farm with good plain tiles and proper hips and ridging and use Iron tile pins with Cartage of tiles and work to be done in a proper workmanlike manner for the sum of eighteen pounds eight shillings and six pence. I quite understood that the laths would be put on ready.' Milicent, with youthful energy and optimism, felt that nothing was beyond her capabilities. On 26 November her diary proudly announces, 'Made the 1st butter'; a few weeks later, a Jersey calf is born. In a letter to Mabel in India, written on 16 December, she sets out her manifesto for her new life at Hancox:

Dearest Mabel – it is indeed great news that you are coming home next spring! It makes me feel years younger, and pounds lighter!. . . I am afraid I cannot meet you in Rome, as I do not suppose I should like to leave the farm. This is what Mr Watts might be expected to say! I am giving my mind to it a good deal, and tho' I may not make it pay, I do not think I shall be badly <u>done</u>. Of course I have to rely upon other people's judgement in buying stock, etc, & if they are foolish, I must suffer for it, but I go into things a good deal, and try and be economical in all the arrangements of the house & farm.

I have 30 beasts altogether, & want 35 or 36. They are so jolly. Uncle Ben thinks Bolton did very well for me – I sent him & Sellers to E. Grinstead fair, & he bought 21 delightful little Welsh beasts called Bunts. They are mostly black - & everybody I have told seems to think they should be a very good buy at the price . . . I think I should find it dull to live in the country now and *not* farm! Of course the outlay is considerable – but it will be such a satisfaction to pull things together & put the place in really good order . . . It is not conducive to poetry or the fine arts to be engaged in mercantile pursuits, but it is not unwholesome, I think! I am sure Ludlow will help me – give him my love, & thank him for his letter.

The reference to 'poetry or the fine arts' relates to two of Milicent's other interests or ambitions. She had loved writing since childhood, and now belonged to a writing group; members circulated short stories, poems and essays on set subjects, using easily penetrable pseudonyms. They judged each other's work and returned it to the author with critical comments. And, like Mabel, Milicent continued to enjoy drawing and painting. She lacked Amy's natural flair, but her watercolour sketches of Hancox and its environs in the 1890s are a lively visual record.

The 'Mr Watts' she refers to was a farming neighbour, William Watts of Caldbec House, Battle. His descendants, the Whistlers, still own Caldbec; our families have been friends for at least five generations. Watts was well acquainted with the intrepid Ludlow girls from the hunting field. He gave Milicent friendly advice:

> The <u>best</u> meadow hay can now be bought for £4 per ton so, if you can get £3 at the stack, the purchaser to pay for Trussing, you will do well I think. Of course, it depends on the distance you have to deliver the Hay, what you should charge for that. Trussing is 6/– per Ton and your Team should have a Pound a day, so charge for any part of that day. Some people are ready to buy Hay, but not so ready to pay for it. Payments should be made in a month from the time of sale . . .! Hope you will find all this as clear as mud.

Milicent was embarking on farming at a particularly difficult time. A series of bad harvests in the late 1870s, plus the introduction of refrigerated ships bringing cheap meat and grain from the USA and Argentina, had made life very hard for English farmers, including Willy Leigh Smith, but Milicent's youthful optimism and self-belief caused her to push harsh realities to one side.

When Mabel and Ludlow returned from India they entrenched themselves at Hancox, and Ludlow shared management of the farm with Milicent. A copy of the Minutes of the AGM of the East Sussex Lean Stock Society for 1893 lists him as a member. Ludlow's ideas were not always successful. He planted the nineteen-acre field with gorse, to provide cover for pheasants, but pheasants don't like gorse and won't shelter or nest in it, so plans for grand shooting parties didn't materialize, and the gorse served only to overrun a perfectly good field. The last of it was grubbed up in 1943, when cultivatable land was turned over to food production. A few scraps of gorse remain in the hedges, and the name lingers on; the field is known as the Gorse Field or Gorsey, joining two other fields named after awkward plants, the Broomy and the Brambly.

All the fields have names, some ancient, some not. The Forstal, or Forestall, is the first field, nearest the house. This was the 'foster field', where very young, orphaned or sickly animals were looked after. The Pett Field contains a round pond, or pett – the Sussex word for a pit. The pond is probably an artificial one created in connection with ironworking. This field also had the older name of Saver, to rhyme with 'lava'. There are also the Knelle (a common local place name), the Post Field (so called because it quite recently had a post in it; before that it was the Chicken Field. It is the oldest field, as you can tell by the high banks that edge it), the Savernake or Savernack, also called the Lavix, and variously recorded in the sixteenth- and seventeenth-century Parish Records as Lavox, Loavix, Gloarix or Gloavix. It was separately assessed for the Churchwardens' Rates, perhaps because of ironworkings. The Roman extraction road for transporting ore or finished iron used to run across it; the long hump of it can still be made out, a swollen shadow across the field.

There was the Woodman's Field behind the Royal Oak, the Glebe, owned by the church and bought by NM in 1908 to complete the farm; the Bottle Field, or Roundel, a tiny field shaped (slightly) like an old-fashioned brandy bottle, the kind one associates with smugglers; it is sunken, because it was once a hammer pond. The Barn Field is self-explanatory, as are the Old Hop Garden and the Maid's Hop Garden, though I don't know who the maid was. The Home Mead lies between the house and the road. Laddie's Field commemorates a carthorse who inhabited it within living memory. The Little Warren, the far side of the orchard, was once a useful year-round source of fresh rabbit meat.

The woods that intersect the fields are also named; the Lavix Shaw which surrounds the Savernack, the Duke's Hall Shaw (pronounced Duck's Hall) and the Parson's Peats. The Lavix contained the Roman ironworkings; the other woods are pitted with small ponds, relics of the ironworking that was widespread across this part of East Sussex from early medieval times until the eighteenth century – the last furnace, six miles away at Ashburnham, blew up in the early 1800s. Bell-shaped holes would be dug to hollow out the seams of iron-bearing rock until the hole became too deep to be safe (about twelve feet) when another 'pett' would be started along the same layer of ore-bearing stone.

In medieval times, the ore, which was called 'mine', was heated until the impurities rose to the surface and could be skimmed off like fat on a stockpot. The solidified skimmings, heavy, black and bubbly-looking, called 'sinders', were used for road-making. Later, French technicians came over from Clermont-Ferrand and Forges-les-Eaux to teach improved smelting methods, adding limestone, which combines with the impurities and floats to the surface, wasting no iron. This slag is light in weight, greenish grey and shiny. The wood named 'Parson's Peats' indicates that once the petts were valuable fish ponds to which the parson had rights. The 'Duke's Hall' is Hancox, a memory of the days when the Sackvilles owned it.

Hancox Farm embraced about 180 acres, and was a mixed farm typical of this corner of England, though somewhat larger than average. East Sussex doesn't possess rolling fertile acres or expanses stretching to a far horizon. Our landscape is made up of small sandstone hills interspersed with woods and copses, a tussocky patchwork that doesn't lend itself to large-scale arable farming. Our Gorse Field is the largest field, at nineteen acres.

Each field is bordered by tall hedgerows of hazel, ash, willow, blackthorn, hawthorn, oak, crab apple, hornbeam, alder, holly and more, threaded with dog roses and honeysuckle. The number of species suggests that the hedges date from before or soon after the Norman Conquest; one species per century is an approximate guide to the age of a hedge. Most English hedges were planted when enclosures replaced strip farming in the eighteenth century, but there never was strip farming round here. Instead, fields were hollowed out of woods, leaving a band of woodland to form the hedges.

The soil is a mixture of heavy Wadhurst clay and lighter Ashdown sand; because the farm is on many different levels the consistency varies from one patch to another, but a typical Hancox field is laborious to work though free of stones. A spring, or ghyll, rises from the steep side of the Gorse Field; it's a seasonal watercourse, flowing in winter and dry in summer, because the geology of the Sussex Weald is a mixture of permeable sandstone and impermeable clay. It's a land of underground streams; the well at Hancox is actually a subterranean river, and if you put your ear to the ground you can hear it. There's an underground reservoir on the farm which supplied all the water for Hancox and its neighbouring cottages until we went on the mains in 1960.

The smugglers believed that the water of the ghyll in the Gorse Field made spirits bear a higher dilution than other water. It trickles down between ferny rocks in a picturesque manner, but despite my aunt Meriel's infant belief that this was the very spot where Moses smote the rock to provide water for the weary Israelites, the spring, like everything else, is on a small scale. There are no great rivers in this part of Sussex, nothing really big enough to swim in. When men were called up to serve in the Second World War, a labourer from the village told my grandmother that of the three armed forces he thought he'd choose the Royal Navy because he was 'used to our river', but 'our river' is only wide enough for a game of Pooh-sticks. Where it runs through our woods, the stream is rusty orange from the iron in the soil. Badgers make use of the Roman excavations and roll in the bluebells and wood anemones. Marsh marigolds, campion, primroses, dog's mercury and stitchwort also flourish, and the air is pungent with the wild garlic I use in every meal between February and May. In early spring lampreys spawn in the shallows of the stream; you can sometimes find a skein of them, twisting away just below the little waterfall. My father cooked and ate some once;

unlike Edward III, he thought consuming enough to die of a surfeit of them would be distinctly hard work.

Two volumes of *The Farmer's Labour and Team Journal* survive from Milicent's time in charge. These ledgers demonstrate how truly mixed and how intensively cultivated a small farm like this could be. Entries were made by Charles Sellers, the overseer, who had elegant handwriting but erratic spelling. He had quite a lot of responsibility. In his account of how his own hours were allocated, he often wrote 'Looking after the Farming Business'. In the first column the labourers' names are entered, then comes a note of how long they spent on each task, and in the final column a record of their pay. There were usually seven labourers. Nowadays a farm this size would be the work of one man, two at most. There were two more Sellers boys, Raymond and Frank, also Frederick Playford, Thomas Herring, Thomas Mast and James Guy the carter boy. Charles Sellers and Frederick Playford usually took home 16/– a week; the carter boy rarely rose above 7/–.

Tasks listed by Charles Sellers include Thiseling, Harrowing, Planting Cabbage, Haying, Rakeing up Rubish, Geting Water for Ploughing, Thrashing, Dung Spreading, Wheat Sowing, Thatching, Draining, Dicking, Beating, Mending Sacks, Snow Moving, Dredging, Roleing the Oats, Pea Hoeing, Weading, Turnip Hoeing, Soliging, Sundry Tying Up Straw, Moleing, Brisking, Tare Cutting and Scuffeling. (The dictionary says that to scuffle means to scarify or stir the surface with a thrust-hoe or horse-hoe, a definition which reads like a line of Middle English verse.) The men are described as spending a certain number of hours 'In the Beans', 'Up Hay Stack', 'At the Hedge', 'With the Horses' or 'At the Well'. Sometimes they help with the Market Garden (our kitchen garden) or they pack up eggs for sale or collect honey from the beehives. They go on errands with a horse and cart – 'To Battle for Mayse and Corn', 'To Boadiam for Beach' (gravel, or possibly beechmast to be used as animal fodder), 'Club Day with Horses'. Very occasionally there's a 'holardy' and once they 'went to Cricket', but by and large they're kept hard at it. Absenteeism or sickness is almost unknown. I only came across one entry when 'Playford, Frederick' was simply 'Unable to Work'. This was New Year's Day, 1900. Could his celebrations have been over-enthusiastic? He received no wages for that day.

The farm, then, was intensely productive, growing a huge range of crops – wheat, barley, oats, hops, turnips, peas, beans, hay and more. Dairy cattle were kept – Milicent was very keen on her dairy – and there were sheep, pigs, bees and poultry. These Farmer's Journals give a picture of agricultural practices which, within fifty years, would almost have ceased to exist.

Few of these crops are now grown locally, but the change that has had the greatest impact on the landscape and the way of life has been the decline of hop-growing. Hops and the brewing of beer played an enormous part in East Sussex life in the nineteenth and early twentieth centuries. Every farm had its hop garden in a valley; at Hancox the Old Hop Garden and the Maid's Hop Garden, both sloping fields facing south, were used in rotation. A few descendants of the hops grow wild in the hedgerows, and in our garden we have a few plants, saved for sentimental reasons when the hop gardens were finally given up in the early 1960s.

Life in Sedlescombe and Whatlington was, as it were, bound up with hops, and this had also been the case at Yotes; Milicent had grown up with hops, and she loved them. In winter, hornbeam wood was made into charcoal for use in the drying kilns. Hornbeam is the signature tree of the Sussex Weald; a hardwood, it was also used for making gear wheels for mills and other machine parts. Sweet chestnut, another tree plentiful in this area, provided poles, which were shaved, their ends sharpened and dipped in pitch. They were then put up in rows to support the hops. In the sheds where cattle were put to fatten there were deep pits known as 'fattening pits'. When these were full of manure, the cattle were deemed ready for market and the manure was dug out and spread on the hops. Later there was the stringing, tying and training of the plants and finally the picking, drying and packing.

The picking, which took three weeks in September, was labour intensive. At Yotes, the incoming hop-pickers, many of whom were itinerant Irish workers, gypsies or other travellers, were regarded as a rough lot; the General refused to allow Mabel to leave the grounds unaccompanied when the hop-pickers were about, even on horseback, though he did allow all three children to take part in the picking, which was a high point of Milicent's year. In Sedlescombe the hop gardens were too small to attract many incomers, though some people came from Hastings to help. Women and children were especially in demand for picking, which required nimble fingers. Alan, my grandfather, noted in his diary in 1946 that the Winters, our tenant farmers, 'can't get women to tie the hops this year, an odd result of some people's being better off'. When I was a child at Mountfield and Whatlington School in the 1960s it was understood that any family could take a fortnight's holiday in addition to the official school holidays. This was a hangover from the days of hop-picking, when the classrooms would have been virtually empty for much of September; the school bowed to the inevitable and granted leave of absence. The last hop-pickers' train, bringing pickers from the East End of London to hop gardens bigger than ours, ran in 1958.

An average worker would pick about fifteen bushels a day. The hops, which had to be picked cleanly – no leaves – were collected in 'bins', large troughs of sacking or canvas slung between two beams on a wooden frame long enough to accommodate four or five pickers on either side. The bins and the pickers were moved along the row as each set of vines was clear-picked, the strings holding up the next lot were cut, and the hop lines came down in festoons. The variety of hop most commonly grown in Sedlescombe was the Fuggle, named after one Richard Fuggle, who discovered it in a flowerbed in the village of Horsmonden. The Fuggle is an especially aromatic hop. (Fuggle, a Bodiam surname, derives from Vogel, a seventeenth-century Dutch drainage expert who drained the marshes in the Rother Valley between Rye and Burwash, and kept the river navigable.) Three or four times a day the measurer transferred the hops from the bins to baskets; the baskets were then emptied into the pokes, which held twelve bushels, and transported to the oasthouse. The number of bushels picked by each worker was recorded either by wooden tallies or by hoptokens, coin-like discs stamped with the grower's number and initials. Willy at Crowham and Ben at Glottenham issued their own tokens, but I don't think Milicent did.

In the oasthouse, the green hops were spread in a thick layer on the slatted floor, about twelve feet above the ground. Beneath was the furnace; the heat had to come from glowing, not flaming, coke or charcoal; the hops had to be dried, not cooked, so the furnace had to be kept at an even temperature day and night until all the hops were done. There used to be an iron bedstead in the downstairs room of our oast because people spent the night there to tend the fire. Such nights became occasions for story-telling sessions, as Rudyard Kipling records in *Puck of Pook's Hill* and *Rewards and Fairies*. The white cowl at the top of the oast, which moved with the wind, carried off excess moisture. Most Sussex oasts are round; they are shaped like giant tagines, and distribute heat in a similar way, so their shape is functional as well as pretty.

Once dry, the hops were raked into the cooling room on the first floor of the adjoining oasthouse. The cooled hops were put into a 'pocket' of woven jute hanging down from a hole in the floor. The pocket had to be strong enough to take the weight of a man inside it pressing the hops down by treading on them. Once the pocket was completely full and round and hard it was closed and marked with the Sussex stamp, a shield with six martlets, and was then ready for market. Martlets are martins; the emblem may be linked to St Martin, patron saint of Battle Abbey. The hop pocket was also marked with the owner's own stamp. We still have Milicent's oval metal stencil – 'M.B. Ludlow, Hancox'. I wonder how many other young women had hop pockets to mark with their own name.

Picking machines were introduced in the 1950s; picking by hand died out. An enormous change in the winter appearance of the landscape came with the introduction of permanent wiring for the hops. Formerly, the hop poles were stacked up against each other in early winter, so it looked as if the fields were full of wigwams.

The white cones of oasthouses still punctuate the view, but nearly all of them have been converted into homes. The oast at Hancox, once a popular meeting place for village lads, who sat round the charcoal fire roasting potatoes at the end of a day's labours, has been most lovingly converted by our friends Christopher and Emily Clarke. Our brewhouse, where in Milicent's time the hops were turned into beer, faces me as I write. It's a brick and tile structure as big as a cottage. At the back is an immense fireplace, used for sausages and chestnuts at my brother Charles's Hallowe'en birthday parties. We use the brewhouse as a woodshed, toolshed and dumping ground for junk. I don't think we'll ever make our own beer. But I love to crush hopflowers and sniff the yeasty smell on my fingers, and I'd love to know what that 1890s brew tasted like.

★

Milicent planned extensive alterations to the house as soon as she decided to buy it. On 7 December 1891, Mabel, homesick in India and longing to have a part in the plans, wrote:

> I like your sketch of the house with the alterations, all excepting the chimney in front – it would not look well – but I feel sure that as far as the look of the house goes – that Mrs McCreath's bedroom is the right place to add on to. I wonder if a chimney could be built up from the ground about where your writing table stands in the drawing room & do give the Hall a fireplace as well – then if the front door was at the side – the Hall would be a comfortable room – Pat the dogs for me.

Several plans were made and rejected. I have an architect's design for a frightful mock-Tudor remodelling which, thank heavens, never saw the light of day – but the aim of them all was the same:

to reorientate the access from the main road to the side of the house, which would effectively enlarge the garden, and to add a drawing room of significant size. Most of the rooms at Hancox were low-ceilinged, small and dark; Milicent wanted something reminiscent of the high-windowed (though chilly) reception rooms at Yotes. It is clear from a bill submitted by Arthur Wells, Architect and Surveyor, Hastings, that Milicent was closely involved in the design, as he charges for time spent in discussion and in redrafting plans at her request.

Eventually, in the summer of 1893, Arthur Wells was given the go-ahead, and a great lump was stuck on the north-western end of the house. It's a mercifully plain brick and tile gabled structure with a handsome solid chimney, but it's uncompromisingly utilitarian from the outside – the long blank wall you see as you drive up to the house is unbroken by windows or any kind of ornamentation. Inside, however, the design is fit for purpose. The new drawing room was fourteen feet six inches high and thirty feet long, with a floor sprung for dancing, and a small but efficient brick fireplace that, unlike the Tudor fireplaces, throws out more heat than smoke. There are large windows at the western end; the room must have been flooded with afternoon light before the trees grew so tall. The windows have slatted wooden blinds which can be rolled up into long boxes in the bedrooms above by means of a hooked pole. The noise the blinds make as they shoot up is a very Hancoxy sound. There's a window at the northern end, too; Milicent set up her easel in its cool and steady light. Victorian painters set great store by 'north light'; the blinds can eliminate all other daylight completely. The design suggests that Milicent was taking her painting seriously.

The whole effect is elegant and airy, if a little formidable. Later, the long walls were able to accommodate the immense breakfronted bookcases which housed NM's ever-growing library. Above the drawing room are two bedrooms, one of which is enormous, and a walk-in cupboard. The joins to the existing house were made with dismal ineptitude; there are all sorts of crannies and gullies which have to be cleared of snow and autumn leaves at risk to life and limb.

Enlarging an already large house may have seemed odd when Milicent was living there with only the servants, the ailing Creathy, and a shadowy companion called Miss Ogle Moore (no relation to NM), about whom I have discovered nothing except her name. But it wasn't long before the house filled up. Mabel became pregnant in India. Her first daughter, Eira – a name calculated to please Uncle Ben – was born at Hancox on 24 July 1892 and christened Eira Leigh Ludlow at Sedlescombe church on 6 September. Milicent was one godmother, Florence Nightingale the other. Uncle Ben, Uncle Willy, Aunt Nannie and Isa were all at the christening party, and I'd love to be able to report that Cousin Florence was there too, taking tea and cake at Hancox, but I'm almost certain that she wasn't.

Mabel and Ludlow's family grew fast. In September 1894 a son arrived, named John after the General; two years later came Amabel Anne, known by her second name, and finally, in 1898, Sylvia.

All four children were born at Hancox. There's a photograph of Mabel and Ludlow on the tennis lawn, holding a couple of white lacy bundles, with a third beside them on the grass – or the third bundle may be a parasol, a shawl, or simply a splodge. The picture is overexposed and it's hard to see detail, but the Ludlows have the air of being well and truly dug in. Upper-class late-Victorian children, with their high-maintenance frills and flounces, their enormous perambulators, their retinue of nursemaids, took up a lot of space. NM's friend Frank Darwin, describing his eleven-month-old son Bernard, wrote on 29 July 1877, 'He can really crawl, and if it were not for his tiresome petticoats he would get all about the floor'; the Ludlow bundles look similarly hampered. There were other family babies to play with. Ben and Charley's second son, Philip, was born in 1892, and on Maundy Thursday, 22 March 1894, Amy gave birth prematurely to Gillachrist.

Milicent was an active aunt. As time went on, she had to assume more and more responsibility, because Mabel's mental state became fragile. I haven't been able to unearth much evidence, but the few references to Mabel and her children I have found always express a slight anxiety, and sympathy for Milicent who has to take on so much. Ludlow was an affectionate father, but he still regarded his own health as precarious, and he took himself off for quite long recuperative holidays abroad.

I have few images, mental or otherwise, of the Ludlow children at Hancox. When Gillachrist – Gilla – was staying at Crowham with his grandparents, he enjoyed coming over to play with them; John Ludlow was just his age. There are photographs of Eira in her pram by the porch, watched over by one of the farm dogs, and of Mabel holding her on the tennis-lawn steps. Eira was a charming baby with a shock of hedgehoggy hair. There's a photograph of John and Anne, posed over a book, looking neat and well behaved. There's a remark of Aunt Nannie's in a letter to Amy, about how pale and sickly her little namesake Anne looks, more like a Londoner than a country child. And there are two tiny snippets from Rose, Milicent's lady's maid. Rose remembered two-year-old Eira standing at the top of the stairs, rattling the stairgate and roaring with all her might. Rose stood at the bottom of the stairs saying, 'Oh no Miss Eira, you can't come down.' The stairgate is still there; it has kept four generations of children in place. It has a distinctive squeak, which I have found useful in alerting me to any midnight escapees. I think that's why Rose's little scrap of an anecdote resonates with me. I can see poor Eira bellowing away at the top of the stairs; the noise the gate made as she shook it with her tiny fists is a deeply familiar sound.

The other little story is about Sylvia's birth. Rose remembered that when the baby was born, it was pronounced to be a boy, but soon this was changed – 'No, it's a little girl.' Rose was very tickled by this. If Sylvia had grown up to be a happy, well-balanced wife and mother, the anecdote would indeed be mildly amusing. But the little I know about Sylvia suggests that she inherited the 'family taint'. I have found only one letter from her, written to Milicent and protesting at being sent to a nursing home by her mother to recover from some sort of breakdown. The handwriting is shaky; Sylvia seems to be iller than she realizes. I think she spent her adult life in one institution or another. The Sutton family, descendants of Anne Ludlow, say that there were rumours of a deranged aunt who wasn't to be seen or talked about. Sylvia did not attend either her mother's or Milicent's funeral. I cannot find her name in my grandparents' address books, and she is not mentioned in Milicent's will. This inadequate but gloomy history makes Rose's little story seem not comic so much as an indication that somehow things were not quite right from the start.

Rose Smith, née Playford, is my memory link with Milicent and those early Hancox days. Rose began her working life aged about twelve, as an 'inbetween maid' or 'tweeny' at Crowham. She was about the same age as Alan, and remembered feeling jealous of him because it was usually her job to ring the bell that hung in the yard to let the farm labourers know it was dinner time, but when Master Alan came to stay, he was allowed to ring it instead. Rose's father was the Frederick Playford who worked at Hancox farm; her mother also worked at Hancox as a washerwoman. The Playfords lived in a single-storey brick cottage on the edge of the farm, right by the road. On her weekends off, Rose walked the six or so miles from Crowham; she wasn't allowed to leave until her work was done, which could be 10 p.m., and she recalled how frightened she was, walking home alone, after dark, through the woods.

She became Milicent's lady's maid, moved back to Whatlington, and became engaged to Isaac 'Ike' Smith, a local carter and drayman; the engagement lasted for about twenty years, before Mrs Playford, Rose's 'difficult' mother, felt able to relinquish her daughter.

After their wedding, Ike and Rose moved into Hancox Bungalow, a prefabricated 'Tudor type' structure bought by Milicent at the *Daily Mail* Ideal Home Exhibition in 1908 and assembled near the Playfords' brick cottage. Its first occupant was a retired governess. In those pre-planning permission days, if you wanted a new house, you just ran one up. NM used to call it 'the hut'.

I can remember visiting Rose there when I was very small. Though she must have been over eighty, she still came in to clean for us a couple of times a week. Rose sat by her stove, walking stick in hand, feet planted wide apart; I remember her wrinkled black stockings, her stout lace-up shoes, the forbidding low-brimmed hat she always wore, indoors and out. It was only removed when she was cleaning. My brother Charles got into trouble for putting Rose's hat on his own head and dancing about in it. Rose's hat was not to be trifled with.

I don't remember the glass case that housed a stuffed hare and a 'tortoose' (so labelled) in illustration of Æsop's fable. I wish I did; my mother has told me about it, and I'm sure it would have impressed me deeply. After Rose died it was given to the grocer's boy, who had long admired it. I have a half-crown piece wrapped in part of a brown envelope on which are pencilled the words 'Little Mifs Carolote'. Half a crown — two shillings and sixpence — was a lot of money for a child in the 1960s, but I kept it in my moneybox and never spent it. It had a certain mystique because Rose had given it to me. Somehow I knew that Rose was a contact with a vanishing world.

Ike and Rose didn't marry until they were in their forties, and Ike predeceased her. When Rose died, my mother was invited to take anything she liked from the bungalow. She took a portrait of Lord Kitchener encircled by a wreath, and a large coloured print of the Boer War Battle of Elaands Laagte, 21 October 1899; this now hangs on Jake's bedroom wall: 'A brilliant and complete success — Splendid Leadership — Masterly handling of cavalry — A charge through the Flying Boers'. I particularly like Major Harry Wright, who though wounded is shown leaning on a hillock calmly puffing on his pipe.

My mother also took a cookery book: 'The New System of Domestic Cookery Containing Full Directions for Choosing, Purchasing, Trussing, and Preparing Food of all Kinds in the most Palatable Form; Including Gravies, Soups, Sauces, Made Dishes, Potting, Pickling, Preserving, Pastry, Confectionery; with instructions for Brewing, Baking, Making British Wines, etc, etc. By A Lady.' On the flyleaf is written 'Mary Sellers, 20 October '75', so perhaps the book used to belong to the wife or mother of Charles Sellers, Milicent's farm overseer. My mother says that whenever she visited, Rose always seemed to be eating or preparing 'slops' – cubes of buttered bread sprinkled with sugar, with warm milk poured over. Perhaps this book put her off making anything more elaborate; the recipes are not for the faint-hearted. 'Take two legs of beef, of about fifty pounds' weight, and take off all the skin and fat', begins a recipe for 'Portable Soup'. 'A pretty side dish' called 'Love in Disguise' involves stuffing a calf's heart, covering it with forcemeat and rolling it in vermicelli. 'To keep Green Peas till Christmas', you must boil them, lay them on a cloth five times double on a table, put them in bottles and cover them with mutton suet, cork them, tie a bladder and a lath over them, and 'set them in a cool dry place. Rosin it down [i.e. seal with resin], and keep it in a cellar, or in the earth.' I think I'd rather have sprouts.

Domestic Cookery demonstrates what a complicated and arduous job food preparation was in the days before fridges and freezers. Cut beef should be 'searched for flyblows', the chine and rib bones of mutton 'should be rubbed every day, the bloody part having been first cut off'. When buying lamb, 'smell under the kidney, and try the knuckle'. The flesh of a boar will be 'hard, tough, red, and rammish of smell'; if a hare is young, its ears will 'tear like brown paper'. When choosing eggs, 'hold the great end to your tongue; if it feels warm it is new; if cold, bad.' To keep eggs, 'place them with the small end downwards in fine wood ashes, turning them once a week end-ways.' As for cheese, 'if old cheese be rough coated, rugged, or dry at top, beware of little worms or mites: if it be overfull of holes, moist or spongy, it is subject to maggots.'

Not only does the 'Lady' make housekeeping sound exhausting, it's also a moral minefield. The cook holds the physical, and almost the spiritual, well-being of the family in her overworked hands. The Lady warns against producing 'savoury and pretty-looking dishes' at the expense of wholesomeness: 'It is at the same time both a serious and ludicrous reflection that it should be thought to do honour to our friends and ourselves to set out a table where indigestion and all its train of evils, such as fever, rheumatism, gout, and the whole catalogue of human diseases, lie lurking in almost every dish.' She rails against the practice, in less well-off families, of keeping the best room in the house – the front parlour – for show only: 'To shut up the only room perhaps in the house which is really wholesome for the family to live in, is a kind of lingering murder . . . What a reflection, when nursing a sick child, that it may be the victim of a bright grate, and a fine carpet! Or what is still more wounding, to see all the children perhaps rickety and diseased, from the same cause.'

The fourth souvenir my mother took from the bungalow was an album of postcards collected by Rose in her twenties. Between them, the pictures on the front of the cards and the written messages on the back evoke the friendships, preoccupations and sense of humour of a working-class Edwardian girl.

Many of the cards were sent by Rose's female friends, who were, like her, in service – Mercy, Jessie, Alice, Olive, Louie, 'Saucy Nan'. Some of these worked or had at one time worked at Hancox. They were all Sussex girls, but some were taken far afield by their employers. Cards were sent from London, Coventry, Ashford, Portsmouth, Croydon, Dumbarton – there are plenty of jokes about sitting on Scottish thistles and looking up Scotsmen's kilts. Rose herself only left Sussex when she went to London with Milicent. She referred to the rest of the world as 'the Shires', which she pronounced 'sheers', and mistrusted travel; when my aunt Meriel went to the Alps and sent her a postcard of a ski lift, Rose opined that 'Miss Meriel was so brave to cross the sea in one of them things.' But she retained an affection for the East End of London, where she accompanied Milicent on her mission work. Several of the postcards feature pearly kings and queens, from friends who knew her taste.

Rose liked to laugh. Most of the postcards are humorous – coloured drawings, verging on caricature, in the style popularized by Donald McGill, or tinted photographs of courting couples in compromising situations. There's little sentimentality. A hideous woman with an eyepatch holds a placard which reads, 'I am blind and the mother of six children by a horrible accident'; her emaciated dog holds up a begging bowl. Grotesque old landladies snatch kisses from their weedy male lodgers or spy on them when they take their baths. Two young men, commercial travellers in a cheap hotel, sit on the edge of their shared bed scratching fleas under their nightshirts. The caption reads, 'We are very busy.'

Fleas, lice and bedbugs are a common source of jokes. 'Scratch as scratch can – fleas potted while you wait' shows a man trying to catch his unwelcome bedfellows in a tumbler. The written message on the back is mysterious – 'hope you will get some more little things what make holes in the chair please do not borrow any of this old man's meat much love from Saucy Nan.' 'We've got no money but we do see life!' declare another pair of young men, and the 'life' they're referring to is crawling over their ragged bedding.

Lack of money is another recurrent theme. A husband sits in bed reading the paper while his wife scrubs at 'his only shirt' in the washtub. A young man in white tie and tails sits darning the seat of his trousers, and his socks are full of holes. A woman empties a man's pockets while he sleeps; a canny Scotsman, looking on, calls this 'the reason why I took to wearing kilts'. Strong drink is a refuge from poverty, though also its cause. A husband guzzles drink in front of his beleaguered washerwoman wife – 'Now, father's got a fish's thirst, which isn't father's fault. /They weaned him on red herrings and half a bar of salt, /Poor Mother wears a lifebuoy – she's afraid he's going to burst, /She hates the drink and begs of him to try and quench his thirst.' One scene is too grim to be amusing. A battleaxe mother stands with her miserable children and pile of baggage under the caption 'Home From The Holidays – Where is Father? (Having a Drink)'.

Courting couples abound, which is not surprising, since Rose was 'walking out' with Ike, and presumably many of her friends were in the same situation. Some of the scenes of courtship are

simply romantic – 'My love's like the flowers – radiant and gay /
But, unlike the flowers, it fades not away.' Heavily clad couples
canoodle beneath street lamps, in woodland glades or by the seaside. They are often subject to a little double entendre – 'When
you get a good thing – Hold tight'; 'I am holding my own'; 'Owing
to "extreme pressure" I am unable to write more.' But courtship is
also a trap. A triptych of 'Love – Courtship – Marriage' shows the
young couple seated demurely with a book on a low wall. 'Dangerous,' reads a half-concealed notice behind them. In the next
frame they're off the wall and entwined on the grass. The notice is
fully revealed – 'Dangerous beyond this.' In the final frame the
couple are struggling with squalling triplets. 'Oh lor',' says the
man, 'I didn't think the notice meant this.'

Babies spell trouble. A wife sleeps peacefully while her husband
administers milk through a length of rubber tubing – 'Is Marriage
a Failure?' the postcard asks. Another father is horrified to be presented with a set of triplets, while his dog exclaims, 'Only three!!'
and the cat asks, 'I wonder how many they will drown?' 'It is not
good that man should live alone!' is a role-reversal joke, showing a
mother lounging on a sofa with a newspaper and cigar while the
father struggles to entertain five noisy infants. This was the era of
the suffragettes, and there are several jokes about women overturning the established order, and some comment on this in the
handwritten messages, too.

In later life Rose was heard to opine that she didn't understand
why people wanted to look at pictures of ladies in their bathing
costumes in the *Daily Mirror* when they could see them on the
beach at Hastings any day of the week, but in her girlhood she
obviously enjoyed a bit of sauce. A fictitious message from a young
man to his fiancée makes an extended joke of the fact that he has
sent her a pair of knickers in mistake for a pair of gloves: 'Oh, how
I wish no other hand would touch them after you have put them
on . . . A thousand young men may touch them, and other eyes
than mine see them on you . . . My sister says she has to clean hers
very often, as so many young men soil them with their hands . . . I

do hope, dear, they are not too small; and be careful, dear, not to
wet them; and be sure and blow into them before putting them
on. Yours with love, Percy.' Girls fall off donkeys and reveal underwear; the wind at the seaside blows up a dress to reveal a substantial rump. 'Shut your eyes, boys!!' begs a fat, moustachioed female
as she makes her way along a high wire above a crowd of male
heads. The complicated Edwardian costumes make it funnier when
a toff leaves the house forgetting to put on his trousers or a lady
catches the train of her dress in a door. And a scene of a Scotsman
clinging for dear life to a rising airship while a matronly figure
looks up his kilt and exclaims, 'My word! If I catch you in an airship! I'll have your propeller!' is unequivocally smutty.

Most of the saucier cards come from Rose's girlfriends, but
occasionally Ike comes up with something a little risqué, as in a
scene with a pretty girl seated on a bank holding a fishing rod. A
young man leers behind her – 'What are you fishing for my pretty
maid?' 'For a nice young man, kind sir,' she said. 'You can fish early,
you can fish late, But you'll never catch one if you sit on your bait.'
This card, like most sent by Ike, is the equivalent of the modern
text message. Ike was working for a butcher in Battle at this time.
'D.R. [Dear Rose],' he writes, 'Just finished 10 pas 9 – see you in
the morning.' In the early twentieth century the postal service was
so good that he could be confident that a card posted at past nine
o'clock at night would reach Rose the following morning.

Ike's messages usually give details of his days off – 'D.R. if fine
I shall come on Sunday so hope you will come to meet me shall
come the long hill way do you want a kitten let me know . . .
all news when I see you'; 'Sorry cant come going to Hooe fetch
Bullocks'; 'Will bring your Boots tomorrow Havant done yet
9 o'clock.' The cards imply that, by 1908, when Rose was almost
twenty-six, they were a well-established couple, but it was another
twenty years before they married. Ike served in the Great War;
when my mother asked about his time in the Dardanelles his only
comment was that 'the sheep had funny ears.' Whether this suggests that he was unwilling to talk about horrors, or whether his

wartime experiences were so far outside his frame of reference that he could not put them into words, I don't know.

It seems to have been the demands of Rose's mother, now widowed, that delayed the wedding. When asked what she wanted for a present, old Mrs Playford always replied that she wanted Oxo cubes, which were certainly easier to manage than the Lady's 'Portable Soup'. At her death, a vast stash of untouched Oxo cubes was discovered. Her insistence that Rose stay at home and look after her removed the chance that Rose and Ike might have had children, but it doesn't seem to have diminished their delight in each other. Their wedding photograph shows a middle-aged couple standing in a field, Rose short and sturdy in a lumpy 1920s suit and cloche hat, Ike with watchchain and buttonhole and very shiny boots, their beaming faces both suffused with happiness.

11. 'A question of life or death'

Milicent, like Roddy, seems to have been cast in the role of spinster. No hint of any suitor for either of them emerges from the family papers of the 1890s. Nor is there any indication that either of them strove to remedy this state of affairs. Roddy, perhaps, was too subdued to express her feelings, but there was nothing subdued about Milicent. In buying Hancox, running the farm, instructing the builders, helping Mabel with the babies, taking organ lessons, keeping up her languages, writing, painting, playing cricket and tennis, hunting, bicycling and taking an active part in the church and in the social life of the neighbourhood, Milicent set herself up as bustling, preoccupied, independent and, perhaps, unapproachable.

On paper she would have been a good catch. She was well connected, had money of her own (the 1891 census describes her both as 'head of the household' and as 'living on her own means'), and she had no parents to raise objections to a suitor. Though not a beauty, her elfin features had a certain appeal. In family letters she is often described as 'a little thing'; at five foot five she wasn't short, but she was very slim, with the handspan waist so prized in the late nineteenth century. I'm sure her waist size was natural; like Aunt Nannie, she would have despised stays. Photographs of Milicent in middle age, as the dignified wife of a senior physician, make her look elegant, even dressy, but as a young woman Amy said she 'looked like a hop-picker'. This judgement is borne out by a portrait photograph of Milicent in her early twenties; rather pleasingly, she doesn't seem to have bothered to tidy her hair for the occasion.

Milicent held missionary meetings at Hancox and sponsored local boys through their apprenticeships, but her desire to do 'good works' was not fulfilled in Sussex. It's likely, too, that she felt the need to escape from an ever more crowded house. While Mrs Mac-Creath was still alive, Milicent felt bound to spend a lot of time with her, thereby gaining Aunt Nannie's hard-won approval – 'I think her quite right to stand by this kind friend of her youth.' The end came on 13 June 1892; Mrs MacCreath was buried at Sedlescombe, and Milicent ordered a headstone inscribed: 'Be thou faithful unto death and I will give thee a crown of life.'

Responsibility for Mrs MacCreath over, she was at liberty to accept a new challenge. She took up work at St Margaret's House, Bethnal Green, a branch of the Oxford House Settlement. St Margaret's was run by women for women. In the 1890s, poverty in the East End of London was extreme. Overcrowding, disease and crime were endemic. Large-scale industry in the area was in decline, leading to a shortage of full-time, steady, long-term employment. Most girls left school at twelve – if they had ever attended at all – and worked twelve hours a day, six days a week in factories, in tailors' workshops, or in the 'sweated trades'. 'Sweating' was a system whereby the manufacture of cheap goods (shoes, brooms, matchboxes) was broken down into simple, repetitive tasks undertaken by the 'sweaters' – the lowest-paid, unskilled labourers – who made up the goods and then sold them on to wholesalers. The work was either carried out at home or in workshops; in either case conditions were likely to be overcrowded, ill lit, poorly ventilated and unhygienic.

The plight of the East End attracted much attention from Victorian philanthropists and social reformers. The university settlements started in the 1880s, such as Oxford House and Toynbee Hall, were not simply charities, though much charitable work was carried out. The principle was that educated, enlightened people, often recent graduates, should establish residential communities in the heart of the slums; through example, they would instil manners, high aspirations and culture in their underprivileged neighbours.

The ideal of 'active citizenship' appealed to Milicent. St Margaret's House organized practical help such as clothing clubs to provide necessities at the lowest possible cost, but it also offered a range of classes and activities for the 'factory girls' – music, acting, painting, Bible study, basket-making, ambulance classes. St Margaret's found 'good' positions as domestic servants for girls from workhouses. Volunteers such as Milicent would pay follow-up visits to check that the girls were settling in well and were being fairly treated. The girls were taken to art galleries and museums, or on trips to the country. Milicent invited large numbers of them to Hancox; we have photographs of forty young women in their best hats, grouped on the tennis lawn with Milicent sitting proudly to one side. Later, when Hancox was let to the Church of England Temperance Society, she took them to Scalands instead. She kept a letter from one Eliza Winter thanking her for 'my <u>lovely</u> time at Scalands Thank you so much for it all dear Miss Ludlow I do feel so much better I am picture-ing the scenery all day long, and the lovely garden I shall never get out of my eyes.'

The ethos of St Margaret's was strongly Church of England but the emphasis was more on active involvement than on proselytizing. Milicent, of course, had no official training, but she was willing to try her hand at teaching, nursing and visiting the sick. Her work carried considerable risks. Bethnal Green was a rough area for a single girl. There were many health hazards; water shortages, for example, occurred often. In the summer of 1894 the *Daily News* announced that 'all sanitation had come to an end' in the East End; drought had reduced the water supply from the standpipes to a stinking dribble swarming with insects. Amy disapproved of her cousin's 'untidy – dirty – rushing life', but Milicent never flinched. She had a real sympathy for those less fortunate than herself, and an earnest desire to make up for some of life's inequalities. The 'factory girls' seem to have regarded her with affection and respect, even if they sometimes tried to take advantage. One unsigned, undated letter gives a taste of the kind of life they led:

And I hope you will not forget that my birthday comes in this month Miss Ludlow for the last letter I had from you you said that you will send me something then so I hope you will not forget your promise . . . a gentleman came down from the oxford hall and told me that you gave him a sixpence to give to me and he said that you said you was coming down to sea me and I was looking for you every day and I said to myself that I will ask the officer of the home weather I could go to the station to meet you. But I made a fool when I got there and asked the porter he told me that the last train had gone. And I came away very sorry and when I got into the home one of my mates whose name is Fred Bathe asked me were my frind was and he that I was trying to run away. With that I lost my temper and struck him in the face and gave him a black eye I was taken before the officer who asked what it was for And I told him that he said that because I went to Brookwood* station to meet you he said that I was trying to run away and he got six cuts with the birch. Afterwards he came to me and gave me his hand to make friends again He is just like my poor, dear mother. Me and him is going for a sailor if I do not get a letter from my sister.

> Varlets are blue
> Roses are red
> You are the best friend I ever knew

I would like to know how my sister is geting on and my brother and father is geting on. So good night xxxxxxxxxxxxxxx God bless you.

*

Milicent got on well with the other volunteers at St Margaret's; she kept letters from many of them, and some became lifelong friends. The most significant friendship was with Ethel Mary

---

* I assume she means the London Necropolis station near Waterloo, which was for use of passengers visiting the enormous Brookwood Cemetery near Woking, created in 1854 to accommodate the overflow of London corpses. I do not know whether Milicent had been visiting the cemetery or whether she was only using the station as a rendezvous.

Portal, who in later years was to play a powerful and not entirely welcome part in Milicent's life.

Ethel Portal was one of the most popular workers at St Margaret's. She involved herself in all aspects of the work, even acting as district nurse until a fully trained candidate could be found. She was six years older than Milicent, and was intelligent, scholarly, with lovely eyes and a beautiful speaking voice. Like Milicent, with whom she quickly became friends, she had experienced more than her fair share of family tragedy.

The Portals were a well-off family with aristocratic connections who lived at Laverstoke Park in Hampshire. The River Test, which flows at the foot of the park, had made the Portal family's fortunes. Originally Huguenots, they had settled in England to avoid religious persecution and had secured a contract to manufacture pound notes for the Bank of England; the beautifully clear chalk-stream waters of the Test were perfect for making crisp notes. Laverstoke House, set in its park, was built for the Portals in 1780; at that time the estate consisted of more than 12,000 acres. The Portals were on visiting terms with Jane Austen's family at nearby Steventon.

Ethel Portal grew up at Laverstoke with her three brothers and two sisters in an atmosphere that combined luxury, learning and 'good works' – the Portals were energetic and benevolent landlords. But of the six children, only Ethel's sister Charlotte escaped illness or early death. Her brother Gerald was a distinguished diplomat, in Egypt and Zanzibar; he was knighted aged only thirty-four. In December 1892 he was directed to Uganda to report on whether that part of Africa should be retained by the British or evacuated. Raymond, the second brother, accompanied him as chief military officer on this difficult and dangerous mission, and died on the journey. Gerald returned to England, sent in his reports, almost completed a book about his experiences (he recommended that Uganda be retained by Britain) but then died of a fever only two months after his return. The *Dictionary of National Biography* describes Gerald as 'a man of handsome presence and athletic mould [who] possessed tact, firmness, and daring'.

The third brother, Alaric, developed the symptoms of 'disseminated sclerosis' (multiple sclerosis) soon after these two deaths. A sister, Katie, was to suffer from the same disease. Ethel herself was often incapacitated by severe migraines. She struggled against these and against associated fits of depression all her life. When not at St Margaret's, Ethel spent her time with her parents at Laverstoke. Her mother, Lady Charlotte Portal, had been devastated by the loss of her sons and, as the 1890s wore on, Ethel found herself less and less able to contribute to St Margaret's and resigned herself to the frustrating life of unmarried-daughter-at-home. On 22 February 1898 she wrote to Milicent, 'It's dawning on me strongly that my B[ethnal] G[reen] days are over – but there, I <u>wont</u> howl.' She was too kind-hearted to resist her mother's insistence on her presence at Laverstoke – 'One simply cant be the cause of tears if its any way avoidable.'

Milicent loved Ethel with an intensity that she bestowed on few people. She did her best to alleviate her friend's wretchedness, and organized expeditions to provide little escapes from home. After one such trip, to see the Passion Play cycle at Oberammergau, Ethel's father wrote to Milicent to thank her: 'Ethel has just arrived, having lost all signs of Headache, & in the highest spirits, overflowing with the happiness of her expedition with you. She . . . is not yet tired of telling me of all your kindness & watchfulness over her – I cannot thank you sufficiently for having contributed so much to lighten her & brighten her forlorn life.'

★

Milicent, a healthy and energetic single woman in a family of complicated invalids, often offered her services at times of crisis. In May 1893 she joined Aunt Nannie and Isa in Perugia. Isa's health had been failing for some time. But Milicent's help was not enough and, besides, she could not stay indefinitely. In August, Isa was no better; Nannie wrote to NM asking him to find a suitable nurse: '[Isa] is dreadfully depressed & she imagines she is going to be paralysed - & then will not use the strength she has to help herself. You can imagine the difficulty with her great weight . . . I should like Amy to interview the Nurse as well as you.' Only a few weeks later, Isa died. Her Italian doctor wrote rather touchingly to NM: 'My dear Confrère . . . Your aunt & her poor friend formed a most extraordinary exemple of friendship, that everyone must admire. It was not possible to have some relation with them without feeling a kind of attraction for both of them.' It was easier, it seems, to feel 'a kind of attraction' for Nannie if you weren't a blood relation.

Nannie's grief was savage. Isa had been 'her own particular One', a softening influence, a buffer between Nannie and the objects of her often ill-founded wrath. My grandfather remembered NM remarking on how very much nicer Nannie had been before she lost Isa. After Isa's death, Nannie had to have the monopoly of suffering; she could not bear to consider that anyone else might be experiencing real trouble. Amy's ill health particularly enraged her.

Amy was not an invalid for the whole of her married life. In 1888 she took painting lessons with the artist Louise Jopling, muse of John Everett Millais and subject of one of his most celebrated portraits but also an accomplished portrait painter in her own right. Mrs Jopling was so struck by Amy's good looks that she asked if she could paint her. The result hangs in the hall at Hancox. It shows a lovely, bright-eyed, glowing young face, with no signs of ill health.

In the early 1890s Amy's bouts of illness grew more frequent and more prolonged. In 1893 she became pregnant for the third time, and both she and NM clearly believed her life to be in grave danger. As the due date drew nearer, Amy wrote a letter to NM to be read in the event of her death, expressing her wishes for her children:

> You will not let them be brought up differently, than they would have been with me, will you? . . . I am afraid I have been unkind very often to your mother but I am so afraid of her influence with them. I think she already has a good deal with Alan. I want him so much to be confirmed & to have <u>definite</u> religious teaching . . . <u>You know how I feel about it</u>? . . . I am sure Alan is big enough to

be a companion to you now & I know he will always be kind to Ethne. I cannot help being a little afraid that when their ignorant mother is not with them they will get to think too much about being clever <u>don't let them</u> . . . <u>Don't be unhappy</u> – you will see someday it is so best You have always been so kind & good to me . . . & I love you very much for ever. Your Amy.

Amy's growing interest in religion, which was to culminate in her conversion to Roman Catholicism, was undoubtedly a cause of tension between her and the 'scientific atheist' Rebecca. Amy's belief that, through suffering, God was fitting her for eternal life was tremendously important to her, hence her reassurance that her death would be 'so best'.

She obviously did not expect to survive her third confinement. On 22 March 1894, Maundy Thursday, she gave birth, prematurely but safely, to Gillachrist. Nannie wrote by return of post, 'It *is* good news: & I am even willing to accept a boy so long as you are well & happy.' But Amy took a long time to recover. When NM took her for a drive in the park in May, it was the first time that year that she had set foot outside 94 Gloucester Place. Baby Gilla, too, was weak and sickly. He was christened at home, aged only two days, because it was feared he would not live. Ethne, eight years older, remembered being summoned home early from boarding school to see her new brother:

Sister Laura Mary bent forward and told me to come round and speak to her. I got up and went round the table as slowly as possible, wondering what I had done wrong. When I reached her I found she had a telegram in her hand, and she did not scold me, but said: 'There is a lovely Easter present for you, at home; you have got a baby brother!'

I asked if it was a sugar baby? I thought it must be some sort of Easter egg and I was astonished when she explained that it was a real, live baby . . . I was made to understand that it was a very important, unusual sort of baby, and I concluded that small babies

were superior to big ones. My father said its name was to be
Gillachrist, and later when I heard him talk about 'the Gilla' I knew
it really was a wonderful baby because to be called 'the' anything
was a sign of importance . . . there was a large iced-cake with real
water-lilies lying on it. I was told that no one had ever had water-
lilies on a Christening cake before.

In August, Aunt Nannie made her first visit to England since
Isa's death. Emotionally, she was extremely fragile. She berated
NM and Amy for neglecting her, though NM had explained that
Amy was gravely ill. 'You and Amy are the only ones of all my
relations and friends, who have failed to write me a kind word. I
cannot now imagine that you can wish very much to see me.' NM
replied promptly, telling her that Amy was too weak even to write,
but this was not an acceptable excuse: 'Amy knew when I came to
England & could have asked you to write. Facts are facts & I cannot forget. Under the circumstances the only thing now is not to
meet. I can face no more pain. A.L.S.' There was a postscript: 'I
should avoid seeing you – if you came here - & you also might find
my eldest brother.' Nannie was rapidly confirming herself as her
own worst enemy, a role that she was to play for the rest of her
long and increasingly sad life. However, she relented sufficiently
to write to tell Amy of her plans for the rest of her stay; she was to
go to Crowham and thence to Hancox & to inspect the baby (John)
which Mabel was scheduled to produce. 'I will write and tell you
what I think of it,' Nannie assured Amy, a touch of the Bad Fairy
in the tone of the promise.

Despite her bouts of illness, Amy did her best to create a warm,
vibrant family life for Alan, Ethne and Gilla. 'Both my father and
my mother seemed to me to be more handsome and more wonderful than other people,' Ethne recalled:

My mother had a gift for saying the right word of consolation
when I was in trouble, but I could not always go to her when
I wanted to.

I was told constantly that I must not bother my father because he was busy, nor worry my mother because she was ill, so the sight of them became rather a treat than an everyday occurrence. For all that, they were the most important people in my world . . . When my mother played the piano . . . I used to run up and down the room and throw myself on the sofa at the end of it. Her playing excited me and also gave me a curious feeling that was melancholy and yet enjoyable. When the music was sad I would walk slowly, saying to myself 'I am a lonely traveller . . . I am travelling right across the world.' And, in imagination, I saw an enormous plain stretching before me, divided by roads and rivers, all sloping away in the distance and looking golden, and rather shiny, like a varnished geographical globe.

These memories date from when the family still lived in the Warden's House at St Bartholomew's, before the birth of Gilla. More than half a century later, on 6 October 1944, Alan visited St Bartholomew's after a German air raid. 'It has been a good deal knocked about. The Warden's house was in ruins. The back wall of the drawing room was gone. I thought of the room as it was when Mama was in it and played the piano to Ethne & me. The room above which was our nursery & in which I was born was open to the sky.'

NM, though so often busy or absent, was an affectionate father. Ethne recalls, 'Often, when I was in the hall ready to go out with my nurse, my father's door would open and he would pick me up and carry me into his room and let me sit on his lap while he made patterns for me with red sealing-wax on a piece of paper. His waistcoat, with a gold chain across it, was like a warm cushion and when his soft fair beard* brushed against my forehead it smelt very faintly of scented soap.'

NM's sociable nature and growing eminence meant that the

---

* NM's beard was especially soft because he never shaved in his life. His hand was considered too unsteady to manage an old-fashioned cut-throat razor – a worrying thought, given his profession.

couple's social life was as active as Amy's health would allow. 'Sometimes,' wrote Ethne, 'my mother would come and say good-night to me dressed in evening dress. I was not allowed to touch her then, for fear of making her untidy, but I used to invent all sorts of excuses to make her stay beside me for as long as possible.' Occasionally they would entertain on a grand scale; a menu survives for an evening party at which the poet W. B. Yeats was a guest: 'Clear soup: turbot shrimp sauce: duck green pease: loin mutton: redcurrant jelly: seakale: ratafia basket caramel pudding cheese soufflés.'

Ethne was a dreamy, untidy, creative child. She spent her early childhood wondering whether she wanted to be an artist or a saint when she grew up. Both were associated with her adored mother. She wanted to be a saint because that would ensure she would rejoin her mother in heaven. Death must have been in the air, though NM and Amy tried hard to keep things cheerful. In 1893, when she was about to set sail for South Africa, in the hope that six weeks in a hot, dry climate would do her good, Amy presented Ethne with a large box of sweets and told her to eat one every day but to save one for her return.

As the 1890s progressed, Amy moved ever closer towards Roman Catholicism. The church she attended, St Peter's in Wapping, was very High Anglican. She believed in early confirmation; Ethne was confirmed aged eight, in a white dress with a net veil. Both Ethne and Alan went to confession regularly – 'when I came out of the Church alone after it,' remembered Ethne, 'I paused by the rosemary bush, picked some leaves off it and then stood quite still for a while because I wanted to prolong the moments during which, I believed, I was utterly free from sin.' Alan, on the other hand, was sometimes at a loss as to how to dredge up any sins. Travelling to St Peter's by underground, he asked Ethne to pinch his arm, 'because then I can say "damn!" and have something to confess.'

Death struck, suddenly and horrifyingly, at the heart of the family. In April 1895, Amy's youngest sister, Dolly, aged thirteen, developed symptoms which her mother believed to be those of influenza. Jenny asked NM to give his professional opinion. He was appalled to find that Dolly had advanced pulmonary tuberculosis; her case was hopeless. NM earned Jenny's lasting gratitude by taking the time out of his busy life to visit Dolly regularly, but all he could do was alleviate some of her suffering. On 12 July she died, at Crowham, where she had spent almost every day of her thirteen years. The rapid course of her illness left the family in a state of shock. Dolly had always been a robust, romping child; Jenny, describing taking her to a children's party, called her 'a large & bouncing person who danced all the time & is not a bit shy'. A strange effect of her illness was to accelerate her growth. In the last few weeks she grew to over six feet tall.

Dolly, two months younger than Alan, had always been a cheerful companion for him on his visits to Crowham. Ethne recalled her child-aunt: 'She never teased, she was tall with long brown hair & was very kind to me. I remember I used to sit opposite her at dinner & she would make what we called the fat-sow-smiling-in-a-ditch-face & make me laugh.' Dolly was buried at Sedlescombe, rather than in the churchyard at Westfield, so that her mother would not have to walk past her grave every time she went to church.

Aunt Nannie contrived to use Dolly's death as a reason to chastise Amy, criticizing her for failing to answer her letter of condolence. The letter had never arrived. Amy made and kept a copy of her carefully worded reply, which suggests that keeping on the right side of Aunt Nannie was considered important. Amy's illness worried Nannie terribly and yet she could not bring herself to acknowledge its seriousness.

She did, however, put Campagne Montfeld at Amy's disposal. It was considered vital that Amy spend long periods in warm climates. Ethne recalled her mother's return from the Cape in 1893 – 'there was Mama, so brown & lovely, waiting for me on the stairs. She said she was much better & had brought me all sorts of things, a wicker chair & table, & six ostrich eggs & a string of ant's eggs . . .'

The travelling put great strain on the family's financial resources; not least because it was unthinkable that Amy should travel even a

short distance alone. It was also desperately difficult for the children and NM to have such long periods of separation. In a diary
she kept during the summer of 1898 Amy outlines the dilemma:

> July 29. Dr Gee came to see me today & stethoscoped me all over &
> then said I was better but not well & I must go out of England
> from Oct to April: that if I stayed at home I should take a fresh
> cold & should not be able to get better then i.e. he certainly thought
> it was a question of life or death. So I suppose that has settled it. It
> is very difficult but can be done I suppose . . . Leaving N & Gilla in
> this house is a difficulty it does want someone to look after it:
> I think myself going away is probably a mistake & it would be bet-
> ter for every one to take the risk of staying at home as I should
> <u>have</u> to if I was say a housemaid.

Much of this diary was written at Down End near Hindhead in
Surrey, a house the family had taken for the holidays. Though
Amy could walk very little and was mainly confined to a bath-
chair, she was able to take pleasure in the activity of the others:
'Roddy walked on with N carrying a basket to buy some chops for
supper & Mrs M [the landlady] dug us some potatoes out of the
garden they were very good. The children have been out all day
Alan & Ethne go off together for hours & this afternoon we had
tea out behind gorse bushes to get away from the wind.' Bicycles
with pneumatic tyres were transforming life for the healthy members of the family. Bella and Lionel took the train to Crawley and
cycled from there to Down End – 'it is about 12 miles but they
seem to have made it 25. Bella finds she went 56 miles yesterday.'
The physical freedom enjoyed by young women of the 1890s was
much greater than that of the previous generation; the bicycle
played a significant part in this liberation.

But holiday good humour could not dispel Amy's anxiety:

> The idea of going abroad has seemed more impossible the more I
> have thought about it. First of all the money part & then <u>if</u> I had

that how could I leave the house to look after itself . . . Then about
Gilla – he is really getting too old for Nurse. She lets him do
exactly what he likes & he is becoming a most naughty little spoilt
child who cries & roars at everything . . . but then again she man-
ages his health well . . . Norman hates talking about the future
with me & hardly ever does. To my mind it is a thing this going
away that ought to be carefully talked over & settled before hand.
but men hate making plans . . . they think things will settle themselves & that means that someone else has all the worry & bother
in this case I don't see how I can arrange it when I know there is no
money.

The 'worry & bother' caused Amy to have a series of dreams about
'curious houses with great staircases & halls & chapels nearly all
ruined'.

In the end, the money was found, and Amy set off for a six-
month stay in Algiers. She hated leaving home: 'I am sure it is not
good for N to be left. He does not look after himself but sits up half
the night writing & then has his food at odd times . . . often goes
the whole day with very little but cups of coffee.' Sadly, it was
easier to leave her four-year-old than her husband: 'Gillachrist has
always lived so much in the nursery that it will not make much difference to him I think. I really have had so little to do with him.'

Amy set sail in early October. Thirteen-year-old Ethne was
taken ill at her boarding school, St Stephen's at Clewer, Windsor,
an Anglican convent. A shy sister was sent to nurse her: 'When she
bent over me as I lay in bed I would try to untie the knots in her
girdle which made her terribly agitated. I asked her what the knots
stood for, and, in the end, she told me. Obedience, poverty and
chastity. "Does chastity mean fasting in Lent?" I asked, but she
blushed and said it was time to take my temperature.' Ethne's
recovery was slow; it was decided that she should leave the school,
and join her mother to winter in Algiers.

She travelled out with two of NM's former patients. 'My father
gave me a box full of little marchpane cakes to eat on the journey.

I knew he had bought them from Buzzards in Oxford Street and I thought it was kind of him to give them all to me for I knew he was very fond of that sort of little cake.' Ethne's only experience of foreign travel had been two days in Bruges with her father and Roddy. She didn't mind being seasick because she was excited by the 'creaking and banging noises made by the boat & by the moans & groans of the French passengers'. Ethne loved Campagne Montfeld:

> a low white building built round a courtyard which had a fountain in the middle. The fountain splashed into a pool which had a tiled seat all round it and goldfish swam in the pool. The walls of the villa were covered with bouganvillia and I used to trim my large Algerian straw hat with its flowers. Behind the villa was a large garden with many orange, lemon and citron trees in it. A pig lived in one corner and I found he would eat any fruit that I threw him, but seemed to like the large sour citrons the best.

There were drawbacks to life in Algiers, such as dull French lessons which Ethne sought to avoid by climbing trees, and the Kaiser's aunt Princess Amelie of Schleswig-Holstein, who was staying with the consul but who, as a former tenant of Nannie's, regarded it as her right to use the garden at Campagne Montfeld and insisted on being curtsied to, even if the curtsier had 'a tea-cup in one hand & bread & butter in the other'. There was a tiresome English boy with smelly breath who tried to kiss Ethne in the stables; another trial was being forced to play the Fairy Queen in the Christmas pantomime in a white dress with silver spangles and getting her wings caught in the stage curtains. But the delicious French food, the yellow canaries hopping in the trees, 'the view of the white town sloping down to the blue bay and the range of mountains to the right, which I knew hid the desert' – all this rejoiced Ethne's heart. NM came out for a time in January, Roddy joined them in March, Alan arrived for the Easter holidays; only poor little Gilla was left behind, in the care of his nurse Eliza Brown.

Amy recognized that her daughter had reached 'the awkward age'. She made an attempt to inform Ethne about the facts of life, but seems to have inherited Aunt Jenny's distaste for the subject. 'When you were born,' she told Ethne, 'I was sorry you were a girl because I knew I should have to tell you this one day.' Her explanation left Ethne 'strangely frightened . . . depressed and horrified', but, oddly, not much the wiser. 'So many problems came into my mind which I could not solve. If babies grew inside their mothers, how, for instance, did they get out?' It seems astonishing that a doctor's child should grow up with hardly any understanding of these matters but such was the case. Ethne read through the medical textbooks that lined the walls at 94 Gloucester Place, but emerged only wondering vaguely why there were so many pictures of babies standing on their heads. NM made notes about pregnancy and venereal diseases in his casebooks, but both he and Amy were true Victorians in their conversational reticence on such subjects. NM, said Alan, could not even bear to hear the word 'vest' mentioned. Aunt Jenny was even more prudish. Alan remembered that, at Crowham, knitting for an unborn baby, 'even a perfectly respectable baby', would be hidden hastily under cushions if a man entered the room.

One unexpected result of Amy's declining health was the reappearance in her life of Uncle Ben. Alarmed by accounts of her, in April 1898 he put Scalands at her disposal; Aunt Jenny stayed there with her and a nurse, and Ben spent a few nights as well. His old affection was revived, and at last he was able to countenance NM. On 25 September he took tea at Gloucester Place with them both – 'so we may finally think the quarrel is made up.' Amy wrote in her diary:

He talked a great deal to me about Lionel – He is so vexed with him for not working & he seems to think perhaps he & W[illy junior] are counting on VS [Valentine Smith] doing something for them leaving them money that may be so but I certainly never heard L say so . . . UB also thinks that P[apa] will have nothing or bearly any thing to leave . . . [he] says the property is mortgaged up to the hilt. In spite of the disagreeable subject of conversation we got on all right & he said he would come on Wed to see Mama.

Alan, then sixteen, recalls his meeting with his great-uncle:

Coming into the drawing room one day I found a fine-looking old man with a white beard and bright blue eyes. 'I don't suppose you know who I am,' he said with a smile. He had been mentioned so often lately that my 'Uncle Ben' was more than a guess. Norman and Amy, to their honour be it said, had never told their children of his bitter opposition to their marriage. In consequence I felt no restraint and we made friends at once, finding a common interest in ships. We had a pleasant talk. After this we met often.

Only one hint was ever dropped about the feud. After Alan's first meeting with Uncle Ben, he told his father, 'I thought he was a very nice old man,' to which NM slowly and carefully replied, 'Not a *very* nice old man.'

Concern and gallantry show through Ben's somewhat abbreviated letters to Amy. He offered her Glottenham for holidays – 'I don't suppose that it would be safe for you to go to Glottenham now but I have sent down a trunkload of coal to air it.' He urged her to winter in County Galway, 'the best winter climate':

Go at once to Cow Lane to the Paternal Acres.
Ireland for ever.
Shamrocks and real rocks and dells.

In March 1900, when Amy turned down the offer of Glottenham in favour of Swanage, he wrote, 'I have no doubt the seaside will be better for you . . . nevertheless Glottenham remains where it is disconsolate.' On other occasions, Amy did avail herself of Glottenham, and Ben was full of questions: 'Do you hear anything about the Light Ry [Railway]? It will be a good thing for Robertsbridge but the natives do not seem to care about having a good station . . . They are stupid, stupid stupid as Barbara used to say.

'Has haymaking ended?

'Has harvest begun?

'When will hop picking begin?

'Are you comfortable and is everything as it should be.'

Such enquiries suggest that Ben was missing Sussex. He was dividing his time between London, where he generally stayed at the Oxford & Cambridge Club, and Southampton; he had installed Charley, Val and Phil at Ryde on the Isle of Wight. His marriage was by now semi-detached. Val had undergone some sort of health crisis; whether physical, mental or both is unclear. He had been removed from school – 'Modern schools are prison houses for mind as well as body,' said Ben – and had then spent time recuperating with Cousin Flora at Bournemouth. Though Ben's involvement with his family was spasmodic he was not estranged from them: 'I think I shall hang on another 10 years as I think it will be better for the children to have someone to start them straight.' He enjoyed seeing troops leave Southampton to fight the Boers – 'Ships full of soldiers leave here every day it is very exciting' – but was concerned about Charley's housekeeping extravagance. He asked Amy, 'As an experienced housekeeper can you tell me on the quiet what ought to be the expenses of one little house, a month. The staff is

'Charlie, Governess 2 children and nurse

'Three servants & boots [a boy to clean boots, see to luggage, etc.]

'Occasional visitors.'

Aunt Jenny, too, became warmer towards Amy in response to her illness. Jenny had always been in frequent contact, but the tone of her letters was often cool and critical. Since Dolly's death she had become more anxious for her eldest daughter, and more helpful. She often had the children to stay at Crowham, and was far more tolerant of the turbulent phases of Ethne's adolescence than she had been of Amy's. When Ben lent Scalands in April 1898, Jenny reassured NM, 'of course we want you to come & settle her, there is plenty of room this is a most elastic

house . . . There is Brandy in the house – also Burgundy I believe.
Tell Amy she needn't be afraid I don't want her – it is what I am
here for in fact - & I should have been so disappointed if anything
had prevented it.'

During the family holidays at Glottenham, Down End, Swanage and Oak Cottage, a rented house in Sedlescombe, Alan and
Ethne worked together on *The Family Magazine*, a mixture of stories, poems, sketches, made-up advertisements, 'Nature Notes',
interviews, 'Letters To The Editor' and round-ups of family news.
(Ethne also produced her own magazine, *The Spark*, which came
out, as she put it, 'sometimes'). Amy spent most of her time in a
bath chair; on 8 November 1899 she underlined the word '<u>walked</u>'
in her diary, indicating how rare an event this had become. But she
was strong enough to contribute drawings and 'Home Notes' to
the magazine, recognizing that its parodic humour helped to keep
up the family's spirits. 'Mrs Moore would be deeply grateful if the
family would change their shoes before coming into the Drawing
Room; the Drawing Room is small & threatens to become a bog.'
She and Ethne together composed a song about four-year-old
Gilla, to the tune of the 'Mulberry Bush':

> Gilla ran up the hill top wide
> all in his little white nightgown.
> A little baa lamb ran by the side
> of Gilla in his white nightgown
> and Nurse went up the hill and tried
> to coax him down in his nightgown.
> But Gilla he sat on the hill top wide –
> with little fat baa lamb by his side,
> and ever so long his nurse defied,
> all in his little white nightgown.

Alan's speciality was the writing of mock interviews with family and servants. One such 'interview' was with Gilla's nurse Eliza
Brown:

I had not far to seek the subject of this interview, picking my [way] over a floor strewn with toys I found her kneeling at a small stool ironing a sheet, there were 2 tables in the room but one had a paper boat & the other a dead mouse tied to a string in the middle, I questioned her as to the reason of this, well you see she said, if I were to move 'is things the child cry & what ham I to do, O he is a trouble, where I was before there [were] 6 of them & they didn't give me 'alf as much worry as 'im . . . get out of my way DO!! She said . . . I ought to 've been out with 'im 10 minutes ago & I've got to change my dress & mend Miss Ethne's frock & get some money out of your papa, & then there's the washing to see to & the stores list to get out of Miss Roddy & your sponge bag to get & if 'e don't stop makin' that noise this minute 'e shall go to bed . . . I 'avent a moment to sit down, I've 'ardly time to 'ave my dinner & they only sends up just enough & no sugar with the pudden. 'What is your favourite beverage' I said. I don't care for reading much she replied. 'No I mean what drink do you like best.' O she said, beer but Ive 'ardly time to get bite or sup . . . What do you want she said, no I cant make you a steam roller out of two bits of firewood & a safety pin, where did I put that coat of yours – there you are maken yourself a 'orrid mess come & be washed . . . seeing I was de trop I departed.

There's also an 'interview' with the 'Dragaunt', Nannie:

Interviewing is always nervous work, . . . I bought a life preserver & a revolver . . . in the greatest trepidation I called at the Trinita dei Monte & rang; an aged Italian answered the bell, him I told my mission, he shook his head sadly but I showed him the butt of my six shooter & slightly reassured he showed me up. My hostess did not rise & I tremblingly announced my desire, to my intense surprise, she not only made no objection, but was even glad; 'I have long wished to let the King of Italy know my opinion of his way of governing his country thousands of times have I called at the palace & never but once have I been admitted, & then it appears,' she said in a voice trembling with rage, 'they mistook me for an

archduchess . . . to compare me to an archduchess really it is too
degrading; I would have you know that I keep my own court &
that I am here supreme, & you, you drivelling wretch, come here
with prying pencil in the insidious interests of your glaring gutter
rag, Joanna remove this wretch, Ayesha, Henri, Laurent all of you
let loose the boar hound, ha villain I see it in your eyes you believe
in vaccination wretch, poisoning wretch begone, my nails are
sharp & eager for your eyes . . .

Though Amy and NM must have supplied Alan with much of
the ammunition – Nannie's devotion to homeopathy and hatred
of vaccination and vivisection were family jokes – they were in
fact very concerned about their lonely, quarrelsome aunt. The
direction their own lives took in 1900 brought forth fresh oppro-
brium. As Aunt Barbara had disapprovingly predicted twelve years
earlier, Amy was moving towards Catholicism. As a girl she had
heard Cardinal Newman preach in Birmingham, and she had been
interested in his ideas ever since. In 1899 she began to receive
instruction from the theologian Father Basil Maturin, and on 14
June 1900, the feast of Corpus Christi, she reached the natural conclusion of her spiritual journey and was received into the Roman
Catholic Church, taking the name Elizabeth after her favourite
saint, Elizabeth of Hungary. She told Alan and Ethne of her decision but didn't urge them to follow her – indeed, she more or less
ordered Ethne not to consider such a step before she was grown
up. But six-year-old Gilla was brought up as a Roman Catholic.

Friends and family were more surprised by NM's conversion,
which followed a few months after Amy's. He disliked discussing
religious matters, despite his deep piety. When Alan asked him,
later, why he converted, he replied, 'I could not desert Mama.'
When he was a very young man, Charles Waterton's faith had
impressed him greatly; Waterton's place as friend and mentor had
been taken by Mr Elwin, an Anglican, but Mr Elwin had died
on the first day of 1900. NM felt himself free to join the church of
Waterton, which was of course also the ancient church of his

beloved Ireland. Rebecca, now nearly eighty and a strong-minded atheist, was not pleased. Nor was the violently anti-clerical Aunt Nannie.

In the late autumn of 1900 Amy set off for Rome, both to avoid the English winter and as a personal pilgrimage. Nannie now spent most of her time in Rome, but it was unthinkable that Amy could

lodge with her after the vitriolic letters Nannie had sent to Willy and Jenny on the subject of Amy's conversion. However, aunt and niece would inevitably come into contact with one another. Milicent offered to accompany her cousin, both to nurse her and to mediate with Nannie.

They left England on 17 November, taking the journey in easy stages. NM accompanied them as far as Reims. Ethne illustrated the expedition in *The Spark*, in strip-cartoon drawings designed to amuse her mother. One shows Milicent and Amy sharing a bottle of brandy in a railway carriage; another has Amy kneeling in a church, holding her rosary, while Protestant Milicent ostentatiously looks the other way with her nose in the air. Such humour concealed grave anxiety. The journey to Rome was the last such journey Amy would ever make.

12. 'My dear Papist'

When Milicent offered to accompany Amy to Rome, she had reached a turning point in her own life. For some time it had been obvious that the ménage at Hancox was not living up to its ideals. It is hard to disentangle exactly what had happened, but it seems that the co-management of the farm had not proved a commercial success, and that Milicent had to give or lend Ludlow significant amounts of money. The Ludlows' marriage was under strain; Mabel's mental health deteriorated with each new baby. In the past, Mabel had recovered from her bouts of mental illness through extreme physical exertion – riding, tennis, dancing – but such activities were not compatible with four small children and the onset of middle age – Mabel was thirty-eight when Sylvia was born. Ludlow still regarded his own health as delicate, and continued to spend a lot of time taking cures.

Milicent, torn between the demands of her work at Bethnal Green and those of Hancox and her sister's family, took drastic action. On the spur of the moment – which was how Milicent usually took decisions – she let Hancox to the Church of England Temperance Society for seven years at a peppercorn rent. The Temperance Society was to have the house, the outbuildings, the garden, the Home Mead for use as a cricket ground and the Little Warren for growing vegetables; the kitchen garden was let separately, and the rest of the land was let to tenant farmers, Caesar and John Winter, for £90 a year. The Winter family continued to farm at Hancox for the next seventy years.

It seems that there was little or no consultative process. Presumably Milicent was exasperated by her brother-in-law's inability to make decisions, so she made them for him. Mabel and Ludlow were thunderstruck. Hancox was home to them, the only home their children had known. Ludlow's farming endeavours had not been an unmitigated success, but they had given him a *raison d'être*. Now, almost overnight, the Ludlows had to remake their lives elsewhere.

There was some attempt to do a deal with the Temperance Society. Milicent, perhaps moved by the Ludlows' plight, changed her mind and offered to buy 'the Drunkards' out for £3,000. Mabel and Ludlow wanted to compensate the Society but considered this too much, and the deal fell through. When Milicent was travelling with Amy in November, Hancox was still a 'burning question', even though the Temperance Society had taken over the house, the Winters had taken over the farm, and Mabel, Ludlow and the children had moved into Scalands, at Ben's invitation.

On 25 October 1900 there was an auction of farm effects at Hancox; refreshments were provided. The sale was organized by J. Hudson, auctioneer of Robertsbridge, 'in association with Miss M. B. Ludlow' – no mention of Mr L. C. Ludlow. 'Tubs, quantity of old iron, old wheels, deal doors, gates, boarding, stack of fagots, quantity hop poles, herdles, fence poles, hoes, grafts & shovels, cart jack beadle, mallock, pich mallock, stack cloth & round ladders, wagon cloths, hay rakes & prongs, spuds, hay knife, pulling blocks, saw, saw horse, combines, troughs, meal bin, cow chains, straps, lamps, trugs, etc etc. Livestock (dairy cows, steers, cart horses, Sussex sow, ducks, geese, hens).' The total raised was £753.12/6. How Milicent felt as she watched her farming dream go under the hammer, history does not relate.

The Temperance Society began its tenancy on 29 September. One of the oddest archival finds I made was a small bundle of letters from the new supervisor, Mr Benjamin Gott, to his fiancée 'Emie'. Why would these letters have been left at Hancox? Once left, why would they have been kept, not forwarded or destroyed? Anyway, there they were, lying unnoticed in a drawer, tied up with a bit of string, and I was pleased to find them, because they provide a small insight into the Hancox Home for Male Inebriates.

The first supervisor, a Mr Porter, had proved 'high-handed' and generally unsatisfactory; Benjamin Gott was to replace him as soon as he had married Emie. In December 1901, Gott stayed at the Wellington Hotel in Battle and walked to Hancox to observe the daily routine. Gott, a Londoner, enjoyed 'the walks in the clear fresh air' and the civility of 'the country folk'. After excellent eggs and bacon at the hotel 'over a warm fire & a neat girl to wait', he arrived at Hancox in time for prayers at eight. 'The organist played the harmonium (American organ) very nicely & they chanted the Psalms!' This took place in Milicent's new drawing room; though almost forty people were crowded into the house, the drawing room, by far the biggest and airiest room, was turned into a chapel, which indicates the Temperance Society's sense of priority.

Gott was shown the men 'netting', which was their occupation on wet days*; otherwise they worked outside. He was most impressed with Hancox, and felt sorry for the outgoing superintendent 'having to leave such a nice home after only 1 year! I would give a good deal to know whether it is all Porter's fault or whether the men are troublesome at times. I fancy we shall be rather watched & shall have to be very careful.' He rejoiced at the thought of installing Emie 'in that snug little room which will soon be ours darling!! So soon now!'

When the Gotts moved in they were joined by a dwarf who was so strong that he could lift any of the inmates – presumably a skill frequently in demand. I have a ground plan of the house under the rule of the Temperance Society. Was the nameless dwarf the 'Second Officer' who slept in what is now my study? My bedroom was allocated to the Gotts, Jake's room was the Hospital, while George and Sam's rooms held five beds each. Altogether there were eleven 'first class' and twenty-three 'second class' beds plus the officers and the Hospital.

There was only one water closet indoors. The only washing facilities were downstairs, opposite the kitchen. A row of eight

---

* Bernard Winter, grandson of Milicent's farm tenant Caesar Winter, has a painting of Hancox oast done by one of the inebriates, so presumably netting wasn't the only occupation.

earth closets was erected in the stableyard next to Mabel's loosebox. The Gotts (and the dwarf?) had their own sitting room, now
our parlour, the 'snug little room' to which Benjamin Gott refers.
The inebriates had two dining rooms; what is now the library
served the bulk of them, while a section of our present dining
room was reserved for the 'better class'. I have no idea whether this
classification related to the behaviour or level of sobriety of the
inmates or to their social standing in their former lives. Our play-
room was the Smoking Room, which inhospitably doubled up as
a Coolroom. On the ground floor, only the kitchen and scullery
fulfilled the function they still have today. Outside, the brewhouse
became a workshop and the coach house (our garage) was a recreation room. Though sleeping quarters must have been unpleasantly
cramped, outside, the inebriates had the run of two and a half acres
of garden plus the three acres of the Home Mead for sports.

I have no hard evidence of the success or otherwise of the venture.
I believe it was generally felt that the close proximity of the Royal
Oak doomed it to at least partial failure, and my mother knew an old
woman who had a childhood memory of a man running down the
road and being told that he was an escapee from Hancox. Ben Gott
did better than his predecessor; he remained in his post until Milicent
reclaimed the house in 1907. In the bundle with Gott's letters to Emie
is a document that suggests he was a conscientious supervisor. It is a
letter written by someone (the dwarf?) who had taken one of the
inmates, J. S. Skinner, to the doctor in Robertsbridge. They had
returned to Hancox very late, and had to account for this:

> The Doctor did not come in till six. We left Robertsbridge at 6.45 &
> arrived here [Hancox] at 7.45.
>
> I hope I did right to exercise my discretion in this matter of
> waiting. I append Dr Hoar's opinion . . .
> <u>Diagnosis</u>:-
>
> Feeble pulse
> Coated tongue

Sour breath
Second heart-beat slightly accentuated
Lungs & chest quite sound
General condition is depressed owing to disordered liver.

Prognosis:-
Keep quiet for a few days & take liver tonic & calomel pills, when
should be better.

*

Milicent and Amy set off for Rome on 17 November 1900. The
journey was mainly jolly. Amy was more amused than irritated by
Milicent's scatty habits and small economies. 'She is the most
untidy creature,' she told NM, 'I should so like to brush her up &
fit her out fresh.' 'M asked for "two small cheap rooms" & we are
at the top looking down a well with no view . . . such is M's way
it amuses me but I am glad she is not tied to me for life.' What, I
wonder, would Amy have thought if she could have foreseen that
NM would before long find himself tied to Milicent for life?

Amy did her best to straighten her cousin out: 'I did up her hair
in the omnibus . . . She started from Lucerne with both boots
unlaced & her clothes thrown on.' From Lucerne they travelled
to Milan and then to Florence. 'M has cheered up & burst into
song! We decide Italy is infinitely superior to Switzerland.' Milicent was fascinated by Amy's conversion. 'M asks me all sorts of
questions . . . I hope I shant convert her I am trying not . . . She
says I am the only RC she has ever really talked to.' They had
'tremendous talks' and a considerable amount of jollity: 'We have
great fun at table d'hôte because we drink cognac & seltzer water
& the old ladies look so shocked'; 'M and I get on excellently
I really think she is enjoying herself very much tell Roddy – she
looks like a tramp but the hotel people (who can't make us out at
all) no doubt think we are mad English.'

Amy could be very critical of Milicent (she told NM, 'the more
I like a person the more I am inclined to criticize'), but she was

appreciative of the efforts her cousin made. 'M bought me a bunch of violets this morning'; 'M is a brick & is simply slaving'; 'Enter M who says we must have some hot <u>Bovril</u> horrible'; 'M was very nice & made me some hot brandy & water & beef jelly! About 9 a.m. yesterday [because I] felt pretty bad after getting up so early.' They arrived in Rome on 26 November and found rooms at the Hotel Beausite. Milicent went to call on Aunt Nannie, but Amy stayed behind. Nannie, still reeling from the shock of Amy's conversion, had made it clear that she should not call until specifically asked to do so. After the fatigue of the journey this edict was a relief.

Once in Rome, Milicent felt the need to emphasize that she was not a Catholic. Amy had a frustrating visit to St Peter's: '. . . the Pope was carried in to bless some pilgrims. [Milicent] insisted on going directly after he came in . . . wh was <u>so</u> Milicenty . . . I stupidly went too to avoid a row! However I <u>did</u> see the Pope please tell Ethne quite near. He certainly is a wonderful old man. I knelt down as he passed, no doubt to M's horror!'

Amy's attitude towards Milicent mixed sympathy, embarrassment and condescension:

I am not quite happy about Milicent . . . she sleeps in the room that has not got enough sun – but I mean to make her change tomorrow. Then her <u>feet</u> hurt her. It seems she has got flat-footed in one foot & has to wear a thing & she thinks the other one is getting bad. <u>Then</u> she is really rather <u>deaf</u> & that worries her I noticed she talked <u>very</u> loud & remonstrated about it as she attracted so much attention . . . She said it is 'a Ludlow peculiarity we all do' so nothing more could be said but once or twice since she said I think I <u>must</u> be getting deaf I cant hear things you can . . . Yesterday . . . we did some shopping <u>think</u> brandy for me & cigarettes for M!! . . . I had to tell M she could not smoke in my bedroom.

Milicent was only thirty-two, but Amy was worried she was turning herself into the type of a dotty old spinster: 'I wonder if she will be a happy or a miserable old woman.'

The summons to visit Aunt Nannie soon came. Amy was shocked: 'She looks so old & shrivelled up. All the servant worries in the world ought not to make anyone look like that.' She was also dismayed at her reception: 'It is a curious feeling to be in a place like this & the only one person I know to hate me! I really felt she hated me today, but Milicent says she doesn't.' Nannie liked to think she held court among the artistic and intellectual expatriate community, but according to Amy the number of her courtiers was dwindling thanks to the airs she put on and her habit of picking quarrels.

After a few days in Rome, Amy's condition deteriorated sharply. Milicent, alarmed, went into her most 'managing' mode: 'This morning I am a little cross with M because she has taken to managing me & saying "now you are to stop in & I am going out. I shall be in to lunch of course you won't think of going out this morning. This afternoon you are to go for a drive till 3.30 . . ." Roddy will perhaps know that phase of Milicent – I have said nothing today . . . but tomorrow M will find a revolution!'

Nannie veered between hostility and generosity. Her new companion, a Miss Burnett, was (in Amy's opinion) 'horrible'. Amy believed that she was bent on turning Nannie against her family, presumably in the hope of personal gain. (Any bounty-hunters counting on being remembered in Nannie's will were in for a long wait; she lived until 1919.) But neither Miss Burnett nor the horror of Amy's conversion could quite extinguish Nannie's feelings for the niece she had once 'loved as a daughter'. She put her carriage and her 'little manservant' at the disposal of Amy and Milicent, and even lent Amy a veil for church-going.

In mid-December, Milicent returned to England alone, feeling that St Margaret's House could no longer do without her. Living alone in the Hotel Beausite was expensive and lonely; Amy hoped to move into the convent of the 'Blue Nuns' at 45 Via Castelfidardo as soon as there was a vacancy for her. Nannie was consumed with curiosity about this plan though her anti-Catholic stance prevented her from asking questions: 'I have been to Aunt Nannie. I was shown into the dining room where the man was laying the cloth. She was

sitting by two or three smouldering logs with the newspaper looking dreadful . . . I see she is fearfully inquisitive about me.'

As the weeks wore on Amy felt increasingly out of touch. She
worried too about her weakening influence over her children — 'I
feel it very much this being put on the shelf whilst I am still alive.'
Alan, in his first year at Trinity College, Cambridge, hardly ever
wrote. His father was already beginning to put pressure on him to
follow him into the medical profession, and this worried Amy:
'. . . we must not expect very much strength of character from
[Alan] — I think he is a good dear fellow but I don't think he has
got *go* in him - & he is very much influenced by other people.'

Six-year-old Gilla had begun at a London day school and was
finding it difficult to learn and conform. With twenty-first-century
hindsight, it seems probable that Gilla was dyslexic. His entire scholastic career was beset by difficulties, though it was obvious from an
early age that he had a lively, inquisitive mind and deep-rooted
interests, particularly in natural history. 'I can see why some governesses think him a fool & others clever!' wrote Amy. At Easter he
was removed from school after one term — presumably his difficulties there had become too great — and educated at home.

Ethne, fourteen, gave her mother regular bulletins about her little brother's progress and happiness. Her surviving letters to Amy
are untidy and ill spelt but full of the kind of vivid detail that Amy
craved in exile: 'Papa has put a picture under your portrait in the
dining room, the one of trees & St Peters in the distance by Mr
Brabazon, to hide the face Gilla drew on the wall.' 'Nurse [Eliza
Brown] has had a bereavement, one of her brothers, he died yesterday she heard this morning she wept a little but as she probably
has'ent seen him for about 30 years perhaps the loss is not so great as
it might be. I was in the nursery consoling her etc, she said, "And
whats so sad is —" (I thought she was going to be very pathetic)
"That I shall have to get a new bonnet" - !' Ethne was a scatty girl,
but she did her best to involve herself with the running of the
household, buying Christmas presents for the servants, entertaining visitors and making sure Gilla had other children to play with.

Ethne's instinct was always to cheer and entertain her mother.
'Give Milicent my love,' she wrote, 'I hope she takes care of you &
amuses you & is kind to you.' The implication is that Ethne would
have made a better job of it.

Ethne missed her mother acutely. There was a plan that she
should join her in Rome during the Christmas holidays, if an
escort could be found. She wrote to Amy, 'Uncle Ben & Ludlow
came to lunch, Gilla was there, of course, he was very good, but
tried to join in the conversation & had to be hushed. Ludlow says
he is going to Rome too, & may be able to take me out.' With sorrow Amy decided that she was too ill to receive Ethne; Ludlow
travelled out alone. Christmas was a bleak prospect. Ethne asked,
'Do you think you could send us each some little thing, that would
arrive as near Christmas day as possible because it would'nt be a
proper Christmas without <u>something</u> from you, you understand
what I mean. Don't forget <u>I</u> don't mind sacred pictures, or even
crosses or even (<u>really</u>) rosaries!'

Salvation came in the form of an invitation from the Pryors of
Weston Park, near Hitchin. Marlborough Pryor, the squire of Weston, was an old Cambridge friend of NM's. He had shown great
promise as a scientist but to NM's disappointment he abandoned
his academic career in favour of running the family business, Sun
Alliance, in London. At Weston he managed his estates and raised his
large family; the social organization of the neighbourhood would
have been completely familiar to Jane Austen a century earlier. 'The
Pryors are a Boon & Blessing to Moores,' wrote Amy, receiving the
news that they had come to the rescue of her children's Christmas.

In her memoir Ethne recalls her first visit to Weston a year or so
earlier. The six Pryor sisters, Nellie, Bessie, Alice, Hilda, Margaret
and Baby (Hannah), all stood in a row outside the front door to
greet her:

> They looked me up and down in a friendly way and someone said:
> 'Good, I'm glad you've got fronts,' by which she meant that I was
> beginning to show signs of adult development . . . I was used to

schoolgirls but had never before met such a large family of sisters and was a little astonished at their intimate habits. Their rooms were at the top of the big house and they had their own bath room to which they all trooped in the morning, leaving the door open, throwing off their clothes and getting in the bath one behind the other, reminding me of pink frogs.

The Pryors filled the emotional gaps in Ethne's life. Mrs Pryor would come up to say goodnight to her when she was in bed:

I thought her neck and arms looked lovely in evening dress and she always wore some sort of gleaming jewel pinned to it. When I hugged her she felt so soft; her arms were soft and the silk or velvet of her dress was soft, and not quite knowing what to call her I gave her the name of 'Mrs Muff'. I found it very comforting to be allowed to hug her, for at home I could not hug my mother because she was ill and though I loved my Aunt Roddy, she was thin and very shy and would blush and edge away if I showed my affection for her.

Life at Weston was much busier and noisier than it was at Gloucester Place. As well as the six sisters there was one brother, Jack, and a number of girl cousins who drifted in and out as intimately as sisters. 'I can still remember,' said Ethne, writing in the 1950s:

my surprise – often pleased surprise, which this family's way of living caused me . . . I think the first thing that really astonished me was the luncheon that was served on Good Friday . . . it was plain boiled salt fish . . . The whole family ate it and then, to my astonishment, it was replaced by a leg of mutton.
    'Thank goodness' someone said, 'that's over' as their fish plates were removed by the footman and I realised that they seemed to consider that salt fish had to be eaten as a kind of penance on Good Friday but that otherwise, no sort of fasting was necessary, for the mutton was followed by a delicious pudding.

Days at Weston were spent riding, bathing in the ponds in the garden, 'sailing' in a boat made by the gardener and named the 'Mary Ansell' after a notorious murderess 'because she upset so easily and a murderess' name seemed appropriate,' and taking long walks on which the girls carried loaves of bread and pots of jam. Indoors they made nougat (unsuccessfully) and a sweet of Alan's invention called 'Weston Delight'. The house and park were filled with animals. Marlborough Pryor had retained his interest in natural history; once, after dining with NM, they were standing in front of the fire and a dabchick hatched out of the egg he had in his pocket. He was happy to indulge his children's desire to keep a variety of odd pets:

> which lived in little cages and were let out to hop about in the hall and billiard room. I remember the Kinkajou the best because he was a fascinating creature during his active jumping life and much wept over when he died. I can see a picture of a great many girls, Pryors, cousins and myself, sitting on the drawing room floor. Some were knitting and many had traces of tears on their cheeks. Suddenly the door opened and a grown-up with a worried face looked in.
>
> 'Ah – ' he exclaimed, 'I see – you know?'
>
> 'Oh yes,' said one of the girls, breaking into sobs, 'he died this morning.'
>
> 'He?' queried the grown-up, looking puzzled. 'But I came to tell you that Granny Pryor was dead.'
>
> 'Oh!' exclaimed someone in a flat voice 'we were crying for the Kinkajou!'

★

NM managed to get to Rome for a short time during the Christmas holidays, but he returned in the New Year. His letters, though very frequent, left Amy hungering for information. 'You don't say much about A[lan]. I wonder how he was looking. I appear sometimes to hear very little about him. I think he interests me more than old books however beautifully written.' She hated relinquishing control over her home: 'Don't let the house get to look like an

Irish cabin with the roof half off. It usually does when I am away.'
She worried about money; her stay in Rome was funded out of
Aunt Barbara's legacy, and there was very little left. She suggested
scaling down their establishment: 'Do you still cling to 94 [Glouces-
ter Place] & 6 servants as inevitable.' She fretted over Ethne: 'I fear
she is lazy & also conceited but that is not quite her fault as she has
been spoilt & kind as the Pryors have been they did spoil her. Then
also she has inherited the Moorian capacity for being able to do any
thing if she likes it! & a wonderful ingenuity for finding difficulties
in the way when she does not like to do a thing.' She urged NM to
visit Ethne when she started at a new boarding school in January,
but chastised him for taking her on an exhausting tour of Cambridge: 'I wonder you didn't kill her – I think you expect too much
from women & girls. Do remember they are not as strong as you 16
colleges!! Did you really take her to 16?'

Amy had achieved her aim and moved into the Convent of the
Blue Nuns. ('My dear Papist,' wrote Roddy from Crowham on
New Year's Eve, 'Do tell Aunt Nanny that Bella wishes to go into
a convent & be Sister something in a blue lined cloak.') She asked
NM not to tell his mother where she was staying, and expressed
irritation when Rebecca sent Alan a book about 'evolutionists' as
a birthday present. NM took an even stronger line. Knowing that
Amy's death must be near, he could not tolerate any kind of attack
on the Faith. 'Burn the development book,' he wrote to Alan,
'there is no help or use or comfort in irreligion.'

Ludlow installed himself in Aunt Nannie's apartment. Leaving
Mabel and the children somewhat in limbo at Scalands (there was
talk of a house at Eastbourne, but nothing had been finalized), he
had come to Italy for an indefinite period for the sake of his health.
Amy was pleased; Ludlow's presence kept the unpleasant Miss Burnett somewhat at bay. Ludlow was never anything but kind – 'he has
just sent me such a nice bunch of blue & white anemones' – but in
Amy's opinion he didn't have 'much in him'. Staying with Aunt Nannie wore him down: 'If you live with a lunatic you get infected . . .
At. N really ought to be shut up . . . He is a good-natured very fee-

ble fellow doesn't think he <u>can</u> stay again with At. Nanny because she feeds him on <u>Duck</u> & does not have enough fires.'

Nannie herself blew hot and cold. 'Aunt Nannie appeared with flowers & sugar plums very weepy & shaky but we got on quite nicely'; 'Yesterday at 4pm At. Nannie & Ludlow came (A. Nannie is a slight humbug as she has told me she can't walk up stairs & never goes out to tea) I was rather taken aback as I did not expect them & was just beginning <u>my</u> tea & also Sister Hilda had left the <u>Altar</u> in my room just as it was in the morning white cloth & everything. However I let them come up. At. N looked like a general officer in this new Helmet bonnet of hers . . . AN was in her most excited & wild state . . . Ludlow looks a poor creature being dragged round by her . . . she really means to be kind. She bought me some <u>lovely carnations</u> & has given me an <u>air</u> cushion which is really a great comfort'; 'She talks about Ludlow as if he was 6 years old what a queer old thing she is.'

Nannie could not bear that Amy's ill health, rather than her own, was centre stage. During NM's visit he had had some very satisfactory medical conversations with her which had soothed her considerably – Madame Helvig, a friend of Nannie's, told Amy that NM was 'a wonderful man' who had 'saved Nannie's <u>reason</u>'. But the sicker Amy grew, the stronger became her aunt's denial of it. 'Ludlow came when my eyes were bad & said "Oh its nothing – Aunt Nannie's eyes are bad & so are mine it is probably all the same thing" She had told him to say so. I was really <u>much</u> amused; it is quite comic sometimes to come across such an absolutely inhuman person.' Ludlow's own ill health did not prevent him from attending a masked ball in Rome. He intended to move on to Florence and urged Amy to accompany him, apparently oblivious of the fact that most days she was too weak to leave her convent room; 'I had to give him a little plain speaking.' Amy thought he looked worn and harassed but did not think there was much amiss – 'does he not chiefly suffer from the dullness of home!!' He seemed blasé about his wife's problems: 'He says Mabel . . . has seen Barlow [the doctor who helped her during her crisis over her first engagement] who says she ought not to be troubled with household cares at present – but he always talks of Mabel as if she had very little connection with him and as if the subject did not much interest him . . . I think he is not at all anxious to return home.'

Amy was fully aware of the seriousness of her own condition. Most of her letters are brave and uncomplaining, and she retained her sense of humour, regaling NM with anecdotes about Father Louis the Trappist, whose one meal of the day consisted of sea spiders, or about the stir caused by the 'improper' statues of water nymphs on the new fountain, or about Sister Hilda's horror when Amy's doctor made a mild joke about a monk kissing a nun. But she could not always keep out a note of reproach:

> After I went out on Sunday . . . my heart felt so bad again - & last night it was very bad after I undressed to go to bed & did not get right for a long time – we even put a mustard leaf on – it was not a pain but simply as if it wouldn't go & I felt suffocating. I felt a rag this morning . . . I have gone back to those strycknine pills after a bottle of the tonic so called. You see it is dreadful to get a letter from you saying "Do get well" when one feels like this . . . I am getting weaker . . . this place on my face, makes me so . . . it still has pus forming – then my temp. is rarely below 100° at night . . . I really think I am getting thinner.

She coughed up blood, soaking thirty-four handkerchiefs in one week. Her invalid diet consisted of milk, brandy and arrowroot, though she was able to eat a little chicken, poached egg, bread and butter and 'pudding'. It is interesting from a twenty-first-century point of view to see that fruit and vegetables were excluded entirely. She was too weak to paint or draw; though she tried to keep her mind occupied with reading theology, Amy admitted, 'There is certainly a monotony in my life that would send a Mabel mad.'

★

Ethne and Hilda Pryor started at a new school together in January – Dane Lodge, St Leonards-on-Sea, a small girls' boarding school where Bella had been a pupil a few years earlier. Hilda had never been away from home before and was very unhappy; her woe infected Ethne. On 19 January, her fifteenth birthday, Ethne wrote in her journal, 'Aye but I'm doleful wilow wilow waley . . . I was never so miserable in my life before.'

Bella warned Ethne that the headmistress, Miss Bishop, was severe to the point of being terrifying, and Ethne soon realized, to her dismay, that she was in the unenviable position of being Miss Bishop's favourite. 'She told me quite soon that she could not be bothered to make friends with ugly or stupid people and . . . one or two of the boarders, who could certainly be so described, were generally ignored by her.' Ethne was neither ugly nor stupid. The cloud of flaxen hair that had caused people to say she looked like a mermaid when she was small had become a thick, fair, rippling waist-length mane. She did not have her mother's classic beauty; with her broad forehead, straight nose and strong square jaw she was considered to resemble Aunt Barbara. She was certainly striking; her big green Irish eyes, creative, dreamy intelligence and potentially tragic home life appealed strongly to the unconventional Miss Bishop, whose behaviour would nowadays be regarded as suspect:

When Miss Bishop told me I had lovely hair I was indifferent, in fact, her admiration became rather a nuisance, for whenever she came by me, she would pull off my hair ribbon because she liked to see my hair flowing freely over my shoulders . . . she [had] a passion for looseness and freedom in every sort of apparel . . . [she] came round behind us as we sat at table, and, undoing our skirts and pulling up our blouses she took out a pair of scissors and cut all our corset strings. She had come to think that the body should not be restricted in any way and made us all give up wearing corsets, also, which was really rather tiresome, she would not let us keep our stockings up with either garters or suspenders and so we used to roll them up under our knees, but they sagged continually and often fell about our ankles. I was glad to be rid of my uncomfortable corsets . . . but . . . I used to spend a long time searching for the hair ribbons

Miss Bishop had thrown away, for I found it more convenient to
keep my long hair tied back with a black bow behind my head.

Miss Bishop was keen on fresh air and exercise. A healthy breakfast of fruit, porridge and 'cereal, which in those days was a nov-
elty, and disliked by most of us' was eaten very early, in the garden.
The girls, unusually, cleared it away to save work for the maids;
they then performed vigorous exercises out of doors under the
scrutiny of Miss Bishop before gathering under a tree to read an
'improving' book – Ethne mentions Marcus Aurelius, and Car-
lyle's *Sartor Resartus* – followed by a chapter of the New Testa-
ment, omitting indelicate verses.

Ethne had not been at Dane Lodge long before Queen Victoria
died. She kept an 'Everything Book', a scrapbook of diary entries,
poems (her own and other people's), drawings, and reproductions
of favourite pictures, and she covered it with a patchwork of pieces
of fabric, pasted on. It is as different as possible from the printed
Letts diaries in which Alan noted details of the weather, train
times, and the number of the hymn sung each day in chapel.
Ethne's ragbag style gives her journal a freshness and immediacy at
the expense of coherent structure:

Monday January 21st 1901 The Queen is very ill, probably dying!
'brain symptoms serious' the last telegram said – I wonder if she
will die –

Had a letter from Bessie [Pryor] today, letters are cheering. I
have hung my crucifix & the rosary up on the wall under Mama's
photograph also the flowers from the Pope's garden [brought
back by NM] - & St Cecilia [a photograph of a statue] is on the
dressing table where I can always see her at once –

I wish I was at home, but its no use wishing – because I shant
be for weeks & weeks . . .

Tuesday Jan 22nd 1901 'The Queen is sinking fast' . . . she will
be sure to die – soon, tomorrow perhaps – how funny it will be!
– I wonder if we shall all have to go into mourning!

It is most frightfully cold here –

I never was so cold before -

Alan's birthday tomorrow I wrote to him tonight. I had a letter from Mama this morning – must stop now & get into bed, I must learn my scripture, Philippians Chap I v.i – ɪɪ –

. . . 8.58 p.m.

The Bells are tolling!

Does it mean the queen is dead – I am almost sure it does –

————

The Queen is dead –

————

We have not heard yet, but it must be the bells would not be tolling for anything else at this hour – Poor Queen, how happy she must be now – And with Prince Albert – The newspaper boys are shouting out 'Death of the Queen official news' (I write in the dark).

Miss Bishop allowed Ethne a weekend off school to watch the funeral procession. 'How jolly it is to be home again & have Papa,' she wrote. She had tea in the nursery, at Gilla's request, and then a cosy evening with NM in the consulting room eating the Brazil nuts and chestnuts he had brought home. At ten at night father and daughter walked the streets of London to look at the preparations for the procession:

We walked as far as Padington & back, Everywhere along the route seats are being put up – the streets were very crowded, some people evedently going to walk about all night, as all the hotels & sleeping places are crammed there are black & purple decorations hung up (decorating is not quite an appropriate word to use, I cant think of another now) & in several places white bows and streamers, they looked rather like lamb's tails – mottos & sweet speeches also here & there, & hardly a house that has nothing, either a moto or bustle cloth or riband or something <u>All</u> the lamp posts along the route, have <u>two</u> very large & fresh green wreaths, the effect is very fine

altogether the [streets] show how much people all loved & respected
Queen Victoria – must stop now its nearly 12.

NM, Gilla and Ethne watched the procession from the windows
of 6 Edgware Road, the home of a doctor friend. The streets were
lined with soldiers; ambulance corps were kept busy as many people
fainted. After a three-hour wait the procession came in sight:

Sir Someone Bradford (I think his name is) the chief of the police
rode first, on a little horse which was very fresh – He is a little man,
with one arm (it was bitten off by a tiger in India papa says) – Then
4 mounted police – then regements & regements of soldiers . . .
then a gap & Earl Roberts [hero of the Boer War] (alone except for
his aidecamp) looking very fine & sad, his arm still in a sling –

The people cheered him a little but were soon hushed & then
remained silent all the while – Then I think came some more soldiers &
then the coffin – Drawn by 8 creem coloured horses, all over gold &
blue rosettes & red with postillions in gold & white with wigs –

It was on a gun carriage, the gun was underneath. The Pall was
most magnificent white & gold – The crown & septre & 2 orbs were
laid on the coffin. The people all took off their hats, & were very silent
– After the gun carriage came King Edward VII, just behind him the
German Emperior (looking very fine on a beautiful white horse) &
the Duke of Connaught – (its nearly 4, I must go to prayers).

The Queen's death prompted Ethne to ruminate on the subject
of the afterlife:

I wonder if when you are dead you can see everything on Earth – I
cant quite make up my mind – It says there will be no more sorrow
on the Last Day but I supose that does'ent mean directly you die.
But if it does, its *so* difficult to understand, But I don't think it can
because, you surely could'ent be so changed as not be sorry to be
parted from your mother – And if I was in Heaven or Paradise or
wherever it is, & I saw Mama crying because I was dead, I am sure

I should be unhappy – I never was afraid of dieing, some people are, I never was a bit. If God said to me Die or Come this Minuet I should'ent be frightened at least not exactly it would be wrong not to be awefully awed of course but I mean I should'ent be in the least sorry to leave this Earth except for all the partings –

I can't write anymore it makes ones head ache so to write a lot in bed.

Death was soon to come much closer to home. Only a fortnight after Queen Victoria's death, Ethne wrote in her Everything Book:

I cant understand it God knows best I supose Mrs Pryor is dead – Everyone loved her so & she was wanted so & did so much good – It was so dredfully sudden – She had a bad throat, a quinsy, it began to be bad on Sunday (last) & now she is dead –

Hilda poor child has gone to London . . . I know its very selfish of me to think of my own sorrow compared with theirs – but I did love her so, Mrs Muff, she was my second mother when Mama was away – it is so very hard, no one knows how unhappy I am . . . its hard to do everything as usual when I am so miserable & thinking of them –

I could'ent do dancing, Miss Bishop wont mind I'm sure . . . I loved Her so, I could'ent dance, now.

Hilda Pryor did not return to Dane Lodge. This forced Ethne to make other friends, and she soon came to like school more and take an interest in things outside her own troubles. On 12 March she wrote, 'Been to lecture by Winstint Churchill about the [Boer] war, rather intresting & amusing I thought but he has'ent a nice voise bad twang - & is a bit conceited.' She stayed again at Crowham during the Easter holidays; the warm spring weather restored her equilibrium:

I am writing this by the open window (Roddy would cry shut it!)

it has been a lovely day in a thin dress [and] no jacket . . . siting
in the garden in April! It is St George's Day, the church bells are
ringing, & the birds are singing before they go to sleep – a little
moth has just fluttered by . . .

The trees far away look blue against the sky which is pink with
the remains of sunset, there is a little white cottage that I can see
with a light burning - & a dog is barking in the distance.

There goes a bat – quite close it sounds as if a grasshopper were
on the lawn . . .

There's a robin siting on the fence, with a very red brest & such
quantities of white tails (rabbits) running up the hill

There goes Ami [tabby cat] on the drive her tail like a soft bottle
brush now its wagging . . .

Here comes a gnat humming by –

I saw 2 wrens fighting on the verander roof, so tiny –

Someone is playing the piano (Aunt Jenny I think) . . .

There is [a] cuckoo . . . There goes Lewis [a black kitten] across
the lawn – Ami has imerged from the bush & is siting in the drive
– she is now walking followed by Lewis, now they sit & look at
each other, now Ami is eating grass.

Lewis lies on the drive looking behind him at a bird now they
both run away as Willie comes in at the gate with Turk [a terrier],
the pipe & his bright new tennis shoes.

The sense of peace achieved by the visit to Crowham did not
last long. By April, Amy was too weak to write her own letters.
She dictated them to Sister Hilda, who added her own postscript
to NM: 'the thing that will do her most good will be to get back
to you again.' NM prepared to fetch Amy back from Rome; he
paid a farewell visit to Ethne, and told her, 'I cannot have you to
worry about too, you must be well and cheerful.' When he got
back to London, he sent her a postcard on which he had written:

> Work on apace apace apace
> Honest labour wears a cheerful face.

At some point during Amy's last weeks in Rome, Aunt Nannie's behaviour caused a lasting rift. The only reference to it I have found is a letter to NM from a friend, Mary Galton. On 27 May, after NM and Amy had returned to England, Mary Galton wrote from Rome a reply to what had obviously been an anxious letter from NM:

> I have only seen Miss Leigh Smith once or twice since you left. She has shut herself up with Miss Burnett and hardly seen anyone . . . all her friends are more worried than ever about Miss Burnett . . . I have no right to interfere in Miss Leigh Smith's arrangements and if she prefers Miss Burnett to all her old friends, well there is nothing to be done – I am very sorry for her for she is not happy – and I am sure is very wretched about the manner in which she treated you and your wife – but somehow has convinced herself that the fault is not hers.

Amy reached England in very bad shape. According to Ethne's memoir:

> she was so ill that they sent for me hurriedly to go and see her. One of the mistresses took me to London and we had so little time to prepare for the journey that I was made to put on a tidy frock on the top of my everyday cotton one, as there was not time for me to change properly. My mother was in bed and seemed, I thought, to be lying very flat in it. The nurse who was looking after her rather offended me by saying that I had grown fat, (she had nursed my mother before and had seen me some months earlier), but my mother laughed and pinched my arm.
>
> 'It's all muscle' she said, and immediately I felt proud of being fatter, instead of being ashamed of it. Although she looked very thin and lay so low in the bed she laughed and talked as she used to when she was well.
>
> 'Do you know', she told me, 'when I first came back they thought I was going to die and the funny thing was, that instead of

saying my prayers I began to wonder whether my sealskin cape
would cut down for you? And I felt quite cheerful all the time!'
She told me to remember this.

Ethne declared that she wanted to become a Roman Catholic
like her mother, but Amy asked her to wait.

'Put all thoughts of it out of your head until you come of age' she
said, 'and then decide for yourself if you really want to become
one or not. Do not be in a hurry, it took me more than ten years to
make up my mind.'

This showed great restraint on Amy's part. She did not allow
herself to capitalize on her daughter's emotional turmoil and push
her into taking such an important step, even though one of her
letters to NM from Rome expresses excitement and delight at
hearing of Ethne's growing interest in Catholicism.

A fortnight later, Miss Bishop herself took Ethne to London
again. 'Mama no better,' wrote Ethne afterwards. 'I wish she would
be, but I supose its right or it wouldn't be.' NM kept going; the
notes on patients in his casebook are as detailed as ever, but he adds
the odd wistful comment about Amy. On 18 June, Waterloo Day,
he sent, as was his custom, two bunches of roses, one red and one
white, to the Misses Somerset, two old friends – 'Miss C Somerset
was a month old when the battle was fought & won at Brussells.
My dear Amy was very weak & ill & coughed a good deal, but
laughed at my remembering Waterloo.'

For August he rented Chilgrove, a house in Marryat Road on
Wimbledon Common; to take Amy further out of London was
impossible. At Wimbledon, Alan, Ethne and Gilla carried on their
usual summer-holiday pursuits, cycling, swimming, sketching,
reading and birdwatching. Amy lay on a sofa by the window so
that she could see the garden. Alan continued to bring out *The
Family Magazine*. The 'news' section records that Bella failed the
Girton entrance exam and that 'Mr Gillachrist Moore has not

increased in wisdom in proportion to his stature.' Ethne contributed a fashion page and snippets of gossip about boarding-school life entitled 'Notes from the Danery'. Roddy, who was in charge of domestic affairs, submitted 'How the Chilgrove Household Might & Perhaps Should & Ought to be Managed'. Most poignant are NM's Nature Notes: 'The robin sings every evening & Mrs Norman Moore enjoys its song & says that she likes it best of any bird's song.'

On the evening of 25 August, Alan and Ethne were called to their mother's bedside. They sat beside her and NM stood at the head. 'The hospital nurse told me my mother would like me to hold her hand,' wrote Ethne, 'and I did so, though she did not seem to be conscious that we were beside her. It was a warm evening and through the open window I heard distant church bells ringing and I have hated the sound of them ever since.' Alan, writing in old age, recalled his last sight of his mother's face: 'The dignity of her perfect features is an abiding memory.'

Amy was buried in the Roman Catholic cemetery at Mortlake. After the funeral NM said to his children, 'Let us draw up the blinds and be as cheerful as we can.' But for Ethne, these days were desolate. 'I was given a black dress with crepe on it and Nurse [Eliza Brown] even suggested that perhaps I ought to have black underclothes. My Aunt [Roddy] and Nurse cried so often that I found a certain relief in trying to cheer them up and in running messages for them.' The faith which brought solace to NM deserted his daughter:

> Though I said a great many prayers and read consoling passages in the Bible and copied some of them onto the pages at the end of it I seemed from this time to cease to believe in Heaven. I found it impossible to imagine my mother existing in another sort of life. It had been my chief delight to please her; I had relied on the interest she took in all I did. Even though I did not perhaps tell her everything, I had known I could do so, if I wished, and now there seemed no one to take her place.

It is a measure of NM's generous and forgiving nature that one of the first people to whom he broke the news was Uncle Ben. The old man wrote back immediately:

I am very grieved but hope she did not suffer much. Please give my love to all and say how sorry I am for them.

Another early recipient of a letter was Milicent, at St Margaret's House. It seems that NM asked her to come and help. She, too, was quick to reply:

My dear Norman – I found your letter on my return – It was very kind of you to write it. It seems somehow natural that Amy with her spiritual nature should have gone on . . . into some higher & better School to be made perfect.

I am coming on Thursday.

Your affectionate

Milicent Ludlow.

13. 'Your tiresome Mil'

NM reacted to his loss by burying himself in work. Less than two months after Amy's death he delivered the 'Harveian Oration' at the Royal College of Physicians, an annual event instituted in 1656 by Dr William Harvey, discoverer of the circulation of the blood, for the perpetual commemoration of benefactors of the college.

To be chosen as orator was – and is – an honour. Most orators chose to give straightforward medical lectures, but NM seized the opportunity to air one of his favourite themes – that the greatest physicians were men of many parts, whose talents and interests all fed into their wider understanding of the human condition, an understanding NM believed essential to good doctoring. His oration led its listeners along byways designed to branch naturally from the main theme and to throw light on the lives and times of the people mentioned.

NM was an avid collector and reader of old books. The oration explored the vast storehouse of his mind and demonstrated his formidable associative memory. For him, the historical figures of whom he spoke were real, breathing people, 'the darlings of my heart and library'. A typical train of association is his reference to Raphael Thorius, a seventeenth-century licentiate of the college and contemporary of Harvey's, who wrote two books in praise of tobacco; Thorius also wrote three poems to L'Obel the botanist who was an apothecary 'known to few of the many who have the Lobelia growing in their gardens'. Those details, and scores like them, may be trivial in themselves, but they are products and illustrations of NM's passionate belief in the interconnectedness of knowledge. It was this power of association that made NM a renowned conversationalist. Alan remembered a gathering in the rooms of a Cambridge fellow, with his father in full conversational flight. 'I'm coming back for some more of this,' said a don when his duties called him away.

The oration was published in a handsome limited edition. NM sent copies to friends; the letters of thanks he received are illustrative of the extraordinary range of his acquaintance. Thus the novelist Henry James wrote from Lamb House, Rye, on 25 January 1902:

> I am ashamed of my delay in acknowledging your so kind and charming memento, but two pleas may perhaps count a little for me. I was in the New Year's overflow, for many days. I was then waiting for the exactly right hour to give to your handsome so equally with elegant little volume which I wished to have enjoyed before writing to you. Success has crowned both my forms of patience and I am free to let you know that your remembrance has greatly touched me, as a sign of old acquaintance surviving muta-tions. It belongs to the class of things that amid the jolts & jars of life give pleasure. And I have read your oration with a lively sense of its taste, of your command of facts, form & interest, a feeling for your kind of problem. Your success is charming & ought to remain the example of the pretty old tradition of the appeal from mere medicine – I mean by the medicus in his hours of ease . . .

And so on. Pat Connell, the estate carpenter at Lake View, in County Cavan, also received a copy. He told NM, 'the book could not be beat.'

★

At 94 Gloucester Place, domestic arrangements were, as Alan put it, 'lapsing into barbarism'. Eliza Brown provided Gilla with stabil-ity, but Amy's absence was acutely felt. Roddy did what she could, but Crowham made constant demands upon her, and her own health was poor. Increasingly, NM looked to Milicent for help.

It was not long after Amy's death, it seems, that the possibility of a more intimate relationship began to dawn on both of them. In December, NM took Alan to Florence for a holiday; a letter Milicent wrote to him there has a very faintly flirtatious tone, or at least indicates that they corresponded about matters other than mere arrangements. She writes of her fondness for the cathedral and for S. Ambrogio in Florence, and says:

> there is no use in telling me that the roof is painted, any more than in pointing out imperfections in one's friends! Of course it is, but <u>so</u> it is, so <u>there</u> it is.
>
> I have no objection to raise to the course of conduct you indicated in S. Ambrogio! Tho' not in my own line, I can appreciate it in other people - !

I don't know what this 'course of conduct' was, but I assume it was some sort of Catholic observance. It seems that NM had been feeling his way into Protestant Milicent's attitude to his faith.

NM made few private notes in the months following Amy's death – indeed, apart from notes on patients he kept no record of his doings at all – but on 26 January 1902 he records that he and Milicent visited the Wallace Collection together. The letters that survive from Milicent from this period begin, 'My dear Norman,' and are signed, 'Yours affectionately, M.B.L.' They show that Milicent was, as usual, being pulled in different directions. As well as working at St Margaret's and doing what she could to help at 94 Gloucester Place, she was *in loco parentis* to the Ludlow children. The shock of losing Hancox had sent Mabel into an incapacitating state of nerves; her state grew worse early in 1902: 'I feel fairly sure that Mabel's recovery will take many months, more likely years,' Milicent told NM on 4 April. Mabel was – I think – being looked after by Cousin Flora at her house in Bournemouth. Ludlow, meanwhile, handled the situation by absenting himself, as was his wont. He returned to the Continent, this time on a sketching tour with Mr Brabazon.

Milicent dashed back and forth between London and Scalands, where the Ludlow girls continued to live under the care of the servants; eight-year-old John was away at school. Eira, ten, had (unspecified) health problems of her own. 'I am making an appointment for Eira to see Mr Cumberbatch next Friday,' Milicent told NM. 'I hope she can also see Mr Spicer. I have a scheme of taking her for a few days to join Uncle Ben at Southampton, and to look up Charlotte at Ryde.' There was no longer much pretence about the state of Ben and Charley's marriage.

Despite the pressures on Milicent, her letters are uncomplaining, and there is an optimistic chattiness in their tone which NM must have found appealing: 'I have just read "Pride & Prejudice" for the first time: how much nicer we have all got since Miss Austen's days. It is astounding to think that my father might have known such people as she describes.' Her mixture of courage and vulnerability aroused his chivalrous instincts; she strove to help and comfort him, but – in his view – she herself needed rescuing. Things moved fast – too fast, perhaps. On 9 June they travelled to Mortlake together to visit Amy's grave. I don't know exactly when NM proposed, but by the time he set off for his annual visit to Ireland in early September, Milicent was beginning her letters with 'My dearest Man' and signing them, 'Your Mil.'

They kept their engagement secret for some time; Amy had only been dead a year, after all. Besides, there was the religious question to sort out. Could Milicent marry NM and remain a Protestant? He saw no difficulty (he never did, when he wanted something badly enough) but she was scrupulous. 'You, I <u>know</u> think it is all right,' she wrote to him on 8 September:

> But do please explain it to me quite fully and [say] what steps exactly you would have to take? I can't bear to think that you would have to ask for absolution for having married me . . . Dear, I don't like to be <u>troubling</u> you about this again . . . but I must fully understand it & <u>why</u> Miss Elliott & Mrs Symons [Catholic acquaintances] evidently disapprove? Miss Elliott said a dispensation should, according to the Catechism, be only given in matters of great urgency or words to that effect. I asked her whether a great wish to marry a particular person was not urgent? She did not seem to think

it was! I could not bear to think that in the eyes of your Church we
were, so to speak, only whitewashed. <u>And nor could you</u>: so explain
it to me, dearest, & I will try & not be stupid.

The year of her engagement was transformative for Milicent.
As she made her own way towards conversion – I cannot detect
that NM put any direct pressure on her – she felt a loosening of
the strong constraints which for years had held her emotions in
check. NM's uncomplicated, protecting, patient love was unlike
anything she had known since the death of her father twenty years
before, and it took her a time to get used to it. Her letters protest
her own unworthiness:

> You see, this is a troublesome woman whom you have elected to
> love! I told you so, all along! But she is quite old enough to enjoy
> being called a girl! 34! Old enough to be wiser than she is. Old
> enough to be so much better. But I think careful treatment may
> somewhat reform her. I may, perhaps, love <u>you</u>: I know I feel I
> love everybody better than I did. I am generally at the wrong end
> of things. If I have said one word that has hurt you, my dear, I did
> not mean it.

There were times when she hardly trusted the reality of what had
happened: 'I begin to think that you are a merman, and will one day
leave me sitting on a rocky shore, while you plunge away into a
deep green sea, and are lost to sight among the white horses!'
   NM's replies are love letters. He did not see his second wife-
to-be as a useful housekeeper, stepmother or amanuensis, though
she gladly took on all these roles; Milicent was the 'dear sharer of
my thoughts'. Perhaps he gave full rein to his power of seeing what
he wanted to see, and overlooking difficulties; if so, he was not the
first man in love to have done so. His letters could never have made
Milicent feel that she was second-best to Amy. She was 'sweet &
kind', the 'good dear girl of my heart'; she seemed to 'radiate affection like a bright little star'; 'dear girl you grow more & more what

I admire every time I see you. You are such a perfectly graceful little lady that I delight to see you move and to see you sit still.' He cast her as Andromeda, chained to a rock; as Calypso on her island; as Thackeray's Princess Rosalba from *The Rose and the Ring* [one of NM's favourite books] in prison, surrounded by toads and snakes who kiss her 'pretty bare feet', all images relating to Milicent in the East End, a beacon of loveliness and virtue in a wilderness of squalor and danger. The fact that Milicent had for many years derived deep satisfaction from her work, and that the 'toads and snakes' were students and colleagues of whom she was very fond, he chose to overlook.

As with the young Amy, NM could not resist taking on the role of instructor. He relished the fact of her relative youth – she was thirty-four, he was fifty-five. He loved an eager pupil, and his serious-minded fiancée had a genuine thirst for knowledge. But she was not a thorough-going bluestocking feminist of the type NM found unfeminine and therefore unappealing. (His mother and Aunt Barbara would have been mortified by how unsound he later became on the subject of suffragettes.) In one letter he gives Milicent a detailed explanation of embryology and then writes, 'you seem to take readily to all kinds of mental food. Dear I like you for this & because with it you have a true woman's feelings as well & like to be petted as well as to talk & are happy when I kiss you & when you give me kisses. It is sweet that nothing is left out in you, dear girl of the beautiful eyebrows.'

Milicent's familiarity, the fact that he first met her when she was a small child, enhanced the charm. NM liked continuity and old associations; Milicent understood much of his frame of reference, and she was closely connected to Amy. 'That you loved her adds to my love for you and that I loved her as you know takes not one bit from my love for you.' Amy's unflattering remarks about Milicent's foibles he was luckily able to put to one side.

Life was made easier for Milicent by the fact that her lover understood something of the intricacies of her relationship with her sister. In September she explained that she could not quickly extricate herself from the Ludlow ménage: 'You see, Mabel is not really well, and if she tries to manage things at Scalands, I fear it will all be very muddley and uncomfortable – and there is the danger of her settling down & refusing to move, if she gets established. That has been a great difficulty all these years – of course, to settle down would be good, if she were quite well, but I think at present she is better away from Ludlow.' The short-term solution was for Milicent to take Mabel to France, first to Beauvais and then to Paris.

The French holiday was only a partial success. The idea was that Milicent would after a time leave Mabel there with a companion, a Miss McCartney, but the reality was different. 'I suggested my going back, but Mabel clearly dreaded my leaving, so what can I do but stay? It really is a great thing that she likes having me, for it is not always so.' On good days they went out sightseeing or visiting, but often Milicent had to endure 'a long rather vague afternoon'.

Milicent was at pains to explain her sense of duty. 'Having so to speak shared Hancox and had a mutual home, it has made me more of the same family with them than is usual in the case of a sister, and we seem to stand or fall together. Just now we seem somewhat toppling.' She chided herself for the peremptory way in which she had brought the Hancox arrangement to an end: 'If only one could have the past again, one would show more consideration . . . Perhaps in another world one will make fewer mistakes – and I shall make fewer when I have you to help me in this present world, I believe . . . I want to see you and be with you – and then I feel less wooden . . . Goodnight, my dear: would you like a kiss for every extra day I stay away?' Milicent's conscience was an active organ. NM was right when he wrote, 'I know for certain that my Mil wants to do right & nothing else.'

After their return from France, Mabel was installed in a London flat – 11 Ridgmount Gardens, near Gower Street. Milicent again went to Scalands to supervise Anne and Sylvia (Eira, like John, seems to have been sent to boarding school by this time). Ludlow

vacillated between the two addresses. 'Ludlow brings a rather dismal
account of Mabel,' wrote Milicent on 7 November. 'She doesn't
seem to be "getting on" at the flat, but I dare say it was really his
presence there which was bad. I don't myself see how with no real
occupation anyone can get their nerves straight.' Milicent rather
enjoyed her quiet domestic Sussex life and the company of the little
girls; 'Here I am, amidst glories of gold & copper & sunshine, and
I think the world a very enjoyable spot, and feel sorry for all the
discords I have brought into it . . . Anne and Sylvia are helping the
undergardener pick up rubbish on the lawn, & I have told the nurse
to leave them to this edifying occupation.' As time went on she
looked forward to married life more confidently: 'Yes, we will
have *very* good times together, and make our home, I hope, a place
of rest & peace, whence to wrestle with forces. Does this sound
uncomfortable. I hope not.' But she continued to deprecate herself, sometimes signing letters, 'Your tiresome Mil.' 'Ah, if you
think so much of me, my dear, you will be disappointed – but
there it is – perhaps a blessed blindness will illuminate you always!'
'When you say you look at my photograph & know me thoroughly
now I think "Poor, misguided man." I do indeed.'

NM's letters, in turn, supply Milicent with his own domestic
detail – Ethne playing the piano; dinner at home with Alan, consisting of curried mutton, potato, jam tart, nuts and coffee; a list
of the wages he paid his six servants, which totalled £141.18/– per
annum: 'It seems a terrific sum does it not – yet it is best to pay
them well I think.' When he dined out at a grand function, he sent
her the bill of fare and an account of the conversation; the letters
show a desire to include her in every aspect of his life. He told her
about his patients – 'Old woman with Bronchitis much better, but
disinclined to go home as husband beats her . . . Idiot aged 4 y . . .
Child with tuberculosis of lung (probably) & emphysema (certainly) very cross, age about 3y.' He worried over Milicent's own
health and the risks of living in the East End – 'Do not eat any
more oysters since every one you swallow gives me an anxious
pang.' One of her Bethnal Green associates was suffering from

quinsy; in reply to Milicent's enquiry about it NM gave her a characteristic explanation: 'Quinsy is short for Squinancy derived from low Latin Squinancia which comes from earlier Latin Cynanche & that from Greek [NM gives this word in Greek letters] which means suffocation or as we might say chokyness.

'Do not kiss her.'

He also found her a good audience for his reminiscences; he described his long boyhood walks in Ireland and told her about Walton Hall and its inhabitants: 'I remember the nights so well & in spring the young herons talking in their nests & in winter the moat frozen & a great silver road of moonlight across the snow covered ice.' In every letter he assures her of his love and constancy: 'Dear you shall be loved and served by your man beyond what you can imagine.' By the end of the year, Mabel and Ludlow knew of the relationship. Whether Milicent told them or whether they guessed the truth isn't clear. What is clear is that they strongly disapproved, and said so. Mabel had never quite shaken off the sense that NM was her social inferior, despite his professional eminence. She had opined that Amy had 'thrown herself away'; now her own sister was about to do the same. Worse, he was a Catholic convert. Mabel adhered strictly to the Low Church Anglicanism in which she had been brought up; the Church was crucial to the social hierarchy which organized her world. Even when suffering from depression, it was still usual for her to go to church twice on Sundays. Both she and Ludlow attacked Milicent about NM. Milicent was greatly troubled; NM tried to soothe her. On New Year's Day 1903 he wrote:

> My own: Mabel has been much to you & you a most good sister to her but you know how a wife's love is quite different to that: much more quite different in every way. It made me unhappy to think you were troubled about her view of me or my faith. Do not look at it in that way dear woman mine. Try & come as close to my heart as ever you can and do not let anything but your own conscience & sense of what is the truth guide you.

Typically, he turned the other cheek: 'My Mil you know however cross or unkind Mabel or Ludlow may be I will never bear
them the least ill will since they are of you.' Milicent allowed
sisterly affection to overcome resentment. On 11 January, Mabel
came for a short stay in Bethnal Green, a rare occurrence: 'Mabel
came after all. She had supper at St Mag's & then came to see Miss
Porter and it was delightful to hear Mabel's laughter coming up
from below.'

In February, Milicent was called to the aid of yet another sickly
relative. This time the sufferer was Roddy. Mabel had improved
to the extent that it was possible to leave England without her,
so Milicent agreed to accompany Roddy for what turned into a
three-month stay in France. It's hard to establish what, if anything,
was wrong with Roddy. Victorian and Edwardian letter-writers
talk about ill health a lot but rarely describe symptoms exactly or
give diagnoses. Roddy certainly believed herself to be ill, but this
may have been her way of attempting to rectify years of neglect.
She had spent her life playing second fiddle, first to her sister Amy,
then to her cousin Mabel. Her spells studying art in London and
Paris had been cut short by family demands, so her considerable
artistic talents had never been fully developed. She had been devastated by Amy's illness and death, but as a mere sister had not had
the solace of being a principal mourner; her grief, and her guilty
feeling that she could have done more to comfort Amy, had fes-
tered. Now, in middle age, she found herself stuck at Crowham
at the beck and call of her careworn mother, her gruff, heavy-
drinking father, and Willy and Lionel, the irritating brothers who
seemed determined not to make their way in the world. Her younger
sister Bella was a cheerful companion, but Bella's no-nonsense attitude and hearty outdoorsiness were the antithesis of Roddy's own
quiet and solitary tastes.

It almost seems as if Roddy decided to allow her health to
collapse. This state of affairs continued for some years. In her
memoir, Ethne recalls how Roddy's invalidism at last came to an
end. It was 1908, and Bella was engaged to a local doctor, Walter

Wynne. Just before the wedding, Roddy asked for his opinion on her condition. Dr Wynne told her frankly that there was nothing the matter with her:

> and, courageously, she immediately recovered. I thought at the time that most people, after such a long period of invalidism would have allowed themselves to alter the habit of it gradually, but Roddy left her sofa immediately; she threw away her wraps and her umbrella and on the day of the wedding ran up the hill after the bridal carriage, throwing rice and waving her scarf till they were out of sight. After that she took to gardening and going for long walks and never again indulged in being delicate.

In February 1902, however, Roddy's invalidism was rampant, so she and Milicent travelled to St Jean de Luz to benefit from the air of the Pyrenees. NM had worried about Milicent's health during the winter, and believed that the change of air would benefit her as well. It was at this time that Milicent decided to put aside her religious scruples. On 3 March she wrote to NM: 'Dearest Man, Don't don't don't worry. I am well. Be so too. It's all quite simple, either permission is obtainable, or not . . . In any case, you know, I am going to marry you in September.'

Milicent had not quite made up her mind to convert, though she was corresponding with Father Basil Maturin, the Irish priest who had guided Amy and who had become a family friend. But she had decided to make her engagement public. She told Roddy, who wrote immediately to NM:

> My dear Norman,
>   Milicent told me yesterday of your engagement – that I knew it already I need not say – I hope & think that you & she will be very happy – you know there is only one reason why I could object & I wont say anything about that. I cant at any rate afford to lose one of the best friends I have & one of the kindest people I have ever met . . .

I have been very nice to Milicent. I am very fond of her though
I think you will allow that I did my duty to you by pointing out all
her faults when I was in London – but I did not realize things quite
besides I was thinking as usual only of myself! I apologise.

Please observe that I do not mention my health in this letter but
I will just say that you have not answered my last two wails & I
require a good deal of consoling on that subject as no doubt you
have found out –

You will be glad to hear that I have given Milicent my views on
the Irish character on several occasions – You did not know what a
serpent you were sending abroad with her.

I don't know quite what the 'one reason why I could object'
could be. I think it unlikely that Roddy had strong views about
the religious question. It seems more probable that, out of loyalty
to Amy, she felt NM had moved on too quickly.

Aunt Jenny and Uncle Willy seem to have taken the news
calmly. Their old hostility to NM had been replaced by generous
goodwill towards him and warm and active grandparenting of
Alan, Ethne and Gilla, active at any rate on Jenny's part. She was
particularly good with Ethne, admiring her originality and taking
an interest in the details of her life with a tolerance she had been
unable to find in her dealings with Amy.

Ethne was at Crowham when she received the news of her
father's engagement. On 7 March she wrote back to him, with a
reasonable show of enthusiasm, 'My dearest Papa – Thankyou
for your letter, I am very glad it will make you happy, I do like
Milicent very much & it will be nice to have her to go about with.'
It took her another week to write to Milicent: 'My dear Milicent . . . It is difficult to express things in letters but I am sure we
shall be very happy together, & we do want someone to look after
us you know, & look after things, & I am glad Papa will be happier, as I am sure he will.' To Alan she was more frank: 'the hardest
part will be . . . when the moon is seen in places where the sun
used to be.'

Ethne was able to be polite on paper, but the news was an unwelcome shock. She had assumed that, young as she was, she would be in charge of the Gloucester Place household when she left Dane Lodge:

> Miss Bishop had talked to me about going home to keep house for my father in a way that had made it seem attractive. I knew nothing about housekeeping and, as a matter of fact, all domestic subjects bored me. We had a few cooking lessons at school but I so much disliked the messiness of uncooked food that I had bribed a friend with chocolates to break my eggs for me and after a lesson on cleaning fish I had refused to go to another lesson . . . To think that I should be in charge of the big house in Gloucester Place made me feel important; I did not forsee any difficulties, but had visions of presiding over dinner parties, dressed in new evening frocks, and taking part in the conversation of my father's learned friends.
>
> It was rather a shock therefore, when I received a letter from my father telling me he was going to be married again. I remember Miss Bishop, when I told her, said sympathetically that it was 'too soon', meaning too soon after my mother's death, and I had immediately thought the same.

Ethne had a kind of false memory of Milicent's arrival at Gloucester Place as its new mistress. 'When I left school and went home I seem to remember walking into the drawing-room and finding my stepmother seated on the sofa dressed in a white satin wedding dress.' She adds 'this cannot have been so,' and thinks separate memories had got mixed up (it was usual for a newly married woman to wear her wedding dress to the first few dinner parties of her married life, and Ethne may have been remembering one of those occasions), but the image suggests how strong her sense of displacement was. More extraordinary is Ethne's belief that she accompanied NM and Milicent on their honeymoon. She did not doubt the truth of this memory, and wrote about it in detail; she had a slight illness, she says, so her father ordered her to stay in the hotel all day long:

He and my stepmother would go out for the whole day and I soon got very bored indoors. We had a private sitting-room with silk panelled walls and ornate furniture, but I had nothing to do and nothing to read except Baedeker [the guidebook]. One day, I could bear it no more, and, taking the Baedeker, I went out by myself to explore Paris. I had not gone very far when I met my father and stepmother, who were horrified to find me out alone. My stepmother said girls never walked alone in Paris, but my father was chiefly shocked that I should have been found standing with a Baedeker open in my hand: 'like any American' he declared.

The intriguing thing about this anecdote is that, though it neatly encapsulates the characters of those involved, it was not true. The honeymoon did begin in Paris, but diaries and letters prove that Ethne did not accompany them, but remained at Dane Lodge. The most likely explanation is that they took her to Paris on another occasion. Ethne's false belief that they took her with them on honeymoon only to exclude her by shutting her up in the hotel reveals the strength of her antipathy towards the marriage.

Alan was also taken aback. His father wrote to him at Cambridge telling him that he should be the first to hear the news, and like his sister Alan managed a polite reply. But his private feelings were that 'it was hard to imagine anyone taking my mother's place.' More able to weigh up the situation than Ethne was, he managed to reason his way into thinking it a positive development: 'However it seemed on reflection to be right. Life for my father had become too difficult. He must often have felt lonely. Milicent was not a stranger . . . the tie of relationship helped.'

Milicent herself wrote thoughtfully and sympathetically to her stepson-to-be:

You will naturally be anxious about anything which must so vitally effect his happiness & well-being, in one direction or the other. So I want to tell you that I am very conscious of the honour such a man as your Father has done me in asking me to be his wife, and to

assure you that I feel towards him in such a manner as should enable
me to be as good a one as it is in me to be. I don't ask you to say
much now; I would far rather hear you say in ten years' time that
you feel it has been for his happiness & for yours too. And this I
hope for.

She went on to commiserate with Alan about his fast-approaching
exams. To NM's bitter disappointment, his son found working for
his medical degree a terrible chore (though he loved all other
aspects of his time at Cambridge) and repeatedly failed exams – he
had nightmares about exams to the end of his life. 'I am afraid just
now you are having a bothering time, with June approaching,'
wrote Milicent. 'Let us hope in some other world the good of
examinations may be made clear!'

One person who could be relied upon not to wrap her true feelings in a cloak of politeness was, of course, Aunt Nannie. I'm sorry
that her letters on the subject don't survive; they must have been
unusually poisonous. Milicent sent a sharp reply, showing it to
NM before sending it on: 'What do you think of the enclosed by
way of reply to At N? Would she see the sarcasm? Or is it un peu
fort?' I don't have NM's reaction, but the following year Nannie's
animus against the couple seems to have taken a more active form.
Milicent wrote to NM saying, 'I told Mabel that if At N liked to
come & see me, I would receive her, "in spite of her abominable
behaviour".' Before the marriage, Aunt Jenny made it clear that
she wanted to disassociate herself from Nannie's hostility. 'I wish
Nanny had not behaved like that,' she told NM, 'it makes me sad
to hear of it . . . I hope she will not come to England this year.'

Uncle Ben's opinion can only be inferred. In July, Milicent
wrote to NM, 'It is dreadful about U.B. I do not regard him as
really sane now, but the turn it takes is most deplorable, & surely
would not have come about if he had not let his mind run so much
on money.' This could mean that Ben objected to the engagement
on the ground that NM was after Milicent's (depleted) money, but
the rather detached tone, and the fact that it is a postscript to a

long letter, not headline news, makes me feel that Ben's 'dreadful' behaviour concerns something else. Milicent's letter, too, is written almost five months after the engagement was announced; it would be odd if Ben had only just decided to be 'dreadful' about it. My guess is that Milicent is actually talking about Ben's marriage. It may have been at this time that his separation from Charley was formalized and Ben may have been creating difficulties over the amount of money he gave her. But this is all guesswork. Ben's attitude to NM's remarriage can probably be summarized by a remark Lionel made three years later when he announced his own engagement to his cousin Agnes Wickham: 'Uncle Ben,' said Lionel, 'disapproves of all marriages so he must just be allowed to have a fit.'

Milicent's female friends and colleagues received her news with delight. There was a consensus that Milicent deserved her good luck: 'You have been sadly rushed about & wearied these last two years & more with all your family anxieties & the care of your sister's children.'

The kindest letter of all came from Ethel Portal, still at Laverstoke with her ageing and ailing mother. Milicent forwarded the letter to NM in raptures. 'Is not this a beautiful letter? Do you wonder that I love her? I know she thinks much too highly of me, but she has, more than anybody I know, the gift of drawing out whatever of good there is in anybody . . . If you only knew the miseries of Ethel Portal's life, you would see how sweet it is of her to write of rejoicing.' It would not be many years before NM came to know the miseries of Ethel Portal's life, and indeed all other aspects of her life, more intimately than Milicent could have wished.

Once she returned to England in May, Milicent's preparations for reception into the Roman Catholic Church began in earnest. Having made up her mind, there was no backward glance. Alan described her attitude in his unfinished life of his father:

Having accepted it her views turned inside out & she became uncompromisingly Roman. Her point of view was exactly that of a convinced Communist: my doctrine is right: since I know this I am not prepared to argue. This attitude was not favourable for making proselytes, & she ardently desired to make them. To do her justice she did not try to force her religion upon people who, she knew, held firmly different opinions but she could not resist shewing the flag now and then. 'You see our churches are no longer ours' was the sort of remark she was apt to let fall.

In this she was in utter contrast with Norman whose real reasons for belonging to the Church of Rome were based on association and sentiment. He loved Ireland; most Irishmen were Catholics, Mr Waterton had been a Catholic and, above all, Amy had become one.

. . . Milicent before a meal would bow her head and cross herself. I remember Norman's noticing and giving two taps to his shirt front, in token.

On 13 July Milicent entered the Priory of Our Lady of Good Counsel at Hayward's Heath. She was to spend two weeks here before being 'received'. It was a momentous time for her. On the first night she wrote to NM:

> And I am in Sussex.
> And in a Convent.
> And I do not think I can be the Milicent Ludlow I have always known. But at all events I am your Mil.

On 31 July, the day before her reception, she wrote, 'This is a serious day. I don't feel particularly fit to be received, but I don't think there is any use in putting it off . . . The nuns really are the nicest possible people. I believe they have all been praying for this unworthy person.' For her new middle name she chose 'Catherine', the name of NM's favourite saint.

A month later, on 1 September 1903, NM and Milicent were married as quietly as possible at St Catharine's RC church, Littlehampton. I don't know why Littlehampton was chosen. Milicent

had been staying in a hotel there with Gilla and nurse Eliza Brown
for most of August, for Gilla's annual seaside holiday; NM had
joined them when he could. Perhaps they chose to marry in a place
that had no particular family associations. They had no guests save
Gilla and Eliza Brown, not even Alan and Ethne. After the ceremony they returned at once to Gloucester Place before leaving for
Paris. Ethne wrote from Dane Lodge on the day of the wedding.
'My love & a kiss to you both – Don't take Milicent <u>everywhere</u> <u>at</u>
<u>once</u> & does she know the Italien for a poultice.'

NM spent the two days before the wedding with Miss Willmott, the gardening expert, at Warley Place. Milicent had given
him a pocket book; in it he noted for 1 September:

> 7.45 Missa Divæ Catherinæ eccl.
> Uxorem duxi Milicent
> Festibus E. Brown. Quidam Hibernicus Flavin Cognem, et
> Gillachrist.
> To 94 G.P. post quam in lutetium Pa.

Nine-year-old Gilla, the only one of NM's three children at the
wedding, is also the only one who left no record of his feelings on
the subject.

14. 'Hancox is the place'

The honeymooners returned to Gloucester Place at the beginning of October 1903 after a month in Paris, Florence and Pisa, and
Milicent immediately set about reforming the household. There
were a lot of people to take into consideration, including the three
children: Alan lived there when not at Cambridge, so did Ethne,
from Christmas onwards, when she left school for good, and there
was Gilla, who had started again at a London day school. In addition, there were Eliza Brown, who was still in charge of Gilla seven
years after Amy had worried that he had outgrown her, Jessie Hern
the Scottish parlourmaid who was addicted to drinking mustard-
and-water; Mary and Louisa, housemaid and kitchenmaid; Santi
Paci the Italian butler and his Cockney wife, who was the (deplorable) cook. After years in England, Paci could not manage English
names: 'when people came to call he would announce something
incomprehensible and we would wonder what strange person it
could be, and then someone we knew well would walk in,' remembered Ethne. Paci was loyal and reliable, and above all he was a
Roman Catholic, but the servants were on the whole 'more odd
than capable', as Ethne put it.

It's understandable that Milicent should have wanted to put her
stamp upon the place, but it's equally understandable that in doing
so she would ruffle feathers. '[Milicent] had a passion for cleanliness,' wrote Ethne, 'and I dare say she found the house pretty dirty,
far too full of books, pictures and ornaments. My father would
not let her touch the books but she put away many of the ornaments and took down a great many pictures. There had been pictures on the walls of the staircase and she removed them all when
the walls were painted and would not put any of them back which
made the place seem bare and empty.' During their courtship,

Milicent had expressed anxiety to NM about her place in Ethne's life: 'I can't expect her to like it all round, but in some ways I hope she will have a better time than she would otherwise.' Milicent and Ethne had many interests in common, but despite Milicent's own independent and adventurous life, she persisted in treating Ethne as a child rather than a young woman, and attempted to impose all kinds of restrictions on her. NM chose to deny it, but the atmosphere between them quickly became strained. 'Because I found my stepmother difficult and disapproving in many ways I would not allow myself to acknowledge that I liked anything she did; nor would I admit that I admired anything she admired.'

Milicent was excited to find herself in charge of Ethne's 'coming out'; she took her duties seriously. She decided that Ethne should 'come out' at the Battle Ball, rather than at a London event. In this way, Milicent was underlining her connection to East Sussex. Hancox was still occupied by the inebriates, but there were already plans to repossess it once the lease had expired. Bills and solicitors' letters show that Milicent continued to have responsibility for the cottages on the estate – one rather defeatist note from her solicitor from 1904 tells her that 'the rain still penetrates the Bungalow [the Playfords' single-storey brick cottage] & I think it is hopeless to attempt to keep it out.' By bringing her débutante stepdaughter to the Battle Ball, Milicent was making a statement about her own future. 'I remember little of the event,' wrote Ethne, 'except that I had the traditional white ball dress of a débutante and that we arrived very late at the ball because my stepmother had declared that in her young days that was the correct thing to do.'

Once 'out', Ethne was required to entertain the medical students NM invited to dinner in strict rotation. 'Before they came he would tell me their names and chief characteristics and hobbies, so that I should know what to talk to them about.

'"Mr Jones," my father would say, "climbs mountains, lives in Tooting. Mr Brown, plays football, comes from Devonshire –."' Milicent was, in Amy's phrase, a 'penuriously extravagant' hostess.

She liked to entertain often, but hated to waste food, so she gave dinners on consecutive nights so that some of the food could be used twice. 'The food at these dinners was a little dull, but fairly good, but I think the wine must have been really nasty,' Ethne wrote. 'I was not allowed to drink any but I noticed that our guests seldom accepted a second glass.' NM was no longer a strict tee-totaller, but he was no connoisseur. 'My father . . . had no taste for it and I remember at one time, when he was feeling tired and thought that some champagne that someone had given him would do him good, he had a glass of ginger beer beside his glass of champagne and sipped them alternately.'

Plans for Ethne's future were surprisingly vague. Ethne herself longed to go to an art school in Paris, but this was vetoed. 'I was given to understand that the life of an art student there was too wild and dangerous for a girl of my age.' NM had never put his daughter in for any public examinations nor steered her in the direction of any particular course of study. Despite her campaigning forebears, she had grown up with the idea that women and careers didn't mix: 'My father had told me that a few very clever women had careers, and about one in particular, who could read Greek quite easily, but, he said, she was very plain and had hairs on her chin and I felt he told me about her as a warning of what might happen to me if I tried to have a career like a boy.' But now, to divert her from the art-school idea, NM made an effort to get her into Girton. As 'founder's kin' her fees would have been reduced. Ethne spent a trial weekend there; it was not a success:

I had hardly spent a couple of hours at Girton when I decided that nothing would induce me to stay there as a student.

I arrived just before the evening meal and met a girl carrying a little bunch of flowers. 'I think Miss So and So is so <u>sweet</u>' I heard her say as she laid the posy by the female Don's plate. That evening at bedtime I was told to partly undress and then to come along in my dressing-gown to one of the student's bedrooms. There we all sat about on chairs, or on cushions on the floor and were served

with china mugs full of cocoa. I had liked cocoa as a child but from
that moment I took a dislike to it; it became symbolic of schoolgirl
behaviour at its worst . . . The same fervent friendships, the same
'crushes' for mistresses, the same living in a herd.

'No thankyou' I said when I got home. 'I should simply <u>hate</u> to
go to Girton.'

Cousin Flora Smith, the rich, childless and usually benevolent
sister of Valentine, took Ethne under her wing. Cousin Flora 'had
been an invalid all her life, the sort of invalid who, beautifully
dressed, lay on a sofa, but who was capable of springing up from it
with great agility and who also was able to enjoy the rather rich
and delicious food served at her table'. Flora was a good singer. She
would accompany herself on the piano, but the effect was marred
by her Skye terrier, who 'would sit under the piano and almost
drown Cousin Flora's notes by a mounting crescendo of howls'.

Flora encouraged Ethne to take music seriously. Singing lessons
were not a success, but Ethne became proficient at the violin and
the piano, and was a second violinist in the Handel Society's orches-
tra. She often had rests of over a hundred bars, but a friendly drum-
mer who had very little to do 'good-naturedly counted out my
rests for me and poked me in the back with his drumstick when I
was due to play'. But art remained her first love. Eventually Flora
chose an art school for her (Cope and Nichols, in South Kensington) and bullied NM and Milicent into allowing her to attend.

*

Amy had been afraid that NM would put undue pressure on Alan
to follow him into the medical profession; her fears were justified. As
Alan explained, years later, in a letter to his fiancée, Mary Burrows:

My father's views were old-fashioned. He held that there were 5
professions open to a gentleman barring special aptitudes for art
etc supposing him to have missed his chance of entering the Navy.
They were politics, the army, the Church, the law & medicine . . .

well for us politics & law were ruled out for lack of money, the
Church for lack of vocation & so there wasn't much choice. I knew
nothing of the army & disliking my imagined picture of it chose
medicine & frankly I wish I hadn't.

After leaving Cambridge, Alan continued his medical studies at
Bart's, but in sad contrast to his father's meteoric rise he struggled,
frequently retaking the exams he dreaded and finding little to interest and much to disgust him in the practical side of the work. He
was a little more interested in the history of medicine and, like his
father, he was observant about the way employment and living
conditions affected health. His medical training took him into the
poorest dwellings of the East End; he made notes in the diaries he
kept every day of his adult life about houses crawling with vermin
and babies dying through ignorance.

For a naval career, Alan should have put in for a cadetship at a
very young age, but it was a great pity that NM did not recognize
the potential for a non-naval career involving ships and sailing, for
Alan had a tremendous passion for all things nautical. His chief
interest was in what he called 'the comparative anatomy of ships'.
He had an encyclopaedic knowledge of the history of sailing ships
and the intricacies of their construction, and he sometimes forgot
that others did not necessarily share his expertise. In the 1920s he
wrote a classic book on the subject, *The Last Days of Mast and Sail*.
Meanwhile, in his twenties, he spent as much time as he could on the
river or sea, or stripping down and rebuilding old boats. His expeditions were not without incident. Quite often he saw bodies floating in the Thames; the bend in the river meant that they congregated
at Greenwich. An old boatswain explained that it wasn't worth
fishing them out since you only got eighteen pence for them.

Alan had a far easier relationship with his stepmother than Ethne
did. Because he was older, and male, Milicent felt less need to control or advise him. He was able to take a detached view; while he
laughed at her foibles, he respected her courage and energy. For
her part, Milicent was warm in her admiration of Alan's unaffected

good nature. She criticized Ethne for being selfish, wayward and untidy, but Alan she described in a letter to NM as 'so simple and good'. She longed for his conversion, and had a (misplaced) confidence that this would one day occur. 'Don't you think he is sure to get the Christian religion in the end? Perhaps we don't pray enough about it.'

Though Milicent's zealotry could hardly have been further removed from Rebecca Moore's 'scientific atheism', relations between the old feminist and her new daughter-in-law were cordial. 'I am very desirous to see you all at home with dear Milicent presiding,' wrote Rebecca from her little house in Richmond. On 23 December 1903 she was at Gloucester Place to celebrate her eighty-fourth birthday with them all; a cake bearing the full number of candles was provided. But she was beginning to feel the weight of her years. She paid her last visit to Gloucester Place in March 1905; in April she developed pneumonia. Milicent and NM were both assiduous about visiting her, and NM provided a nurse. 'I had hoped she was getting over the attack,' wrote NM in his casebook. '- I had been with her every night – On Monday May 8th I left her at 9.40 for work in London & she kissed me & though weak I hoped to find her a little better but she became suddenly worse & Milicent & I went at once on receiving a telephone message at 7.45. We arrived at 8.45 she had died at 7.50. May she rest in peace.' A niece of Rebecca's wrote to NM, 'How her bright intellect remained the strongest part to the end.'

Rebecca's 'bright intellect' and unshakable principles had carried her through an era of change and turmoil. Her grandson Alan wrote:

When she was born in 1819 George III was king. Travel, as for the preceding millennium, depended mainly on sails and horses. Fires were lighted and guns were fired by flint and steel. Executions were frequent and public. There were no anaesthetics. She was 12 when the Reform Bill was passed. She was 17 when the Atlantic was first crossed by steam. Railways were rapidly displacing coaches in her twenties. She was in her fortieth year when <u>The Origin of Species</u> was published and in her fiftieth when compulsory education was introduced. In her sixties the discovery of the part played by micro-organisms in disease and other pathological processes was giving medicine precision and revealing new possibilities in surgery. She saw the first photographs and the rise of telegraphy. She saw the telephone come into every day use, electric light and trains and railways. Bicycles with pneumatic tyres had made a quiet revolution since she was 70. Six years later motor-cars were dashing about at 12 miles an hour. Probably she thought X-rays more interesting than them or the moving pictures. One can be sure she had read of electrons, and wireless telegraphy.

Unlike many old people, Rebecca accepted, even welcomed, change, and never complained. 'I never saw her out of temper,' wrote Alan. 'Her faith in progress and in the goodness of human nature was unbounded.'

Though Rebecca had averred that she would simply 'go out like a candle', NM and Milicent, of course, believed no such thing. Decisions taken about Gilla were guided by the fact that he was the only one of the three children to be brought up as a Catholic. For NM, the biggest wrench was relinquishing the idea of sending him to Eton. NM, having reluctantly left school at fourteen, had a reverence for the place; he was fascinated by the traditions of such an ancient establishment. Sending Alan to Eton had had a great significance for him; luckily, Alan had loved it. As a 'wet bob' he hadn't needed to trouble himself with the team sports at which he did not shine; instead, he spent hours on the river, a marvellous freedom for a teenage boy.

But if Gilla was to be a true Catholic, Eton would not do. In 1906, NM withdrew his name from the waiting list. 'How silly of me to fret about it,' he wrote to Milicent. 'I am clear that it is right & that also there is a false glamour about Eton to me. It looks like a heaven of boys but is not one. It is a nice place but the true heart of all is not there.'

A year after his father's remarriage, the sheltered, rather isolated nursery life that Gilla had always known came to an abrupt end. A Catholic boarding prep school in Bournemouth was chosen for him, called Ladycross. Milicent, who did not in any case like power-sharing, decided that when Gilla went away to school, Eliza Brown would be surplus to requirements. Psychologically, her timing was poor, and she seems to have broken the news tactlessly. Eliza had served the family faithfully since Gilla's birth; she was credited with having saved his life during his sickly babyhood; she had done her best to hold things together in the desolate aftermath of Amy's death. Ethne remembered her fondly and gratefully, though her air of 'unbroken calm' could be exasperating. 'She seldom showed any emotion. I remember that at Christmas time, when she was given some present which we all knew she really liked, all she would say was: "thank you, I'll put it away." And it would go into the top drawer of the chest of drawers where she kept her treasures. Once a week she had an afternoon off and used to visit a friend called Miss Lacey. Once, when I asked her what they did, she replied: "we 'as a nice cup-er tea, then we takes off our bodices and lays on the bed."' Given her marching orders by Milicent, Eliza broke out of her usual reserve. NM was away in Ireland at the time. He wrote to Milicent, 'I was sorry to hear of Nurse's hysterical attack but I feel what we are doing is necessary for the child's good. Of course she had thought of staying on always & indeed so had I till it was clear it would be wrong.'

This was in September 1904; NM had taken Alan and Ethne to Northern Ireland. Their ultimate destination was Rathlin Island, but on the way they visited many of their father's boyhood haunts. 'There were so many recollections in it that I could hardly keep from crying,' NM told Milicent. In his eagerness to show his children the places that meant so much to him, he – as usual – overlooked the fact that he was wearing them out. Ethne remembered forcing her eyelids apart with her fingers as she tried to listen to the facts her father was telling her about every town and village they passed through, in a variety of horse-drawn vehicles. The

holiday was by no means restful. Reaching Rathlin Island involved
a long voyage in an open boat, through stormy seas. They stayed in
a primitive cottage; the beds were so flea-ridden that Ethne preferred to sleep on the floor. 'The bracing air of Rathlin made us
very hungry,' remembered Ethne, 'but even so, I found it difficult
to eat the cheesy-tasting potato cakes which were as heavy as lead
and the strongly-flavoured hard boiled eggs. More than once I was
given one with a half-formed chicken in it but I was so ravenous
that I ate what I could even of that sort.'

Meanwhile, Milicent was having a less adventurous though
more comfortable bucket-and-spade holiday with Gilla at Seaford.
'I hope you grow intimate with the Gilla it will be so good for
him,' wrote NM.

The holiday at Seaford was ten-year-old Gilla's last taste of freedom before he started boarding at Ladycross. The few letters I have
from this time show what a problem spelling was for him, a fact
which his father often bewailed. On 12 November 1905 he wrote
about his confirmation: 'The name I took was St Alutious I no that
is not the rite way to spell it we were confirmend by the Bishop of
portsmouth . . . I can not think of anything else to say.'

In obedience to Amy's dying request, Ethne had put thoughts
of conversion to one side until she reached adulthood. In 1906,
aged twenty, she returned to the idea, influenced less by her father
and stepmother than by a combination of her mother's memory
and the influence of some glamorous older friends, the Miss Fitzgeralds, who were Irish Catholics. 'I forget to whom I first confided my decision to change,' Ethne wrote, 'but I remember telling
my stepmother about it one day when we were putting some flowers
in water in the back drawing room. She blushed with pleasure. "It
was the one thing you lacked," she exclaimed, and I was surprised
by the affection in her voice and, I am afraid, not grateful for it.'

Ethne was prepared for conversion by Father Basil Maturin, the
Irish priest who had advised both Amy and Milicent. His eloquence swept her doubts and worries aside. What, for instance,
should she do if she found herself at Crowham on a Friday, and

Aunt Jenny had prepared a specially good meat dinner? 'Was it cowardice to eat it up for fear of hurting her feelings, or ought I to have refused the cutlets and asked for fish, even though I knew it was unobtainable at short notice? . . . Father Maturin . . . said it was more important to please my grandmother than to fast and gave a special dispensation for when I visited Crowham.'

Ethne stayed at the Haywards Heath convent, where Milicent had been prepared. It was a closed order; the nuns were only allowed to receive visitors when building works were being carried out, which meant that rebuilding was often called for. 'Chère Mère', the cheerful Mother Superior, became Ethne's close confidante; Ethne's religious fervour was, for a short time, strong.

Gilla, who never seems to have had any doubts about his faith, wrote to Milicent near the end of his summer term, 'Now I know that Ethne is a Catholic sumhow it makes the days go much faster. I am longing to sea her.' On the other side of the sheet he adds a postscript expressing a recurrent family concern: 'IMPORTANT NOTICE DON'T LET FATHER overwork himself and get ill.' He sent a separate letter to his father on the same day. On the back of the envelope he wrote in large letters, 'THIS TIME NEXT WEEK WERE SHALL I BE OUT OF THE DEPTHS OF MISERY.'

*

Mabel and Ludlow maintained their frosty attitude towards Milicent's marriage. Though ties were never completely severed, for the next few years the two couples met only rarely. From Scalands, the Ludlows had moved to Glottenham, put at their disposal by Uncle Ben. In the summer of 1906 they were hosts to Aunt Nannie, and also to Willy and Jenny. This was a major coup for Jenny; it had been years since she had persuaded Willy to leave Crowham even for a day. Ben gave his blessing to the gathering but he did not join them; he was frail and tottery and forgetful, and spent most of his days at one or other of his London clubs.

Aunt Nannie, having deprived herself of affectionate contact with Milicent, turned her attention to Bella, now in her twenties and still living at Crowham with her parents. Physically, Bella resembled her oldest sister, Amy, and Aunt Jenny took many photographs of her with her head wistfully tilted sniffing roses or fingering apple blossom. But her delicate appearance was deceptive. She was a robust, humorous girl – Alan called her Bella the Jester – who was cheerfully dismissive of many of the family's 'sacred cows'. At Gloucester Place, describing an intellectual parlour game called the Quotation Game, Amy had once reported to Alan that 'Bella got on very well because she simply & quietly cheated.' Alone amongst her sisters, Bella escaped the family curse of weak lungs. This was probably thanks to her penchant for outdoor pursuits. Old Willy disapproved of his daughter's habit of cycling all over the country, but it may have saved her life. Aunt Nannie approved of Bella's disregard for the limitations her parents tried to impose. She went to watch Bella take part in an all-female cricket match and treated the twenty-two cricket girls to a grand tea afterwards.

However, not even Bella always escaped the ire of the Dragaunt. Ethne described Aunt Nannie at Crowham. She was 'a thin, upright, long-faced person who dressed in black silk and seldom smiled . . . When she was really annoyed she would not speak at all and Bella and I once had to sit through a silent dinner because we were going to a dance and were dressed in low-necked dresses of which she disapproved.' A typical argument between the elderly brother and sister occurred on the same visit:

They were disputing the points of the compass.

'I know, and I beg to inform you,' said Aunt Nannie (it was her favourite mode of address), 'that <u>that</u> is the north' and she pointed to a corner of the dining room. Grandpapa disagreed, pointed to a different corner and said he could show her a compass to prove he was right. Willy [junior] was sent to fetch the compass and came back with two or three. Aunt Nannie barely glanced at them.

'I <u>know</u> . . .' she repeated. 'And the compasses are wrong!'

Another version of this story has Nannie surreptitiously attempting to alter the direction of the compass needle with the blade of a knife.

*

Uncle Ben's travelling days were over. He lived in a set of rooms at 37 Bury Street, St James's, where he was looked after by servants, and was often visited by Ludlow, and by Dr Neale, his companion on the *Eira*'s final voyage. He divided his days between the Reform and the Oxford and Cambridge Club, where he read the newspaper, conversed with all comers, and dozed by the fire. His ability to recognize people and remember names declined rapidly. NM often saw him at the club or in the street; sometimes Ben was friendly and lucid, but at other times he showed no recognition. This enabled NM to watch him unobserved. It is sad to find Ben loudly denouncing his cousin Valentine Smith – Valentine, the energetic and generous brother of Flora who had joined Ben in many of his adventures and offered large amounts of his own money for the relief of the *Eira*. In December 1906, when Milicent was convalescing in Switzerland, NM told her of a further encounter: 'I looked up & there was the Polar Bear very old, [he] shook hands and said "I hope Amy is better I was sorry to hear she was ill" & I said "Yes Milicent" & he said "Yes Milicent" quite sensibly. I said "I will tell her you asked" & he said "Yes do." '

The problem was that this increasingly erratic old man still had power over his own considerable fortune and over the lives of his sons Val and Phil. Val joined the Navy, but the venture was short-lived and seems to have been followed by some kind of mental breakdown. At the beginning of 1907 he was at Deal, apparently receiving a course of psychiatric treatment from Risien Russell, a doctor from Demerara. Charley wanted her son to go to Cambridge that autumn; Ben said that he would not pay for Cambridge, but that Val could live with him 'and become a life member of the Royal Institution'. This does not sound like a suitable arrangement for a boy of nineteen.

Eventually it was agreed that Dr Risien Rutsch should be

authorized to decide whether Val was fit enough to go to Cambridge. He declared that he was; Ben agreed to pay; and Val went up to Trinity in October. A year later, NM, at the club but this time unrecognized, eavesdropped on a conversation Ben was having with another old man. He jotted down some of their talk on a couple of postcards. The two old men agreed that their children were 'a good deal of trouble'; 'Yes, if they're not old enough to have any sense.' 'My son was in the Navy,' said Ben, 'now he's at Cambridge going in for singing.' 'That won't do,' said his companion. 'No regular system there.' Ben appeared to agree. 'Children are very troublesome, very very – they begin to have wills of their own when they're growing up.'

NM's scribbled notes are hard to decipher, but it looks as though, when asked how many children he had, Ben replied that he had only one. The remark about Cambridge shows that Val was the one he was thinking of. Either I've misread the notes, or Ben's dementia had caused Phil to drop from his mind. Or, possibly, relations with Phil were so bad that Ben disowned him. There were other rumours, too. My mother was told that there were bullet marks in the panelling at Scalands where one of the sons had tried to shoot his father. Whether or not this is true, the very existence of the story indicates the extent of the family dysfunction.

Over the next year, 1909, it became clear that Ben was no longer fit to manage his own affairs. Charley tried to get a legal injunction to transfer control to Val, who had come of age. She was worried that other people were writing Ben's cheques for him, including, possibly, Ludlow. Ben had had a good business brain. Of all his siblings, he had been the one who knew how to make his money grow. Now, aged eighty-one, he would authorize people to sign cheques on his behalf and forget ten minutes later that he had done so.

As the eldest son, Val was the natural person to take responsibility for his father's affairs. But Val's history of mental illness, combined with the fact that he was sent down from Cambridge (history doesn't relate his crime), caused members of Ben's inner circle, including Ludlow and Dr Neale, to attempt to put a legal block on his rights. The court found against Val. Charley, naturally, was indignant; she asked Milicent what she should do, and Milicent prevailed upon NM to examine Ben to establish the truth about his mental and physical fitness.

On Christmas Eve 1909, NM called on Ben in his rooms in St James's. The very fact that Ben showed, at most, only intermittent recognition of the man he had first admired, then reviled, feuded with and been reconciled to, illustrates the extent of his degeneration.

NM sent a copy of his report to Milicent. He was received at Bury Street by Dr Neale and Ludlow, who then left him alone with the 'patient'. 'He received me most courteously & offered me his own chair which I persuaded him to take. We conversed chiefly by the help of a speaking tube on account of his deafness.' Ben did not understand why he was under scrutiny. He thought it had something to do with 'one afternoon in Scotland' when he went 'up a valley . . . had a lunch & some speaking & singing went on . . . someone gave me my health & I had too much to drink.' He could not name Dr Neale, who had left the room only minutes before, and said that Ludlow was 'the General'. 'He then said that his sister was coming from Rome & he should not leave London until he had seen her & then said "General Ludlow knows that."'

Ben was vague about his age and his address:

He gave me the name of his place in Sussex Scalands but could not tell me when he had last been there . . . I asked him what family he had & he said he had two boys. I asked him how old they were & he said someone said the eldest was 17 but he doubted it and thought he was less than 17 & that he had never thought much about it . . . I asked where Mrs Leigh Smith [Charley] lived & he said 'the other side of the water'. I asked what water he meant & he said 'the river that goes into the Thames'. He said he had not seen her for more than a year. He said he had forgotten how long she had been away from him . . . He said there had been a difference. I asked what the difference was & he said he would rather not say

but he 'gave her much more money'. (Evidently he was thinking of
the separation & not of the present enquiry.)

Ben could not name his solicitor and seemed all but unaware of
the dispute in question:

> I asked him if there had been any question about his fitness to man-
> age his affairs. He said he should not bother about a little thing like
> that but dared say there had been any amount of squabbling . . .
> I asked if he had signed any letter or paper opposing proceedings &
> he said he had forgotten all about it. He said he should not think
> anything of it because if you paid attention to that sort of thing
> you might always be worried . . . He said he could not help laugh-
> ing at anybody wanting to know about his affairs.

NM spent about three-quarters of an hour with Ben. The old
man could not say what his income was or how near they were to
Christmas, but he showed NM a map of the polar regions and was
able to point out where he had been. For NM there was great
pathos in the spectacle of his old opponent, a man who had had
unshakable belief in his own powers, reduced to dependency on
those he had once sought to control. But his spirit, though subdued, was not broken: 'He could not tell me when he last went on
an Arctic expedition, but said if anyone asked him to go he would
very likely go again.'

Nowadays, given NM's intimate and intricate connections with
the 'patient', the writing of this report would be considered unethi-
cal, as it was to be used as evidence in court. But in the event the
report was almost certainly fair. NM had always been able to
detach his professional from his personal life. Medicine, as he told
Milicent, 'does not exclude even the greatest of villains from its
charity'; besides, NM never bore grudges, and had long ceased to
regard the old Polar Bear as a villain.

A couple of weeks later, on 12 January 1910, Val's appeal against
the ruling was heard. NM was present; he described the proceedings

to Milicent: 'I got there at 11.10: a room high up in the labyrinth of the Law Courts: about half as big again as our dining room here. At a table near the fire an old man Fischer with a secretary sitting beside him: In front of him a big table & on the opposite side seated in wigs three Counsel.' NM drew a seating plan. Besides the lawyers and clerks there were Dr Neale, two other doctors and Val himself. When NM arrived the junior prosecuting Counsel was talking about Val:

said he was sent down by the authorities of the University & spoke of him as 'this boy'. The Master who seemed a kindly old man said, 'Mr ---- You have used an expression you ought not to have used this gentleman is of age.' The Counsel apologised . . . The Master said 'it is not fair to use the expressions you have used to prejudice this young man I have read the affidavits & his affidavit & I am of opinion that nothing took place which can justly be urged against him. He did not act wisely. Young men often fail in wisdom but it is right to be careful what is said about a young man just entering life & the evidence you have produced does not justify any reflexion on Mr Valentine Leigh Smith's character . . . I may say at once that I am inclined to appoint him as the natural person to look after his father's property: his father is clearly unfit & unable to do so & if left to himself is the kind of person in his present state likely to get into the hands of designing persons. I do not like at all the way in which persons who had no particular right to do so have signed cheques for him. It would be a very grave slur upon his son not to appoint him . . . but . . . as it is a considerable estate & he has no experience it will be an advantage to him to have the help which the official solicitor's experience can give him' . . . Then all rose. Neale spoke to me good-humouredly said he disagreed. Woollacombe's clerk (Woollacombe was the solicitor acting against Val) said 'Not fair: I think we shall appeal.'

I ought to have added that the master said Uncle Ben ought to have better rooms & be made much more comfortable than he is; & that he should order him to have more spent on him . . . It looks

as if Uncle Ben has generally thought Ludlow was your father.
They evidently don't think Ludlow so innocent of trying to gain
influence as you do . . . I went to Morpeth Terrace [Charley's London flat] & saw Val who was giving lunch to a Father McKenna.
. . . Val had telegraphed his mother. He said 'I knew Milicent
would do all she could for me' & spoke nicely to me . . . It seemed
very just & kind & sensible the whole thing I thought.

Shortly before Amy's death, Ben had told her in a letter that
he meant to hang on another ten years to see his children had a
'straight start' in life. The ten years had passed, but Ben's hopes for
Val at least had fallen miserably short.

Meanwhile, Milicent and Charley had grown close. They were
exactly the same age, and their shared religion was a strong bond.
In recent years they had both shared the experience of falling from
Ben's favour, and of struggling to bring up difficult adolescents.
Milicent, always energetic on behalf of the people she approved
of, was assiduous in her attempts to help Charley deal with Val's
difficulties. When Val was in London Milicent carted him off to
concerts and recitals and invited him to meals at Gloucester Place.
Alan co-operated with her attempts to prevent the strange young
man from drifting out of the family's reach. He, too, organized
outings with Val, and Val seems to have enjoyed Alan's company as
much as he enjoyed anybody's. Alan was able to look with amusement at his cousin's eccentricities, even when they disadvantaged
him. On one occasion, Alan set out on a journey across Sussex on
foot. Val lent him a rucksack, in which he put a cold pheasant for
Alan to picnic on. Val walked the first lap of the journey with him
– pointing out a stone wall, which, he said, kept tumbling down,
and would never be sturdy because it had been wrongfully built on
common land – and then bade him farewell. When, after several
hours' walking, Alan sat on a tree stump to eat his meal, he found
the pheasant was cold indeed. It was raw. 'I had bought a bottle of
ginger beer, & this with some bread, some nasty meat lozenges &
some chocolate had to serve for lunch.'

Aunt Charley reciprocated by taking a great interest in the lives of Alan, Ethne and Gillachrist. The boys found her amusing and appreciative; with Ethne she was a little too controlling. Like Milicent, she seems to have felt more need to influence Ethne than her brothers, and Ethne's dreamy untidiness was irritating to the neat, elegant, well-organized Frenchwoman. In 1906 she invited Ethne for a long stay at Pont de l'Arche, her house near Rouen, the aim being to improve Ethne's French. Ethne enjoyed larking about with Phil, then a schoolboy at Eton, but the visit ended badly. Phil dared Ethne to swim across the Seine; she succeeded, and both Phil and Charley were impressed, but Ethne caught a chill and was soon seriously ill. Charley called in a nervous young doctor, whose embarrassed attentions made matters worse. A hired nurse sat by Ethne's bedside incessantly munching baguettes (she had 'eating diabetes', she explained) and failing to raise her patient's spirits: 'My last patient was just like you . . . just your age . . . just twenty, she was . . . she had fair hair, just like yours . . . she made a beautiful corpse.'

Ethne became delirious. Alarmed, Charley sent for NM and Milicent. Milicent wanted to take over the nursing, but this was not a great success. 'She was even more modest than the young doctor and seemed determined not to catch a glimpse of my body. She dabbed some soap onto my chest and only half wiped it away, all under cover of the bedclothes; consequently, I was left feeling damp and sticky.' NM wisely ordered the cessation of all treatment. 'All you want,' he told his daughter, 'is to be left in peace.'

Earlier in the same year, Milicent had herself been taken ill while staying at Pont de l'Arche. She had had a slight haemorrhagic attack, but had made a good recovery. However, in October, at Gloucester Place, she suffered a more severe haemorrhage, and tubercule bacillae were found. NM's feelings can be imagined. The discovery of penicillin was many years in the future; NM ordered the only kind of treatment then known to help tubercular patients. As Amy had done, Milicent was to spend the winter months abroad. But instead of sending her to a warm climate he

installed her in a specialist convalescent hotel at Davos in Switzerland, where all the guests were either sufferers from TB or their
friends and companions.

It was decided that Ethne should accompany Milicent. Aunt
Jenny protested, anxious lest Ethne should catch the disease, but
Ethne longed to go, because her Catholic friends, the admired
Miss Fitzgeralds, would also be there. A friend of Milicent's came
too, a Miss Bryant, who (according to Ethne) was very ugly and
smelled of oatmeal, but Ethne did not have to spend much time in
uncongenial company. The invalids lay on their sunny balconies
encased in fur bags for a specified number of hours each day. They
clutched hot water bottles; hot water pipes ran the length of the
balconies. The snow lay thick; the days were bright and crisp, but
at night the temperature sank to as low as −34°F. Here Milicent sat
from November to April, drinking milk to fatten herself and reading the letters from NM that arrived up to three times a day. Miss
Bryant ran errands and kept her company while Ethne and her
friends spent the days skating, tobogganing, riding in horse-drawn
sleighs, drinking cherry brandy and chatting in the bright sun
while the band played on the shore of the frozen lake. Ethne never
tired of sketching the mountains, which seemed to change colour
every time she looked at them, but she had to use pastels rather
than her usual watercolours because 'even sitting in the sun the
water in my pot would freeze.'

It was at this time that plans for the reclamation of Hancox got
under way. NM was seriously worried about Milicent, and thought
that the only way to give her a healthy future would be to get her
out of the sooty London air as often as possible. For the schoolboy
Gilla, too, Hancox would be a far healthier place than London in
which to spend his holidays. Gilla spent as much time as he could
birdwatching and collecting eggs, nests, bones, butterflies and
insects; to give him the run of the fields and woods of Hancox
would be ideal. NM himself needed quiet and seclusion. He was
about to embark on the writing of his great *History of St Bartholomew's Hospital*, which he had been preparing for years. Besides, he

longed for a place he could truly call home. He wrote to Gilla, 'Hancox is our home too when I give up this house [Gloucester Place] & grow old I hope to live there altogether. Old Mr Waterton used to say to me when I was a very little older than you are "Normando" (so he called me) "when you are old I hope you will have a place in the country & then you will enjoy the birds & will remember me as you sit in the sun or walk about" - & now Hancox is the place.'

Thinking about Hancox helped the months of separation pass more quickly. 'You and I are so close,' NM told Milicent, 'that space is nothing . . . How fortunate about Hancox if we had it not we should have had to take a country house.' NM's letters are as loving as ever. Writing from Bart's, he tells her that 'I ordered some coffee & biscuits & had them by a fine fire here. I have put a chair to represent you my own dear Mil.' Alone at home, he tells her of the substantial solitary dinner he has eaten – soup, partridge, mashed potato, bread sauce, cauliflower, apple pie, custard, bread, butter, 'reddishes' and coffee – wishes she were there to share it, and concludes 'I love Alan Ethne & the Gilla [but] it is you that makes life most to me.'

These are not the letters of a man who feels he has hurried into an unsuitable marriage. As well as showing his affection, NM clearly enjoyed communicating with his wife about his work, his social life, his reading, his feelings and opinions on a range of subjects. He continued the dinner parties for medical students in her absence, and sent her the menus, on which cigarettes were included as well as smelts, goose and apple pie; NM disliked smoking and considered it unhealthy but social convention decreed that at a gathering chiefly consisting of young men, cigarettes would be served. In one letter, NM wrote, 'I wish I were a poet to describe really some of the things I see,' to which Milicent replied with fervour: 'You need not wish you were a poet, for you are one, or you would not see all you do see. I suppose to express it all in verse is another part of the same gift . . . But surely to feel & see is the inner essential part.'

Milicent's letters show her frustration at having to relinquish the reins of the household. 'Do tell the cook to feed Alan up. Wd not soup the last thing be good for him? It is so important in every way.' 'Please give Mrs Hyland orders for what you want for Lent and see that <u>Paci, Jessie & Eleanor</u> (our 3 Catholics) <u>have what is right provided for them</u>.' But long before Lent, Milicent organized the servants' Christmas long-distance. NM, Alan and Gilla joined Ethne and Milicent at Davos (Paci wrote to Milicent assuring her that he had packed enough warm underclothing for her menfolk) so the servants had the run of Gloucester Place, where they were to feast, not to work.

Christmas at Davos was much enjoyed. Alan and Gilla loved the winter sports, though NM's attempts to ski revealed that he had no sense of balance whatsoever. Ethne describes him lying flat on his back in the snow 'contentedly smiling. "I feel," he said, "like the knights at the Battle of Crécy, who, when they fell down, could not rise because their armour was too heavy."'

Back in England in January, NM set about sorting Hancox out; the inebriates were due to vacate the premises on 1 July, and there was a lot to be done. After his inspection of Hancox, described in Chapter One, NM abandoned his hopes that the restoration and redecoration could be carried out by the inmates: 'From the look of the inebriates I do not think it wd be much good to let them do much.' Alan was enthusiastic about Hancox and involved himself fully in the plans. 'I like the oak beams very much,' he told Milicent. 'I think it is a house which lends itself to simple furnishing & plain walls & that kind of thing.' Milicent was heartened by the efforts being made on behalf of her beloved house. 'I thought a good deal about us: you & me,' she wrote to NM. 'Won't we have a good time? I think we ought to have a second honeymoon after all this! Bless you. Your own M.'

The mountain air had the desired effect upon Milicent. Before she arrived at Davos she weighed 7 stone 7lbs, fully clothed in heavy Edwardian dress. By 14 February she weighed 8 stone 2lbs, a significant improvement – though still not much, especially compared to Ethne who, though only an inch taller, weighed two stone more. Ethne had been a thin child, but had become quite a buxom young woman. This was not surprising if Alan's account in his *Family Magazine* of her usual lunch is to be believed: 'Daily she eats two hot crumpets, a cup of Bovril, ginger beer, several éclairs, & perhaps a doughnut or two & then purchases a few chocolates to sustain her during the afternoon.'

By mid-April Milicent was strong enough to return home. The prospect cheered NM greatly: '11th April. When I got home there was Alan teaching Gillachrist the Greek Alphabet over tea . . . soon you will appear here again dear star, moon, sun of Gloucester Place.' Ethne would have spluttered with indignation over this last comment. Spending the winter with Milicent had done little in bringing them closer; now, in the spring of 1907, the Miss Fitzgeralds invited Ethne to join them in Italy, but she did so in the face of familial disapproval. NM and Milicent had expected her to help with getting Hancox ready and looking after Gilla, hardly a tempting prospect for a girl just turned twenty-one. 'Perhaps she is like me, rather a selfish person; or perhaps it's only the excitement of youth,' NM wrote to Milicent.

Once home, Milicent threw herself back into her busy life. In 1905, NM had been made Senior Physician of St Bartholomew's, though he never used the title, declaring that all physicians had equal status. Milicent enjoyed the role of Senior Physician's consort, which included the attending of many functions; she handed out the prizes at the St Bartholomew's Hospital sports day. She involved herself once more with her 'factory girls', inviting them to tea and getting up little plays for their entertainment.

Throughout the summer Milicent made frequent visits to Hancox, sometimes with NM, sometimes with Alan, to inspect the work in progress. Alan took photographs with his Box Brownie. Emptied of its furnishings, stripped of its Victorian wallpaper and plaster, the antiquity of the place is strongly felt.

The 'drunkards' had left their mark. The main staircase is ornamented with carved Tudor 'poppy head' finials. Each one is a little different; they march in rhythm from the ground floor to the attic, and when I was a child I thought of them as witches' heads, and always used the other staircase if I could. To me their malign presence was balanced by the benignity of the faces of the family portraits which overlooked them; the poppy heads were almost like my ancestors' evil twins. At the entrance to the attic, where many of the drunkards slept, one poppy head has been snapped off. That would be hard to do; they're tough, solid carvings that have survived hundreds of years. That broken finial is perhaps expressive of the explosive feelings that must have simmered in the house, despite the best efforts of the Church of England Temperance Society.

NM and Milicent spent their first night together at Hancox on 3 September. Alan soon joined them, travelling by train with his bicycle, Paci and 'eleven portmanteaux'. NM bought a visitor's book bound in red leather with marbled endpapers. In gold letters on the front is the Irish expression, *CEAD MILE FAILTE* (A hundred thousand welcomes). On the first page NM wrote another sentence in Irish, which means 'the members of the clan of Moore'. All five signed their names beneath it. Work on the house was by no means finished, especially on the ground floor. 'There is a room ready for you with a fine view from the window. The hall & the Dining Room & the drawing room are not yet ready but we have a cheerful sitting room upstairs,' NM told Gilla. Alan revived his *Family Magazine*, renaming it *The Nebula*, subtitled 'The Crowham Courier and Hancox Herald'.

The magazine records the discoveries at Hancox – the old panelling hidden beneath the Victorian wallpaper, the thirteenth-century pillar, the recess for concealing smuggled goods. In the Christmas number for 1907 the news was that:

the parquet has been laid in the Hall & dining room, mostly of teak, but oak in parts of the Hall. The new panelling for the wall between the hall & dining room was found to be unsatisfactory when it arrived from Crippses Corner [a village a couple of miles off] & as far as it is concerned the work is at a standstill. Some admirable carving by Mr Collier which completes a damaged design has been put up over the Parlour fire place. The said fire place has been enriched . . . with a fireback with a design of anchors & with a date 1588 [the date of the rout of the Armada]. A Latin inscription containing a chronograph & initials is in course of construction by Mr Collier, but we reserve a description till our next number.

This was the inscription described in Chapter One: *Nisi dominus ædificaverit domum in vanum laboraverunt qui ædificant eam.*

The reclamation of Hancox was, on the whole, a period of rejoicing. Alan loved everything about the place. Toiling in London over his medical training, he wrote in his diary, 'I wish I were at Hancox.' He and Milicent tried to make a stand against the floodtide of NM's books that soon engulfed the house, but they knew their cause was hopeless. 'It was amusing at first before nearly every room became a library trying which should be a sitting room and which a dining room,' he wrote wistfully. He bicycled to Rye and bought a ship's bell to hang in the hall; we still ring it now, to summon far-flung people to meals. Arriving at the house alone one summer's day, Alan's diary records, 'Hancox was looking beautiful. I thought the birds seemed to know it was deserted and were bolder . . . As I passed through the Hall . . . I struck the ship's bell that hangs at the foot of the staircase. I wonder why. In a sort of protest against the silence perhaps.'

Alan and Milicent were brought closer by their shared enthusiasm for Hancox. They shopped together for fabrics, flooring material and wallpaper. For Milicent, it was important to refashion Hancox as a fit setting for her married life. It needed to change, not just because of the ravages of the inebriates, but because of the memories of her ménage with Mabel and Ludlow. From the lack of references to the Ludlows in Alan's diary and from the absence of their names in the visitors' book, it seems that the coolness continued. 'Mabel's letter is rubbish,' NM wrote to Milicent at one point, but the nature of the 'rubbish' is lost. However, as only overnight visitors signed their names in the book, the lack of

Ludlow signatures does not mean they never came to Hancox. After several years of living in one or other of Uncle Ben's properties, Mabel and Ludlow had at last acquired a home of their own, Beech Green at Withyham, near Tunbridge Wells. This is easily close enough for a day visit, even without a car. Nonetheless, there's a sense that Milicent kept them at a distance.

Alan, for whom long-standing associations were always important, enjoyed the easy access to Crowham that Hancox afforded. Lionel, now married to his cousin Agnes Wickham, worked (to Aunt Jenny's disgust) as a chemist at the recently founded cordite factory at Aruvankadu in the Nilgiri Hills in India, but the three unmarried siblings, Roddy, Willy and Bella, still lived at Crowham in much the same way as they had always done. Alan went out shooting with Willy (who was by far the better shot); Roddy and Bella often bicycled over and practised archery or croquet on the Hancox lawn.

For Gilla, too, the link with Crowham provided a happy sense of continuity. Having been rejected by the naval academy at Osborne, he started at the Oratory School, Birmingham, in September 1907. The regime at the Oratory was fairly harsh; homesick and nervous, Gilla took comfort from thoughts of future holidays in Sussex. 'I am getting much more used to it,' he told his father on 30 September, 'but still things take rather a long time to get past . . . I felt quite relieved when yesterday I saw a robin in a tree and a blackbird flying overhead with a bit of something in its mouth . . . I am so looking forward to next holidays at Hancox.' His next letter sounds a little more confident, and is also wholly typical: 'Can I learn boxing as there is a class. I think it is 10/– extra a term. A boy has given me a heron's egg it is about 2ins long and light Blew in colour. Can you tell me if a bird called the Hoopoe, and another one called the Golden Oriole have ever been found wild in England. Would it be possible for me to become a <u>Naturalist</u> . . . when we live at Hancox we must have some animals.'

Gilla's love of natural history was his great point of contact with his father, who patiently answered his youngest child's many questions about birds and reptiles, and filled his letters to him with explanatory sketches. He sent him a collection of essays on Charles Waterton, which he had edited. Gilla loved it. 'It makes me long to go to the Oronoco and Amason, who knows perhaps some day I might, anyhow I wish I could, don't you think that next holidays I could sleep on the floor with a block of wood for a pillow . . . Please answer about the skin of the Bussard.' Once at Hancox, Gilla kept ferrets and attempted to breed lizards. There is a photograph of his bedroom, its walls ornamented with horns, skulls, feathers, and pictures of creatures of all kinds.

NM's letters to Gilla show an ability to enter into the boy's concerns; he also selected details of his own activities that he thought would be of interest: '1st June 1908. This morning I went to St James' Palace to what is called a levee. The king sits on his throne & you walk up to him & your name is read out & you bow & then walk on. There were many officers in uniform & naval officers, and Mohametans from India in turbans, & two Mandarins with pigtails & such a small Japanese.' But NM was unable to relax about Gilla's poor academic performance; he admonishes him for his weak spelling, his indistinct speech, his supposed laziness: 'work work work always always always very very very hard for you are backward for your age & so need to work harder than most boys.' Milicent's letters lay on more pressure: 'I do hope the work is getting better this term. I can't bear Father always being disappointed about it, so buck up.' The first letter Milicent sent Gilla at the Oratory perfectly sums up her style of stepmothering: 'I do hope . . . that you will like the Oratory very much, & get every good from it, & always be known as one of the straightest & truest boys they ever had.' There is an echo here, whether conscious or not I don't know, of old Ben Smith's planting of the five firs at Brown's, one for each of his children, in the hope that they would grow up as 'straight and true' as the trees themselves.

*

Ethne was the one member of the family who did not enter into the general enthusiasm about Hancox. She painted a rather good watercolour of it, which she gave to Alan for Christmas, and she contributed to his magazine, including designing elaborate covers for its Christmas numbers, but in Milicent's presence she kept up a façade of indifference and boredom. 'I did not care much for the drawing room,' she wrote in her memoir, 'which I thought stiffly arranged but my own bedroom there delighted me, but unfortunately I could not say so . . . it became understood by [Milicent] and my father that I did not like Hancox and I was neither generous enough nor brave enough to tell them that there was much of it that I liked very much indeed.' Despite her attitude towards the house, or towards its chatelaine, Ethne liked the area and had plenty of local friends. There was one family in particular, the Sayers, who 'helped me to enjoy myself more than any others'. The Sayers, unfortunately, brought out Milicent's snobbish instincts. She raised objections to Ethne's spending so much time with them. "In my young days," she said, "one did not know the B----s" (mentioning Mrs Sayer's maiden name). And I lost my temper and retorted:

'"I don't care who Mrs Sayer is or was; she has a very kind heart."'

Perhaps NM intervened, for after this Ethne's intimacy with the Sayers was allowed to continue unchecked. There were two daughters and two sons, and they cheerfully incorporated Ethne into their social life. The business of Mrs Sayer's life was to see that her daughters were prettily dressed and having fun; in a straightforward, unscheming way she was on the look-out for husbands for them, and it was through this family that Ethne received her first proposal of marriage:

The young man was a cousin of the Sayers, a tall thin youth who did not attract me at all. He was a good dancer and at the dance at which it happened we had just danced all the supper dances together and were resting in the corner of a large empty tent. I was sitting on a little hard chair and was leaning against a tent pole when suddenly the young man remarked that he wanted to tell me

something and hoped I would not be offended. I had no idea what
he was leading up to and told him he could say anything he liked.

'Look here – ' he said, 'A few days ago I asked Miss --- if she
would marry me, but she doesn't seem able to make up her mind,
and, if you'd have me, I'd much rather marry you than her?'

He was sitting rather behind me on another little chair on the
other side of the tent pole; we were both facing the side of the tent
and he started kicking the pole as he spoke, not looking at me . . .

'I'm afraid I couldn't,' I said at last. He was silent for a moment
and then asked:

'Are you really serious? May I see your face?'

It was dark where we sat and he pulled a match-box out of his
pocket, lit a match and held it up. This made me want to laugh but
I tried to look serious.

'You are sure you are not offended?' he asked as the match flick-
ered out.

'No, of course not – it's . . . it's . . . nice of you,' I stammered . . .

'May I give you just one kiss?' he asked.

I drew back.

'I never have been,' I said truthfully.

'Just one, to show you aren't offended,' he urged, and very reluctantly I said he might. He bent forwards and pecked my cheek; his
breath smelt of claret cup and tobacco and I was glad when at that
moment the music struck up in the next tent. I jumped up quickly
and he followed me towards the dancing tent. I heard, not long
afterwards, that Miss --- had eventually made up her mind and that
he had married her.

Only marginally more romantic was Bella's engagement to the
family doctor, Walter Wynne. One day in 1908 Ethne arrived at
Crowham to be told that Dr Wynne was in the garden.

' "He is with Bella down by the cucumber frames," said Roddy,
"and either she is consulting him about her varicose veins, or, he is
asking her to marry him."

'The latter was correct and they were married soon afterwards.' ̄

Alan remembered finding Bella 'wild with delight' at the prospect of escaping Crowham, and Aunt Jenny saying of Walter Wynne, 'Bella thinks he's a cock angel, but I don't.' Bella was a matter-of-fact person who enjoyed country life and wanted to establish a home of her own in the neighbourhood in which she had grown up. It must have occurred to her that, despite her good looks and cheerful disposition, she was now in her late twenties and her choice of husbands was necessarily limited. Walter Wynne was quite a bit older; judging from photographs he had few physical charms, but he seems to have been a steady, sensible man who shared Bella's sporting tastes, and the marriage turned out well. For the wedding – like Amy's, it was held in Westfield church – triumphal arches were erected across the road, including one from the local Cricket Club featuring pendent stumps, bat and ball.

An important guest at the wedding was Aunt Nannie, who had made a special effort to be there for the sake of her – currently – favourite niece. Lionel was there too, on leave from the cordite factory with Agnes, baby Medora and her ayah. Lionel had always declared himself an atheist, but, he said, he was quite ready to swear he was a Unitarian if Nannie would make him her heir.

'On Bella's wedding day,' Ethne recalled, 'Aunt Nanny seemed quite cheerful and it was only as the bride and bridegroom were leaving the house that her brow darkened; she had caught sight of a bag of golf clubs . . . Though severe, she was also sentimental, and she expected, I felt sure, that honeymoon couples should do nothing but hold each other's hands; it had shocked her to think they might play golf.

' "They will forget to use them," I said, knowing how unlikely that was, but Aunt Nanny believed me and a storm was averted.'

★

The family had always spent Christmas Day in London; the ritual was that NM took the children to visit patients in the wards at Bart's; they then went on to Wapping, where they visited some of the pious but impoverished old ladies whom Amy had known before returning to dine at home, usually with guests who would otherwise have been on their own. In 1907 they went to Hancox straight after Christmas and prepared an entertainment for local children. 'Hancox became inhabited soon after last Christmas,' reported *The Nebula*:

> and revels began almost at once . . . at incredibly short notice scenery was painted, & properties were prepared, & in little more than a day, certain children of Whatlington, having been first filled with tea, gazed upon a series of presentments of certain episodes of our national History. They saw a druidical sacrifice. They saw King Alfred lay the foundations of English cookery. They heard the alarums & rout of Hastings, & beheld the death of Harold on the stricken field, & the trading of his body. They saw King Richard gloomily despondent in prison, till roused to hope by the strains of his musician, & they saw the Abbot of Robertsbridge bring his ransom, which perhaps some of their forgotten ancestors helped to pay. Finally, in a scene of ecclesiastical & military splendour, they saw King John set the seal on those liberties which we all enjoy. A Christmas tree and presents followed.

The family at once began to take an active part in village life, even though they still spent far more time in London than at Hancox. Whatlington was, and is, a small village; the population was 281 in 1921. Most of the labour force were agricultural labourers, gardeners or servants. A few men were employed at the gypsum mines a couple of miles away in Mountfield; this was a better paid job, but unhealthy and dangerous.

The upper part of the village, to which Hancox – or rather, the half of Hancox that wasn't technically in Sedlescombe – belonged, straddled the main London to Hastings road, now the A21. This road was created in the early nineteenth century as part of a defence system against Napoleonic invasion; in the mid-twentieth it was still sometimes referred to as the 'New Road'. A tiny scrap of the old, pre-nineteenth-century road is still preserved on our farm, a narrow green tunnel between flowering hedgerows.

In the 1820s, six coaches left London each day for Hastings. The journey took between eight and twelve hours, and Whatlington was reputed to be the coldest spot between London and Hastings. This I can believe. As the stage coach began to go downhill from the Royal Oak, Whatlington's one pub, the driver would say to the outside passengers, 'Turn up your coat collars, gentlemen; we have reached Whatlington.'

In 1907 the public buildings in the village were the small Early English church of St Mary Magdalene, the wooden Church Room (later the village hall), a water mill, a grocer's, a tiny post office which sold sweets and cigarettes, a chapel which was built for members of a Wesleyan sect called the Countess of Huntingdon's Connection, and a forge where horses were shod, farm machinery repaired or an iron rim put on a wheel. Hancox Farm sold its milk to villagers; the Forestall, the first Hancox field, was used as a public cricket pitch. Various clubs and societies were active; Sunday School was well attended. The Bonfire Society was vigorous. East Sussex, for hundreds of years the centre of the gunpowder industry, still commemorates 5 November in style. Most of the towns and villages have their own Bonfire Society; the members march in procession in fancy dress, carrying flaming torches, at the Guy Fawkes events that run throughout the autumn. Whatlington still has its society, but it no longer has its own bonfire. Until 1950, however, it did; the bonfire was in another of the Hancox fields, just behind the Royal Oak, and Milicent was called upon to light it. The parade would be led by the landlord of the Royal Oak dressed as John Bull and riding a white horse.

Another, very different kind of society was the Whatlington Benevolent Society. Formed in 1874, it was vitally important in the days before the Welfare State. Members paid 1/6d monthly, and 2/– on quarter nights. This entitled them to 10/– per week for twenty-six weeks if they fell sick, and 6/– per week for a further twenty-six weeks if they were still ill enough to require it. Once a year all members were invited to a dinner, 'to be paid for out of the funds of the Society, whether the member is present or not'.

There was also an annual procession. 'Every member shall attend the club room by ten o'clock on the Anniversary Day, to receive his equal share of the funds, and to walk in procession; any member behaving disorderly while so doing, to forfeit One Shilling.'

Living conditions in the village were quite primitive. There was no gas or electricity; houses were lit by candles or oil lamps. Cooking and heating water was done on the kitchen range. Most people had a copper heated by a wood fire to do their washing. Drinking water was a problem; some houses, including Hancox, had their own wells, but for most there was the daily walk to the spring by the Church Room to collect water in buckets or cans. Water for non-drinking purposes was collected in tanks fed by rainwater from the roof. Tin baths were placed in front of the fire and filled via kettles; afterwards, the dirty water went on the garden. Indoor lavatories were rare. Most people used a shed at the bottom of the garden, with a rough wooden seat and an iron bucket underneath, which was emptied each week into a hole dug in the garden. Squares of newspaper were used as lavatory paper.

Milicent, brought up at Yotes Court, had a thorough understanding of the duties and responsibilities that went with owning the largest house in a small rural community, and she seems to have been a conscientious and respected landlord and employer. Several documents survive showing that she gave financial support to local boys who wanted to join the Navy or undertake training for specific trades. She also quickly reimmersed herself in the social round; many of the local families who attended the same gatherings had been familiar to her since childhood. Alan's diary for 1908 shows how much he enjoyed Sussex life. A hard winter meant that 'all our water is melted snow,' but it also meant skating on the Pett pond and tobogganing in the Gorse Field. He often went shooting, canoeing or riding with Milicent. He attended various garden parties and the village flower show, where the Hancox gardener won five prizes, and hugely enjoyed taking part, with Ethne, in a pageant at Pevensey Castle got up by Brabbie's sister Mrs Combe. 'I was in the landing of William the Conqueror scene, & in the one of the surrender of the castle by Bishop Odo in wh. Ethne also was. In this . . . the part of King William Rufus was taken by Major Prendergast.'

A highlight of 1908 was NM's decision to buy a car. The journey from Gloucester Place to Hancox was laborious; a cab, bus or long walk to Charing Cross, a train journey of nearly two hours, then another four-mile walk or bicycle ride from Robertsbridge station. Sometimes they hired the Royal Oak's wagonette, but this was not quick. In August, NM obtained a 'laundaulet' on approval from the Fiat company, having beaten down the price. 'Today in the evening the motor arrived,' wrote Alan, 'very fine, about 20 h.p. 4 cylinders, with electric light in the "cabin" an engine room telegraph to the driver & a speaking tube. The front seats in the "cabin" fold up & stow away very neatly & the sitters face inwards.' It was not considered that NM or Milicent, or even Alan, should drive this splendid vehicle. Instead, Paci added 'chauffeur' to his job description. 'The FIAT co. have lent a mechanician to assist Paci for a week.' Milicent ordered a black suit of livery for Paci, which she felt would go well with the bright blue of the car. Soon, the journey door to door would be made in less than three hours, except that frequent punctures caused hold-ups, and refuelling took a minimum of half an hour. A pattern was established. The family and Paci travelled to Hancox by car, the servants took the train with Mr Willett, the ginger cat, in a basket. Rose Playford and her mother were the skeleton staff at Hancox, along with the gardener, but the other servants travelled to and fro.

All seemed well. Milicent had regained her health and her home. Her stepsons were reasonably settled; Ethne was difficult, but at least she had embraced the True Faith. NM flourished at Hancox. He loved the garden, the birds and butterflies, the pure air, the peace. He made great strides with his history of St Bartholomew's. It would have seemed impossible to Milicent that only a few months later her happiness would be threatened by a new and unimagined danger.

15. 'The Land of Love'

'What a delightful holiday we've had mimil. I enjoyed every hour of it.' So wrote NM at the end of the summer of 1908, the first summer spent at Hancox. 'Mimil' is an abbreviation of 'my Milicent', and is one of several pet names. Another is 'Marzocca'; I haven't traced the origin of this (the internet only comes up with 'coffee machine'), but it seems to have something to do with cats. Staying in a rather luxurious house without Milicent, NM wrote, 'two fires & five electric lights even do not make up for one pair of Marzocca's eyes – dear dear thing.' Five years after their wedding, the letters give the impression of a strong, trusting, communicative marriage. Ironically, it was Milicent who inadvertently introduced trouble.

Ethel Portal was in poor shape. Laverstoke, the beautiful and beloved family house, had passed to a cousin after her mother's death. Her brothers were dead and her sister Katie, to whom she had once been very close, had married a man, Sir Francis Scott, whom Ethel found dull, narrow-minded and critical. Besides, Katie had developed multiple sclerosis, the disease that had already killed her brother Alaric; the combination of her illness and her husband led to what Ethel saw as a miserably isolated existence. Ethel herself had never been strong. Her rheumatic attacks and her debilitating migraines became worse as time went on. Though only in her forties, she led the life of a much older woman. She lived with her maid, Katrine, in a flat near Westminster Cathedral, 82 Carlisle Mansions, and though she kept in touch with many friends and travelled when she was well enough, she often felt her own life to be lonely and confined.

In the autumn of 1908 she became very seriously ill. I can't work out what the illness was, but Milicent thought it was life-threatening

and begged NM to take her on as a patient. She also invited Ethel
to stay with them at Gloucester Place until she was better. Before
she took up residence, on 18 November 1908, the day after her
forty-sixth birthday, something happened between Ethel and NM
that changed the nature of their relationship.

Once she was installed at Gloucester Place, other medical opinions were sought. On 3 December she was moved to a nursing
home at 5 Bentinck Street. Two abdominal operations were needed;
Ethel was described as being 'in a critical condition'. Both NM and
Milicent were in constant attendance over the next few days, but
they had arranged a trip to Egypt over Christmas and New Year,
and on 10 December they departed, leaving Ethel in the nursing
home, out of danger but still weak.

The first of Ethel's letters to NM is dated 28 December. She
sent it to him in Egypt. It is far more than a letter of thanks from
a grateful patient to a kind doctor:

> I want to try & write a few lines just for your eye alone . . . thro' these
> long days & nights full of discomforts and tiredness theres one
> thought that helps me all the time & it's the thought of you. Over &
> over again when I am near the end of patience I call back the sight of
> you – your voice – your words – your touch. & you are never too far
> away to help, & every night I say Goodnight Norman – dear Norman
> – & think I feel you hold my hand & tell me night wont last forever.

In her next letter she refers to *Antony and Cleopatra* – 'I always
liked it, but never loved it as I do now.' NM had placed a copy
of the play under her pillow as a farewell gift. It looks as though
she and NM had already adopted Shakespeare's lovers, no longer
young, separated by circumstances and by continents, as parallels
to themselves.

The affair – I can't truthfully call it anything else – would not
necessarily have been obvious to other people. NM's status as medical adviser was an effective smokescreen. Sir Francis Scott wrote
him a letter full of gratitude for taking on the case of the sister-in-law

he regarded as something of a liability. And NM's children had grown up with the knowledge that their father had many female friends of all ages; he always had done, even in Amy's day. They were also accustomed to his spending a great deal of private time with his patients; his style of doctoring was to find out as much as he could about the whole person, rather than simply treating a set of symptoms, so his regular visits to Miss Portal's flat after his return from Egypt would have surprised no one. What the servants thought is another matter. Ethel's maid Katrine must have understood what it meant when she was asked to prepare the flat for Dr Moore's arrival and then make herself scarce; she must have noticed that among the letters she brought to her mistress each day there were usually one or two in the same handwriting. But what of the servants under Milicent's command? Ethel writes, 'I felt almost as if I were still sitting beside you in the car holding your hand & wishing I could just drive on & on like that for ever,' which makes me wonder what Paci thought. Were the hands held discreetly beneath a rug? Were the passenger seats out of the driver's sight? A glass screen separated the driver from the passengers, but surely there was a mirror? Or did the employing class simply rely on their servants to play deaf and blind?

And what about Milicent? Letters to NM addressed in Ethel's familiar handwriting were delivered almost daily. NM could probably rely on Milicent not to read them. He could have destroyed them, but he didn't. Milicent's hallmark was her extreme moral scrupulousness. But while she might not have read them, she must have known of their existence. At the very least, she must have felt put out that her dear friend now wrote so much more often to her husband than to herself.

In late February 1909, Ethel went to Pau, on the edge of the Pyrenees, to continue her convalescence. The letters show that the affair had progressed: 'You have got into every crevice & corner of me . . . my life-giver has given me life of body & mind & whatever else there is'; 'I do feel that I have found my home after many wanderings & that home is in the arms that have held me & comforted

me & the big loving heart of the greatest man I have ever known';
'It is the Land of Love - & that is the atmosphere I am breathing &
living in - & in that land I keep close to Norman – & hold my arms
round him & feel him closer & closer to me & nothing can come
between or destroy that perfect rest. Or I come closer still - & now
it is Life – glorious thrilling burning Life – And it all begins & ends
with Norman – the Norman that I love.'

I wonder how NM justified his behaviour to himself. His letters
to Ethel have not survived, apart from a few scraps in a box of odd-
ments Alan inherited when she died. These include verses he wrote
for her. On one in which NM imagines Ethel preparing for bed,
Alan has pencilled, 'Destroy?' NM's casebook for this period contains only one note about her: 'Feb 10th 1909 EMP said she never
expected to be alive today.' Ethel certainly believed that NM saved
her life; what more potent aphrodisiac could there have been?
Ethel Portal was brave, clever, well read, interested in antiquity,
still handsome, suffering and adoring. It is natural that NM, a
busy, harassed man in his early sixties who had been through a lot
of troubles, should have found it hard to resist what she offered,
but I cannot detect that he made any effort to resist. The vow of
loyalty to his future wife that he had made at Glastonbury on his
twenty-first birthday, which he had made a point of renewing
when he became engaged to Milicent, let alone the marriage vows
he had made in church – these were not strong enough to with-
stand the fact that quite suddenly, and for the first time in his life,
NM had found his soul mate.

There never seems to have been the slightest idea that he should
end his marriage. Neither wanted to hurt Milicent at all; Ethel
must have been jealous of what Milicent had, but she had always
been, and for the most part remained, very fond of her. For the
rest of his life, NM's letters to Milicent continue to be grateful,
respectful and affectionate. But the promises he had made her –
'You have my whole heart dear one and never shall have less'; 'All
there is in me dear I give you & if you rest on me I will not fail you'
– had undeniably been broken, whether she knew it or not.

There is no sense at all that NM was tortured by guilt. He must have twisted the facts into a shape that satisfied his conscience; as Alan said of him, 'NM has great difficulty in believing what he does not approve of & readily believes in what he wishes to be true & so lives in an unreal world. This makes him suffer much when reality will not be gainsaid & obtrudes upon his fancied universe.' I imagine that he 'cleared' his affair with Ethel in his own mind because he had always held friendships in the highest esteem, making almost a cult of them. Now that he had found *the* friend above all other, he perhaps told himself that to deny their intimacy was to desecrate the shrine of friendship, and would therefore be a barbarous thing.

'Reality', in relation to his affair, never did 'obtrude upon his fancied universe', because the two women in question played the game. I think Milicent turned a blind eye partly because her sense of propriety would not allow her to investigate the truth too closely, and partly because NM was always to her the Great Man, someone whom one did not judge by the usual standards. Her role had always been to protect him, not to expose him. I cannot believe Milicent felt no sense of hurt or loss, but I think she buried her feelings so successfully that she managed to continue in a marriage that was far from being merely a façade.

Ethel, for her part, acted wisely. She knew that she could never truly share NM's life; she knew that her feelings for him would have to be kept secret from the outside world. But she also knew that she could become tremendously, vitally important to him, as long as she always behaved impeccably and kept herself under control. Whenever she mentions Milicent in her letters – which is not very often – her tone is invariably one of sympathy and concern. She took a warm but unobtrusive interest in the lives of Alan, Ethne and Gilla, and made sure she was always a valuable dinner guest at Gloucester Place or an easy, appreciative weekend visitor at Hancox. Ethel Portal knew how to sing for her supper. But, as with Milicent, a great deal had to be suppressed, and it took its toll. When my mother asked my grandfather, Alan, why he thought Miss Portal had migraines, he replied, 'Because she couldn't have NM.'

Ethel first stayed at Hancox in April 1909, after her return from Pau. Her warm thankyou letter to Milicent shows how much she wanted all three of them to have their cake and eat it:

'Dearest Milicent . . . I loved being with you – as I always do - & always did – whether in the wilds of B[ethnal] G[reen], the scorching streets of Munich or the peace & beauty of Hancox – we've seen a good many different phases of life together haven't we? - & the last is the best of all – So here's to many more such times - & at this point I would raise my glass if I had one – but I wave my pen instead – first wiping it on a little round penwiper which you gave me in 1905.

So began what amounted almost to a ménage à trois; Miss Portal became so much a part of the household that Gilla remarked, 'It's almost as if Papa had two wives.' The fact that this innocent comment has survived in oral tradition, via Alan, shows that for him at any rate it was received with a certain amused uneasiness.

Ethel was entranced by Hancox, which she regarded as NM's natural habitat, the best place for his physical, mental and spiritual health. The day after writing her letter to Milicent, she wrote to NM:

And then I got up & saw two swallows – the first that have been seen here [at her sister Katie's house] - & they had passed over Hancox yesterday & saw you standing on the bowling green & heard your greeting & hurried on because they knew I would like to hear their news. . . 3p.m. the 2nd post has just come & brought me 2 letters - 2 good helpings of happiness
     - 2 good whiffs of Hancox air
     - 2 good handshakes from Norman – no, not that – 2 arms round me & the distance between us annihilated . . . Dear I wish you hadn't got to leave Hancox on Monday – I wish you could look at that thrushes nest a few days more & sit on the tiles in the sun & fix up the boxwood shuttle - & hear a few more evening concerts from the blackbirds – How glad – how very glad I am to be able to

picture you there - & to know the room where you are writing & the landscape you see as you step out on to the lawn - the panelled room you will pass as you go to & from yours -.

The panelled room, furnished with a sumptuous day-bed as well as a regular bed, became the room Ethel always used on her many visits to Hancox. NM and Milicent slept in the big bedroom above the drawing room, just a short flight of stairs away.

★

Reconciling herself to Ethel Portal's frequent presence was not the only strain on Milicent's emotions at this time. Ethne had started at Cope and Nichols' art school in South Kensington, which at least meant that she was out of the house for several hours each day, but relations between her and Milicent did not improve. NM floundered as a father. He showed appreciation of his daughter's talents – he gave her a piano for her twenty-first birthday, he had a poem of hers set to music – but he seemed unable to treat her as an adult with a right to her own tastes and opinions. Under the influence of the fashion-conscious Miss Fitzgeralds, Ethne took to wearing face powder. One day, as she was about to leave the house, NM pulled her into his consulting room and, licking a corner of his handkerchief, rubbed it off. ' "Good!" he said, "I thought you had a skin disease!" ' His attempts to create harmony between stepmother and stepdaughter were heavy-handed:

> She [Milicent] found a good many things of which to disapprove and I knew that often she was right, but her indirect method of finding fault annoyed me so much that it made me unrepentant. Our conflicts came to a climax one day, and though I do not remember the cause of our argument I know we shouted at one another until, feeling I could bear it no more, I left the room in a rage banging the door behind me. I rushed up to my room and played the piano to calm myself. My father followed me and told me that there were quarrels in some families but that he would not have a quarrel

in his family and I was to go downstairs and tell my stepmother
that I loved her. I stared at him in astonishment.

'I will go and beg her pardon for being rude,' I said, 'but I can't
tell her I love her because it would not be true.'

Milicent may have sensed that Ethne's religious enthusiasm was
waning. Ethne's life as an art student was full and active. The art
school's object was to train students to the standard required by the
Royal Academy School, and Ethne had ambitions in this direction.
Teaching methods were dry and conventional, with much drawing from casts of Greek and Roman statues using careful measure-
ments. Ethne, untidy, impulsive and original, found this side of
the work 'most tedious', but she enjoyed the life classes despite the
fact that the models were elderly and plain. She enjoyed, too, the
relative freedom of a student's life. She could travel through London alone, at least during daylight hours; she could buy her own
lunch and fraternize with other students of both sexes, though
when she took friends home their speech, manner and dress often
incurred Milicent's criticism. Edwardian dress codes were astonishingly strict. Ethne sported an orange silk scarf to make herself
feel 'artistic', but she never dared be seen in the street without
gloves. Soon an interest of a new kind had come into her life which
helped to push religion to one side.

The awkward young man at the dance excepted, Ethne seems to
have reached her early twenties without romantic adventures. She
had met plenty of young men – fellow students, brothers or cousins of her female friends, her father's medical students – but she
remained strangely innocent, even ignorant. Amy and Rebecca's
long-ago attempts to instruct her in the facts of life had been
ineffectual; Milicent, needless to say, was too prudish to help. 'She
told me I must not walk down Piccadilly or Bond Street alone, but
did not tell me why. I wondered vaguely if there were still rough
men like highway robbers who might hit me on the head and steal
my watch. As soon as possible after I had been told not to, I walked
down Piccadilly and along the Burlington Arcade, but as nothing

unusual happened I decided that my stepmother must have some private and probably "snobbish" reason for forbidding it.'

The change in Ethne's life came suddenly. She had maintained her friendship with the Pryor family, but on her frequent visits to Weston Park, Jack Pryor, the only boy, had been a shadowy figure, often away at Eton or Cambridge. But when she stayed there in the summer of 1909 and he helped her judge some schoolchildren's drawings at the village Flower Show she was 'surprised to find that I liked him'. He invited her to a party – 'In his letter he said something about hoping I would be his faithful female friend, which pleased me.'

She did not tell NM or Milicent about this development. Their attitude towards Ethne's marital prospects seems to have been ostrich-like. They did not entertain the idea that she would marry anyone but a Catholic, and yet they must have known that the vast majority of the young men she met were not Catholics – indeed, suitable Catholic men were in extremely short supply, and they do not appear to have gone to any pains to ferret them out. Ethne was now twenty-three, striking to look at, friendly and popular. The inevitable outcome does not seem to have crossed their minds.

Troubles arrived not as single spies but in battalions. Alan's diary records a dramatically blighted Christmas. After the usual charitable visits to the hospital and to Wapping, they had dinner at home. 'Near the end of dinner the new parlourmaid Mary Mahoney, suddenly fell; we thought in a fit. She did not come to & we performed artificial respiration . . . But she was dead. We telephoned to Scotland Yard, & after a time the coroner's assistant came & later a vehicle & some men who removed the body.'

Milicent fell ill, perhaps partly as a result of the shock. She recuperated at Hancox, but the news from Crowham was bad. Old Willy Leigh Smith was becoming rapidly weaker. Alan, aware that his grandfather could not live long, sat with him a long time asking him for stories from the old days. Alan wrote the stories down in a big leatherbound manuscript book in which he pasted in cuttings or wrote down anecdotes, rhymes and anniversaries – anything that appealed to him.

Willy recalled his childhood in Hastings, when his father, old Ben, owned the houses on either side of St Mary-in-the-Castle, the church that is set into the middle of Pelham Crescent. One house was for the children, the other for adults; guests were asked which they'd prefer to stay in. Willy remembered his governess, Miss Spooner, who could sing very beautifully; at Christmastime she sang in the street, a window went up and, to her embarrassment, a half-crown piece was thrown to her, which she returned. Willy wondered if he could produce a similar result so he went out and began to sing a Christmas song, but up came a policeman who said 'You, young man, none of that noise.' He remembered his father telling him that when he, the Pater, contested the parliamentary seat of Rye against Sir Lacy Evans, the Conservative, 'two fine fishermen & doubtless on occasion smugglers said "We and our mates, sir, will capture Sir Lacy Evans, and carry him out to sea and keep him there until the election is over if that would be any service to you."' He told Alan that he had asked an old farmhand at Crowham whether the rumour was true that he had been accustomed to hide smuggled goods in the stone tombs in Westfield churchyard. 'It's as true as Gospel,' replied the old man. 'And you know,' said Willy, 'his bringing in the Gospel like that tickled me.'

Willy's stories show that he had a good rapport with his estate workers. He talked of old Adkins, who was breeched* at about the time of the Battle of Waterloo, and could remember his father setting him in the doorway holding a broom handle to keep the French out. Adkins could remember the tenants' dinner at Crowham, to celebrate victory over Napoleon. Willy talked, too, of old Ben Hilder, born in 1806, who lived in a little Gothick cottage halfway up the drive at Crowham; his job was to open and shut the gate across the drive. Hilder had been in the Grenadiers as a young man and was on duty in the streets of London when the Houses of

---

* Taken out of petticoats into breeches, i.e. transferred from infancy to boyhood.

Parliament were burnt down. 'On the day of Robertsbridge fair long ago,' Alan records, 'my Grandfather decided to enjoy himself so he went to old Hilder who lent him his gabardine, as the long smock frocks used to be called, & the two of them went to the Fair. My Grandfather enjoyed himself greatly and danced and drank vigorously nobody suspecting him, at last the band sent round the hat, & he now greatly elated and on the best of terms with all the world put in ten shillings and so discovered himself.' He talked, too, of a cobbler called Blundell, Hilder's nephew, who was apprenticed when young to the cobbling trade by Aunt Nannie, and who 'attributed his success in life to her'. It is pleasant to read of someone whose contact with Nannie was wholly benign. Milicent must have felt the same, for she made the cobbler a present of a picture painted by Nannie, a view of Venice from the sea.

Willy told tales of his shooting and riding exploits, of a hard ride for help the night of Amy's birth, of how he used to ride the sixty miles to London, riding one horse and leading another, of his dogs and his cattle. Alan, with his strong desire to capture moments from the present before they slipped irretrievably into the past, gives a picture of Willy as he last saw him: 'My Grandfather engaged in the conversation just recorded, sitting before the fire in an upstairs room at Crowham. He complained much of the cold & had a rug round his shoulders fastened in front by a brooch of two buttons each shewing a swallow in flight, the two being beak to beak, & as usual had a black skull cap on his head. On his left was a table covered with books and with a siphon of soda-water, a jug of lemonade & a tumbler on a tray.' The room was hung with guns – old-fashioned muzzle-loaders – and old farm implements; on the mantelpiece was a portrait of a favourite dog. His room was not entered by the grandchildren without much trepidation. Gilla wrote in his own scrapbook, 'I always remember my Grandfather as being very enormous and with a kind of good-humoured gruffness. He used to come into lunch and roar at me – why don't you drink <u>beer</u> – beer's the stuff.' Ethne remembered that 'Grandpapa . . . looked alarming to me when I was very young, but, in spite of his deep voice, bald head, and the white beard which spread over his ample chest, I soon found he had a twinkle in his eye. He used to call me 'Mount Etna' because he said I exploded suddenly.' In the family archive, of the five Leigh Smith siblings Willy is the one who has left the least behind him. I have only two documents in his handwriting, one a letter to Milicent about apple varieties, the other a letter he sent to his brother Ben and his family in December 1896. It is characteristically blunt:

> A merry Christmas and Happy New Year to you all. I don't go in for cards. Dear Ben I have heard that you are going to take a house some where on the SW coast — we think of taking a small house after Xmas most likely at St Leonards — hope you are all well and jolly . . . Nanny is very doleful and very poor she says — I hear she has taken a most extensive & expensive house at Rome — which seems absurd for one person. She has not furnished her spare rooms so I suppose does not want anyone to stay with her. We have Bella home from school now. Would they be obliged to take her at Girton if she could not pass the exam? I don't think she could. Yours WLS.

Willy was the most ordinary, the least remarkable, amongst his siblings, but his personality was strongly stamped upon his little kingdom at Crowham, and when he died on 5 February 1910 (attended in his last illness by Bella's husband, Dr Wynne), his death marked the end of an era for the village which he had hardly left for more than half a century. He was nearly seventy-seven when he died, which was in those days regarded as 'a good age' to have reached; given his lifetime of smoking and drinking it was surprising that he lived so long. His loss was felt. His obituary stated that 'his geniality and heartiness coupled with an undemonstrative charity, will cause him to be greatly missed in the parish.' If NM thought of his old father-in-law's mean-spirited and tight-fisted behaviour during the days of his courtship of Amy, he kept such memories to himself. To Gilla he wrote, the day after the death, 'We [himself and Milicent] walked to Crowham yesterday evening &

dined with Willy [junior] & Roddy & tried to cheer them as much as possible. Then we walked back threading our way across the field through the Forge Wood with a lantern Willy lent us. It blew & rained fiercely all the way back here . . . We shall all miss your grandfather he was so kind & good-hearted a man. May he rest in peace. With love my dearest boy.' It says much for the stamina of NM and Milicent that, aged sixty-three and forty-two, they walked the six miles back from Crowham to Hancox on a stormy February night.

Willy's funeral took place on 9 February, at Sedlescombe church, because Dolly, his youngest daughter, was buried there. Alan recorded in his diary, 'The coffin was carried by farmhands & that sort of people, 6 in number, including George Dann [the Crowham coachman] in smocks. [The smock or round-frock was the traditional wear of the Sussex labourer. It was the Gore-tex of its day, though more 'eco-friendly'. The back and front of the garment were identical. White frocks were worn on Sundays or for mourning; a plainer one of a dark colour was worn on weekdays over corduroy trousers tied under the knees with string or with a calf-strap. The smock was warm in winter and cool in summer; it could be worn over several layers. It was made of coarse calico impregnated with linseed oil which made it waterproof. The embroidery on the chest, back, shoulders and wrists was called gauging or honey-combing; for the smocks to be worn at weddings or feast days it was elaborate, with motifs worked into the design; a red handkerchief was worn round the neck. The everyday smocks had large pouches which held tools, bales of string and the like.] Present were Roddy Willy Aunt Dora NM Milicent Noel [Wickham, Dora's son] Mabel Bella & Walter . . . & others.' Aunt Jenny, the widow, isn't mentioned. Neither of Willy's two surviving siblings was there. Ben was now beyond any such excursion, and Nannie would have considered a rushed journey to England in the depth of winter to be out of the question.

Gilla, who was at the Oratory School in Birmingham, did not get leave of absence. Ethne was not at the funeral either. In January she had been 'on probation' at the Royal Academy, but had failed to win a place. As soon as her exams were finished she went to Weston. She recalled in her memoir that she and Jack took long walks together. 'One day as we were walking towards the Park wood he pointed to a pair of partridges which were running into the wood.

' "They have started to pair," he said. Then he took me into the summer-house in the wood and asked suddenly if I thought I could marry him.'

Ethne said 'Yes' without hesitation. 'I was afraid I should be a bad housekeeper, but he said that would not matter. When we went into lunch we announced that we were engaged and someone . . . laughed and said that anyone might have guessed that from our ruffled hair.'

The Pryors were delighted, but NM and Milicent immediately made difficulties when Ethne broke the news to them, a few days before Willy's death. It seems odd that they apparently did not see it coming. The match seemed a very natural one. Jack's father was one of NM's oldest friends and one of his most favoured travelling companions, despite strongly expressed differences of opinion on some issues. NM had welcomed and encouraged the friendship between the Pryor children and his own, and was grateful for the family's kindness during the final stages of Amy's life. NM was himself beloved by the young Pryors, who looked forward to his visits as occasions of great hilarity. But Jack was not a Catholic – indeed, he was anti-Catholic – and for NM and Milicent that outweighed everything else, especially when Ethne announced that she was going to renounce her own faith. 'She told me that she was going to marry Jack Pryor & that she had ceased to be a R.C. wh. latter is causing trouble,' wrote Alan in his diary with typical understatement.

Immense emotional pressure was piled on to Ethne. 'I do not know how many talks I had with my father,' she writes:

but I remember clearly one of our final interviews. It was in the Consulting room, a bright fire was burning and my father stood

23. Rose, née Playford, and Ike Smith on their wedding day, married at last after a courtship of two decades.

24 & 25. One of the postcards from Rose's collection.

26. Hancox from the south, taken by Alan in 1909.

27. Repairs being carried out to the north end of Hancox in 1915.

28. The kitchen garden at Hancox in 1909. The great barn can be seen in the background.

29. The hall at Hancox being renovated after the departure of the 'inebriates', 1907. Taken by Alan with his box Brownie.

30. The hall with its new panelling; the '*Nisi dominus*' inscription can be seen.

31. The parlour fireback. The fireback was donated by a grateful patient whom NM had treated for gonorrhoea.

32. The main staircase at Hancox, showing the poppy-head finials.

33. NM speaks to an audience while Milicent (*seated to his right, holding flowers*) looks on proudly. Probably taken at Bart's in about 1908.

34. NM as President of the Royal College of Physicians, 1918.

35. Ethel Portal.

36. East End girls from the Bethnal Green settlements on a visit to Hancox in the 1890s. Milicent is sitting on the grass at the extreme left. Milicent's friend Alys Pearsall Smith (later the wife of Bertrand Russell) wrote of a similar gathering that 'the girls were wild and rude beyond anything one could conceive of', but this group looks orderly enough.

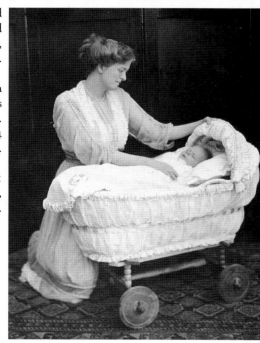

(*top left*) 37. Alan aged 15, Ethne aged 11 and Gillachrist aged 3, taken in 1897.

(*top right*) 38. Gilla aged about 6, with his nurse Eliza Brown. Taken by Alan at 94 Gloucester Place.

39. Ethne in 1911 with her first baby, Johnnie.

40. Alan at Hancox riding his 'ordinary bicycle', as penny-farthings were sometimes called.

41. Gilla on the Tennis Lawn at Hancox in 1914.

42. Mary Haviland, *c.* 1911. 'Val thinks she is such a <u>modern</u> girl,' said Aunt Charley.

43. Alan in his cabin on board HMS *Sagitta* in 1915.

44. Mary Burrows, taken at the time of her engagement to Alan. 'She made me think of wood nymphs,' wrote Ethne.

45. Alan and Mary's wedding, April 1922, at The Palace, Chichester. NM is standing on the far left. Next to him, seated, is Mary's aunt and surrogate mother ''Tedith''. Milicent is seated on the right; standing next to her is Mary's father Winfrid Burrows, Bishop of Chichester. The pageboy is Ethne's son Mark.

with his back to it. I said I was quite determined to marry Jack and that as I was now quite sure that I did not care whether I was a Roman Catholic or not I would stop being one . . . And I visualised a picture of Sundays at Weston, the family walking to Church, Mr Pryor striding down the aisle to read the lesson and then dealing out sixpences to all of us for the offertory; once a member of the family, I thought, how could I creep off to mass in a distant town? Mass in Latin, incense, priests and the confessional, all seemed incongruous, quite out of place in the picture of Weston Sundays that I had called up . . . My father's voice interrupted my thoughts.

'You cannot mean it?'

What had I said? I had said I would stop being a Roman Catholic.

'I do mean it,' I said.

My father walked up and down.

'You can't give it up,' he repeated and suddenly I found that he was crying, with his head on my shoulder. I stood quite still. I felt calm because I had no doubts, I knew that whatever my father or anyone else did or said, I should not change my mind. I was sorry to distress my father and yet I was almost angry; a scene like this ought not to happen.

Ethne was just twenty-four; though ignorant and inexperienced in many ways she showed a mature and prescient understanding of what marriage to the squire's only son would mean. Her father's behaviour seems blinkered, babyish and selfish; I find myself in full agreement with her that 'a scene like this ought not to happen.' And yet I also feel a pang of sympathy for NM. Becoming a Catholic had been the crowning decision of Amy's stricken life. Ethne's decision to follow in her mother's footsteps had been a deep joy to NM; her renunciation of the faith must have felt something like a second bereavement.

His objections were, of course, powerfully reinforced by Milicent. 'I do not think my stepmother ever argued with me,' wrote Ethne, 'though I felt that in the background she continually urged my father to be firm. He was so easily moved to tenderness that without her prodding I believe he would soon have begun to relent towards me.' Ethne was not allowed to see Jack, though they could write to each other. Milicent decreed that Ethne should return to the convent at Haywards Heath, doubtless hoping that the kindly 'Chère Mère' would persuade her to change her mind. But Ethne refused to go, feeling that to do so would be 'a waste of time and probably a waste also of emotion'. It may seem extraordinary that NM, having endured the restrictions that the Leigh Smiths placed on his courtship of Amy, should in his turn try to control his daughter in a similar way, but the strength of Catholic feeling in the household can be judged by fifteen-year-old Gilla's remark — 'It's quite on the cards that Ethne's damned.'

Ethne and Jack took matters into their own hands. While NM, Milicent and Alan were in Sussex for Willy's funeral, Ethne remained at Gloucester Place, alone except for some of the servants. She telephoned Jack — telephoning had not been expressly forbidden, perhaps because the telephone was in the entrance hall and so, normally, no private conversation would have been possible. She told him of Milicent's attempt to get her into the convent. Jack was horrified by this 'tyrannous move' and announced that he was coming round at once to take her away to Weston. 'I could not help being pleased, and ran upstairs to get ready. Having just gone into mourning for my grandfather all my clothes were new, and as I put on my black mushroom-shaped hat I was glad to be able to go away with Jack looking tidy.'

After the funeral, the rest of the family returned to London to find, as Alan wrote in his diary, 'Ethne gone, and an appalling letter from Jack to NM. I to Stevenage by the X o'clock train from Kings X and . . . arrived at Weston at half past midnight. I saw Mr Pryor in his bedroom, he having gone to bed, and then Jack came down to the smoking room and we discussed the matter till about a quarter to III when NM arrived, he having first gone to the Pryors' flat in London. After much discussion we retired at about IIII a.m.'

Ethne agreed to return to London with Alan the next day, to wait until some kind of agreement could be reached. ' "If this wasn't happening to us," said Jack to me before I went, "it would really be very funny." ' A meeting was held at Gloucester Place between the two families, which Ethne was not allowed to attend. Alan, it seems, was the voice of reason – 'It was really due to him that any agreement had been reached and we felt very grateful to him. I remember when I thanked him I said that when Jack and I were married we would put up a statue to him in our garden.'

The agreement was that Jack should go to Peru for three months, to see to the family business out there, and that if the couple still wished to marry when he returned, they should be allowed to do so. NM admitted that because Ethne was of age he could not forbid the marriage, though he vowed never to give his consent. Before Jack sailed for Peru they were allowed to meet at Gloucester Place at stated times, for half-hour periods. Ethne was not allowed to wear a ring, but:

> Jack bought me a little pearl necklace which I thought was more lovely than any ring. When he opened the round, pale blue velvet case, took out the necklace, showed me its little emerald clasp and then fastened it round my neck, I was too happy to speak. When he went abroad he arranged that a series of letters, which he had written, should be posted to me, so that I got one every day when he was on the sea and unable to write to me.

With this kind of attention to detail, it is not surprising that Ethne's feelings did not weaken. The time dragged. She worked in a shared studio and took frequent short holidays to stay with friends. She also went on house-hunting expeditions with Aunt Jenny and Roddy. After Willy's death a momentous decision was made: Crowham was put on the market. Even more extraordinary was that Willy junior moved into a house in Hastings, the first time in the forty-three years of his life that he had set up home independently. Jenny and Roddy rented a house in Mayfield, a pretty village within easy reach of the Ludlows at Withyham. They named their new home 'Croteslei', the ancient name for Crowham as recorded in the Domesday Book.

Milicent suffered several severe bouts of illness during 1910. The horror of Ethne's engagement and her suppressed feelings about Ethel Portal must have contributed to her malaise. In May she wrote to Gilla from Hancox, 'I found being carried up & down stairs so horrid that I have had <u>your</u> bed put in the drawing room near the big window . . . I feel very weak when I stand up, which I don't do often!' This letter has an uncharacteristically querulous tone. Gilla was now the only Catholic child and she turned to him for comfort. She confided to him her worries about NM: 'I don't think he is so cheerful as he used to be, tho' I hope this may get better – You must cheer us up!'

Sad though NM was about the sale of Crowham, and sadder still about Ethne's loss of faith, the unchecked stream of Ethel Portal's passionate love must have been a source of secret solace. Her letters show how she longed to enter fully into his life, how she tried to imagine what he was doing at all hours. 'I hope its sunny at Hancox but I suppose the red creeper is beginning to drop its brilliant leaves & the swallows are having their last discussions as to the day on which they start . . . And the Red Admirals & Tortoiseshells have chosen their nettle leaves in friendly neighbourliness - & the small copper we saw has laid its eggs on a delicious sorrel leaf & ended its glowing little life.' She did all she could to foster the feeling that she and NM were inextricably linked: 'It gives me such a keen pleasure when I see that the same wave of feeling has swept over us both at the same time – as if your spirit had heard mine calling out to you.' She often uses the image of a love-knot binding them both; 'just give a little pull to your end of the cord to test it – you can feel how tight & firm it is cant you? It didn't slip by one hairsbreadth.' If NM's letters responded in kind – and I am sure they did – then, at some level, Milicent must have sensed it.

Ethel spent much of the summer in France, visiting cousins

in the Lot et Garonne district. NM saw her off on the SS *Ortolan*
(with some subterfuge – Alan's diary for this day innocently states
that his father went to Oxford) and gave her three roses, one pink,
one red, one white. Ethel's letters from France are unmistakably
erotic. Coyly, she refers to NM in the third person:

> . . . when I found myself quite quite alone with [Norman] & talked
> to him à coeur ouvert & nestled up close to him – closer & closer
> – till he could not draw a breath without my feeling it - & how
> happy it made me . . . happy all over – inside & out - & body &
> soul – every inch of me happy from the feel of you . . . every day
> finds me tugging harder & harder at the string – longing more &
> more for the actual presence of you – the touch of you -.

NM had taught her a little Irish, and she often put in Irish words
as expressions of love.

Having been forced to accept the likelihood of Ethne's marriage
to Jack, NM tried to make the most of the time he had left with
his daughter, and apart from refusing to discuss wedding arrangements, he seems to have treated her kindly. In May, King Edward
VII died (he bore a striking physical resemblance to Willy Leigh
Smith – or perhaps that should be the other way round). George V
succeeded; 'that stupid little drunkard', Ethel called him in a letter
to NM. Ethne and NM rose early on the morning of 20 May to
see King Edward's funeral procession, as they had done for Queen
Victoria's. They watched the procession from Apsley House. On
23 May Alan's diary records, 'NM dined with Miss Portal & afterwards went, taking Ethne & me, the 4 of us, in the car to Hampstead to look at Halley's Comet, wh. was a feeble affair, though
many people were looking at it; it did not surpass a first magnitude
star, if it was as bright.' Milicent at this time was ill and at Hancox.
I doubt that she would have enjoyed that phrase 'the 4 of us'.

Ethne's long summer of waiting came to an end at last. 'Jack
came back. I rushed off to meet him at the station, went back to
Weston with him and all restrictions automatically came to an end.

He told me he had ridden a hundred miles on horseback in Peru to catch the boat home and that unfortunately the horse had died because it had been given a drink when it was tired and hot.' In mid-September, NM and Milicent reluctantly allowed Jack to stay for a weekend; Ethne wanted to show him her old haunts. The sale of Crowham had just been completed; Ethne, Jack, Alan and Gilla paid a valedictory visit. For Alan it was a deeply felt loss, but for Ethne, though there was sadness, there was also a symbolic severing of links with her old life that felt appropriate. Ethel Portal wrote sympathetically to NM – 'I shall be thinking of you tomorrow & Sunday enduring [Jack's presence],' but she included a tactful reminder that the young man might be a decent human being despite the religious difference: 'the best I can hope is that . . . you will find signs of an honest & strong character - & that he realises how Ethne's happiness will depend on him.' Ethel, a strong Anglican as a young woman, seems to have become more or less agnostic. Though she could never share NM's faith, she had assured him that she respected it: 'dear never think I could mind your talking about religion. I should be withered up inside entirely if I couldn't respect & admire all that is real to anybody I love & I'm not withered up entirely yet.'

The wedding was fixed for Wednesday 12 October, but as neither NM nor Milicent would acknowledge that it was happening Ethne had to make all the arrangements herself, with some help from Cousin Flora, in an atmosphere of semi-secrecy. NM gave her a cheque for her trousseau but it was not enough. (This was not simple meanness on his part. Ethne had run up small bills at various shops during her student days, which she had been ashamed to admit to. She had to discharge her debts from her trousseau money.) Hilda Pryor came to the rescue and made her a present of a set of new underwear and nightgowns: 'She had them made for me and they had pale blue ribbon run through two or three rows of insertion at the tops of the petticoats and night-gowns and round the legs of the knickers.' Milicent was determined to show no interest, which was a waste as she loved that sort of thing. When the wedding presents began to arrive, Ethne caught her 'eyeing the parcels in the hall rather enviously'.

As the wedding day approached, Milicent worked herself up into a frenzy. Aunt Charley, a sympathetic co-religionist, did her best to calm her. '[Aunt Charley] was so kind and nice,' Milicent wrote to Gilla on 6 October; 'My dear, we all, you & we here, are having a trying time. It can't be helped. We must pray. Please write to me, I get rather wretched at times . . . We shall all be happier when it is over, I expect.'

NM and Milicent did not attend the wedding. Ethne remembered lunching with her father on 'coffee and dry toast' at twelve; he said nothing about the ceremony that was to take place that afternoon. 'I was too happy and too much excited to think coherently when I left him and walked through the hall, though I did think, for a moment, that it was a little lonely going out alone like this to my wedding.' This is another moment when the emotional truth of Ethne's memory overrides the literal truth. It is true that she left her father behind in the house, but Alan states clearly in a letter to Gilla that he escorted Ethne from Gloucester Place to Cousin Flora's house in the Cromwell Road, where she was to dress. Cousin Flora provided a more substantial lunch, attended by several Pryors.

Cousin Flora seems to have taken over the role that should have been Milicent's in helping Ethne plan the wedding. She gave Ethne 'a stole of sable skins lined with ermine' to wear with her going-away dress; it cost £40, an extraordinary sum when one considers that Paci's annual wage was £54.12/−. The wedding dress was 'of white satin tight as a sheath, its yoke was embroidered with pearls which, I was to find later, dropped off in showers'. The maid who helped Ethne to dress 'had a cold in her head and sniffed persistently while she did my hair. She put it up in rows of little curls on the back of my head. My veil, an old lace one lent me by Jack's sisters, was fastened round my head with a band of silver ribbon and orange blossom and my only jewel was Jack's pearl necklace.' Alan, who gave Ethne away, described her attire to Gilla with masculine brevity: 'Ethne looked very pretty, she was all over things that looked like pearls. She had something old and something new, something borrowed and something blue, her veil was old, most of her things were new. I don't know what she borrowed, and I only know the blue by hearsay it being hid.' Presumably that was the blue ribbon on the new underwear.

The ceremony took place at the Church of the Annunciation in Bryanston Street, which was known as the Quebec Chapel. Amy had often worshipped there when she was not strong enough to get to Wapping. Alan and Ethne arrived in a Daimler, which Ethne had hired. 'I gave Ethne my arm and we walked up the aisle doing our best not to walk too fast, with people on each side who were a blur merely. Hilda Pryor was the only bridesmaid.' Aunt Jenny, making a firm statement of allegiance to her favourite grandchild, took the place of 'mother of the bride'. Ethne recalled, 'As Jack and I knelt on the Chancel steps the way in which the choirboys hooted the responses like little owls made me want to laugh.'

Afterwards, Alan told Gilla, 'there was a general move to the Great Central Hotel, where we had champagne and tea and coffee and wedding cake and other refreshments.' Alan's list of those present suggests that disapproval of the marriage was not widely felt. Charley, Val and Phil stayed away, and so did the Ludlows, but there was a smattering of Bonham Carters, Smiths and Nicholsons as well as Jenny, Roddy and Cousin Flora. There were, of course, plenty of Pryors. Friends of NM's turned up; they must have been aware that to do so was a faint act of defiance. Ethne's fellow art students came, as did schoolfriends and Sussex friends such as the Sayers; most touchingly, the servants from both London and Sussex were there in force. To Ethne's regret, there was not time to greet everyone. She changed into her going-away dress of soft dark blue and an enormous matching hat 'quite as wide as my shoulders', then Jack hurried her down the stairs:

'Hurry up or you'll miss your train,' someone said . . . and I could only wave to a group of people I suddenly saw on my right; I was sorry I had not time to shake hands with them for I saw they were all people from Sussex.

At last, Jack and I were alone in the car. The first thing I did was to take off my wedding ring.

'Just so that I needn't feel superstitious about it,' I said, but as I took it off I had a feeling that now I really was free, not only from superstition but from many other restraints. I gave the ring to Jack and held out my hand and asked him to put it on again.

So Ethne's memoir ends. The evening after the wedding, Ethel Portal dined at Gloucester Place. Her presence was no doubt cheering for NM; less so, perhaps, for Milicent.

16. *Arma virumque cano*

'We came back yesterday & Lor', I wish you'd been here, Royalty isn't in it,' wrote Ethne to Alan on her return from honeymoon. Marlborough Pryor, Jack's father, owned 3,700 acres at Weston and was a popular and benevolent landlord; the bride of his only son was greeted with an enthusiasm that hardly seems to belong to the twentieth century:

> We were met by <u>our</u> motor (done up & very elegant) & then when we reached the very beginning of the village we found a triumphal arch all lit up & the entire population cheering us! They insisted on pulling us the rest of the way, so the engines were stopped & they stuck on a rope . . . we were then pulled on with the whole village running along beside us letting off fireworks as they went! & cheering loudly . . . on every gate post was placed a lighted turnip with a smiling face & lanterns hung all along the drive & the house was all lit up – After tea we went out & saw most magnificent rockets, & the Church bells rang & we shook hands & grinned all round. Then we went to a big field on the way to the church where they'd made the biggest bonfire I've ever seen.

A few days later a reception was held at Weston Park to meet the bride and groom and to admire the wedding presents. Five hundred villagers were fed on 'tea and beef', and on an enormous cake made specially by the Pryors' cook. She made a small version and sent it to Gilla at the Oratory School, where it was very gratefully received. The wedding presents ranged from 'magnificent' diamonds for Ethne and the title deeds of Lannock Manor for Jack, from Marlborough Pryor, to a lace handkerchief for Ethne from Gilla's old nurse Eliza Brown. Alan and Gilla clubbed together on an antique chest of drawers, but there's no mention of a present from NM or Milicent.

The wounds inflicted by Ethne's defection healed very slowly. NM began to feel his age; both he and Milicent suffered from a series of illnesses, which in NM's case usually involved laryngitis, a sore trial for the great communicator. In 1911 the time came for NM to retire from Bart's; he felt this deeply, though his gloom at the reminder of advancing years must have been mitigated by the letter Ethel Portal sent him on his sixty-fourth birthday: 'Here is my birthday kiss – right on your lips – lingering there long – mingling my life & breath & soul with yours – telling just that one word love . . . It feels almost as if you were still in the room as you have been these two happy happy days . . . & if you were, it wouldn't be just 3 fingers & thumb [i.e. her writing hand] that would be trying to give you all my love.'

NM's retirement, of course, made little or no difference to his workload. He was appointed Consulting Physician to St Bartholomew's and was Emeritus Professor in medicine and a hospital governor. He was Secretary of the Literary Society, Librarian of the Royal Society of Medicine and President of the Samuel Johnson Society. He gave many lectures, including the 1913 Linacre Lecture on 'The Physician in English History'. And all the while he was working on his immense *History of St Bartholomew's Hospital*. In this he was helped by both Milicent and Ethel, Milicent working on the index and the more scholarly Ethel seeking out and transcribing scores of ancient charters.

The significance of Hancox for all of them continued to grow. For Ethel, it became almost a fantasy land, one where – despite Milicent – she claimed her own cocooned space: 'In the bowroom – in the garden – in "my parlour" – up & down the house – I am going over it all again & feeling the happiness that you gave me - & can see the bright crimson leaves against the grey wall & smell the delicious scent of a wood fire - & hear my Norman's well-beloved voice - & almost – but not quite – feel his touch.' It is extraordinary that only a fortnight after this letter was written, Milicent and Ethel were sharing a holiday in a rented house near Worthing while NM was in Ireland: 'I am thoroughly enjoying having Milicent here,' Ethel told NM: 'We talked all day and all the evening without stopping.'

NM's flexible mind and apparently companionable, rather than masterful, conscience enabled him to maintain Hancox as the backdrop to a happy marriage as well as a setting for his extramarital romance. (While Gilla found nests of dormice in the wooden summerhouse in the orchard, NM and Ethel used it as a trysting-place. No trace of this structure survives.) 'I wish you were here,' he wrote to Milicent from Hancox in all sincerity. 'Your sitting room has a big fire by which the Gilla & I had tea & eggs. Now I write in the bowroom with a good fire & there is one in the parlour & in the dining room & in your bedroom . . . The drawing room is all set for lectures. The traveller's joy was lovely in the woods . . . great grey tracts of it as if it had climbed the trees young & had remained to extreme old age which of course is the fact. Hancox is delightful within & without. Its only defect being the want of you.' I'm interested to note that husband and wife had separate bedrooms – earlier in the marriage they had shared – however, this was a far commoner arrangement then than it is now, and doesn't necessarily indicate a breakdown in relations.

Milicent's letters show that her energetic spirit was still very much alive. She enjoys picking hops and mushrooms – 'what sport you are missing!' – and longs to sleep out of doors: 'I got so far as hawling out the little camp bed. But I know you did not seem to like the idea when I suggested sleeping in the hammock, so with extraordinary virtue I will desist till Tuesday. By which time I can hear from you. The nights are so splendid, I don't see that it will do me anything but good.' Though nothing like Ethel's outpourings, Milicent's letters are still addressed to her 'Dearest Man' and usually contain at least one expression of affection – 'C'est toi que j'aime.'

For the teenage Gillachrist, Hancox was the bright gleam on the horizon at the end of the long, harsh terms at boarding school.

'What a comfort Hancox exists'; 'I'm simply longing to go down to Hancox again'; 'When you are making plans please bear in mind that I do want to go to Hancox . . . very much indeed.' The regime at the Oratory School was one of cold water, punishment, hard and uncongenial work, and much prayer. 'I am looking forward to coming home very much,' Gilla wrote to Milicent in December 1910, 'because I have had the roughest and hardest term I have ever had.' Schoolboy behaviour, it seems, was not much subdued by constant threats of punishment, be it in this life or the next. Gilla's diaries record fights, thefts, and acts of bullying and petty vandalism. 'After tea Gilpin's hair was smeared with a disgusting concoction of tea, salt, mustard, pepper, etc'; 'On arriving in the refectory one has to be . . . jolly careful someone does'nt [steal] your knife or glass or anything else in that line that may happen to look better than the one your neighbour has been provided with. The best plan I think on the whole is to lick everthing immediatey you get into your place.'

Being 'sent up for the rod' was an almost daily occurrence. Boys were 'swished' with a birch, or caned, or hit with a hockey stick, or 'spanked' with a wooden racket two inches thick – this last was regarded as the most painful weapon. Punishment was meted out for academic failure as well as for failing to put one's gym shoes away, breaking bounds, reading prohibited books, or any act of insubordination. Bullying seems to have gone unpunished. 'I was spanked for fooling in the game,' Gilla records. 'I had on

   i. my trousers
  ii. my shirt
 iii. my pocket handkerchief
  iv. pants
   v. pants
  vi. pants

I did put in a lot more, only Boylan gave me a spank and it sounded like a pillow so I took a lot out.' It seems that the masters, known by nicknames such as Bones, Ticky and The Hog, got wise to such ruses; later diary entries mention bare-fleshed chastisement: 'the victim lowering his unmentionables . . . receives his allotted number of strokes.'

The attitude among the boys was broadly Philistine: 'Young Ward hasn't come back yet and people say it's because he's afraid of being licked for having a father who writes books,' Gilla told NM, and Gilla himself was 'chased for being a naturalist' and challenged to fights on the grounds of his Irish descent. But school life was not unrelieved misery. Gilla made friends easily. Despite having been a sickly child he grew tall (six foot one) and strong, and enjoyed the horseplay. He describes with relish fights involving pillows, oranges, books, pellets and 'little puppy biscuits' – sometimes, the targets were the bald pates of the priests. He enjoyed the Debating Society, speaking in favour of vivisection and free trade but against conscription. Evenings were enlivened by ghost stories and secret feasts: 'Simpson and I are sharing a small feast tonight. Toffee, chocolate beans, caramels, and jujubes [similar to fruit gums].'

The Oratory would have failed today's Health and Safety standards on every count. '20 Feb. 1908. Very high wind – the floor of Fr Tristan's room fell in he fell through John's [the headmaster's] room right down to the instruction room came out at bottom unhurt. I walked through a passage just as I had got through the ceiling fell in'; '20 May 1908: Fire in the lounge, great hole burnt away in the floor'; '7 Feb. 1911. Shaw fired his pistol at the wall in the school room this morning it made an awful din.' The dormitories were bitterly cold, and the quality and quantity of food was erratic. Every February a flu epidemic laid low many of the boys. However, the priests showed some respect for the individuality of their charges. Father John, the headmaster, told Gilla he was 'a rum chap' but helped him to set up a Natural History Museum with custom-made glass display cases, a library, and a programme of lectures given by boys (including Gilla, on 'extinct mammalia') and masters. NM and his naturalist friends, who took a kindly interest in Gilla, sent skeletons, nests, eggs, books and stuffed animals to stock the museum. There was an aquarium, too, but this caused problems because someone would keep spearing the catfish with a poisoned arrow (an exhibit), and neglect during the holidays meant that specimens were too often found floating belly-up at the beginning of term. On the whole, though, the museum was a thriving concern. Its committee was often riven with dissent, but it was shown to visitors with pride, and it survived Gilla's time at the Oratory.

Catholicism was woven into the fabric of the day – 'Benediction in the afternoon. Sausages' – and observance was of course compulsory, but a certain amount of discussion was tolerated. One of the priests told Gilla that he 'believed Darwin's theory'. Gilla's piety remained intact: 'Retreat begins. Lovely jaw [lecture or sermon] all about Heaven and Hell'. He asked Milicent to send Hancox flowers for the chapel. At her urging, he prayed for Alan's conversion, and received, apparently with pleasure, the news that she had turned his bedroom at Gloucester Place into an oratory. NM's letters to his youngest child are affectionate and full of detail about birds and beasts, but a shadow is cast by his attitude towards learning. NM was unable to attribute Gilla's repeated academic failures to anything other than laziness: 'I wish that you could think of work. When you have acquired the power of hard work & attained some knowledge you will be better able to see how you ought to spend your life . . . think of your work & not of yourself.'

Although Milicent's letters to Gilla also urged him to 'buck up', she did try to soften NM's attitude towards his scholastic failures. In August 1908 she wrote to NM, 'Certainly his report is bad, and disappointing . . . He has, of course, a very bad memory . . . of course he is very thoughtless in one way . . . But in other ways he is most thoughtful: he has really shown fine qualities in my illness – great consideration, and a great sense of responsibility. He has character.'

The thought that Gilla might not be able to get into Cambridge worried NM terribly. 'I often think of you,' he wrote on 7 May 1911, 'and hope you are working every day & hour so that October year may see you at Alma Mater Cantabrigia.' NM, in many ways broad-minded, showed no flexibility or imagination when it came to planning his sons' futures – all he could think of was that they would replicate his own youthful experience.

The irony was that Gilla was not idle. His notebooks, which he called 'Hodgepodge', are full of intelligent observations and competent sketches. He often pursued subjects of his own accord: 'Oct. 22nd 1910. Did some more on the Earthworm what a very interesting animal he is.' He had great difficulty mastering mathematics, Latin grammar and English spelling, but his problems with spelling didn't hold him back from enjoying reading and writing. He had the family taste for recording impressions and events, the same instinct for locating his personal history in a wider context. In one diary he records his earliest memories: 'Sitting in my perambulator in the front hall at 94 waiting to be wheeled out to go into the park and Papa coming and pretending to give me apples from the ones painted on the front door.' He remembers horses running away, seeing a steam omnibus, people getting too close to a blazing railway car and the firemen turning the hose on them, 'seamonsters' at the Hippodrome, the Christmas tree at home and 'being given Prince the wooden horse by Mother'. Amy, however, is absent from his memory of his fourth birthday:

> It was a very foggy day indeed and the ellectric light had only just been put in and of course when it was most wanted it failed and we had to light candles – and sat down to tea and there were four candles on my cake and I rather think they were stuck in reels of cotton. And Alan going out and getting me a brass cannon. Later on Father fired it off. He put it on the window ledge of the consulting room and I stood on his writing table then he took a piece of paper which he light from the fire and touched it off. It fell over on its muzzle I remember.

Gilla was fascinated by his great-uncle Ben. Dementia had placed the old man beyond anybody's reach, but Gilla read books on polar exploration: 'I want to go on an Arctic expedition perhaps I may some day who knows?' He struck up a friendship with Hugh Frewen, a Sussex neighbour (and cousin of Winston Church-ill) who though only in his twenties had travelled much in Africa and had at times ruled a Nigerian province. Frewen had brought back many trophies to his house, Brickwall in Northiam, includ-ing live animals; Gilla was very impressed that gazelles were allowed to wander freely in the drawing room. The young explorer corre-sponded with the schoolboy – 'I got a ripping letter from Hugh Fruin who was in Nigeria all about gaselle shooting' – and gave him exhibits for his museum. A beautifully mounted skeleton of a monkey is still at Hancox.

Gilla had a strong sense of duty, but he remained uncowed by academic pressures from home and school. The receipt of every end-of-term report resulted in a 'row', in which he stood up for himself. He expressed himself forcibly in a letter to his father on 9 July 1912, near the end of his time at the Oratory:

> I was very much surprised at your letter this morning . . . Every one of [the Masters] will bear out that I've done my very best in this exam and I cant do more than that can I? I know you think I've got a sort of geneus only I'm too lazy to use it, but the sooner you get rid of that [idea] the better . . . By taking up the attitude you are taking, it doesn't make me want to work any harder in fact rather the reverse, until you cease to look on me as a sort of lazy hound who doesn't care a hang for your feelings or his own success you wont encourage me a bit . . . The fact is you've always looked on me as if I was ten years old . . . you never have understood that I'm not quite such an ass as not to want to get on.

School holidays began in London, where Gilla renewed his acquaintance with the inhabitants of Regent's Park Zoo: 'Got round the keper in the small mamel's house first he took a coati mondy out of its cage and shewed it to me then a Kinkajou he took me behind the house were there were two more coati's I saw a very fine wild cat and some badgers two of which were a funny

colour not quite albino he also fed the otter.' Gilla kept creatures
of his own: 'I went to Gamages to try and get a tortoise to eat the
black beetles in the kitchen but could not so I bought two Japanese newts.' (Not, presumably, to fulfil the same function. I doubt
whether in any case a tortoise would have done the trick; my own
childhood memories tell me that tortoises eat mainly buttercups
and lettuce.) Gilla already had two tortoises which lived at Hancox, Mahomet V and Abdul Hamid. He kept lizards in London
and ferrets, obtained from Crowham, at Hancox; he built the ferrets 'a refectory'. He searched the fields for caterpillars, frogs and
snakes; Rose Playford remembered with great amusement how he
used a grass snake to give the cook a scare. This was a good-natured
prank. The cook was very fond of Gilla, who used to stand in the
kitchen doorway, rubbing his stomach and pulling a face, until she
relented and supplied him with between-meals sustenance. That
snake is still at Hancox, blackish and bottled. I've never felt justified in throwing it away.

At Hancox, Gilla went shooting with Alan, Willy junior and
the farm boys, and occasionally with his father who, he noted with
surprise, was 'quite a good shot'. He sailed with Alan, and played
tennis or croquet 'almost every day'. He went riding with Milicent
and took long walks in all weathers, often walking to Crowham or
Hastings. He cycled too, and experimented with Alan's penny-
farthing, bought more as a curiosity than as a practical means of
conveyance. He sketched, and decorated his bedroom wall with
a frieze of swans, ducks and geese. They're still there, and will
remain there as long as I have anything to do with it.

Gilla's desire to spend time at Hancox was always strong, and at
the end of 1910 it became stronger still. At the time when Ethne
was settling down to a happy married life, and NM and Ethel Portal were privately celebrating two years of intense romance, Gilla,
aged only sixteen, met the love of his life. '29 Dec went to dance
at the Adamsons. Was introduced to Mary Haviland ripping.' The
following evening they met at a dinner at Battle Abbey, and on
New Year's Eve Mary's parents hosted another dance. 'Best of the

lot,' wrote Gilla. 'Asked her if I could write to her reply in affirm-
ative.' He ornamented the endpapers of his diary with endless rep-
etitions of 'MKH' – Mary Katherine Haviland.

Mary was the same age as Gilla; when they met, she was still in
the schoolroom, and wore her thick dark hair 'down'. She lived at
Brightling Place, a handsome early-nineteenth-century house in
the same village where General Ludlow and Bella had married,
and where Barbara was buried. The Haviland parents seem to have
been pleasant, conventional Anglicans, active in the parish, protective of their only child and not ambitious for her. Mary spent
most of her time at home with Miss Young, 'Youngster', her
beloved but comically inept governess.

Things moved fast between Gilla and Mary. On 5 January 1911,
Gilla bicycled to Mayfield to visit Roddy and Aunt Jenny: 'Called
at Brightling Place on the way mkh mkh mkh mkh ripping ripping ripping ripping.' I'm sorry to report that the next day, spent
with his grandmother and aunt, was 'deadly dull', but on the way
home he called on Mary again and was smitten afresh: 'I fall deeper
into the mire. N.b. funny sort of mire.' He consulted Aunt Charley as to whether she thought it would be a good idea for him to
kiss Mary. Charley's reply was encouraging. On his last day in Sussex, 17 January, he was asked to tea at Brightling Place. The compliant Miss Young retired early, and 'I had Mary alone for an hour
in fact two hours. Did it on the verandah just before going away X
It was beastly leaving her simply beastly.' (I take this to mean that
a kiss was exchanged.) Two days later he returned to the Oratory.
'Rotten train. Here I am. DAMN!!!!!'

The very next morning brought 'a ripping letter from Mary . . .
She sent me her <u>love</u>.' The correspondence blossomed, to the envy,
I imagine, of Gilla's schoolfellows. She sent photographs, too; she's
a round-faced, sweet-eyed girl with a heavy jaw and a friendly,
toothy smile. In one photograph she's holding Peter, a wire-haired
fox terrier Gilla ordered for her from the Army and Navy Stores. He
confided in Ethne, and she wrote back sympathetically, sometimes
enclosing a postal order to help with the expenses of courtship.

Gilla stored Mary's letters in a black tin box. On the lid he scratched two mottoes, '*Nitor In Adversum*' (Edmund Burke's tag, adopted by NM) and 'Faint Heart Never Won Fair Lady'. The latter features in an Edwardian board game we have called 'The Prince's Quest'. Perhaps Gilla played this in his childhood. It's based on the story of the Sleeping Beauty; each prince sets out on a path beset by magical dangers. Their quest ends with a battle through the briar thicket that surrounds the sleeping princess. In courtship, Gilla, like his father before him, saw himself as a dragon-slayer, a faithful knight who would prove himself worthy of his lady's hand.

Mary's letters, frustratingly undated, contain plenty of teenage fervour. 'Just heaps & heaps & yards & bushels, & gallons & acres & stacks of love, from yours till hell freezes.' An only child, she obviously enjoys having Gilla to chat to. She writes matily of the perils of being female – 'You may be thankful you aren't a girl when its windy. Oh it is awful when your skirts all blow up, & your hat blows off, & your hair gets in your eyes!' – and of the difficulties of conducting a love affair in secret – 'I used to take your letters to bed with me . . . but twice I left the wretched thing under my pillow & found it in the morning put out in my room, found by the servants when they made my bed. I felt such an ass I never dared do it again!'

She shows a girlish preoccupation with her weight: 'Everyone thinks I'm getting so thin & look ill!!!!! Think of me getting thin. I'm awfully pleased only I'm afraid it won't last long. I'm pining for you I s'pect Gilla dear'; 'I didn't really mean anything about Joan being fat, but she is fatter than I am, much! I was weighed on Friday night in St Leonard's after tea at Addisons too, & was pleased to find I'd only gone up 3lbs since last June.' I particularly like this letter, for two reasons. One is that 'Joan' was well known to me – Joan Ashton, then living at Vinehall, later Joan Whistler, granddaughter of the Mr Watts who had advised Milicent about farming practices. Mrs Whistler was a tremendous character in my early life, forceful, opinionated, funny, interested in everything. Her grandchildren are friends of mine. The second is that, in my child-

hood, tea at Addison's, a large shop in Hastings, was a great treat.
I remember going there with Hilary, my late aunt, and eating a
round thing made of pliable chocolate, miraculously filled with
cream. It was a bit like a giant profiterole without the pastry, and
I'd never encountered anything so luxurious in my whole life.
Addison's, too, featured in General Ludlow's diaries and in Milicent's memory, and catered for family weddings until the 1960s.
Joan Whistler, when I knew her, was certainly not slender, and
I imagine that any weight Mary Haviland lost pining for Gilla was
quickly regained, judging by another letter: 'I wish you had been
here for tea tonight – in the schoolroom. We had eggs, new bread,
tea-cakes, honey, blackberry jam, shrimp paste & <u>Devonshire cream</u>.
Doesn't that make your mouth water.'

Mary's letters are full of affectionate concern – 'I wish you were
ill here, I'd nurse you with great energy' – but they are also the
letters of a very young and inexperienced girl. She seems sometimes to have been taken aback by Gilla's ardour: 'Gilla dearest,
don't be cross . . . It isn't that I find it hard to imagine your feelings
to me . . . but when I am with you I forget . . . that I am anything
more than just a pal to you . . . You must try now & think how a
girl feels – that she loves a pal and is proud of him . . . but she likes
him indifferent to his sex.' This cannot have been exactly what
Gilla hoped to hear. Gilla correctly identified Miss Young, the
governess, as a potential ally, and sent her boxes of chocolates,
with the instruction to Mary, 'see she doesn't eat them all at once.'
'Youngster' was, in her charge's opinion, 'the brickiest brick that
[ever] existed.' But Mary's educational predicament would have
horrified an Aunt Barbara. 'I make out the timetable at the beginning of each term, & I always have to tell her how to arrange her
book that she keeps marks etc in. I always set my own prep . . . I
get very interested in my prep when I'm doing it alone, but when
Y. is here in the room & I'm doing it its awful 'cause she talks
hard about her hats or her bills or something & I talk back.' But
'Youngster' fulfilled a valuable role in Mary's somewhat restricted
existence. 'Bad luck for you losing your special pal,' she wrote

to Gilla after one of his friends had left the Oratory; 'Before Youngster came I had an awfully lonely life. I'm dreading the time when I put my hair up & haven't got Y. Oh its horrid, absolutely horrid when you feel you oughtn't to be alive & that you weren't wanted.' Gilla's unswerving devotion must have done much to dispel that feeling.

The summer of 1911 was famously hot. Gilla spent much of it at Hancox. He neglected his diary, but compiled a summary of the highlights:

1. Birth of John Walter Peregrine [Ethne's first son].
2. Strikes.
3. Wasps.
4. Heat.
5. Mary Katherine Haviland
   Tennis
   Dance – when the dance was over I went back to B.Place and slept the night there in a room opposite Mary.
   Cricket match – Mary was scoring just behind me.

This list is followed by a poem touching on the melancholy of parting, which has been carefully scribbled out.

Mary's behaviour is usually 'ripping' ('She was ripping in the car'), her absence invariably 'beastly'. Gilla often comments on the limits of his ability to express his feelings verbally – 'To Brightling to see Mary for the last time till we meet again. It couldn't have been better and she is – to put it in words is impossible.' But the simplicity with which he describes the affair is touching in itself. On 26 October 1911 he goes for a long solitary walk from school into the hills beyond Birmingham. 'One view with the mist and rain on it looked just like the view out of my window at home and I imagined that Mary was just over those hills.'

Obviously, I don't have Gilla's answers to Mary's letters. But a few scraps do survive. There's a pencilled note in his handwriting, apparently planning a clandestine meeting in London, suggesting hiding 'if necessary' and pretending to arrange to meet a friend. There's also a note which seems to be a timetable of prayer. Of all the obstacles that lay between them, the difference in religion was likely to be the greatest. The note suggests that Gilla was praying hard for Mary's conversion. Could she have been hoping that things would move in the opposite direction? Describing a wedding she attended in July 1911, she told him, 'When I eat the wedding cake & was told to wish I wished something to do with you but I won't tell you what it was.'

I also found the rough draft of a letter Gilla wrote to Mary towards the end of his schooldays. This gives a clear picture both of life at the Oratory and of the frank and easy intimacy that usually characterized their relationship:

My d.M. Thursday night.

I'm writing to you for once in a way during prep cause I've just got your letter and I feel sort of inspired. Your letter didn't come until 3rd post . . . I got one of the men to get it for me while tea was going on and he brought it under a bread plate without telling me, and put the plate down on the table and of course when someone asked for the bread and the plate was moved away there was the letter underneath and of course everyone grabbed at [it] . . . Yes you must be pleased at having done with the dentist, and I hope you're improving your American accent, when is the play on the 5th isn't it? Good luck. I hope your French girl will be away when I come and see you cause it always sends me into fits of laughter when I hear other people talking French and oh it would make me feel so horribly shy – It snowed again today just as we had started playing football and its like living in an icehouse, about 15 people are down with flue . . . I'm absolutely determined not to get it this term cause there simply isn't time. It wouldn't be so bad only fogs and wind and snow always give me sore throats which are horrid things aren't they? I'm simply <u>longing</u> and <u>longing</u> for Cambridge now, and whenever I go into any of the masters rooms here I always try and find out how much their armchairs and things cost for my rooms . . .

Sometimes in bed I have awfull mental fits about whether I'm going to pass or not really I get hot all over, that reminds me I had such an odd dream the other night I dreamt that you and your Pa came to lunch at Hancox at least I invited you and didn't tell my people and then when you arrived my ma [Milicent] was furious and said you'd got to wait till we'd had lunch and then if you would each sing a song she might possibly let you have the remains. Then your Pa said 'Oh I'm going up to the Royal Oak to have some beer' and you said 'So am I' and I was awfully shocked then your Pa opened the front door to go out when he suddenly turned round and said 'Why there's fire engines full of beer in the drive' and everyone screamed out 'don't let him drink it the horses have got scarlet fever' and then I woke up and that again reminds me that during the cold weather they gave us ½ an hour's soak [lie-in] which = ½ hours extra bed. Ripping word soak don't you think exactly describes it doesn't it?

Mary sent an account of a dream of her own, one full of foreboding:

Gilla dear I had a most <u>awfully</u> vivid dream about you this morning . . . you & I & Dr & Mrs Moore . . . motored to Rye & we had lunch at an inn place in the garden on a lawn. You went away before we began lunch, & you were all right then, & then you came back to us & sat on a seat & I looked at you & you looked <u>awfully fearfully</u> ill, all sort of shrivelled up & white, & no one said anything or took any notice & I leaned over to you & said Poor old dear I am sorry or something like that and Dr Moore saw me and said Tut Tut. Then you got more & more ill & shrivelled up & I howled . . . What were you doing at 7.30 to 8 this morning? It was <u>horrid</u>. I kept thinking about it all the morning. Hope it didn't mean anything.

*

Following the departure of Ethne and the retirement – with some loss of income – of NM, Milicent decided to reduce the number of servants at Gloucester Place from six to four. 'We may have to

do a little more for ourselves but that will not hurt us!' she wrote
to Gilla. Milicent was busy enough already, but she throve on
activity. She was a commandant with the Red Cross and a committee member of the St Bartholomew's Women's Guild, she was
Treasurer of the Choral Society of the Catholic Women's League,
and in 1913 she took on a weightier responsibility. She told Gilla:

I am on a Committee at the Local Government Board on District
Nursing in London, to represent the Cardinal. I am awfully proud, &
need taking down! In consequence of the job I went round in Ber-
mondsey one morning with a Catholic nurse, it was *very* interesting, but sad – A baby recovering from pneumonia in a box (it was
all right in the box!) the father who has been turned off his job . . .
several little girls standing about, and the mother out at work trying to keep them all.

Running two households and keeping up with friends and
acquaintances and with the extended family also took up a huge
amount of Milicent's time. She continued to involve herself closely
with Charley, Val and Phil. Bella, a cheerful but overworked doctor's wife at Northiam – she kept only one servant, to everyone's
astonishment, and rose at six to do the housework – produced
three babies in quick succession. 'Bella had a daughter (female),'
Gilla wrote carefully in his diary. The family often came over to
Hancox, Bella driving the little ones in the pony trap.

Lionel and Agnes were still living in India, where Lionel was head
chemist at the cordite factory. They sent their two pretty dark-
haired daughters Medora and Nancy back to England, where they
were shuttled between various sets of relatives, Milicent taking her
turn. Aunt Jenny and Roddy, at Mayfield, still had to be consoled
for the loss of Crowham; Willy junior had to be supported in his
brave attempt to manage alone in rented rooms at Hastings – 'There
is no bathroom which is rather beastly,' he complained to Alan. Alan
himself had become a reluctant medical inspector of Hampshire
schools, and had taken lodgings in Basingstoke. Aunt Jenny wrote

to him, 'It's funny to think of you living at Basingstoke which I have never thought of as anything but a railway station where you change for everywhere can you really live in it & have you got a nice lodging with two rooms so that you don't have to eat your dinner in the waiting room?'

On 31 December 1912, Eira Ludlow arrived at Hancox with the news that Uncle Ben was sinking fast. For some time he had lived at Frognal in Hampstead, cared for by two male attendants, and, it seems, supervised by Mabel and Ludlow and by Dr Neale, the ship's doctor of the *Eira*.

Ben died on 3 January 1913, aged eighty-five. The coffin was brought to Sussex by train. Aunt Charley slept at Hancox; on the morning of 7 January she and Phil and Alan and Milicent drove to Robertsbridge, where the funeral procession started, and climbed into the waiting carriages. Ben was buried in Brightling churchyard, near Barbara and Aunt Dolly Longden, the maternal aunt who had helped to bring him up. Alan noted on his nautical greatuncle's behalf that 'on the way a distant view of the sea near Beachy Head was had with bright patches on the water where the sun struck through the mist.'

NM did not attend the funeral, whether due to pressure of work, or out of respect for old enmity, or to grasp the chance of a day alone with Ethel I don't know. Roddy, Mabel, Ludlow and Bella were the other family members present, beside a few more distant relatives and a good many villagers. Val's absence from his father's funeral was neither commented on nor explained.

Milicent wrote a full account for NM and posted it to him at Ethel's flat:

Dearest Man,
    . . . All went without a hitch . . . There was a large cross of flowers from Charlotte & a wreath of daffodils from Aunt Nannie. Dr. Neale represented the Geographical Society . . . yet there was something aloof about the whole thing, as if he did not really belong here . . .

Charlotte is resting on her bed. She suddenly realized she was very tired. Dr. Neale seems to know 'all about' the will. Val gets most, Charlotte what seems to me quite good, but Phil only £150 a year. Dr. Neale spoke with great assurance. He was in the carriage with Alan and me, seems to be a good sort of man. Alan heard Phil told, & says he took it quite well. . .

P.P.S. After tea Charlotte produced a précis of the will & read it, if you see her <u>do not mention</u> that we heard about it first from Dr Neale, as I did not. She might not have liked it.

Crowham gets nothing, tho' if both Val & Phil had died, the Crowham family would have succeeded.

Old habits died hard. Milicent still talked of Aunt Jenny's family as 'Crowham', though Crowham had been sold three years before. The gross value of Ben's estate was £110,781 – about £10 million in early twenty-first-century terms. This was nothing compared to his cousin Valentine Smith, who had left an astonishing £2 million when he died in 1906.

Val moved into Scalands, alone except for the servants and an Irish wolfhound called Jim. His father's legacy meant that any thoughts of earning a living could be safely abandoned. 'Val is a remarkable person,' wrote Alan in a (later) letter to NM; 'He has great abilities, & has thought upon & is read in many subjects I should hardly have suspected him to be interested in. He is however obsessed with the notion that the English are an incapable race & that Englishmen are not worth knowing . . . It's difficult to determine wherein his defects lie: not precisely in character, though partly. He tries to do all he can to please, but does not like to have his opinions questioned.' At Scalands Val was able to shield himself and his 'defects' – which in my opinion amount to Asperger Syndrome – from the outside world. He lived in seclusion, creating an oak plantation and playing his flute, spinet and clavichord. When Gilla visited he loved poring over Ben's photographs and other Arctic memorabilia with Val, and listening to the *Eira*'s musical box, imagining the comfort its sound must have brought to the stranded crew.

'Aunt Charley is making the house very pretty,' wrote Alan after a visit to Brown's in April. She converted one room into a chapel. Charley's Catholic faith was deep and unquestioning, though she edited out the bits that didn't suit her. 'Charley, how <u>can</u> you believe all this nonsense about the Assumption?' my father remembers his father asking her at lunch one day. 'Oh no, Alain, eet eez lies, all lies,' she assured him. But the 'lies' didn't spoil the great joy she found in worship. 'I don't <u>love</u> Jesus the way Charlotte does,' said Milicent wistfully to Norman, my uncle. While Ben lived, however mentally incapacitated he was, Charley would not have dared to create a chapel at Brown's, let alone invite outsiders to use it, but on 22 November 1913 Milicent proudly sent Gilla a newspaper cutting. 'A new Catholic centre has been opened in Sussex at Robertsbridge, where Mass is now said on Sundays and holidays of obligation at the residence of Mrs Leigh Smith. Mass had not been celebrated at Robertsbridge since the Reformation.'

*

Gilla claimed to work ten hours a day for his Cambridge entrance exam, and his efforts were rewarded. In October 1912 he went up to St Catharine's, his father's old college. Cambridge was a release and a revelation. 'I think Cambridge is the rippingest place on earth,' he told NM, 'Goodbye yours very busy and very happy Gilla.'

Undergraduate life suited him well. He rowed for the college, and attended riotous 'bump suppers'; 'Some people a bit screwd Bartlett got DT [delirium tremens?] and started firing off a revolver . . . Knight finally captured him but he shot himself with his own arm. Most of his furniture smashed.' Gilla hired a motorcycle and explored Cambridgeshire: 'Started across Gog & Magog hills through an awfully pretty village of white houses with thatched roofs which made me feel quite ashamed to be on a motorbike.' His two greatest friends were Leonard Ward-Price and Jim McNaught Davis; they were fellow members of a dining society called the 'Entre-Nous'. Their letters, often on the subject of girls, show an easy, relaxed friendship. 'Went up to the [boat]

sheds,' wrote Gilla in his diary, 'and bathed with Ward-P & lay on
the roof sunning ourselves & watching the damsels go by.'

But university life was not unalloyed pleasure. At that time all
undergraduates had to pass the dreaded 'Littlego', an exam requir-
ing mathematics, regardless of their choice of degree subject (Gilla's was natural science). Gilla failed the Littlego, twice. Pressure
from home became intense. Gilla, realizing that his ambition to
become a naturalist was unlikely to earn him a living, considered
an army career; Mary Haviland's approval of this plan strengthened his resolve. He consulted his father, but NM refused to discuss the matter:

> Your Littlego disaster distressed me much for it looks as if you
> had accomplished nothing in your first year. I certainly under-
> stood you meant to work hard at Cambridge when you went up.
> You must get through in October.
>
> I feel no heart to talk about military affairs for all future proceed-
> ings seem too absolutely uncertain in view of these repeated failures.

Gilla replied with defiance tempered with a genuine attempt to
see things from his father's point of view:

> If you judge me as a whole and as a son by the Littlego I'm either a
> madman or else utterly worthless and no use to anyone and if that
> is the case you'd better forget all about me and get me a post as you
> once suggested as a grocer's mate. I don't think I am mad though . . .
> I may be mathematically mad and worthless but there are luckily
> some other things in the world besides maths . . . I find that I can
> enter the Army without taking any mathematics at all . . . As for
> the Littlego I . . . fully realize what a beast I've been over it . . . but
> I only ask that you wont judge me absolutely by that . . . Of course
> if you've any objection to the Army as a profession I wouldn't think
> of going against your judgement but otherwise I want to put my
> name down as soon as possible . . . <u>DO</u> cheer up you know these
> things <u>really</u> are <u>not</u> tragedies they are only your affectionate son

> choosing his profession
> Gilla
> . . . An owl is hooting on the backs.

Gilla joined the Officers' Training Corps and spent several weeks of the summer of 1913 and 1914 at army camps. To the great relief of all, he finally passed the Littlego in October 1913. 'So that's done,' is the only comment in his diary.

★

94 Gloucester Place had come to seem unnecessarily large. A house on the other side of the street, number 67, fell vacant, and NM and Milicent decided to move. 67 had one storey fewer, but being a corner house it had more light. Milicent masterminded the move, in September 1913, while NM was in Ireland. 'I am really glad to be leaving 94,' wrote NM. 'It was too big perhaps but anyhow had some sadness in it from which 67 will be free as Hancox is.' He felt guilty about avoiding the upheaval of the move. 'Do little enough . . . Be happy,' he urged.

Busy with the move, Milicent was also obliged to resume her role as an active aunt. Eira, Mabel's eldest daughter, had had to have several operations to remove sections of jawbone diseased by an infected mosquito bite. Her ordeal, and the scars it left, sent Mabel into a new depression. Milicent stepped in, and Eira, Anne and Sylvia became frequent visitors at 67 Gloucester Place and at Hancox. Their brother John, following in the Ludlow tradition, had chosen an army career and was training at Sandhurst. The girls were jolly holiday company for Gilla. They came to Hancox; he took them to the sea at Pett Level and introduced them to his local friends, including Mary. '19.4.14 Spent the time after tea dancing on the lawn & blowing a coach horn; finally driven away by gnats.' There are faint hints that sixteen-year-old Sylvia was already showing signs of 'the family taint'; she often withdrew early, blaming an aching head or general feelings of malaise, but Gilla and eighteen-year-old Anne, who was exceptionally pretty and lively, would talk late into the night. On 16 June 1914 Gilla introduced her to his friend Jim McNaught Davis, who fell instantly in love.

'McNaught' relied on Gilla to create opportunities for meeting: 'July 4th. Just heard from the Precious Anne. Gad, I hope she'll be with you when I'm there: lived in a dire state since camp. Let me know if she's coming . . . many thanks you old brick.' McNaught's intentions were serious – 'By heaven Gilla lad I w'd give anything to have her as my wife' – but he realized he had little chance of impressing the Ludlow parents, and though Anne wrote to him, he feared that his hopes were 'madness'; 'You know Gilla I don't think she w'd marry me if I had pots of Brass: As it is you know I am a penniless devil: & at the best can only hope for a few hundred from the Pater.'

Gilla and Mary still regarded themselves as a couple, though when Gilla went up to Cambridge Mary seems to have insisted on a cooling-off period. They still exchanged letters, but less frequently. There's an intriguing letter from Mary, dated 3 December 1913, sent to him at Cambridge:

Cheer oh you'll soon be 21. [Gilla was 19.] I know its rotten not being independent. I want to be too. But don't worry you soon will be.

You mustn't have these morals about women. I shall have to speak seriously to you when we meet. I can see that.

Have a good time with the girl and have the lights out. Think what I've always told you to do . . .

It will do you good and her too.

The ways in which language is used to describe human relationships has changed so much over the last century that I hesitate to put too obvious an interpretation on this.

It seems that the bond between Gilla and Mary was quite widely acknowledged. 'Nov. 18 '13. Mrs LS [Aunt Charley] & mother talked about us again,' wrote Mary. 'She knew about last Sunday because Val had told her but said she was not going to tell your people because they would not like it. She said your father was "much against it" & "Milicent was not quite sure." She then said "Val thinks she is such a <u>modern</u> girl." Whatever that may mean I don't know but it does not sound very flattering!!' Mary's name is not once mentioned in any of NM's letters, but an obscure reference in Gilla's diary suggests that she had become the subject of family rows.

A desire to win Mary's heart and hand once and for all lay behind Gilla's decision to join the Army. Mary did not share Gilla's naturalist tastes; his notebook records that she possessed some 'rather decent rabbits', but her interest in animals didn't extend beyond pets. She did, however, think highly of the courage and discipline of soldiers. Though Val thought her 'a modern girl', Mary was conservative by instinct ('March 7 1912. Isn't the strike rotten . . . And aren't the suffragettes simply awful. It makes me ashamed to be a girl. I think they ought all to be taken off to an island in the middle of the Pacific!') For her and for Gilla, defending the honour of King and Country was a high calling. In the summer of 1913, when Gilla made his decision to join the Army, no one foresaw how soon he would be called upon to put his ideals into practice.

*

It all happened so quickly. Gilla spent July 1914 at Hancox. His days were filled with the usual summer pursuits. 'To Brown's with some flowers for the chapel then to Battle & picked up some cartridges from the station then on to Crowhurst & met Papa. Got three rabbits in the nineteen acre after tea, came back & had a game of croquet with Milicent. A very hot day.' This is a typical diary entry. But on 25 July a different note crept in, for the first time: 'In the evening began to realise the foreign situation.'

NM was quick to realize that they were on the brink of a cataclysm. He had not, till then, kept a regular diary, but on 31 July he began a war journal in a large, red-bound manuscript volume. It was to be both a public and a personal account of momentous events. At Hancox, on 2 August the parlourmaid Lily Chandler came in with the news that Russia had mobilized. That evening Ethel Portal sent a telegram: 'Germany occupied Luxembourg Reported repulse of Germans by French near Nancy: unofficial.

Ethel.' 'I did not wait dinner,' wrote NM, 'but went to meet Gillachrist at Robertsbridge in the car & stopped at Vinehall where they [his friends Lord & Lady Ashton, Joan's parents] were finishing dinner (& I ate a green fig). They grew more serious . . . as they thought of the telegram.' He went on to Robertsbridge station, where he sent a reply to Ethel: 'The clerk came out to me on the platform & said "Is this telegram in code or cipher for we have orders not to send any such?" No I said it is in Gaelic I will read it to you & so I did & he was satisfied.'

The train was over an hour late, but:

the Gilla . . . stepped out gaily and we got in the car & drove to Browns. He said that a commander R.N. was in the carriage with him & told him that the Germans had broken neutrality & that probably the French & Germans were at war & we should be so soon.

At Browns were Mrs Leigh Smith [Charley] & Alan & Father Geddes S.J. [Charley usually had a tame Jesuit in tow] . . . & Philip Leigh Smith [just arrived] from Paris via Havre. They were anchored four hours & detained by a British Destroyer which called them to stop & again said Why the Devil don't you stop? So they stopped & their wireless apparatus was removed. Phil just caught the train, which was crammed, at Paris. He thought the French seemed depressed about the war & heard talk of the probability of defeat.

Two days later NM added:

At our aunt's request I painted on the window end of the oak beam over the fireplace to commemorate the beginning of war & our meeting together at Brown's:

ARMA – VIRUMQUE – CANO*
A.D. IIII. NON. AUG
MCMXIV

* The opening line of the *Æneid*: 'Of arms and the man I sing.'

We had a supper of cold chicken & duck & potato & other meats & apple pie . . . & then Alan, Gillachrist & I all the men of the house of Moore (for I suppose Ethne's little Johnnie is a Pryor) drove off to Vinehall which we reached about 11.40. Lord Ashton & Lady Ashton & Joan in shawls & dressing gowns came down & learnt the news & then we came to Hancox & at 1 a.m. I went to bed leaving Alan & the Gilla talking.

To supplement her telegram, Ethel had written a letter. She had spent the day in the British Museum: 'As I gave back my book to the attendant in the inner circle, a fellow attendant just returning I suppose from the all-important Museum Tea said to him "They're shouting 'War declared' outside" – "Oh" said my man – "If that's true, I've lost ten bob."'

Two days later, on 4 August, Roberta, the housemaid at Glouces-ter Place, telephoned with the news that 'Master Gilla had got a commission in the Army & Master Alan was to be appointed a surgeon in the Navy.' Another telegram arrived: 'Ultimatum sent to Germany respect Belgian Neutrality or we declare war at mid-night Ethel.' She wrote to NM the next day, 'So the suspense is over at last & we are at war & such a war as never was before . . . Your two brave boys are coming to dine here tonight . . . Pride in them & heartache for them fill my mind . . . All my love is flowing out to you . . . I think if they were my own boys too I could hardly be feeling with you more strongly & tenderly.' This is as close as Ethel came to expressing the longing that must always have been present, the desire to have shared NM's life fully, to have been his wife and the mother of his children.

Alan and Gilla saw a lot of Miss Portal while they remained in London awaiting orders. 'We had a measuring with the tape meas-ure round the chest,' she wrote, '& there was very little difference between them in spite of Gilla's more stalwart appearance.' The young men were impatient for action: 'The poor boys are evidently chafing at the delay as to their destinations, but they were so cheery & charming – My two Abyssinian swords . . . were drawn & used to show a sword exercise. Then we all went to the bathroom & washed off some inches of Abyssinian dust.' Ethel compared the mood in London with the gung-ho jollity she remembered at the beginning of the Boer War: 'The general atmosphere is one of great solemnity & sadness . . . We have at last realised that war is not a joke nor a melodrama.'

Small signs of war began to appear. A band of children in Ethel's street marched 'to a biscuit tin drum with a Union Jack flying . . . making a great noise'. Ethne wrote that the Pryor girls were in floods of tears because their hunters had been taken for military use. Their lamentations were augmented by the fact that Jack was worried about the fate of the family business. 'I feel as if we were all people in a H. G. Wells novel! . . . I should say there was quite a chance we might all be ruined. I don't mind for us . . . but . . . the girls say "we shall never get married when we are all penniless spinsters." ' Her three-year-old Johnnie 'shot a piano tuner . . . quite rightly suspecting him of being German. The P.T. didn't mind a bit & asked J. how old he was, but he had to go & ask Nanny.' Troops of soldiers were soon marching down Gloucester Place singing 'It's a Long Way to Tipperary'. NM and Milicent offered Hancox as a hospital; their offer was declined, which was just as well as it's hard to imagine a more unsuitable building. Alan, helped by Hammond the chauffeur (Paci had retired) and Murduck, a local builder, erected a flagstaff in the Forestall to fly the Red Cross flag, should the offer be accepted. The Prussian landlord of the Ostrich Inn at Robertsbridge was interned.

When aeroplanes flew over Hancox, the whole household turned out to look; it was several months before they were treated as commonplace. NM's journal contrasts the warm, peaceful days and nights of August with these portents of catastrophe. 'Aug.13. After dinner Gillachrist heard what he thought an aeroplane & we went out but it was too dark to see; a lovely starlight night. The great bear partly about the drawing room end of Hancox & Cassiopeia's chair above the middle. I saw one bright meteor. We sat on the teak seat but heard no more, came in . . . The

Gilla read Wood's Achievements of Cavalry . . . & I some of Dorset's poems.'

The day after this, Gilla went to Brightling Place to take his leave of Mary. He then went on to Lannock to see his sister Ethne. Mary wrote to him there:

My dear Gilla, here are the photos will you send back whichever you like least. I know you will hate both at least I do. It was very nice of you to come yesterday . . . I wish I could have got off more but it is so difficult especially with Pa's eye upon me and things have not been very smooth at home just lately. Thunder has been in the air. . .

I shall keep your pin very safe and value it very much. I hope you didn't mind parting with it. It was rather a shame to make you but I do like having it.

Don't forget all about me. I shall think about you very often. You are squinting at me now, about 3 inches off my nose.

Good luck to you all the time in everything and if you can tell me where you are I shall very much like to know . . .

I think that's all my parting words. Thank you, once more. Good luck to you, and my love.

There was no chance that Gilla would 'forget all about' Mary. He sealed and addressed his reply but did not post it. It is unlikely that Mary ever saw it, though in some ways it was the letter of his life:

I was awfully glad to have been able to see you yesterday and I really honestly didn't know how fond I was of you till now.

I do love you Mary dear as much as its possible for a man to love anyone, but I like just to feel it and not to think of the hows and the whys. I hope you'll always keep just a little bit of yourself for me whatever happens . . . rotten clumsy things words but please try and understand what I mean. I know you will as a matter of fact and it will be a tremendous standby whenever I want anything to back me up. Remember that its because of you that I've got into the army and it means a very great deal to me and I look at it in a mediæval sort of way. . .

Take care of my pin and yes do, give it me back when I come back and if I don't come back or come back without having been to the war at all stick to it.

Goodbye for the present. I wanted to kiss you yesterday just to spite the German Emperor and a lot of other things as well most frightfully.

Ever yours Gilla – with ever so much love.

★

On 21 August Alan set off for Chatham, where to his disgust he had been appointed surgeon in the Royal Sailors' Home, which had been turned into a naval hospital. 'I've at present got a job of perfectly incredible dullness,' Alan complained to Gilla. 'The Barracks isn't bad; the atmosphere is very Naval & I hear the band play "a life on the ocean wave" every morning at viii, & I sometimes get a glimpse of the said wave as represented by an upper reach of the Medway when I go to the front door of the Temporary Hospital for a breath of air . . . I have a comfortable bed & the bathwater is hot & the food is plentiful & good so that I'm as well off as an ape at the zoo.' Alan longed for a posting on a ship. As the weeks went by the tedium of Chatham grew worse. 'This is the damndest hole on earth. I don't wonder the blues get drunk. They do.'

Others, enviably, were seeing action. John Ludlow was off to the Front with the Inniskillen Fusiliers. Gilla's friend 'McNaught' was with the South Wales Borderers. Phil Leigh Smith rather improbably became a dragoon, and turned up at Gloucester Place in spurs with a huge sword. Phil's readiness for action was questionable. Milicent, whose enthusiasm for her Red Cross nursing knew no bounds, gave a vivid discourse at dinner on the subject of stopping bleeding, with the result, as she told NM, that 'poor Phil fainted right off! I caught him as he was falling sideways and laid him flat, etc. & he soon came to & eat a good dinner.' It seemed out of the question that Val should join up, though he talked about becoming a Special Constable.

NM had set off for Dublin on 24 August, where he had agreed to mark medical examinations. On 1 September, their eleventh wedding anniversary, he wrote to Milicent from Glaslough, the friends' house where he was staying, 'the flower garden is gay before the window & beyond are the fine old trees & the lake & it only wants you walking round the fountain to make a perfect view. Sunshine, flowers, ripple on the lake; back one comes to the horrible war.' Milicent, at Hancox, celebrated the anniversary by broaching 'our usual pound of wedding cake'. She appreciated her absent husband's expressions of affection: 'It's something to be thought incomparable even once in a lifetime!'

On 26 August Gilla was gazetted to the 2nd battalion of the Royal Sussex Regiment as a second lieutenant. The news filled Aunt Jenny with a mixture of pride and anxiety: 'I'm afraid Grandmothers can't take as cheerful a view of things as the boys themselves they seem to me quite wonderful in that respect – My first remembrance of War was my brother fighting against the Russians [in the Crimea] & now my Grandson fights <u>with</u> them & a very good thing too. I feel that they are a tower of strength.' On the thirtieth the regiment was ordered to Dover for training. On 13 September, a Sunday, NM and Milicent, driven by Hammond, motored from Hancox to Dover to spend the day with Gilla.

They drove across Romney Marsh, bathed in early autumn sunshine, paying two sixpences at tollgates on the way. 'Some two miles out [outside of Dover] we were stopped by two soldiers with fixed bayonets & an officer. He asked whence we were if we had a camera with us & then let us go on.' Gilla took them to St Paul's, the Catholic church, and installed them in the front seats. He was in charge of the Catholic soldiers. 'The priest preached a sensible sermon about the importance of a clear conscience amid the dangers of the field.' After mass, Gilla led his men up to the castle, then joined NM and Milicent for a cold luncheon at the Lord Warden Hotel. Then they all went to 'Fort Burgoyne where Gillachrist eats & sleeps & saw a large encampment of guns & horses & looked down on the men of war in the harbour & at the fortified hill on the opposite side of the town.' They walked down to the sea and 'paused to look at the French coast which was very plain . . . we saw some smoke blown along the coast & heard the boom of great guns.' Hammond opined that these were French guns practising. 'The Gilla showed us a barbed wire entanglement round a field of turnips watched by a sentry.' Back at the harbour, 'A steamer the Invicta came in with no one on the deck & stopped at the usual landing place for passengers. A special train of two first class carriages was waiting. A big wig (it might have been Lord Kitchener but I could not see his face well) & about 3 gentlemen & 2 attendants without luggage walked into the train looking serious & saying nothing & off it started.'

A week later, Gilla again lunched at the Lord Warden Hotel, this time with Mary and her parents. This rather formal encounter cannot have been wholly satisfactory, though he was allowed to walk with her to show her the ramparts while Mr and Mrs Haviland drank their coffee. A letter from Mary expresses how hard she found the farewells: 'I have done nothing but say Goodbye lately. It is really awful but everybody has gone now. So we've nothing to do but make shirts & pretend we are happy when we all know we're not . . . I'm fearfully proud of having a real live soldier really going to fight but I shall be most thankful when it's over and he's back – safe.'

Letters of support for Gilla poured in. He stored them in his kitbag. 'Keep your head & put Vaseline on your toes,' advised Ethne. 'My dear you are both noble fellows & I love you with all my heart,' said NM. Alan, the other 'noble fellow', was lugubrious: 'I hope you'll dodge the bullets, but if you don't, it's a question whether you're much worse off than having pneumonia in 50 or 60 years time, wh when it came would be just as much "today" as today's lunch.' Aunt Charley sent a volume of R. L. Stevenson's poems. On the first page she inscribed Joan of Arc's dictum: 'The soldiers must fight, but God gives the victory.' 'Milicent & I have been talking a great deal about you,' she told Gilla in her letter. 'It will be in a very special way, that the soldiers will be remembered in the white chapel at Brown's.'

Gilla wrote to his father to ask for £5 to pay for a sword and a sleeping bag. Milicent offered him a cork mattress, but this cumbersome article was refused; his kit already weighed over 60lbs. On 24 September he left for the Front. NM was in a committee meeting at the College of Physicians when he was called to the telephone. It was Phil, to say that Gilla would be leaving Waterloo for Southampton at 5.30. NM asked leave to depart, and took a taxi to Waterloo. 'I found Gillachrist on Platform 8. He was going with a draft of officers: & beyond leaving from Southampton knew nothing of his destination . . . The dear Gilla & I walked up & down . . . Phil came up & he & the Gilla laughed over his being a dragoon & so it was time & Gillachrist got in & off went the train. The dear boy looked very well & happy & sent his love to Milicent & to Alan.'

At Southampton the officers were billeted at a hotel; they slept on the floor of the billiard room. The next day Gilla was given his kit on board ship. 'The Normania is her name she is the ordinary mail packet and not a transport so we are doing things like gentlemen.' They docked at Le Havre on the twenty-seventh, 'entrained at about 5.30 got rations for 3 days . . . The people everywhere are very kind & interested in one. They wave and talk to one all along the line.' The next few days were spent mainly in trains, with intervals of idleness at seaside towns. 'Wasn't given any orders. So didn't do anything in the morning except play noughts & crosses on the shore with Goring.' Fred Goring was a friend and fellow second lieutenant. They bathed, took a boat out, and talked to French soldiers in a bar. The weather was clear and bright, and food was plentiful. It was an encouraging start to the war.

They made their way slowly, with frequent stops: 'French nurses a great attraction at Angers.' At Versailles a porter fell under the train and was killed. On 8 October they 'woke up to find that we were at the railhead. Got out and had some tea and stood round a fire. Guns could be heard in the distance. Presently loaded up in a motor lorry.' Here, at Mont-Notre-Dame, near Reims, Gilla saw the first dramatic sign of the enemy presence, a looted cottage the interior of which had been destroyed 'to an extraordinary degree'.

From now on, war began in earnest. They moved on to the Aisne and into the trenches, heavily bombarded with 'coal boxes' – shellburst, usually from a heavy gun, causing a cloud of black smoke. Gilla and three other officers slept in a cave and ate on the edge of a trench. Members of Gilla's platoon were dying around him. His letters home, scribbled in blunt pencil on flimsy paper, play down the horrors to some extent:

> 18th October. Thank you so very much for your letters you would think it extraordinary to see them delivered under shell fire we've had plenty of the latter by the way and it isn't exhilarating though it did me no harm. What an extraordinary individual the British soldier is and out here his one idea when he isn't fighting seems to be to make tea and not even German high explosive shells stop him . . . I can't help thinking that its rather a priviledge to have taken part in if not the greatest the biggest battle in history you cant think how one longs to get home but war isn't all horrors and when one is in the middle of them it cheers one up when one thinks why one is there.

NM, who had returned to Ireland for more examining, may have been reassured by the remarks of an Irish reservist who had been sent home wounded: 'What was it like? "Oh it was like the best pantomime you ever saw. The food was very good. I weigh a stone more than when I went out." He was going out again as soon as he could.' But Gilla and his men, the men of D Company, were feeling the strain:

> 15th October. An ominously quiet day. Stood to at about 10.30 the whole regiment in the road just behind the trenches. There had been some shrapnel wh we heard afterwards did the French some damage

i.e. French who were coming to relieve us. We waited in the road for about an hour. Every moment I expected the Germans would open fire. They threw some lights and one or two snipers loosed off but nothing happened luckily there was a thick mist wh must have saved us . . . we did a forced march to Bourg across the river . . . Breakfast and to sleep (much needed) in some straw in a loft . . . passed several very deserted villages some of the houses burned out.

They entrained again, and arrived at Pont de Briques, near Boulogne. There they remained all day in a siding. 'People came and brought us bread and went into the town and foraged for us . . . several trainloads of Belgian refugees passed us and many troop trains went on ahead of us several full of Indian troops.' On the nineteenth they reached Cassel, about twenty miles south-east of Dunkirk. 'Marched up to the town and billeted in the Casino from which there is a magnificent view . . . This is a very fine little town very clean with a decidedly Flemish look about it.' Hill-top towns being rare in Flanders, Cassel became General Haig's HQ. The next day they marched over the frontier into Belgium. It seemed as if the whole country was on the move. 'Past us there came a continual stream of refugees in carts & wheeling barrows, French curassiers with breast plates, chasseurs, infantry, motor cars, some mounted with guns, horse & mules . . . Now we are waiting for a meal at an inn after having billited our men. As usual the French occupied every billet in the place & had to be turned out.'

Gilla slept in comfort 'on the sofa in the drawing room of a well-to-do Belgian', at Boesinghe but the next day he had to go and dig and then occupy trenches. On the twenty-fifth they marched from Boesinghe to Ypres, forty thousand men under General Haig, and 'Billeted there in a house full of fruit . . . Had a look at the town wh I admired very much.' Gilla visited the medieval Cloth Hall and the cathedral and went to mass in the open air. Less than a month later, on 22 November, the Cloth Hall was flattened by the Germans.

This was the last day of anything approaching comfort. Danger once again became constant: 'Saw a great flaming mass fall out of the clouds heard later that it was one of our aeroplanes . . . A coal box fell about 20 yds from me killing Ainsworth's horse.' Gilla commanded 16 Platoon D Company and Fred Goring 15 Platoon D Company, each in charge of fifty men. On 29 October, Gilla wrote to NM and to Ethne. 'This is a war,' he told his father:

The amount of ammunition wasted at any rate by the Germans is extraordinary and even when one is well shelled the casualties are extraordinarily small provided one is well dug in. Though at the time the noise is terrifying . . . It's a bit cold at night but I'm frightfully fit and there is generally plenty of food . . . Your letters are most frightfully peaceful and refreshing. I think anyone who gets through this ought to know how to appreciate small things and life will be very much happier.

His letter to Ethne is bleaker in tone:

Goring is sitting in the bunghole next to me . . . In this war one is always under fire. It's a most extraordinary thing that the guns never stop either by day or night . . . There is a battery just behind at the present moment which sort of takes ones insides out & feeds them back again every 3 mins . . . By jove one will know how to enjoy life if one pulls through this. The only way to stick things is to live entirely in the present out here and not think of the future bit . . . When is Jack coming out? Hope he doesn't.

One does see some extraordinary things. Hope I'll tell you about them some day. I chewed your chocolate this morning. (Crash). There are bright spots occasionally & mails is one of them. I['m] sure my coy [Company] men would deeply appreciate a jolly old cake (not really old) you know large and round & solid the sort Alan likes on his birthday.

These letters were never sent. The following week was one of incessant action and very little sleep.

30th October. In the morning the enemy suddenly began to drop coal boxes on us. Result a disorderly retreat to the other side of the road just as bad there however. Got the men together after a bit and formed up on a hill. There to make things more cheerful they burned a light and then with a wail of pipes finally the brigade formed column of sorts & marched down the road towards Ypres. The enemy putting a little shrapnel into us. We turned off to the left and made an attack on a wood. We did not know for certain where the enemy were but at last got within about 100 yards of them. I had a shot at one and missed him. Shaw killed R.I.P. I was with him at the time. [Gilla was binding Shaw's wounds when he was hit for the second time] . . . We finally retired and took up a position in a wood near a farm from whence we had started.

Four officers, including the colonel, were killed on this day. The position was too thinly held. Out of 1,750 members of the battalion, only 380 remained, and the enemy got through the line. The next day was as bad:

A good deal of shelling all day finally the Germans got round our left & we retired got mixed up with another regiment made a line on some high ground until they dropped coal boxes right into us. Had a narrow shave retired back to main road. There collected some men and came up again and finally found the regiment in some woods. Very fine to see the Highlanders advance across an open field with fixed bayonets. Woods all round & a glorious sunset . . . a great many dead. Finally all the battalions got together and advanced into the wood. We tried to retake our old trenches but failed. D Coy . . . ran for it. Got men together behind a farm . . . v.tired.

They retreated into a wood two miles back and dug themselves in. November the third was a quieter day: 'Spent most of the time digging a dug out. A wren came and had a talk with me.' The next three days were spent in the trenches under heavy bombardment.

The constant noise wore the men out and Gilla found it hard to keep them awake and alert.

On the morning of Saturday 7 November the Sussex marched out about two miles to the south-east of Ypres. There were many little woods, crisscrossed by dangerous paths. Gilla and Fred Goring were in one of these woods and were discussing what might happen next when an unseen sniper shot Gilla through the heart at a range of fifty yards. He died, said Goring, instantly.

Goring took Gilla's wristwatch and the contents of his pockets: his pipe, his diary (filled in up to the last full day of his life), the unsent letters to NM and Ethne, and two photographs of Mary, one head-and-shoulders portrait, the other a snapshot of her holding Peter, the terrier Gilla had given her. Gilla's body was buried by the roadside that evening. An hour after his friend's death, Goring was struck by a shell fragment on the side of his head. He was well enough to write to NM: 'Dear Dr Moore, I hope that I am not the first to break the painful news of your son's death to you.' He was.

★

In November 1999 a group of us, sixteen family members, my father being the oldest and my son Jake, still in his pushchair, the youngest, travelled to Ypres to commemorate the life and death of Gilla, the uncle and great-uncle none of us had met. We went round the museum in the Cloth Hall, beautifully rebuilt to resemble as closely as possible the great medieval structure Gilla had admired. We visited Toc H at Poperinghe, listened to the Last Post, and found Gilla's name on the Menin Gate, one of the long, long list of soldiers whose bodies had not been recovered. My cousins Tom and Henry Oliver worked out as accurately as they could the spot where Gilla must have fallen. We found it, and my niece Helena, the youngest there capable of so doing, attached a cross of poppies to the nearest tree. What struck me most was how quietly domestic that agricultural landscape was – how similar, indeed, to the fields and woods of Gilla's Sussex boyhood.

17. 'A monstrous inconceivable war'

At 3.30 p.m. on 7 November 1914, when Gilla was shot through the heart on a road through a wood south-east of Ypres, NM was visiting wounded prisoners at Bart's; his visit coincided with one from the King and Queen. Alan, who had left Chatham for Lowestoft as surgeon to the *Halcyon*, a minesweeper, was attending the funeral of a trawlerman killed in an accident. Ethne, alone for once, was in the drawing room at Lannock, curled up with a book by the fire and, she said, thinking of Gilla.

Fred Goring's letter did not reach NM until four days later. NM wired Alan at once – 'Our dear Gilla is dead.' Alan recorded in his diary: '11th November, 1914. About v.20 I got a telegram from NM saying that Gilla was dead. I saw him last on 21 August. R.I.P. I am proud of him and not ashamed of my tears.' The next day NM went to the War Office to see if he could find out more. 'An officer did all an officer & a gentleman could do to find out for me & showed me the list of Nov. 8 which had on it the names of Goring & of McGrath of the Sussex Regiment wounded but not the Gilla.' That evening, NM stood alone outside 94 Gloucester Place looking up at the window of the room in which Gilla had been born.

On the thirteenth, mass was said for Gilla at the Sisters of Charity in Seymour Street. NM and Milicent were followed there at a respectful distance by 'our kind Irish parlourmaid Lily Chandler'. They paused and touched the knocker and door handle of 94 'just because he had often touched them'.

Letters of condolence poured in; I've counted 321. 'They make me think better of mankind,' wrote NM 'and vow never to speak or think harshly of any one again.' Bessie Belloc, now eighty-six, wrote, 'My dearest Norman and Milicent – I am inexpressibly shocked & troubled. My age prevents me from being seen in

London frequently; but I am always true to all of you. Alas! What a monstrous inconceivable war.'

'He was the nicest boy I ever knew,' wrote Jack Pryor, now serving with the Hertfordshire regiment; 'We always thought Johnny was like him I hope he will grow up like him too.' Alys Russell, wife of the philosopher Bertrand Russell who would later be imprisoned for his pacifism, wrote, perhaps surprisingly, 'He has given his life for his country, & we can feel nothing but gratitude to him, & reverence for his high courage.' The headmaster of the Oratory praised Gilla's 'simple manly piety . . . we may be sure that God will give him now a reward exceeding great for his faithfulness.' Father Dulley, Amy's old friend from St Peter's, Wapping, recalled 'Dear Gilla! I baptised him before he was 2 days old . . . We little thought of his destiny then, & of the great world-convulsion in which he would so gloriously give his life.' The letter from Gilla's Cambridge friend Jim McNaught Davis is marked 'Passed by the Censor' and is written in pencil under shellfire from an unspecified place in France. McNaught told NM what he most wanted to hear: 'he could not have died for a nobler cause! honour! his country's honour: he wished – when the time came – to die on the battlefield fighting a just cause . . . Our last year at "Cats" together was most happy: we became REAL friends, very fond of one another & told each other all our ups & downs: so you will understand how deeply I feel his going from us.' He signed the letter with a Catherine wheel, to symbolize St Catharine's College – a detail NM would have appreciated.

Alan wrote to Ethne, 'It does seem queer to think it's you & me again & no Gilla . . . This is a bloody war. I felt as we entered it that each must reckon to part with everything & to count on anything retained at the end as a gain. Gilla I know was ready for anything.' Ethne understood: 'It was beastly difficult writing to Papa. I thought, as you say, it's just you & me again. I feel we've all got to lose something or the war won't have got its fill, the devil it is. I still feel that Gilla must turn up on a motor byke one day – one cant realize it properly – but I also feel dying cant be so bad

somehow if someone so lively & like oneself as Gilla has done it.'
Ethne wrote a poem and sent it to her father:

> What, these black robes and this weeping?
> Are we then to mourn him so?
> Out among the leaves late fallen
> Gold and Purple clad I go;
> Never more decay in autumn,
> Death in winter will he know.
>
> Away with pomp! I hear his laughter,
> Or its memory on my Ear!
> Of our blood, a son, a brother
> Yet a hero scorning fear!
> Ah his laughter! It will surely
> With the spring come back each year.

★

'Milicent has been an angel,' NM wrote; tragedy brought them
closer. Milicent was generous in her grief, and able to comfort others. She told Aunt Charley how much Gilla's many visits to Brown's
had meant to him. She drew comfort from Gilla's popularity; as she
wrote to Alan, 'It is a great comfort to think of his clean good record,
and how fond everybody is of him, our servants, Charlotte's Lena,
even Val's cook – he brought cheerfulness with him.' Gilla's death
must have reminded Milicent painfully of the death of her brother
Harry at a similar age, a promising young man just launching into
life, but her public-spiritedness meant she was able to think of the
distress of other people, and she did not forget Mary Haviland. In all
the many and loving words NM wrote in his letters and in his journal about Gilla, he never once mentioned the brave young woman
who meant so much to his son. It may be that his silence was intended
to protect Mary; it would have been bad for a young girl's reputa-
tion to have had such an intimate relationship, but my feeling is that
Mary didn't fit into the version of Gilla's life in which NM wanted

to believe. Milicent, however, wrote to her almost as soon as the news arrived. Mary at once wrote back, a careful, loyal letter, modest in its claims on Gilla, grateful to Milicent for thinking of her:

My dear Mrs Moore,

It <u>was</u> so kind of you to write your self & tell us about Gilla. I am so awfully sorry for you & Dr Moore. It is so dreadful that one can't realise it at least I can't believe that he will never come over here again. It is such a short time since he was here, when he came up to say Goodbye, & then we saw him again at Dover only a day or two before he went off. He was so absolutely happy and keen wasn't he? & so longing to be out there. I had four letters from him from France, but of course he couldn't tell very much – only one felt all the time that he was perfectly happy & I only hope he was happy up to the very last moment & we know he is happy now.

It does seem so cruel that people like that should have to be chosen. I wonder sometimes whether people can ever have the spirit of pride, & even gratitude that they have been allowed to give something. It must be splendid to feel like that.

If you do hear any more about it would you tell me some time not when you are dreadfully busy as I am sure you will be now but later on. I should be so awfully grateful if you would tell me anything there is to know about him. We had been such friends always, & I am so proud, & so are we all, that we did know him so well.

Yours affectionately
Mary Haviland.

Her request for more information was granted; there follows a second letter, dated 23 November, thanking Milicent for bringing her up to date.

Mary's mother also wrote to Milicent: 'His devotion to Mary was wonderful. Gilla always seemed so absolutely <u>good</u>, I used to feel it. Do you know what I mean? I am so very glad to have known him . . . I wonder what their future would have been?'

★

NM's journal, begun almost as a public document, became a log of the stages of his grief. He pored over the details of his son's short life and sudden death; it was absolutely necessary to him to believe that the sacrifice had been worthwhile. At no point does he question the justice of the war, and he turned away from those who challenged what Wilfred Owen was to call 'the old lie – *Dulce et decorum est/Pro patria mori.*' In his efforts to make sense of the loss, he gathered every scrap of information that he could find, pasted maps into his journal, pored over the Allies' progress – or lack of it – in the Ypres area. It helped him to place Gilla's death in the context both of national and of family history. 'Nov.30. What a great battle and how grand to have a part in it. He is at the head of the family of this time a worthy grandson of Robert Ross Rowan Moore who did so much to establish happiness and diminish servitude by his speeches for Free Trade all over England and Scotland.' Though it is true that Robert Ross Rowan did further the cause of political freedom, and more specifically saved hundreds of poor Irishmen from the horrors of indentured labour, I find it extraordinary that NM should thus link his faithful, honest, high-minded son with the feckless, selfish father who never troubled himself about the child he never saw, but NM could not let go of his idealized version of his father, and at times of trouble he took refuge in ideals.

An anxiety hovers in the margins that NM had been too hard on his youngest child, that he had failed fully to appreciate his virtues and talents. A determination not to repeat that mistake made him cling fiercely to Alan, almost idolizing him. From the day of Gilla's death till the end of the war, NM wrote to his surviving son every single day. If he was ill – as, increasingly, he was – he dictated a note to Milicent or Ethel Portal. Sometimes the letters were lost in transit, or delivered weeks or even months late, but the many that survive endlessly assure Alan of how much he is loved and valued.

His telegram breaking the news on 11 November was followed the same day by a letter:

My dearest Alan,

    Our own dear Gilla is gone from us. A letter came this morning from F.Y. Goring of the same regiment who says 'I was just by him when he was hit: a bullet hit him through the heart so he died a painless death' . . . My Alan you know how fond of you both I have always been; & I know you were of him & of Ethne. I have written to her. I never thought of the Gilla being the first [to go] of those names we wrote in 1907 Sep 9 in the guest book at Hancox. It seems a very short life as if only 94 to 67 Gloucester Place yet he did in it all that came to him to do . . . God preserve you my Alan.

Over the next few days he wrote, 'I shall remember him every day I live. Do not ever forget him. He loved you so much'; 'Your letters are the greatest help & comfort to me . . . They help to make life worth going on with'; 'I have found one volume of the Gilla's notes. I did not know half that was in him.'

NM never felt alone in his grief. 'All I can do is to love you more & more,' wrote Ethel Portal, 'my own dearest bravest truest Norman – whose sons must needs be brave & true also.' But despite the comfort he drew from so much warm support, and his own powerfully optimistic temperament, there were moments of bitterness and anger. On 27 December he wrote in his journal:

In the evening I finished the French yellow book [a volume of diplomatic documents 'relative to the events and negotiations which preceded the opening of hostilities']. It seemed to me as if the discussions of ministers and diplomatists, emperors and kings, and the mobilization of vast hordes of men and the outbreak of war, were parts of a tragedy all leading to the death in an instant of my dear pure bright noble heroic Gillachrist. That is how the vast convulsion looked to me as I read this record of it. The German emperor, his Chancellor, and his ambassador seem a group of fiends like those in Milton.

NM collected Gilla's personal effects and stored them in a tin trunk. That trunk is in my study at Hancox. It's a time capsule, a compression of the ingredients that made one short life. Though Gilla's body was never recovered, his kit bag was returned, and Fred Goring brought back the contents of his pockets. In the trunk are his belt, his gun harness, a pair of army socks, stiff and brittle now. His watch is preserved in an envelope on which NM has written, 'The Gilla's watch. God Bless Him.' There's a small cardboard box containing the present that was sent to every soldier, a handsome tobacco tin, embossed with a portrait of Princess Mary and the names of the Allies – Belgium, Japan, Russia, Montenegro, Serbia, France, Imperium Britannicum; Christmas 1914. Inside is a pipe wrapped in tissue paper and a card printed with a sprig of holly and the words, 'With best wishes for a Happy Christmas and a Victorious New Year from The Princess Mary and Friends at Home'. On the lid of the box is a typed message – 'It is regretted that non-smoker gifts are not available.' How times change. Gilla was an enthusiastic pipe-smoker, but the packets of tobacco in the tin remain intact; the present arrived after he was dead.

There are booklets of instructions to infantry officers, a Catholic prayer book, and letters and certificates concerning Gilla's brief army career. There's also much evidence of his Victorian infancy and Edwardian boyhood – letters, sketches, photographs and diaries. There are some pathetic postcards from Amy, putting a brave face on things during her sunny winter exiles – 'My dearest Gilla . . . It is very nice and sunny here how I wish I could send you some in a letter . . . There are more [beggars] here than I ever saw and they each have two babies and one little boy like you!! . . . There is a French cat jumping on Papa it can't understand English, Poor thing!!' There are his 'Hodgepodge' notebooks, lists of exhibits in his 'museum', and a hawk's hood, a fierce and delicate thing.

There's a receipt for the purchase of Peter, the wire-haired fox terrier Gilla ordered for Mary from the Army and Navy Stores, also the order for a box of sweets (price 2/6d) he sent her on her birthday. There are dance cards on which her name appears more than anyone else's. And there's the letter he wrote her on 16 August, on the brink of his departure, the letter he sealed but never sent – 'I do love you Mary dear as much as its possible for a man to love any one.' NM, it seems, could not bring himself to send this on, but neither could he bring himself to destroy it.

★

Fred Goring was sent to recover from his head wound at Osborne, once Queen Victoria's holiday home on the Isle of Wight, now a military hospital. On 14 November, NM and Milicent travelled down to see him – via Waterloo Station, the first time NM had used it since he had said his last goodbye to Gilla in September. Goring, on his feet but with his head in bandages, told them, 'very simply and kindly', the story of Gilla's last days. He handed over Gilla's belongings – his pipe, his watch, the unsent letters, his diary and the photographs of Mary. All of these NM noted in his journal, save that he didn't mention the photographs. They admired the magnificent view from Goring's window, thanked him warmly, and departed.

In December, Phil Leigh Smith came home on leave and helped NM in his ceaseless quest for information. Gilla, said Phil, was killed in the wood of Zwarzleene, south-east of Ypres between Zillebeck and Kleine Zillebeck, about a hundred yards to one or other side of the high road between those villages, 'not the road which joins them but on a road running with one of them on each side of it'. On 20 October, Phil had seen the 1st Army Corps led by General Haig march through Poperinghe forty thousand strong; Gilla would have been amongst them, though Phil didn't spot him. Phil, a Catholic like his mother, had made sure that mass was said for Gilla at the Front. He came to Gloucester Place to point out on the map all the places where Gilla had been and gave them his own journal to read. At breakfast, NM noted, 'our yellow cat came in. He looked at Phil in uniform looked again & walked towards him just touched his leg & walked on to the window. It was evident that the uniform suggested something, a memory of the Gilla I think, to him & that the touch satisfied him it was not applicable to Phil.'

Phil's war experience had, in NM's opinion, made a man of him. Being fluent in Russian and German, he was employed as an interpreter, but this was not a soft billet; he spent most of the next four years at the Front. In response to a request from Alan, who wanted to be able to imagine what Gilla had gone through, Phil described what being under fire was like:

I have not yet had time to get accustomed to it or to get over the first sensation. The three chief causes of discomfort when under shell-fire, are – one's consciousness of complete helplessness in the matter of avoiding the shell, the realization of what a very small & readily annihilated amount of 'gun-food' one would make if hit, & the horrible hiss of this invisible missile suddenly arriving as if from nowhere & bound Lord knows whither. The effect upon one of all this combined with the natural dread of an abrupt departure from this world is to produce a thirst caused by the suspense & a peculiar feeling of lightness caused by the relief when each shell is safely passed – or lodged in somebody else.

Hardly a day went by without bad news. Sons of NM's friends, Alan's contemporaries at school, Jack Pryor's best man, Hancox neighbours, Gilla's friend Jim McNaught Davis, shot through the lung – a brutal resolution to the problem of his infatuation with Anne Ludlow. Milicent had supported the romance, writing to McNaught to let him know that Anne reciprocated, but Ludlow and Mabel had continued to disapprove.

Rose Playford's cousin was drowned, not long after Gilla's death. She told Milicent about it, using her idiosyncratic punctuation:

Dear Madame . . . you no doubt saw. In the paper that. my cousin's body was. washed up at.Kethole. Reach the River Medway. The Admiralty have done there Duty. in every.way. 1 brother went by. motor car from Mountfield 8 oclock Sunday morning and brought him to Mountfield Church at 3 oclock for burial we now. know he rests in peace. from the wild. waves of the sea his cloth's

was still on and they. cut out his Stripes Gun Star and badges the
letters in his pocket were both from his mother. which she as got all
of it they sent her they gave him his Naval Honours. Firing over him
on leaving Chatham. this side Mr Page had his choir and they sang
God Save the King on entering the Church . . . he had 4 brothers
there and they lowered him in the grave themselves. one brother he
was In Canada and one. in the Army which could not be there.

Alan later remembered Rose saying that the body was returned to
the family on the condition that 'we didn't unscrew'.

Early in 1915 came news of a less heroic kind of death. Willy
Leigh Smith had collapsed and died of a cerebral haemorrhage
while staying at Mayfield with his mother and Roddy. He was
only forty-eight and, though he was overweight and unfit, his
health had given no real cause for concern; his death was a complete shock. The extent of Willy's war effort had been to write to
The Times suggesting that the troops should be supplied with thin
white overalls and caps to make them invisible in the snow, but
though, as NM wrote to Milicent, 'he was not a man of use to his
generation,' he was mourned and missed. 'He showed kindness to
the Gilla,' said NM, 'so I think kindly of him.' Aunt Jenny was
deeply distressed. As NM wrote, 'She wd have sacrificed all the
rest for Willy: Roddy included.' She wrote to Alan:

> Your letter of this morning was so welcome to me coming as it did
> to lighten the gloom of one of the most miserable days of my life
> – the day of my poor Willy's funeral . . . Of course I knew it was a
> wasted life & so did he there was so much goodness & kindness in
> him really. Think how he liked all animals & birds - & children too
> – but I don't want to distress you about him – your life has had &
> is having quite enough sorrow – danger too in it – only I want you
> to know that he always liked you very much.

She linked Willy's death to the giving up of Crowham – 'he was
quite wrapped up in that place & never got over the pain of leaving

it.' For Jenny, as for Roddy, Bella, and of course NM and Milicent, Alan became the focus of pride and anxiety: 'Keep well and
as safe as you can dear Alan. I can't lose anybody more.'

Everyone looked forward to the imminent arrival of Ethne's
second child, though a pall of anxiety hung over this event too,
because Ethne was suffering from an untimely attack of measles.
'I feel as if all babies now ought to be boys,' wrote Aunt Jenny, 'to
prevent the race of mankind being quite blotted out but I'm afraid
she'll be disappointed if its not the "Sophie" she talks of.' No
'Sophie' appeared; if Ethne was disappointed by the boy born on
25 February she kept her feelings to herself. Johnnie, three and a half,
was more candid. 'Johnny is . . . much disgusted its not a sister & says
he is going to write to the Stork to bring a sister as soon as possible
"we'll keep the brother as well & then we'll be 3 in nursery" "I
don't think Mummy wd like that" says Nanny "then she needn't
come into the nursery" says the heartless child.'

The baby escaped the measles, but Ethne was confined to bed
for three more weeks. NM came to see his daughter in her London
nursing home and read her Alan's letters while she lay surrounded
by iris stylosa, violets and daffodils. Alan was now on board the
HMS *Sagitta*, a minesweeper that in her former incarnation had
belonged to a French duke who had left ninety pairs of trousers
on board when he gave her up. The *Sagitta* moved up and down
the coast from Lowestoft to Scapa Flow looking for mines and
submarines. In addition to his medical duties, Alan was in charge
of coding and decoding messages. On 22nd February the *Sagitta*
was attacked by sea planes, which were kept at bay by rifle fire.
Ethne listened to her brother's adventures with envy – 'Didn't I
always want to be a boy!'

Ethne wanted to name the baby Gillachrist. 'I have always thought
it a pity,' she told Alan, 'to absolutely shut up all the doors & never
to mention anyone who is dead, as the Crowhamites do - & I feel
calling this creature Gilla will be like putting a wedge in one of the
doors to keep it open.' But people shied away from using the name;
the baby was addressed as Squeaker, Gillette, Gillikins or plain

Baby. At the last moment, on the day of his christening, Ethne
gave in and called him Mark, with Gillachrist as a second name.
But she told her father that privately he would always be her little
Gilla.

*

Once she had recovered from childbirth and measles, Ethne took
on as much war work as she could, dividing her time between
nursing at the Maples Hospital in Hitchin and tying up parcels for
wounded airmen at Suffolk House near Marble Arch. Milicent
continued as a commandant in the Red Cross; Hancox was the
headquarters of the local branch. Normanhurst, Lord Brassey's
vast château near Battle (where Aunt Jenny had long ago refused to
let Amy stay), was now a hospital; Milicent would cycle over to do
night duty there, often relieving nurses made of less stern stuff.
Beech Green, the Ludlows' house, also a temporary hospital, was
full of wounded Belgians. The Ludlow girls sometimes nursed
there, and Eira also nursed at a Tunbridge Wells hospital. Mabel,
intriguingly, 'patrols the streets at night', NM told Alan, but 'does
nothing whatever by day for her own girls'. He doesn't say which
streets, or what the patrolling was meant to achieve. Perhaps her
mission was similar to Aunt Charley's. Charley had gone to Rouen
early in 1915 and had been shocked: 'France is swallowed up by the
war to an extent we don't realize,' she told Alan. 'I heard a French
soldier looking on [at the arrival of British troops] remark: "Ils
sont heureuse les Anglais, pour nous, pas de repos jusqu'à ce qu'on
soit blessé" . . . Rouen . . . is practically an English garrison town
. . . The English alas! drink horribly . . . The Tommys seem to
have made drinks for themselves of cider with rhum & absinthe
. . . I saw some revolting looking men – Also the dealings with the
factory women are bad.' Later in the year she returned to France
'to look after young women' as NM rather vaguely put it, under
the auspices of the YMCA.

   Bella, at Northiam, had her hands full with four very young
children and her doctor husband, who now had to work without

an assistant, but she helped at Great Dixter, yet another large house turned into a hospital, and she took in soldiers who were passing through the village on their way to the coast. 'One lot were rather rowdy. We heard they had been paid the day before, anyhow some of them got very drunk & made a great row at the Inn, & broke open cases of beer & stole the bottles . . . One of our men . . . was beastly sick,' she told Alan. Such behaviour did not deter the robust Bella: 'I think most people are beastly stolid to them, after all they are going out to fight for us, & we might be cheerful to them!'

Aunt Jenny was faint-hearted. She risked a faintly flirtatious wave at a Tommy who called out to her 'Hullo Mother, 'ave a bite of my apple!' (to Bella's amusement), but she would not allow Roddy, aged fifty-three, to nurse at the local 'Tommie's Hospital' on the grounds that she might catch cold walking there. Roddy had to content herself elsewhere. 'Roddy is very busy with all sorts of irons in the fire – a working class with some grand name – I know she wears a cap & apron & makes pyjamas for soldiers.' The servant shortage meant that, like most women of her social class, Roddy had to take on a larger share of the domestic chores than ever before. Jenny was disgusted at the unpatriotic behaviour of their cook: 'I had the displeasure of hearing Ethel's banns read out in church on Sunday. She ought to be ashamed of herself appropriating a Chauffeur to herself when they are so much wanted – & that's what Aunt Nanny says too.' Aunt Nannie, now well into her eighties and dividing her time between London and Torquay, seems to have confined her war effort to tirades against the government.

Joan Ashton of Vinehall worked filling shells at the Vickers Maxim munition factory. When the glare damaged her eyes, she switched to driving ambulances. Ethel Portal's migraines ruled out any such work, but she wrote letters to boost the morale of many soldiers and sailors who had been pupils at the school she funded at Freefolk, near Laverstoke. Only Val Leigh Smith remained aloof from the war. 'Val will not talk of the war but only of music and the like,' wrote NM. He did not declare himself a conscientious objector, but he remained unmoved by the zeitgeist that drove nearly all the men of his class and generation to join up. 'I wonder if you saw Val on leave?' Phil asked Alan in April 1915. 'It is pleasant to think that whatever wars & slaughters convulse & transform this world, we shall always be able to fall back on Scalands serene & unaltered.' I can't decide whether his tone is sarcastic – it probably is – but the picture he paints is certainly an accurate one. NM's journal entry for 29 August 1915 records Val's characteristically idiosyncratic hospitality: 'Milicent, E. M. Portal & I had luncheon at Scalands with Val who gave us mead to drink. Afterwards Miss Portal on the clavichord & he on the flute played Handel & I read some poems of Nahum Tate (one quite fine on a skeleton) & a speech of Macaulay's on the Dissenters Chapel Bill, which had been printed with the rest of the debate and given to Benjamin [Smith, MP; 'the Pater'].'

On 7 May the *Lusitania*, a Cunard liner bound for Liverpool from New York, was torpedoed by a German U-boat. She sank within sight of the Irish coast, with a loss of 1,153, mainly civilian, lives. One hundred and twenty-eight of the dead were Americans; although the USA did not join the war until 1917, the outrage of the *Lusitania* was a significant step in strengthening anti-German feeling. 'This sinking of the *Lusitania* has given one a distinct sense of personal enmity to the Germans,' Aunt Charley wrote to Alan – all the more personal because amongst the drowned was Father Basil Maturin, the kindly Irish theologian who had prepared Amy, Milicent and Ethne for reception into the Roman Catholic Church; he who had been so flexible about the matter of Ethne's eating meat on Fridays to spare Aunt Jenny's feelings. 'I see him at Oxford with his quick eyes and delightful abundance of speech,' Aunt Charley told Alan. Father Maturin, who was not wearing a lifebelt, was seen administering absolutions as the ship went down. His last act was to hand a child into a lifeboat with the instruction, 'Find its mother.'

NM was as busy as ever. He struggled on with his *History of St Bartholomew's*, in preparation for which he copied a thousand medieval charters by hand. Every time he came across an Alan, such as 'Alan the goldsmith', he would send his own Alan an account of his long-ago namesake. At night he would walk the streets of the City to reconstruct the hospital's links with twelfth-century London; one of the very few benefits of the war was that the darkness of the streets and the great reduction in traffic made it easier to imagine its ancient past. He served on medical and educational committees, was Secretary of the Literary Society, Librarian of the Royal Society of Medicine and Harveian Librarian at the Royal College of Physicians, and represented the College on the General Medical Council. As Consulting Physician, he still spent a lot of time at Bart's; he remarked on the cheerfulness of the wounded soldiers. He sometimes ran into Henry James, who was a ward visitor despite his angina and advancing years. It is hard to imagine a mutually satisfactory conversation between a wounded Tommy and the supreme novelist of inaction, but at least James tried.

NM's activities relieved the pressure of his grief, but thoughts of Gilla continue to pervade his journal. He followed the movements of the Sussex Regiment with keen interest. On 16 May 1915 he met Sir Foster Goring, older brother of Gilla's friend Fred. Sir Foster gave a bleak account of the latest engagement:

[He] told us the Sussex regt had been engaged last Sunday & had lost 500 men & more as well as 14 officers. The Colonel Green was not hit & Goring the Gilla's friend escaped also. The regiment assaulted the German trenches where the enemy had been since October & which were therefore well fortified. The British guns began a desperate bombardment at 5 a.m. & went on for three quarters of an hour. There were many British casualties from short fuses in our own shells.

The distance between English & Germans was 250 yards & the intervening ground covered with obstacles. The Germans were not cowed as expected & the Sussex were met by 'a hellish fire' & shot like rabbits & so could not take the trenches . . . [Fred Goring] was not wounded but Captain Villiers whose company he was then commanding was wounded & every other officer of the company killed ... This Sussex slaughter depressed me so I read some of [Standish] O'Grady's Irish catalogue & its fine translations to ease my mind. There will never again be such an Irish scholar as he is.

NM commissioned a memorial tablet for the cloister at the Oratory School. It was made of 'red marble rosso antiquo with a border of alabaster', and inscribed:

PRAY FOR
GILLACHRIST MOORE
SECOND LIEUTENANT ROYAL SUSSEX REGIMENT
SON OF
NORMAN AND AMY MOORE
WHO WAS BORN ON HOLY THURSDAY, 1894
AND FELL IN THE BATTLE OF YPRES
ON NOVEMBER 7, 1914.

His attempts to sort through Gilla's books and papers were sometimes too much for him and he had to take to his bed – 'I was knocked over by the feeling of the Gilla's loss.' He noted the anniversary of every significant date: 'September 12. I thought a great deal of the Sunday corresponding to this last year [when he and Milicent had spent the day with Gilla at Dover] & could not help thinking of the lines

The Flowers o' the Forest, wha ay shone the foremost,
The prime o' the land lye cauld in the clay!'

It was in nature, and in particular the woods and fields of Hancox, that NM could find most comfort and feel closest to Gilla:

As I was sitting on a gate near the Maids Hop garden I heard a wren in the hedge & looking up saw it. I said to it 'are you any relation to the wren that came into the trench to talk to my dear Gilla?' (as he wrote in his diary two or three days before his death). I spoke in a natural tone. The wren came on to a bough quite close to

me . . . I looked at its head & eye & its beautifully marked grey &
brown plumage & its pretty cocked up tail & it stayed a long time
& then quietly went away. It quite seemed as if the bird felt with
me & I expect the wren the Gilla saw behaved in the same way.

*

In July, NM had had a prostatectomy. After four weeks in a nursing home in Hinde Street, near Manchester Square, he spent the rest
of the summer convalescing at Hancox. 'How glad Hancox must
have been to see its Lord returning,' wrote Ethel Portal. 'I hope all
the Red Admirals came out and made evolutions round you & the
scabious waved & bowed in greeting.' Extensive repairs were under
way. The entire north wall had to be dismantled and rotten plaster
and woodwork removed. NM enjoyed chatting to the workmen
and admiring them as they manœuvred great beams of Sussex oak
into a pattern of horizontals and verticals. Despite the disruption,
NM wrote that 'Hancox always does me good it seems so quiet
and peaceful.' The shortage of manpower meant that the look of
the place was changing; NM remarked with pleasure that the
uncut lawns had an Irish air. In response to food shortages, potatoes
(the variety was Aran Chief, at Miss Ellen Willmott's suggestion)
were grown in NM's 'butterfly bed' amidst the zinnias and the
yellow phlomis. When gooseberry blight appeared in the kitchen
garden, Milicent patriotically reported it to the police.

The weather was glorious, and it felt good to sit breakfasting
with Milicent in the garden – NM sitting on his African throne –
when she returned on her bicycle from a night's nursing at Normanhurst, or to watch the harvest coming in; 'A great cart of corn
has just come into the barn contrasting its yellowness with the red
tiles.' But there was no absolute escape from the war. Aeroplanes
overhead were now so common that the household no longer
turned out en masse to inspect them, and the booming of the guns
in France could be heard by day and night, a distant shudder that
rattled the windows at the southern end of the house.

Alan spent 1915 on board the *Sagitta* as she moved up and down the east coast destroying mines. The danger was constant, but compared to what Phil Leigh Smith and John Ludlow were enduring in the trenches, Alan's daily life was luxurious. He had plenty of time for his journal, and for his attempt to learn Italian by reading Dante. (Milicent sometimes sent him letters in Italian, which must have been a welcome leavening.) The threat from mines and submarines caused Alan less anxiety than his unconquerable seasickness. When woken by the steward's boy, he would anxiously look at the two razor strops hanging on the cabin bulkhead. 'One swings easily, the other, wh is used for a patent razor, does not. If the patent strop is moving I may feel seasick, if only the ordinary one swings I probably shan't.'

As well as his medical duties, Alan was in charge of decoding signals, ordering meals in consultation with the steward and, ironically, dealing out tobacco. Food was plentiful, if monotonous (soup, potato pie, blackcurrant jam roly-poly and cheese was a typical meal); port, Marsala, beer and ginger beer were usually on the officers' table. Boredom was an enemy. Alan spent a great deal of time pitching the medicine ball on deck for exercise, playing with the ship's cat and pet monkey, and entering into idle conversation with his fellow officers.

Alan was not impressed by the way the Navy operated. He considered that many practices were outmoded or otherwise unnecessary and were carried out for form's sake only. His journal is intended as a plain factual record, but frustration with the tedium of life at sea and anxiety about the way the war was going seep through. The horrors of the Front reached him through his friends on leave; they told him that soldiers would deliberately wound themselves to escape the trenches, even though the penalty if caught was execution, or that the average length of life of an artillery horse was five days. On 18 June 1915 he summarized the state of the war and found little cause for optimism:

The Russians are being driven back. Lwow is threatened. At the Dardanelles we have a very heavy task, perhaps greater than we can carry through. The French however seem to be making some head-way in the West. The losses are great. The great difficulty . . . is the adequate supply of ammunition. It has been found that modern artil-lery uses shells at a far greater rate than had been expected. Artillery is the decisive arm in land warfare as at sea. The chief use of aircraft has been found to be that of discovering the enemy's positions to our artillery. Dropping of bombs seems to have much less effect than might be thought. Zeppelins dropt some 90 upon a crowded East End district of London lately & only 5 people were killed. Machine gun fire has been found to be most valuable. Long range rifle shooting is seldom practised. The bayonet is frequently used, the sword very seldom & officers have given up carrying them.

At sea the threat of submarines keeps the main fleets in port & prevents a close blockade. The enemy's submarines especially prey on our merchantmen & fishermen as many as 43 of the latter being by this means sunk in one week . . .

I think our seamen are unduly hampered by Whitehall. Now that Winston Churchill is gone there may be less of this.

Each man was issued with an identity disc on which was stamped his name, rank and religion. Alan had his stamped with G.O.K., standing for God Only Knows. This suggests that his belief in a beneficent universe was not watertight. And yet, amidst the vast-ness of sea and sky he was able to discern something greater and more lasting than the world-convulsion in which he found him-self. He wrote a poem:

> The light that never was on land or sea.
> Yet have I seen it in a type or shew
> When under stormclouds comes a sunshine glow.
> And once in war I watched the goods ships go
> From English cliffs, and o'er the straits expanse
> A darkling raincloud stretched to dim seen France
> That seemed to yoke in heaviness and pain
> Two labouring nations: and then came the rain.

Soon 'neath the clouds shone forth the low sunbeam
And lightened all with such a lovely gleam
That drenched in liquid gold the air did seem
And looking round there hung the heavenly bow
And I rejoiced and thought now sure I know
And have the meaning found:
Though half the world lie waste & near & far
Unchecked & onward sweeps the flood of war
The world shall not be drowned.

18. 'England best my heart contents'

Alan struggled to overcome his seasickness until December 1915, when he admitted defeat and asked for a move. His commander said he was surprised Alan had stuck it out for as long as a year, and arranged for him to be placed at the Chatham Barracks. Here, part of his duty was to examine recruits and reject those unfit for active service. Enlistment was still voluntary – the law was not changed till May 1916. 'By means of advertisement, wheedling, flattery & threats large numbers have been brought to enlist, & a not inconsiderable number hold back,' Alan noted.

At home, the deprivations of war were making themselves felt. Coals and some foodstuffs were in short supply. Aunt Jenny reported to Alan that Roddy was up to her eyes in making 'weird jams' out of unlikely ingredients, and fretted about coals, fearing that on cold days she would have no option but to stay in bed. Milicent decreed that there should be only one fire lit in the house, aside from the kitchen range. At Vinehall, Lord and Lady Ashton economized by giving up coffee. Hammond the chauffeur joined the Royal Naval Air Service as a mechanic. His wife and children continued to live in the flat above the garage at Gloucester Place, but NM gave up the car. Air raids increased. At Lannock, Ethne spent nights under tables in the drawing room with her little boys and the servants. In Gloucester Place, the servants ran out to watch the Zeppelins, or crowded on to the roof; 'Roberta says she wouldn't have missed it for the world,' Milicent told Alan.

In Newcastle, Alan noticed female taxi drivers, and girls pushing municipal handcarts dressed in yellow regulation tunics and trousers. In London, NM commented on women bus conductors (who looked, he said, 'tired'), and female waiting staff at the Reform Club, that male bastion. But it was still sometimes possible to escape the evidence of war. 'We went to Brown's,' NM told Alan on 9 July 1916, 'and were met by our Aunt [Charley] in a bright blue dress. We walked about the garden full of roses & white lilies & then had tea & strawberries. The room the strawberries & the ARMA VIRUMQUE [NM's inscription to mark the outbreak of war] all made me want your presence – strange that such different things should all press the same way.'

Alan was rarely absent from his father's thoughts. Earlier in the year NM had visited Cambridge, so strongly associated with both his sons and with his own youth. 'There was a flaming planet in the sky & Mercury & a bright star in another quarter as I came away & stood on the hall steps & surveyed the dark great court of Trinity & thought of you. I had had a look at your window before & as I came back here down Queen's Lane saw a lamp alight in what were the Gilla's rooms & loved you both my dear sons.' NM often wrote of Gilla as if he were only absent, not dead. To mark the second anniversary of the declaration of war, he took himself off to Buzzard's in Oxford Street, where Alan, Ethne and Gilla had lunched in August 1914, the last time the three of them had been together. NM 'had a cup of chocolate alone yet in all your company . . . I do not believe anyone ever had three nicer children. I sometimes feel as if I ought to have earned & laid by more money but when I think of you three I am content.'

★

Alan was ordered to sea once more, aboard the Q2, on 30 May 1916. The 'Q ships' were decoy ships equipped for the destruction of submarines. The Q2 was really the Aberdeen liner the *Intaba*; the government paid her owners £4,100 a month for her. Alan was disgusted that they accepted this vast sum. Alan could not reveal anything about his mission to his family – which was a good thing, he thought, as the truth would have made his father extremely anxious – but he described the ship in his journal:

We pretend to be a merchantman . . . The plan is to steam along a trade route in the hopes that a submarine will appear and tell us to stop . . . The stokers not on watch are trained to make a rush for the boats. Meanwhile the gun crews are to go to their stations & keep out of sight & the marines are to assemble . . . out of sight. Everyone is in plain clothes, except the ordinary ship's officers. Then if a submarine comes within a thousand yards the order is to be given & down the sides are to go, & out the 12 & 13 prs [pounders] are to swing, the skylight aft is to slide forward & the 4 inch & the other guns wh bear are to open fire & the marines are to pick off whom they can. The white ensign is to be hoisted.

In the event of catching a submarine, prize money of £1,000 was to be divided amongst the crew, who numbered 113.

No such excitement occurred during Alan's four and a half months on board, which was perhaps just as well: 'I don't think most of us want to meet a submarine yet, with our 4 inch gun limited in its fire, our explosives that no one knows how to handle, & with two of our guns not yet on board . . . What makes us rather gloomy also is the expectation that if we are sunk we shall not be allowed to get away in the boats.'

The Q2 sailed from Milford Haven to Malta and the North African coast via Queenstown (now Cobh, as formerly) in Ireland, then from Queenstown up to the Hebrides. NM tried to guess the route from the riddles based round place names and the natural history observations Alan put in his letters. NM continued to write every day; often the letters could not be delivered for weeks, and Alan would find great bundles of them waiting for him at the end of a voyage. Trying to imagine what his son was experiencing, NM wrote a little verse:

> To plough the waves & cut the foam,
> Among sunfish & sharks to roam
> By day to watch the diving gannets
> By night the shining of the planets
> Yet always in my mind you stay
> Or are you near or far away.

★

In October, Alan was ordered to leave the Q2 and report to the Hoy Battery No. 1 at Stromness on Orkney, where he was to be in charge of the little hospital. Ethne provided an excellent veal and ham pie from Fortnum and Mason's to sustain him on the long train journey north. Alan was interested to find that the islanders, who regarded themselves as Norse, not Scottish, still used some words from their own largely vanished language, such as 'peedi-oddy' (tiny), 'eeryoy' (great grandchild), 'quoy' (a walled culti-vated enclosure), and 'orra' (other or odd).

> The people commonly own their farms & thirty to fifty acres of land for wh they have no title deeds but succession for immemorial genera-tions. The older farms, have one storey with a low pitched roof made of great slabs of stone, on wh is turf heather & the like with stones to keep it down. The byre is part of the building & sometimes people & cows have a common entrance. There is one room with bunks, a peat fire . . . & no ceiling . . . Oxen are used for carts & ploughing . . . Spinning wheels are common. There are hardly any trees. Peat may not be sold.

The hospital served the islanders as well as those posted to the Hoy Battery. Alan also boarded ships where there was illness or injury. On one drifter, the skipper, Buchan, who came from Peter-head, 'speaks a dialect that I have difficulty in understanding at times. He could remember the Eira & said he had talked with men who had sailed with Uncle Ben, & that he was still spoken of at Peterhead, & I gathered kindly remembered.' As the winter wore on Alan found life on Orkney something of a trial. Roads were primitive, but he had to get about a great deal. Weather conditions were extreme – he wrote to Milicent for extra warm pyjamas – and evenings were spent cooped up with uncongenial companions: 'Burrell has been pro-moted to lieutenant. He wants taking in hand. Yesterday he pro-duced a bottle of scent & scented his letters'; 'Major Storey to-day said he disliked reading. A few days ago he said he disliked talking. He has however no objection to eating.'

★

On 7 November 1916, Milicent received a letter from Gilla's Cambridge friend Leonard Ward-Price. 'It isn't only on the anniversary of his death that I remember dear old Gilla,' he wrote. 'Of all the men I have met in my life I feel that Gilla is the most charming, the most manly & the most gentlemanly, & my feelings for him have only grown stronger now that he has joined the gallant dead.' The number of those known to NM and Milicent joining the gallant dead continued to grow. 'Wardy' himself, seconded from the 4th Dragoon Guards to the Royal Flying Corps, was soon to go on a mission from which he never returned. On 9 December, Milicent received a barely legible letter from Mabel about John:

> Dearest Milicent,
>
> I had this wire from W.O. [War Office] yesterday 'Regret to inform you that 34 Casualty Clearing Stn reports Dec 7th that Capt J.C.Ludlow, Innis.Fus. was admitted with gunshot wound head-compound fracture – dangerously ill, further news sent immediately on receipt – Regret permission to visit cannot be granted.'
>
> I got this at T[unbridge] Wells, & came up at once & I went to the W.O. yesterday & found the reason for refusal to visit is because casualty Clearing Stn is right at front line – but I'm hoping to go as soon as he can be moved –

John had walked into the dressing station, and at first seemed to be making progress, but on 15 December he died in hospital at Rouen of this, his third war wound. NM wrote in his journal that John 'had become a captain & adjutant in the Inniskilling Fusileers & was a nice brave, open-hearted boy. May he rest in peace.' With John's death, Milicent had lost not only a dear nephew, one with whom she had been closely involved in his childhood, but also the last male Ludlow, a promising career soldier who had been expected to follow in the tradition of his grandfather the General. 'He leaves a very bright memory,' she wrote to Alan.

John's death made NM cling still more closely to the thought of Alan. Two months later Ethne provided a cheering piece of family news. On 25 February 1917 she gave birth to a third son, Matthew, a birthday present for two-year-old Mark. In May, Jack Pryor, now a lieutenant-colonel, was awarded the DSO. The following year Ethne received an MBE for her war work. She was surprised, she told her father, to find herself such a grown-up person when she still liked to eat toffee and run down hills.

Six months of continuous chill on Orkney took their toll on Alan. In May 1917 he developed pleurisy. Once discharged from hospital, he recovered, slowly, at Hancox. The roads, almost empty of traffic, and the landscape, unkempt for lack of manpower, were marvellously tranquil. The need for a tonsillectomy extended his sick leave still further, and it was 24 September before he returned to duty, at Haslar hospital in Gosport, Hampshire. 'There are a great many cases of neurasthenia [shell shock] coming in – most unsatisfactory people to deal with,' he wrote to NM. One patient complained 'of seeing tigers & eels turning summersaults in the ward'.

Alan was pronounced fit to return to active service, but it was stipulated that he should be posted to the Mediterranean. In November he was ordered to join HMS *Grafton*, somewhere near Port Said. Alan was to be Medical Officer for 60 officers and 704 men. As he prepared to leave England his heart was heavy:

Thus has the falling away of Russia [due to revolution] & the weakness of Italy altered all prospects & renewed the waning strength of the enemy who appears if not to triumph yet to be victorious. The gloom of winter weather matches the hardship & stress of the times, but the play is not played & Acts IV & V may retrieve the past & see villainy punished.

It was all very well for the doctor to decree that, due to the poor state of his lungs, Alan should serve in a warm climate, but to reach HMS *Grafton* he had to endure greater physical hardship than he had yet encountered. He and his company crossed from Southampton to Cherbourg on 18 December 1917; it would be seventeen months before he again set foot on English soil. On arrival, he and nine other officers slept in a wooden hut without furniture, mattresses or any means of heating; in twenty degrees of frost, sleep was elusive. So it continued to prove as they made their way slowly through snow-covered France in a train with broken windows. Alan had been ordered to inoculate the men against typhoid before they left England but as the vaccine had gone missing this had not happened. Now, the vaccine turned up, and Alan found himself frantically inoculating as many men as he could on the platform whenever the train stopped. He had been supplied with a portable 'Tommy's cooker', so he supplemented his rations of bully beef and bread with hot coffee and soup. 'I don't think I have had an hour's consecutive sleep since leaving England & . . . have not had a wash in hot water,' he wrote home on 22 December, 'nevertheless it is all like a huge picnic & everyone is cheerful . . . you would hardly know me . . . such a red eyed blue faced object.' Alan was impressed by the attitude of the men, despite their tendency to 'bolt for the wine shops' at every opportunity; 'I understand . . . more how the British Empire arose from Englishmen just settling, managing for themselves & being on good terms with the people already there.'

On Christmas Eve they reached Toulon. The snow had gone and the landscape had changed.

The roofs were low-pitched, great jars stood by the farms & there were olive trees & red earth & aloes and cactus. We saw many black troops in the blue French uniform who greeted us with cheerful smiles & all we passed were friendly . . . [at] Nice . . . we stopped & were given tea by Red Cross people, English & American, on the platform. Here we received quite an ovation, people mustering outside the station & cheering us as we went by. One girl kissed her hand to us with an indescribably graceful gesture.

The mood changed when they crossed the border into Italy. The snow returned and the friendliness vanished. The sullen attitude of the Italians was attributed to envy; the Italians, Alan thought, considered the British to be living in luxury while they endured endless shortages and hardships. Italian railwaymen boarded the train at night and robbed the British troops as they slept. 'I was prepared to like the Italians & their country,' Alan wrote to NM, 'but to get an idea of both I shd think to imagine yourself in the Orkneys among Sinn Feiners would produce it. It is clear that England upholds the war.' Those bound for Egypt, including Alan, were put aboard the *Leasowe Castle* at Taranto. It was a luxurious ship. Alan's suite of rooms had been fitted out specially for the Queen of Greece. 'I am writing in a beautifully panelled little sitting room & near by is a large bedroom with a shore-going bed . . . & opening from that a spacious bathroom. On the deck in both rooms is a thick piled carpet . . . I expect I shall have a good deal to do as we shall have some 2000 men on board – many of them Egyptians. We have also a hundred & fifty nurses.' The journey was dangerous. 'Every one has orders to wear their life belts night and day.' Not long after Alan left the *Leasowe Castle* she was sunk, with great loss of life.

They docked at Port Said, where Alan joined HMS *Grafton* on 10 January 1918. His first task was to inoculate the crew against bubonic plague. The ship seems to have been on standby in case of an engagement; much of the time the crew were in the dark about the purpose, if any, of her movements. She made her way down the Suez Canal to the Red Sea, stopping on the Asiatic side at Tor, a quarantine station for pilgrims returning from Mecca. The Cockney officer in charge of the quarantine station 'inquired whether we could furnish a football team to play the men in charge of the wireless station'. Alan and others set off to explore. 'On a mound just outside the town I found a human femur & a number of other bones & was seriously thinking of taking some on board for use in first aid classes when I noticed some hair sticking up through the sand & advised our moving on . . . This was the first time that I ever set foot in Asia.'

At Akaba, a town in what had been Turkish territory, they landed by a noticeboard with 'Chatham Pier' written on it. Akaba was dirty and evil-smelling, and full of Bedouins with camels.

'Nearly every man has a pretty good rifle & ammunition . . . they loose off at any time & at any mark . . . The Bedouins have a certain picturesqueness, but many are ragged & villainous looking.' An 'elderly' Captain of Sappers appeared, who said that the Bedouins were supplied with food and ammunition by the British, but that 'they were not particular on which side they fought.' The Captain pointed out three Armenians, the only survivors from a village where the Turks had burnt alive nearly all the inhabitants by driving them into barns to which they set fire.

Alan's days mixed fairly heavy medical duties (he was in charge of organizing all the supplies, bedding and so on for the sick, as well as treating them), and decoding and censoring. However, he still found plenty of time for sightseeing and relaxation. At Yanbo he admired coral reefs, and commented on people richly and colourfully dressed carrying silver-hilted swords and 'light battleaxes', small girls with rings through their noses, Sudanese slaves following their masters. On the *Grafton*, a canvas bath was erected on the upper deck large enough to hold forty-eight men; Alan also took every opportunity to swim in the sea, as was his lifetime's habit. He rode – both camels and horses – and went on shooting expeditions with other officers. They bagged sandpipers, shoveller ducks, snipe and quail, but failed to hit the vultures.

In Egypt he admired, particularly, the Sphinx, attended a very British garden party at which the Duke of Connaught handed out medals, and bumped into an old Cambridge friend, Warde-Aldam, 'whom I thought to be in France. He thought I was in the North Sea.' A leitmotif of Alan's wartime journal is being hailed in farflung places by men who say 'Weren't you at Eton?' or 'Aren't you a Trinity man?' It was in Egypt that Alan had his first go in an aeroplane. He was taken up about 2,000 feet and did some turns and a short nose-dive. 'The sensation was delightfully exhilarating . . . Flying feels very safe.' Since eight airmen at this particular flying school died within a month his confidence seems misplaced, especially as on landing a 'fine spray of spirit' was observed issuing from the engine. His instructor told him that 'one of our airmen chal-

lenged the German Immelmann, a famous fighter, to single combat
in France. The challenge was accepted & on both sides the guns were
quiet. The encounter took place at a great height & lasted 4 seconds,
the German being shot down in flames. The Englishman threw two
wreaths after him. Isn't that Homer brought up to date?'

News from Europe filtered through slowly: 'March 26 1918. We
are getting news of tremendous fighting in France . . . The scale of
the battle is so great as to pass the powers of the imagination.'
HMS *Grafton* was on alert to take part in the capture of Haifa, but
this plan was 'abandoned due to great pressure on the Western
Front'. As the weeks passed, conditions on board deteriorated.
Great heat swelled the sicklist 'to eighteenth-century proportions';
the temperature in the unventilated sickbay reached 100°F (38°C)
and Alan had to wage battle against ants, rats and cockroaches –
'the ship's cockroach is an intelligent insect clever at taking cover.'
'This ship is not really inhabitable under war conditions at sea.
We have to close up all scuttles to darken her & that means no, or
next to no, ventilation so you can't sleep below. The quarter deck
is impossible owing to the rain of cinders from the funnels so we
crowd into odd corners.' At Port Said, plague and typhus were
rife: 'all intercourse with natives is forbidden.' Even the Admiral
succumbed to the heat, issuing orders clad only in a towel – 'not
one of the largest towels either'.

★

In 1918, life was better for NM than it had been since Gilla's death.
He served on a pensions tribunal which considered the cases of
men applying for war pensions on the grounds of ill health,
whether mental or physical. He heard a total of nine hundred peti-
tions; the work suited him well, as at the heart of his medical career
lay a belief that the health of an individual was inextricably bound
up with his interests, occupation, attitude of mind and relationships with those around him. On the tribunal he listened carefully
to each case history and made, usually, merciful judgements; in his
notebooks the term 'malingerer' is sparingly used.

1918 was the year in which NM's medical career was crowned. On 25 March he wrote to Alan, far away in the Red Sea:

> I wished for you here today & by the fire after dinner for I was elected President of the College of Physicians . . . West arrayed me in the gown of black satin & gold lace . . . I am glad thus to have attained the top of my profession by the vote of physicians & not as a result of any favours. I then presided for the remainder of the meeting & then took a taxy to 67 G.P. & made Milicent happy with the news. We gave each maid servant a sovereign. So this is my addition to the family honours. I hope you like it.

Alan did like it. 'MY VERY BEST CONGRATU-LATIONS,' he wrote when he received his father's letter a month later. 'You will be the best President they ever had . . . I hope your term of office will see the victory of the allies.' Ethel Portal gave a tea party to celebrate the event – 'her maids had put up "A Happy Day" & made a sponge cake with apricots & chocolate on or round it. Milicent came too . . . A most pleasant celebration,' NM wrote, somewhat incongruously, in his medical casebook.

The presidency was the high point of his life as a doctor; the completion and publication in the same year of NM's *History of St Bartholomew's Hospital* was the fruition of his antiquarian labour. Advance copies of the two-volume history, handsomely bound in red linen, arrived on 14 October – NM and Milicent took the books to show to the tomb of Rahere, the twelfth-century founder of Bart's, as a homage. The history, which was very well reviewed and which even today is eminently readable, had repaid patience as well as hard study. NM had begun it in 1881, before Alan's birth. It had suffered about twenty years' delay because W. H. Cross, the clerk of Bart's, had prevented NM from having free access to the records, for reasons that remain obscure. Rather than quarrel with this unreasonable man, NM waited, and was at last allowed to see all he needed. When the history came out, the obstructive Mr Cross was still alive; 'I mean to give him a copy,' NM wrote in his journal. Of the first six copies, he gave one to Milicent, 'who had made the index & cheered the work often on its way', and the remaining five, all inscribed, to King George, Queen Mary, Queen Alexandra (the Queen Mother), the Prince of Wales, and Viscount Sandhurst, the Treasurer of Bart's. This distribution suggests not so much ardent royalism on NM's part as a desire to remind the Royal Family of the importance of Bart's and their historic links with it. A day or two later another copy arrived. 'After dinner I took it to Ethel, who was delighted to receive it. She has paid for all the plates in the book.'

NM, now seventy-one, was still well enough to enjoy the honours his presidency brought, such as dinner with the King and Queen at the Guildhall to celebrate their Silver Wedding. Signs that his health was beginning to fail were just starting to appear. He does not dwell on his illnesses in his journal, showing more anxiety about Ethel Portal's – he records that in 1918 she suffered 101 severe headaches, compared to fifty in 1914 – but he often had to take to his bed, usually with bronchial complaints. His intellect remained active though his body failed him. 'When I find Henry James too thin a writer,' he wrote, characteristically, to Alan from his sickbed, 'I turn to Nota Latinae an account of abreviations in Latin M.S.S. of the early minuscule period 700–850 by W. M. Lindsay a book with an almost terrific air of veracity.' In the same letter he described the paintings he could see from his bed:

> The Cornfield at Scalands given to me one evening as I was leaving her house in Blandford Square by Aunt Barbara. The reproduction of Daubigny's sketch of a flock of rooks on bare trees given to me by her in memory of an evening when I met that great painter at her house . . . The one I like best is Ethne's birthplace by your mother. Her pictures I like more the more I look at them, & so I do the early ones of Aunt Barbara.

NM's life, he said, 'as I look back on it by the flaming light of these days seems to have been a very sit at home at ease one. Yet I have no ground of complaint in the least for it has been rich in people beyond all likelihood.'

★

In August 1918, HMS *Grafton* spent several weeks in dry dock at Malta – not pleasant, as Alan explained to NM, because in dry dock 'you have no drains, even the washing up water has to be carried ashore to be emptied.' Still, for the first few weeks his duties were light, but in September influenza broke out, a foretaste of the epidemic that was to sweep across the world during the winter of 1918–19, killing millions of demoralized and undernourished victims. In the first week of the outbreak, Alan sent 140 men to hospital, but found to his dismay that the influenza cases were crowded into the surgical wards. The hospitals were so badly run that many tried to conceal their illness to avoid them. It was a relief when the *Grafton* was ordered back to Italy: 'There was a pleasant smell from the shore quite different from that of the East, a European smell.' For the next few weeks the *Grafton*'s job was to carry troops to and fro across the Aegean, to Mudros, Stavros, Salonika, Kephalo. One day 'four monks from Mt Athos wearing brimless tall hats came alongside in a curious boat. They were taking oil & corn to some people who were starving in Bulgaria.'

Reliable news was hard to come by, but it really did seem that the war was drawing to an end. Messages for Alan to decode came thick and fast: 'The rumours multiply & there is excitement in the air.' Alan's life was complicated by the presence on board of a 'lunatic' who chased people with a bayonet and threw all his clothes and bedding through the scuttle of his cell.

At Salonika they embarked 1,500 troops for Imbros. Salonika looked grand from the sea, but proved to be 'smelly and burnt out'. The terrible sufferings of the Macedonians were revealed. An estimated ten thousand had died, mainly of starvation, at Karalla; the stench of their burning bodies was dreadful. The Bulgarians, it was said, 'spared no woman above 12'. As they sailed past Mount Olympus, Alan was in conversation with an Irish colonel named Maxwell, who told him:

much of interest concerning the country about Salonika. In time of peace there is much brigandage & citizens are snatched away from their own houses & held to ransom. If it is not paid an ear is sent in, further delay brings a second ear, & after that only immediate payment prevents murder . . . In the war we have employed bands of these comitadoes, but they are unsatisfactory, preferring to plunder rather than to fight . . . He spoke of the horrible cruelties of the Bulgars & how the civil population died of starvation, coming over to our lines & we not able to admit them so that they died then & there; & how ill-treated our prisoners were so that of one batch of 70 in a month half were dead. The Greeks fought well he said & the Serbs too. The latter he said never touch the women when they conquer a district. The Bulgars act otherwise . . . Once he took a German trench & in it were the bodies of 10 women still warm. He had often seen the Germans kill our wounded.

On 5 November, Alan wrote in his journal, 'The war is ending so fast that we can hardly realise it, the more so because . . . we have seen no English papers later than of September 28th.' At home, confidence had been growing throughout the autumn. NM had been responsible earlier in the war for removing and safely storing the pictures and other treasures belonging to Bart's; in October he proudly brought them out of their hiding places. On 9 November he wrote to Alan, 'The Germans have a few hours more in which to accept or reject the Armistice. I expect they will try & dodge it someway but I feel great confidence in Marshall Foch as a man who will stand no nonsense.' As NM wrote, Alan was in sight of the Gallipoli peninsula, sailing past the plain of Troy; he spotted two mounds, the alleged tombs of Achilles and Patroclus.

On the tenth Alan heard a wireless report of Lloyd George's victory speech, given in the Guildhall the day before. NM had been there in person, as a guest of the Lord Mayor. He described the event in his diary:

I dressed in levée dress . . . [and] drove to the Guildhall. The Lord

Mayor received his company in the library . . . From the end my name President of the Royal College of Physicians was called out & a third of the way to the dais a second usher asked me to stop & after a breathing space shouted my style a second time. Everyone was not cheered & I was so I suppose some friends or old students must have noticed me. I reached the Mayoral Throne & after bowing to his Lordship was introduced to the Lady Mayoress . . . an alderman told me that fur on his gown was of the very best sable . . . A fanfare of trumpets announced Lloyd George & loud cheers. Soon after we went into the great hall . . . The dinner was wholesome & not too profuse. Then speeches: A. J. Balfour in a dignified serious & impressive strain surveyed in one extensive view affairs from Siberia to the North Sea. Geddes 1st Lord of the Admiralty of a resolute bulldog appearance told us that ten days ago the German fleet seemed about to come out & fall on. They were ordered to do so but would not come so that was the end of the German navy. Lord Milner spoke smoothly: his best passage was where he told of the resolute nature of the British army. After a little the citizens grew impatient & shuffled their feet . . . Then the prime minister. I had never heard him before – A fine speech often applauded, deserving applause in its thoughts, in its style, in its delivery from beginning to end. What rare fifth act to crown this huffing play. The speech itself in that old hall with its civic marbles [statues] with its roof hung with banners with the chief man of England speaking seemed not a mere relation but an actual scene in that fifth act of a long drawn terrible drama. 'The German messengers have not been able to reach Marshall Foch so I have nothing to tell you I had better stop here & go no further.' Cheers sent him on. It was a dramatic beginning. He told that Kaiser Wilhelm & the Crown Prince had abdicated & then made it clear that the acts of war were those not only of the rulers but of the German people themselves & that they too must answer . . . They must agree by 11 on Monday at latest. There would be no alteration in the terms of the Armistice. If they did not accept their defeat would be greater: the fighting would go on: the allies were determined to conquer them. He had been a week at Versailles. He had walked in its beautiful woods the leaves were falling & day after day the crowns of kings kept falling . . . He spoke of our young men who had fallen (& my dear Gilla I remembered you). Geddes had praised the Navy & the Q.2. men & that with me was for Alan.

Lloyd George hoped for better times & a league for peace among nations.

It was a noble speech . . . some of the force of Bunyan in it – no flourish no bombast – not too fast nor too slow but just right. Clear throughout – that of a mind which had been thinking of these great tremendous terrible events & of nothing else. Cheers & more cheers greeted its end . . . We had to wait about the porch for more than an hour. Out came the Lord Chancellor with the bag of the Great Seal & his huge mace & three or four judges in fullbottomed wigs & scarlet gowns & knights & aldermen & Henry Fielding Dickens the Common Serjeant [Charles Dickens's son] whom I liked to see for his celebrated father's sake & the honour of literature. & so we drove home a dark cold night.

It is extraordinary to reflect that in 1918 it was usual never to have heard the voice of the prime minister.

Alan, coaling – always a messy and uncomfortable process – at Mudros, heard the news of the Armistice confirmed at a quarter past ten on the eleventh, when a signalman came into the wardroom with a message: 'Hostilities will cease on the whole front from the 11th November at 11 o'clock. The Allied troops will not cross until a further order the line reached that date & that hour.' This was followed two hours later by a signal: 'The mainbrace is to be spliced in celebration of the conclusion of the Armistice with Germany.' 'This was followed by cheering & ringing of the ship's bell,' recorded Alan; 'The ship is now getting tuneful under the effects of rum.'

Aunt Charley was writing to NM at the very moment of the announcement:

As the Robertsbridge train came in just now into London, the

great flag of England actually being hoisted on Southwark Cathedral tower told me the great hour was come – All along flag after
flag went up & on the tops of all the warehouses dense masses of
work people waving to the train in sheer joy – And instantly my
thoughts went out to dear Gilla – he who has given all to give us
this day of fulfilment – the very place where he fell emphasises it
– that front & that battle were the real barriers to the enemy and
have in the end given us victory.

*

Alan's war did not end with the Armistice. It would be months
before the seas were safe. The frustrating uncertainty about the
Grafton's movements – orders were frequently countermanded –
and the relentless progress of the influenza epidemic meant that
daily life continued to feel grim, despite the huge sense of relief.
Alan gave vent to bitterness and cynicism: 'Hardly anyone trusts
our political leaders & most fear that the enemy will be gently
dealt with. If he be not punished then no one ever should be punished again.' Alan, by nature peaceable and fair-minded, expressed,
like many others, a thirst for vengeance born of four long years of
hardship, danger, grief and loss. 'I am sorry that Germany has not
been pillaged,' he wrote to his father: 'I hope our guns kept up a
heavy bombardment to the last moment. I don't feel the faintest
spark of pity for the Germans & like to think that though fighting
is at an end yet winter is before them hungry & heartbroken.'

The next few weeks took Alan and the *Grafton* to Constantin-
ople ('I suppose I am one of the first Etonians to see it under European domination'), across the Black Sea to Sebastopol, where the
German flag was flying over the town and 'people for the most
part had not heard of the Armistice,' and to Nikolaev, where he
worked as an intelligence officer. 'Our immediate business was to
check the Bolsheviks . . . An army of 10,000 Bolsheviks is 20 miles
off. In the town are some 600 loyal Russian troops. There are also
Germans who are to be got away.' Alan was instrumental in brok-
ering a peace between these factions. They moved on to Odessa,

by no means out of danger – there was a large German minefield off Odessa which 'complicates navigation in the dark'.

Alan had been told he would be sent back to Egypt. He was amazed and delighted when on Boxing Day he received the order to return home. On his leaving the *Grafton*, the captain told him that he had made 'the best impression possible'. His progress back to England via the Mediterranean was extremely slow, including a wait of several weeks at Spezia while his ship, the *Endymion*, was repaired.

It was in Spezia that he received news of the death of Aunt Nannie at the age of eighty-seven. 'She was never directly unkind to me,' was his fair and guarded comment. Nannie, born six years before Queen Victoria came to the throne, had managed to hold on just long enough to witness the birth of a new era. Despite a lifetime of anxiety about her health, it was only in the last few months of her life that her activities were truly curtailed by illness and she was con-fined, as far as I can make out, to Torquay. Though she had alienated many, she remained attached to Bella and her family, to Mabel's daughters, and to Lionel and Agnes's two girls, Medora and Nancy. At intervals throughout the war she would turn up at Mayfield, as Aunt Jenny reported to Alan: 'Fancy Aunt Nanny paying us a surprise visit the other day . . . What she did *not* know was that all our Flys have been taken off for wartime - & nothing but the most unsuitable & tipetty little carts left in the village – poor Aunt N – she didn't look the right woman in the right place, in one of them.'

There is some evidence that old age mellowed the fearsome free-thinker. In March 1919, Milicent was surprised to receive a letter from Margaret Howitt, one of the circle of radical women that had included Barbara, Nannie and Bessie Belloc, asking for a mortuary card of Nannie's, 'to hang up in the hotel (for pilgrim soldiers) at the Grotto at Lourdes'. Few people would be less read-ily associated with the Grotto at Lourdes than the virulently anti-Catholic Nannie, but the letter went on to explain:

Last summer or spring I received a joyous letter from your Aunt saying that Mrs Lionel Leigh Smith [Agnes] had unexpectedly

arrived safe & sound in London from India; & as a thanks offering
for her prosperous voyage she sent me a cheque for £5.0.0. . . .
to . . . help some poor folks. I replied that as it was a thanks offering for a journey I thought if some other traveller could be helped
it would be most appropriate. I knew that to send a Catholic soldier to Lourdes for his leave made him intensely happy . . .
Although probably your Aunt would have better understood an
English holiday for a Tommy she took it very graciously.

Margaret Howitt ended this unexpected letter with a reminiscence
of a long-ago holiday in Germany in which Milicent had taken
part: 'You have left a very melodious memory. I can still hear your
singing as we returned from that mountain valley ramble.'

'I shall be interested to hear of Aunt Nanny's will,' wrote Alan, 'I
hope . . . that all is not left to the society for the prevention of drainage in malarial districts.' But Nannie's will was more even-handed
than might have been expected. All the surviving nieces and
nephews were remembered. Bella and her four children received the
largest share; the rest received £2,000 a piece, including Milicent.

*

Alan finally reached England on 20 March and got to Gloucester
Place for a celebratory dinner party the next day. England, he
remarked, looked as if she could do with a lick of paint. The general shabbiness, cold dull weather, and a huge amount of red tape
to be disentangled before he could re-start civilian life all muted
the euphoria of homecoming. He had come back to a country full
of unrest. Returning servicemen felt neglected; coalminers went
on strike; even the police attempted a strike. 'Many people,' wrote
Alan a few weeks after his return, 'think we are on the verge of
revolution & indeed last Sunday seeing Aunt Charley & Sir Wilmott
Herringham sitting by the fire in the kitchen at Brown's boiling
eggs, there being no servant but the gardener, made me realize that
a revolution was actually going on, though so far not a violent
one.' Alan was struck by the rapid growth of new and radical ways

of thinking, political, social and scientific. In May, staying with friends in Cambridge, he was fascinated by the conversation of W. H. R. Rivers, the psychiatrist and social anthropologist who had treated soldiers for what would now be called Post-Traumatic Stress Disorder at Craig Lockart War Hospital. His patients included the poets Siegfried Sassoon and Wilfred Owen. 'Rivers told us something of the new experimental psychology wh science he said had advanced more in the last 4 years than in the previous 100,' Alan told NM. 'Apparently our conception of mind has to be completely altered. A great deal of the work is due to the war. He says that on the whole army officers were sensible in their treatment of misbehaviour, recognising often that it was beyond a man's control . . . It is a new world wh looks as though it might have very wide influence upon such matters as criminal law. What it is all based on is the operation of the unconscious mind wh profoundly affects the conscious & sometimes comes to the surface.'

Alan had great difficulty in establishing a place for himself in this confused and confusing new world. His experiences of the last four and a half years had convinced him that he was not suited to a Naval career. When he was finally demobilized in June he wrote in his journal:

> I feel a vague disappointment. I suppose when abroad I had pictured a definite triumphal finish & instead we have delays & apparent weakness of statesmen & for myself a couple of weeks leave & then not very congenial work leading to nothing pleasant that I can forsee . . . It may be that feelings of this kind are widespread & are the cause of strikes & unrest. Certainly were my circumstances less easy I should feel inclined to kick against the existing order.
>
> My chief regret in leaving the Navy is that I regret it so little.

His distaste for medical practice remained as strong as ever, but he did not feel qualified for any other work, so he took up a temporary post for the Willesden Urban District Council, working at a medical advice centre for mothers and their children.

A very bright spot in the gloom was the news of a further
honour for NM. In April 1919 he was made a baronet. A suspiciously
large number of baronets were created by Lloyd George, who was
widely believed to take cash for honours, but as Alan hinted in his
letter of congratulation, this was not the case with NM:

> It is right that the state should set the seal of its approval on serv-
> ices that are so well recognised by all to whose knowledge they
> have come. You will now become known to many in whom for-
> merly your name roused little curiosity, & your fame will increase
> to their benefit who, attracted by a title, by hearing of you & by
> meeting you will learn of how much greater worth are nobility of
> character & learning. I am naturally reticent with you in such mat-
> ters but I am delighted to have an occasion on which I may express
> myself without restraint.

The question now arose as to how NM should style himself.
Should he be Sir Norman Moore of Whatlington, of Hancox, or
should he adopt an Irish name, such as Rowallan, where his father's
ancestors had lived? Alan rejected the Irish idea as too tenuous.
'The only question about Hancox is whether so small a place
should be used, but as it was in time past a gentleman's house it
might be I think. I like any sort of title to be a reality & think the
attaching of a territorial name when there is no attachment to the
territory a practice to be discouraged. If however Hancox is what
Milicent likes if it be thought suitable by the Heralds, Hancox let
it be, but if not then Whatlington.' 'Sir Norman Moore of Hancox' was the final decision.

NM derived deep satisfaction from devising his coat of arms,
subject to the approval of the Royal College of Heralds. Heraldry
was one of the many interests he shared with Ethel Portal and long
and detailed were the conversations they had on the subject. Naturally, he chose as his motto Edmund Burke's '*Nitor in adversum*': 'I
strive against adversity.' For the crest he chose a Moor's (negro's)
head, both as a pun on his name and as a reference to his family

involvement with the campaign to abolish slavery, atop a sheaf of corn, in homage to Robert Ross Rowan Moore's championing of the Anti-Corn Law movement. The Red Hand of Ulster is included in the top left-hand corner of the shield – this is a symbol of baronetcy – as are two more sheaves of corn and a band of three gold stars, taken from the crest of his grandfather William Moore. These stars also appear in a small piece of panelling in NM's 'scriptorium', the room at Hancox in which I am now writing. An oblique reference in one of Miss Portal's letters gives the impression that these stars represent herself, NM and Milicent, but I could be wrong.

On 2 July 1919, NM and Milicent went to St James's Palace to see peace finally proclaimed to the cheering crowds, and NM wrote the last entry in the third of his big red-bound war journals. On 19 July peace celebrations were held at Hancox to which the whole village was invited. Alan's description of the day bears the stamp of many an English summer event. The afternoon began with a service of thanksgiving on the tennis lawn: 'The vicar hurried away afterwards, saying that to stay would distract his mind from his sermon for the next day. but there would be few to notice it. Then there were sports in the Forestall. The races were started by George Dann with an old single barrelled muzle loading fowling piece. Rain fell increasingly but tea was eaten under trees & the races run at last.' The sports included a husband and wife arm-in-arm race, and a tug of war, married v. single. Competitors for the sack race were asked to bring their own sacks:

Then the people assembled in front of the house for prize giving . . . during wh the rain began to fall fast. So we invited them into the drawing room & held the prize giving there. There must have been 150 people in the room . . . Those of the village who had served were given a small gift each. I received mine first, a cigar case. NM made a short speech, saying how perhaps the young children present would remember the peace celebrations when they were 90 . . . When we had finished . . . we went to the Woodman's Field

where the bonfire was lit [by Milicent] & blazed well & some fire-
works were let off. A fiddler . . . played in the wet until two of his
strings broke. I lashed to one of our gate posts a paraffine torch that
I carried in a procession before Queen Victoria at Windsor in honour of her 80th birthday. It lit up the drive for the people going to
the bonfire. We could see the glare of a fire before Battle Abbey
gates, another in the direction of Netherfield, & another towards
Sedlescombe.

The torch still lingers at Hancox in a dusty corner.

*

When Alan's temporary job at Willesden came to an end at the
beginning of October he felt himself to be badly in need of a holiday. Lionel Leigh Smith had just returned from India and had settled with Agnes, Medora and Nancy at Ludshott Common in
Hampshire in a bungalow he built himself. Alan had not seen his
uncle for six years; he decided to walk right across Sussex to visit
him. The country was still in a state of unrest, with a threatened rail
strike and rumours of Bolshevik infiltration, and Alan's personal
prospects were no brighter, but the Sussex countryside was still
able to work its old restorative magic. The walk took seven days
and ended when Alan, enquiring at a laundry on the Grayshott
road, was told:

> to go to the wood & take a path through it. I returned found the
> path & almost at once caught sight of a house through the trees. I
> hastened on, passed out of the little wood & entered an enclosure
> bounded by a low earthen rampart. Before me was a man digging
> & when I could see the line of his cheek I knew it was Lionel . . .
> We went into the house to find Agnes & I sank into a comfortable
> chair before the fire too tired to help in laying tea.
>
> So my journey ended as journeys should with a meeting again,
> a welcome, & good cheer.

Alan composed a poem, part of which he carved on his walking stick – a celebration of the fact that, for all the difficulties and disappointments of his life, the war had ended and he had come home:

> Though I have seen three continents
> Yet England best my heart contents
> And had I all my choice & will
> Twixt Dungeness & Selsey Bill
> I'd wish to pass my days.
> The very names can weave a spell
> What music rings in Arundel
> And where across the plain you 'scry
> The clustered roofs & church of Rye
> To mention is to praise.
>
> Near Brightling Needle take your stand:
> Look forth upon the favoured land,
> On village, shaw & field.
> The happy life rejoicing there
> Breathes up an influence to the air
> Like incense from the Weald.
>
> And this good county of my choice
> Has for my ear a secret voice,
> As one who in a lovely face
> And form perceives a special grace
> Which others cannot see
> So all the wealth of streams & downs
> Of woods & farms & little towns
> Of Hancox, Scalands, & of Browns
> Is magical to me.

19. 'I feel he is happy somehow'

Alan's poem, and the walk that inspired it, were both influenced by Hilaire Belloc – indeed, the route Alan took consciously followed the journey Belloc describes in *The Four Men*. Aged forty-nine in 1919, Bessie Belloc's son had become one of the most celebrated writers of his generation. In 1877, when Hilaire (or Hilary, as he was known to family and friends) was six and a half, Barbara had sent General Ludlow some of his precocious poems; a few years later Amy had described him to NM as 'a queer youth'. Nowadays he's chiefly remembered for his *Cautionary Tales* ('The chief defect of Henry King/was chewing little bits of string') and for a handful of much-anthologized poems for adults ('Do you remember an inn, Miranda?'), but he was also a novelist, essayist, historian, journalist, MP and iconoclast. His hugely forceful personality and doggedly old-fashioned way of living won him many admirers and many enemies. He had spent much of his childhood at his mother's cottage near Arundel, and Sussex traditions and the Sussex landscape were very close to his heart. He bought an old house with a wind-mill, King's Land, near Shipley (described by Alan as 'not unlike Hancox'), where he lived without electricity or running water.

From 1919, Belloc and his circle played an important part in Alan's life. Phil Leigh Smith had become friendly with Belloc's children; Mrs Belloc had died young, leaving Hilaire the devoted but unpredictable father of five. In September 1919, Alan met one of the Belloc daughters, Elizabeth, whom Phil had invited to Scalands. (It was a sign of the times and a mark of the unconventionality of the Belloc family that this very young woman was allowed to go and stay unchaperoned with a young man who was not related to her.) Alan was struck; 'A very pleasant pretty little thing, charming in fact. Phil & Miss Belloc & I walked up to the great beech tree wh Miss B. and I climbed. She climbed better than any girl I ever saw.'

After his great walk Alan took up a new post, as medical referee for Stepney, but he liked it no better than the last job. He was restless, and escaped from East London to Sussex at every opportunity. It seemed to him that, at thirty-seven, he had made no progress in life. '31st December 1919. So ends this year with the outlook very bad in Europe & my own prospects as bad as they can be . . . I loathe & detest my profession & have no ambition therein but to leave it.'

Early in 1920, Val Leigh Smith put two-thirds of his estate on the market, including Glottenham – possibly to pay tax bills. He retained Scalands and four hundred acres; Brown's he made over to Aunt Charley. Alan visited Scalands in May: 'I found Val playing the clavichord. We went & looked at the Eira's boat wh had been removed from the barn at Glottenham & now lies near the kitchen garden . . . The whale's jaw was set up by the tennis lawn.' The boat has since rotted away, but the whale's jaw still forms an eccentric entrance to the tennis court at Scalands.

Phil had passed his Foreign Office exams with distinction and had been posted to Russia. In the summer of 1920 he was home on leave. He, Alan and Elizabeth Belloc went on expeditions together, such as rowing on the Thames at Eton; 'Miss B. was very diverting talking on all manner of subjects loudly & convincedly.' Soon, Alan's courtship began in earnest. In his own view he was financially no fitter to marry than he ever had been, but he recognized that 'faint heart never won fair lady.'

Phil Leigh Smith was a lively companion. A very good dancer himself, he persuaded Alan to take lessons, and dragged him along to all sorts of social events that Alan would by natural inclination have avoided. The Bellocs were a boisterous family. Visits to King's Land were characterized by singing, feasting, cheerful arguing and the recitation of rollicking verse, as well as strenuous physical activity – Elizabeth climbed to the end of one of the windmill's sails, to Alan's admiration.

Belloc himself came to stay at Hancox on 3 January 1921. Alan, who was by this time hoping he could regard the great man as a future father-in-law, recorded the visit in detail. Both Belloc and NM were celebrated conversationalists; though NM's powers were in decline, he could still keep his end up. Alan was anxious that the somewhat austere catering arrangements at Hancox would not suit the bon viveur – Milicent's youthful liberality had been reduced by wartime shortages to an almost Lenten parsimony:

I bought a bottle of Chablis as we had no wine in the house & carried it in a German bomb bag. I had bought two in Hastings for the very small sum of 5d each. Belloc when he saw them asked me to get him a dozen wh I did & two haversacks besides. In his letter acknowledging their receipt he said it was good fun spoiling the Germans for that was what it amounted to.

He had arrived when I reached Hancox & presently he & NM & I walked into Sedlescombe to look at the Brabazon pictures . . . We returned to Hancox to tea. Belloc talked on a number of subjects, particularly political corruption of wh he drew such a picture as to make one think he a little over-estimated the rottenness of our government. NM evidently thought so & withdrew from the conversation . . .

Belloc also talked of the Jews. He denied that they had a real religion – I mean that their common bond was one of dogmatic theology – it was, he said, a way of life & having no ideals they were sad. It was, he added, worthwhile learning the Jewish profession of faith in Hebrew for the fun of repeating it in restaurants & noting the effect. Once he said he was at an auction & a ring of Jew dealers was keeping the prices down. So to help the lady whose furniture was being sold he bought a little table for £5. 'It won't be much use to you at that price,' said a Jew. Belloc at once repeated their sacred formula, wh. Disraeli pronounced on his death-bed, & the man turned quite white. 'They don't know it is known,' said Belloc.

Belloc enthusiasts take great pains to claim that his opinions about Jews don't amount to anti-Semitism, but to a twenty-first-century sensibility the distinction is a subtle one, and reading this account I was relieved when the conversation changed direction.

Belloc had brought only a very small hand bag & asked to be excused dressing for dinner. When we came to the meat course he said he was very sorry but that he could not eat hot meat in the evening. He was offered eggs or cold beef & chose the beef of wh he eat very heartily. He drank also three bottles of beer & a good deal of Chablis.

Afterwards we sat for coffee in the hall parlour. He refrained from smoking a cigar because NM cannot stand the smoke.

. . . We talked of the resurrection of the body wh Belloc said was not so difficult to conceive of as of the continued existence of the discarnate soul. I told him that I had once challenged a Jesuit to shew why the definition of the dogma: that the resurrection body was the same body as the earthly, should not have been worded in exactly opposite terms, seeing that it was recognised that as far as material went it must of necessity be quite different. I have been unable to get a conclusive reply to this question & Belloc's answer was not entirely satisfactory to me. He said that the definition meant that the new body would be human & not something totally different . . . He said that the scholastic doctrine that the soul was the form of the body was difficult.

Belloc was a Roman Catholic; Elizabeth's sister Eleanor was a novice at a convent. Alan was the only member of his immediate family never to have been a Catholic. His questions suggest that he foresaw problems in proposing marriage to someone the details of whose faith he could not accept:

I asked him how he reconciled the statements of Christ touching the end of the world – wh in the event did not take place – with either on the one hand the divinity of Christ or on the other hand the inspiration of scripture . . . He had not however the eschatological passages clearly enough in his mind to give a decisive reply.

He said that inspiration was not literal, for if taken literally certain statements, particularly in the O[ld] T[estament] were clearly untrue, that every animal was represented in kind in the ark, for instance. It was however, he said, necessary for a Catholic to believe all the miracles of the N.T.

At dinner NM & he talked of Darwin. Belloc said that Darwin's theory had been offered at a time when the scientific world was ready for the doctrine of tranformism, a doctrine that seemed so plausible. Many facts however could not be explained by it & he spoke of Fabré's work on insects & the incomprehensible things that some of them did. What theory would account for an insect's standing on its head for no apparent purpose. NM praised Darwin & said he was not devoid of religion & spoke of an old Irish reaper who liked him &, he thought, had some hopes of converting him.

This was an itinerant Irish labourer, one of a group who turned up at Down House every summer to reap the harvest. Darwin enjoyed talking to this particular man, who made efforts to convert him to the 'True Faith', as NM recounted. Alan continued:

Belloc is fond of sailing & we had some talk about the price of sails & sea stores . . . We spoke of the decay of the art of seamanship. He said it would all have to be learnt again. I said I thought it was too far gone for revival & inquired if he thought that sailing ships would really come into use again. He said he thought they would. He spoke of the approaching material decline of our civilisation. I asked him if he thought we should fall in to dark ages as set forth in Edward Shanks' book <u>The People of the Ruins</u>. He said he did not think we should fall so far as that but that he regarded a measure of decline as certain . . .

He said that 1921 should prove an interesting year with the Irish business to settle & the French attitude to Germany. For if Germany does not make reparations according to the peace treaty, the French will occupy the Ruhr Valley. France, he said, is the greatest force in Europe.

NM spoke of companies & their dinners. Belloc said that the company of Inn Keepers had asked him to write them a song & that he intended doing so. He said he would like to be a member of their company.

While talking of Darwin he said that by collecting facts you could uphold almost any hypothesis & that he & [G.K.] Chesterton once collected instances to try & shew that as a rule great men were bald.

He went to bed early, being tired & took with him to read Thackeray's Book of Snobs. He said he did not think that Thackeray would live as a writer because the conditions of life about wh he wrote had become so much changed, but that Dickens who wrote about an imaginary world would last.

Other topics of conversation during the visit included Northerners ('they are Barbarians'), the Reformation and the pockets of Catholicism surviving in rural Sussex long after the towns had become Protestant, Glastonbury (Belloc was inclined to believe the tradition that Christianity had been preached there in apostolic times), the honours system, and his boyhood memory of having met an old woman [daughter of Montgolfier the balloonist] who had witnessed the storming of the Bastille. 'I have seldom met a man,' concluded Alan, 'with whom conversation is so enjoyable.'

Three days after this visit, Phil persuaded Alan to join him at the Ashtons' ball at Vinehall. The evening proved to be one of the most significant of Alan's life. They dined before the ball with the Combes at Oaklands; among the diners was Miss Mary Burrows, only child of Winfrid Burrows, Bishop of Chichester. Elizabeth was not at the ball, but Alan enjoyed himself nonetheless: 'The dance was a capital one & the first since my childhood at wh I have danced more than one or two dances . . . There were no chaperones & no programmes . . . I could hardly get Phil away when our cars came & I was loath to depart too.' Miss Burrows and the improbably named Miss Idina Papillon were the girls who suited him best as dance partners. The very next day he went to another ball, where he 'danced chiefly with Miss Burrows'.

By this time Alan had changed jobs again; he was medical inspector of Sussex schools. The work itself was of no great interest to him, but he preferred being based in Lewes to Stepney, and he enjoyed extending his knowledge of the Sussex villages. He usually travelled by bicycle, and often lunched with the local vicar ('country parsons generally have an ample midday meal'). Many of the parsons were well informed about local history and customs, subjects which interested Alan. His workload was not excessive; he had time for sailing, canoeing, exploring, and seeing friends. Money was still a worry. In his lodgings at Lewes he lived frugally; his total annual income for 1920 was only £409.4/3, much less than his father had been earning more than forty years earlier, when Willy Leigh Smith had deemed him too poor to marry Amy.

Alan was encouraged by the fact that the Bellocs were an unconventional family who cared less about such things than most. (Belloc himself spent money as fast as he earned it, and died, in 1953, with little to show, in pecuniary terms, for his prodigious and acclaimed output.) Elizabeth seemed to be returning Alan's advances. He confided in Milicent, who took a sympathetic and surprisingly sensitive interest in affairs of the heart – except, of course, in the case of Ethne and Jack. He told her he hoped he would have a particularly good piece of news in time for her fifty-third birthday on 8 March.

It was not to be. Passages concerning Elizabeth have been cut or scribbled out of Alan's diary, but it is clear that he proposed, and was refused. To Milicent he wrote, 'there is someone else'; later he wrote in his diary that Elizabeth had vowed never to marry, and offered to take a bet on it. Whatever her reasons, Alan was astonished, and deeply wounded. He refused to accept that Elizabeth would not change her mind, and outlined to Milicent his plan for winning her back:

> If I am to win her yet I must behave in a manner that will appeal to her . . . I must try & get a little happiness into my life . . . If I am to be natural again I must get my longing for her beneath the surface a little – I must, superficially, care less whether I win her or not &

to this end it will be well for me to see as many young women as possible so that the image of Elizabeth may become somewhat blurred. Then I may get back to the old high spirited intercourse & she may realise that she has made a mistake.

Milicent shrewdly helped to supply Alan with distracting young women – or at least, with one particular young woman. Mary Burrows's mother, born Mary Talbot, had been a fellow worker with Milicent at St Margaret's House in the 1890s. Ethel Portal had been a close friend of hers; one of Mary Talbot's sisters had had to break off an engagement to one of Ethel's tragic brothers. Milicent had a photograph of the three of them – herself, Ethel and Mary Talbot – at St Margaret's. When in 1895 Mary had become engaged to Winfrid Burrows, the Principal of the Leeds Clergy School who had been active in the establishment of the Oxford House Settlement in Bethnal Green, Milicent had gone with her to help choose the material for her wedding gown, which was made up by the Bethnal Green girls.

Mary Talbot's background was political, intellectual and very Anglican. Gladstone – 'Uncle William' – had married her great-aunt; her father John Talbot was an MP. Her grandfather, Lord Lyttelton, had been involved with Barbara's campaign to get Girton College off the ground; Mary herself had been a student in the 1880s at the newly formed Lady Margaret Hall, Oxford. Mary was intelligent, humorous and full of virtue. Her aunt, Lucy Cavendish, used to say that Mary made her a heretic because she could find in her no trace of original sin.

Mary Talbot's marriage to Winfrid Burrows was intensely happy, but it only lasted thirteen months. Her pregnancy gave no cause for alarm, and she wrote her last entry in her diary on 22 May 1897, the day she went into labour: 'Lovely day – shall associate this time with floods of sunshine –' Not long afterwards she started to have convulsions, was chloroformed, lost consciousness, and barely understood that she had given birth to twin daughters before she died.

One baby was stillborn. The other was named after its mother. Little Mary inherited her mother's warm brown eyes and gentle smile. Her father's special darling, she grew up surrounded by devoted love, tempered by a careful adherence to the teaching of Christ. Winfrid never remarried, but invited his sister Edith to be housekeeper for him and surrogate mother to Mary and to four little cousins whose parents lived abroad. Mary, like her mother, went to L.M.H. When Alan met her she was twenty-three, living with her father and aunt in the Bishop's Palace at Chichester.

I imagine that, for Milicent, a bishop's daughter with aristocratic connections was the next best thing to a Catholic bride for Alan. Milicent was charmed by Mary in herself, and deeply interested in her for her dead mother's sake. She took trouble to put Mary in Alan's way. Alan was immediately responsive: 'Miss Burrows was the one person I felt could at all take Elizabeth's place in my mind,' he wrote to Milicent. In his diary he noted, 'A letter from Milicent, writing of Whitsuntide she wrote, ". . . I should like to invite Miss Burrows for say 3 nights during that time, if you approve - ?" Directly I read it I knew I approved very much.'

The Whitsun visit to Hancox was a success. Milicent accompanied Alan and Mary to Rye, where she tactfully withdrew, leaving them to walk out to Camber Castle unaccompanied, 'our conversation impeded by our absorption of two enormous bullseyes'. Later, at Hancox, there was a meeting of fifty Red Cross members. Alan addressed the gathering; his speech was well received. Mary thus had a chance of observing him from a distance and of introducing herself to the local community. The audience were socially mixed; Lord and Lady Ashton and the Combes were there, but so was Mr Emeleus, the Battle chemist, Rose Playford and her mother, the Winters (the tenants at Hancox farm), and Mr Questier, the village builder and digger of wells.

'Life,' wrote Alan, 'is often like sailing up one of the creeks of Chichester harbour; the channel appears impossible as you look ahead but you go on & it opens out as you progress.' Throughout the summer of 1921, Alan's life opened up with a speed he never thought possible. Memories of Elizabeth were still painful, but her image was being replaced. Doing up a parcel, the purplish-blue wrapping paper conjured an image of Mary in a dress of a similar colour, worn on her Whitsuntide visit.

Alan bought himself a motor bicycle, which increased his freedom. The adventurous Bella also had one, a Royal Ruby 2-stroke. On it she came to visit Alan at Lewes, a round trip of seventy miles. (To me, there is no more succinct illustration than this of the change in the lives of upper-middle-class women during the period covered by this book. Amy was Bella's older sister, and it is impossible to imagine Amy on, or even near, a motorbike.) In August, Alan had a poisoned toe surgically opened, and convalesced at Hancox; with NM and Milicent he went over to Bateman's at Burwash, to call on the Kiplings:

> R.K. is like his pictures only more so – short bald & with bushy eyebrows. One can well understand his being called Beetle at school. He did not shew an atom of conceit. He is a good listener. We talked about his water mill wh now lights him with electricity, & whether or not it was the mill mentioned in the Doomsday book . . . We talked about the early days of cars. The Pryors had a steam car wh once belonged to him & about wh he wrote a story called Steam Tactics & this I had been in . . . His knowledge of ships . . . is not profound.
>
> I liked him but can understand why some do not. [Hilaire Belloc was very antagonistic towards Kipling, which is probably what Alan had in mind.] I am glad to have talked to so famous a man for his fame is really very widespread. All sorts of people who have read hardly anything have read Kipling.

When the Kiplings visited Hancox, Rudyard admired the house greatly and asked NM questions about 'nearly every picture'.

In late September, Mary came again to Hancox, this time at Alan's invitation. They still did not use each other's Christian names. 'Miss Burrows has a gentle sweetness that is most captivating,' wrote Alan. 'To put down my own thoughts seems almost an impiety.' After this weekend NM wrote a letter of encouragement to Alan: 'I meant to write to you yesterday to say how much I think you get on as a conversationalist & how much I enjoyed your talk, & that of Miss Burrows . . . Miss Burrows was delightful to walk with: to talk with and to see & there seemed a rare goodness in her disposition & a fine store of learning in her mind.' Though full of good intention, such a letter shows how dominant NM's influence still was in the life of his son, who was approaching his fortieth birthday.

By now Alan's mind was almost made up. Though he declined an invitation to lunch with Aunt Charley for fear she would quiz him about Mary, he continued to confide in Milicent, who urged him to write to Mary taking up her suggestion that he invite himself to stay a weekend at Chichester. His visit was settled for early November. A few days before, he consulted his friend Gemmell: 'I asked him if he could keep a secret & he guessed at once my intention. He told me just what I wanted to know about expenses & was encouraging. He pays a rent of £75 a year, keeps 2 servants & a car & a motor bicycle on less than £1,000 a year, & the car alone costs £120.'

The fateful weekend arrived. As Alan approached Chichester on the Friday afternoon, the day's heavy rain cleared:

Looking west from Drayton station were the rails all glistening with wet & on the horizon a broad stretch of crimson lake, almost, with a delicate yellowy green above, & stars.

I was met by one of the Palace gardeners who carried my luggage . . . At the door of the Palace was a friendly & welcoming butler. [Tea was served in the drawing room.] The Bishop is an able looking man with white hair and a somewhat aquiline nose . . . His sister is much like him . . .

My heart sank somewhat when I saw the great 50 foot long drawing room & the stateliness of the Palace wondering whether possibly its Princess could be for me.

It being a Friday there was no meat at dinner, after which Mary played the piano. The Bishop's evening dress included buckled shoes. The panelled dining room ceiling was decorated with 'great roses & coats of arms & other devices'.

The next day began with:

prayers read by the Bishop in the exquisite little chapel. Mary played the organ. Then breakfast about IX. The Bishop wore a purple cassock.

After breakfast Miss Burrows [Mary's aunt, who she called 'Tedith] proposed an expedition. I soon found that it was to consist of Mary & myself. Miss Burrows lent me her bicycle. We bicycled in sunshine Northwards till we came to the beginning of the hills. We left our bicycles in a chalk pit & climbed the hills. We saw some rabbits & picked a handful of mushrooms. Our destination was two mounds at the top of a hill wh Mary told me were believed to be the tombs of Danish kings killed in a battle fought in the valley below [Kingly Vale]. This valley soon lay beneath us like an amphitheatre with dark yew trees growing in it. The view broadened but Chichester spire dominated the foreground. When we reached the mounds we could see to the N. rolling hills & autumn woods under the great clouds, & South below us was the green valley, Chichester spire to the left a little, the sea with the plain before it, the mud shining in the creeks of Chichester harbour & the distant Isle of Wight. The w'ly wind was keen so we sat down under the lee of the westerly mound.

I knew the time was come to speak. 'I want to tell you something,' I said, '& to ask you a question . . .'

Mary said that she needed time to consider her answer, and that she needed to think it over out of Alan's presence, but her manner gave him 'great hope . . . Was ever a declaration of love made in such perfect surroundings? . . . We got up. The mushrooms were squashed.'

They returned to the Palace, and spent the rest of the day trying to behave as if nothing had happened. At tea the Bishop lightened the mood by reciting:

> There once was a glutton at Crediton
> took pâté de foie gras & spread it on
> (pause)
> a chocolate biscuit
> He said I will risk it.
> His tomb bears the date that he said it on.

The date was Guy Fawkes Day. 'Remember remember the fifth of November. Shall I ever forget it. I slept very little & a gale aided the agitation of my mind in keeping me awake.'

The next morning Alan got his answer. 'After breakfast Mary beckoned me into her sitting room. We stood together by the fire. Then she said "The answer is Yes."'

They both wrote at once to NM and to Milicent. Their letters arrived the next day, 7 November, the seventh anniversary of Gilla's death. 'Such is the mercy of God that he has given us perfect happiness on a day of tears,' was NM's reply to Mary. Milicent wrote ecstatically:

My dearest Mary,

It is great good news, & we thank God for it. It is so delightful & seems wonderful & strange. Was it for nothing that I went with your mother to help her choose her wedding gown? My dear, I do feel in a kind of way a responsibility to her about you – But she would have liked Alan if she had known him . . . Of course we won't say anything till your Father gives his consent. NM has already resisted the frightful temptation of telling Ethel Portal, who arrived soon after the letters!

Our dear Gillachrist fell this day in 1914 at the Great Battle of Ypres, but we <u>like</u> to feel his coming, as it were, into this family happiness. He adored Alan . . . and there is nothing sad about his dear memory.

Alan described Gilla to Mary:

He was very merry & lively & intensely interested in birds . . .
Birds were to him what ships & boats are to me. Scolastically he
was an utter failure, even worse than me wh is saying a good
deal . . . but everyone liked him & no one ever dreamt of calling
him a fool or dull save only examiners . . .

When the news [of Gilla's death] came I was quite knocked
over. I am not ashamed to confess that I used to find myself in tears
in the street. We have his diary, with his outrageous spelling, kept
up to Nov 6 1914. The place where he fell was fought over for four
years & he has no known grave.

It was quite impossible to associate him with death, their meeting meant a lessening of one's idea of death . . .

One other thing about him now. He was in love with a girl
called Mary.

*

The engagement could not be made public until the Bishop had
given his consent. On Armistice Day, Alan asked him for his
daughter's hand and he, of course, agreed – 'so we became formally engaged on this great anniversary.' Alan bought Mary a
ring, three rubies and two diamonds, and they had their photographs taken at Elliott & Fry. 'It is odd to feel one is someone else,'
wrote Alan, 'as though I had been hydrogen & had met oxygen &
was now one of the ingredients of water.'

Meeting Mary's innumerable cousins, aunts and uncles was a
time-consuming but interesting business. Many of her relations
were prominent in the Church of England; Alan, who had been
reading Trollope, perhaps in preparation, was amused: 'Never
have I met so many of the higher clergy.' The bishop, Alan was
relieved to find, was more than ready to laugh at Anglican absurd-
ities. He showed Alan 'a high church manual of self-examination
for children in wh the child is directed to search its conscience for
the shortcomings of its sense of smell "Have I allowed myself to
say or think that I don't like incense?" ' A post-Christmas stay at
the Palace, with several of Mary's cousins, was full of a sense of

exuberant fun that was sadly lacking at Hancox now that NM's health was giving cause for concern.

For Alan's family, the engagement was a cause for great rejoicing. The dark war years really seemed over at last; the future looked real and promising. Alan had written to Ethne with the news as soon as he could: 'Doesn't it shew the danger of dancing? . . . You know I keep a pretty tight hold on myself – but I've let myself go over this. I am a very lucky man to be loved by such a darling as is your sister-in-law to be.' Ethne wrote, after meeting Mary for the first time:

> But of course, you could not have married before because Mary would not have been old enough, and who else could you marry but Mary?
>
> . . . To be conventional, I think she is charming: to be matter of fact I think she is full of sense & wit & kindness, and why didn't you tell me she was pretty?
>
> To be poetical, she made me think of wood nymphs . . . Yes, my dear boy, I am completely satisfied: If I had been given the job of creating a wife for you, I should have tried to make her in the image of Mary.

★

The wedding date was fixed for 26 April 1922. Mary's youngest aunt, Peg, had married the Earl of Antrim; Peg offered them Glenarm Castle, their home near the Giant's Causeway, for the honeymoon, and the offer was gladly accepted. Mary was examined by a London doctor and pronounced fit to bear children.

The months of the engagement were spent house-hunting, receiving and acknowledging wedding presents, and of course in the deeply enjoyable process of getting to know each other's tastes and foibles. 'If I were ordering a perfect dinner,' Alan told Mary, 'I should begin with either pea soup or scotch broth. Then would come either whitebait, preferably devilled, or salmon, hot & then curry with plain boiled potatoes, & then mince pies or a blackcurrant pudding with thin cream or milk, & then sardines on dry toast . . . Here is a dinner I shd hate: very white soup, boiled fish messed up with white sauce, pork with mashed potatoes & artichokes (not the sort you pull to bits) with white sauce, meringues, welsh rarebit.'

Reading the list of wedding presents as published in the *Sussex Daily News* makes me smile, as I recognize many things we still have at Hancox; I'm glad to know that we have the clergy of the diocese of Chichester to thank for our unlovely but useful mahogany sideboard. Mabel and Ludlow gave 'two odd dark green glass bottles. They look like the sort of thing the careful hussife would keep in the still room for cordial waters. Mead or cowslip wine I can fancy being poured from them.' One bottle survives, and I'm very fond of it, but I wish I knew what had happened to the 'rabbit menu holders' or the 'iridescent china sardine dish'. We still use the Wedgwood dinner service donated by Aunt Charley. The servants at Hancox gave a set of china for early morning tea; 'Mrs Playford pointed out . . . that the two cups are not the same size "one for the lady & one for the gentleman".' Alan took the Hancox servants over for a tour of the Palace and its gardens, and they all came to the wedding too. Val Leigh Smith, however, declined his invitation: 'I looked in at Scalands. Val was playing the spinet – characteristically he did not look up when I came in but went on playing. He doesn't think he'll come to the wedding – says it is too far.'

Alan and Mary spent the weeks apart, but were together most weekends either at Chichester or Hancox, or on visits to their various relations. Mary had spent several weekends at Hancox before she discovered that it had a bathroom, but its whereabouts had not been revealed to her; 'it is so far from the bedroom you occupied that we felt it was too far to ask you to travel,' Alan explained.

Just two days before the wedding, Alan, at Lewes station, heard 'someone call "Alan Alan" & looking round there was Elizabeth hurrying after me. She was just back from France & was between two trains. How strange that she should appear now. Her manner was unaffectedly friendly. I am experiencing much friendship in these days.'

The wedding, in Chichester Cathedral, caused considerable excitement in the local papers. The social revolution set in motion by the Great War was far from complete. 'In view of the distinguished parentage of the bride and bridegroom,' gushed the *Portsmouth Evening News*, 'the wedding created great interest throughout the diocese of Chichester and in a much wider area, and was one of the most important and imposing marriage ceremonies that have taken place in the Cathedral of recent years.' 'Beautiful and Impressive Ceremony' was the headline in the *Sussex Daily News*:

> Leaning smilingly on the arm of her father, the bride made a wonderfully pretty picture as she slowly passed up the aisle. She was charmingly attired in a Venetian dress of cream embossed velvet georgette, with a pearl girdle, and with a train of the same embossed velvet georgette falling straight from the shoulders, and also a single wreath of orange blossom holding in the veil of beautiful old Honiton lace, in which her grandmother, Mrs Burrows, had also been married. She carried a lovely bouquet of lilies of the valley, and her only ornament was a pearl necklace.

Mary had four adult bridesmaids and two little ones, all cousins of hers. The big ones wore 'lilac charmeuse with quaintly draped bodices caught at the side with clusters of gold grapes, and overskirts of gold silk lace with long loose sleeves, and coronets of gold roses and grapes (the gift of the bridegroom). They carried bouquets of mauve irises tied with ribbons to match.' The two younger bridesmaids were 'very dainty in lilac charmeuse dresses with pale gold net with a trail of gold grapes at the yoke, and wreaths of tiny gold leaves on their heads'. They carried posies of anemones and wore amethyst drops. There was a solitary pageboy, Ethne's middle son, Mark, aged seven. He wore 'violet velvet knickerbockers with a silk frilled shirt to match, and purple shoes and socks'. In one of the wedding photographs he is sticking out his tongue at the camera, perhaps in protest at the knickerbockers.

Milicent, revelling in the grandeur of the occasion, wore 'a black soft satin dress with a coral waistcoat and a black hat with coral feathers'; she carried a bouquet of coral-coloured roses. Ethne was artistically attired in a grey gown with a dark blue and silver belt and a painted straw hat, plus a black satin cloak with a silver collar. The reception at the Palace passed in a blur of hand-shaking, then Mary changed into her going-away outfit, 'a silk crocheted dress of medlar brown with a long fringed girdle falling below the skirt', plus a Paisley cloak and hat. They spent their wedding night at Gloucester Place, where champagne and supper had been left ready for them. The following evening they boarded a train at Euston, bound for Stranraer. At dawn the next morning their luggage was searched for firearms before they caught the *Princess Maud*, a screw steamer bound for Larne, to begin their fortnight's honeymoon at Glenarm Castle. An old fisherman who invited them to take tea with him in his one-roomed cottage said to Mary, 'I like to see you sitting there, you look so pretty,' with which Alan heartily agreed.

★

The excitement and delight over Alan's wedding could not mask the fact that NM's powers were declining fast. Though I cannot find any direct statement to confirm this, it seems that he was suffering from Parkinson's disease. His handwriting, which had been large and loose, became tiny, cramped and spidery; the change is first evident early in 1920. His movements slowed; walking became an effort. He complained that his memory was failing; he found it difficult to call to mind the right word, detail or anecdote he needed to make a point. Writing, walking, talking, remembering – all had been essential to NM's sense of purpose and enjoyment in life. Luckily he was still able to read.

Ethel Portal's health was more of a worry than ever. NM felt it as a personal failure that he had found no lasting remedy for her headaches, though she always said that his letters and visits were her best medicine. But between headaches her feelings for him burned as strongly as ever. 'I thought,' she wrote to him on

26 March 1920, 'how I would like to have a large & steady yacht to go round the world with you observing parrots . . . I think we could spend quite 3 months observing them on our own Pacific island – lying on the sunbaked sand dearest - & looking up at them in the cocoanut palms . . . And of course we wouldn't be thinking of parrots all the time would we chéri?'

By the end of 1921, NM was beginning to admit defeat. 'Talked to Milicent of giving up speaking & Presidency,' he wrote in his casebook, 'but it racks me to think of it. May God guide me.' On 8 April 1922, shortly before the wedding, NM's friend and medical adviser Dr Fletcher took Alan on one side and 'told me how serious was NM's condition'. Alan decided to act. The next morning, 'Milicent did not come down to breakfast & I told NM I thought he had better not seek election again. We rung up Dr Fletcher & he kindly came round & we talked the matter over & decided that he should give up. One reason for not doing so was that thereby he would lose £200 a year without wh the house in Gloucester Place can hardly be maintained. It is of course disappointing to give up as it means the end of his career & of public life.' Aunt Charley came later in the day to offer moral support, and then 'Miss Portal called just as she was leaving. I like Miss Portal & I like Aunt Charley but they do not like each other.' Milicent felt the change almost more than NM. 'Milicent was much cast down & I fear she will have a difficult time getting rid of the house & moving . . . I am very sorry that the house must be given up.'

With her usual energy, Milicent set about altering Hancox to make it their headquarters rather than their holiday home. A big Tudor fireplace in the pantry was excavated and internal walls were rearranged so that this fireplace could be in the front hall. It was fitted out with a large, grand, iron fireback bearing the arms of the Dukes of Dorset, similar to one at Knole Park. Gilla's old bedroom was turned into a chapel; Milicent had plans to create a 'Catholic centre' at Hancox, as Charley had done at Brown's.

'NM . . . is slow & his face frequently becomes set & expressionless,' Alan noted in July. A month later he wrote, 'I am afraid

NM does not improve. He is ageing much . . . He can hardly write. When I came back in 1919 he was vigorous & active. Now he seems unhappy & can do hardly anything. I am very sorry Mary should never have known him at his best.' NM slept badly, and Milicent, who insisted on doing the nursing herself, was worn out by the broken nights.

Aunt Jenny's decline kept pace with that of her son-in-law. She came to Alan's wedding; in June, two months short of her eighty-fifth birthday, Alan took her out in the sidecar he had bought for his motorcycle once Mary had said 'Yes'. But by December she was 'deranged'; 'she thinks she is no longer at Mayfield & that round about are houses all alike containing copies of her pictures & furniture.' She died in August 1923.

In October, NM wrote Ethne a shaky letter, coherent but with an uncharacteristic spelling mistake:

> My dearest Ethne,
> Thankyou for your partridges.
> Two painted laidies
> 6 red admirals
> 2 peacocks
> 4 tortoiseshells
> are living on my butterfly bed.
> I admire the Painted Laidies most.
> Has your garden any painted laidies.

These were the last days that he was able to enjoy pottering about the house and garden. On 19 October he and Milicent went to stay with Alan and Mary in their new house in Lewes, 'brought by Mrs Whitefoord [a Hancox neighbour] in Ld Rothermere's car, a huge grey Rolls Royce'. Mary was pregnant; the news was, of course, very welcome, but could not cure NM's restlessness and depression. They went on to Bath, hoping that the change of air would do good, but NM caught bronchitis and Milicent was seriously alarmed.

They returned to Hancox. NM's next letter to Ethne shows a

deterioration in his physical and mental health; it is very hard to read:

> I enjoy being here yet get no sleep.
> I have just being down the well.
> I am glad Mark [Ethne's son] know about butterflies, I wonder if he has painted ladies & hummingbird hawk moths.
> A sparrowhawk killed itself against the glass. [Irish words: possibly 'I myself or any other'] could not cure it.
> I must stay here for a while & will later see you.
> I am not fit to travel just now. But you shall hear anon.
> I did not know how much I was done up.

On the envelope, Ethne has pencilled 'Papa's last letter'.

Most of the thousands of letters NM wrote to Ethel Portal have disappeared, but a few scraps remain in a box, together with poems he wrote for her, and letters to her from Ethne, Alan and Milicent. One undated letter may be the last he ever wrote her with his own hand:

> The luncheon bell . . . How I want to see you dearest of friends.
> Alan's Mary is charming I like her more & more.
> As for your poor Norman he feels as if his life was to end every morning & slowly gets better as the day gets on.

Ethel came to Hancox in mid-November and her visit did him good for a time. But it was clear to Alan that there could be no long-term improvement. Though he never seemed in doubt about the people closest to him, NM became easily confused and had delusions. He was anxious about what he saw as his poverty, and said that the remembrance of old family quarrels was making him ill. 'I have long dreaded this time,' Alan wrote in his diary on 12 November. '. . . The real parting is now. It is very distressing to see him & to know he knows me & yet somehow cannot get in touch with his intellect. Love & affection can reach him still, but letters & real conversation are failing more & more. If it were not for Mary I shd be in great distress & loneliness.' A week later, Alan thought his father 'much under the influence of the opiate that he is obliged to take . . . he does not realize how ill he is . . . We walked a little in the garden very slowly NM leaning on my arm & talked a little about flowers & the like.' Alan knew that the end was in sight. 'We have lost him, his image becomes dimmer & soon we shall see him no more. I have a feeling of unreality when I address a letter to him.'

Milicent's state of mind made the situation worse. The long-suppressed difficulties of life as a stepmother and of her triangular marriage rose to the surface. She became jealously protective of NM and would hardly leave his side. Alan told Miss Portal, 'I wish I knew what was best about Milicent . . . She is so jangled . . . that she is inclined to make difficulties & produce a wrong atmosphere.' Alan was particularly irritated when Milicent held up a crucifix for NM to kiss, when he could see that what his father wanted was a drink. Ethne, who spent much of the second half of November at Hancox, found it frustrating that at first she was allowed so little time alone with her father. Milicent was using religion as an excuse to keep people away from NM, claiming that only Catholic sympathy was of any use. Ethne, wiser in her dealings with Milicent than she had been as a girl, exercised tact and patience, and at last persuaded Milicent to take more rest and entrust others with the care of the invalid.

When Alan arrived on 22 November, NM called out, 'Oh Alan I'm dying.' Alan summoned Ethel Portal, who paid what she must have known would be her farewell visit on 23 November. After that, she and Ethne entered into a kind of epistolary conspiracy to keep the image of Ethel present in NM's mind. 'My dear,' wrote the daughter to the mistress on 24 November:

Just a line before I go to bed – He knew me – and I have been with him most of the evening – I made M sleep till 12 . . . I gave him your love & he looked pleased & said something about not tiring you – later he began to talk Irish . . . He said 'two good friends' in Irish, so I said 'Yes, you and Miss Portal' & he said 'Ethel, you saw

her?' and again I gave him your love. He had oysters & champagne &
said they were good — Alan and M are evidently on each other's
nerves — I am a buffer — I must go to bed or I shant keep soft — &
buffers must be soft . . . I feel he is happy somehow.

Ethel replied at once:

> Bless you for your letter.
> I love to hear every word I can of the best friend any lonely
> woman ever had . . . The only hope I have for him is that he may
> suffer less & less . . . I suggest that you drop 'Miss Portal'. . . of
> course I should like it best if you would always make it Ethel to my
> face too . . . to him anyhow do.

Alan wrote to Ethel Portal on the same day: 'Milicent who can't
be persuaded [to trust] the night nurse would stay up all night but
is gone to bed this morning . . . Aunt Charley is coming down to
Scalands & will come over. I am glad for M will be able to blow off
religious steam . . . It has been the greatest comfort for me that
you were with him in the last days of his consciousness.' Charley's
presence helped. She was able to offer Milicent 'Catholic sympathy' and to act as a safe conduit between Milicent and her step-
children. Ethne, who had always found Charley too 'managing' and
self-centred, was glad of her company now. 'I have a little altered
my judgement of Aunt Charlie,' she told Ethel. 'She has behaved
very well these 2 days & shown more insight & understanding than
I credited her with.' On being told of Charley's arrival, NM whispered that he should like to see her. 'She went up to him & he
seemed to know her,' wrote Alan. 'He whispered to Ethne, "She is
a good woman."'

NM spent the last few days of his life drifting in and out of
consciousness. On the twenty-seventh Ethne reported to Ethel:

> He knew us early but has been in a sort of stupor since — Quite
> comfortable & peaceful — Yesterday he was better & smiled - &

seemed altogether *happier* – not even imaginary worries – yesterday a.m. he said to me 'that tall nurse only gives me things out of little cups, I'm hungry' wh was the longest thing he'd said . . . I feel the last flickers were happy ones . . . M stays upstairs – Now he's unconscious I don't mind – I was with him a lot yesterday & whispered about you in his ear. I'll write again . . . Thank you for allowing me to Ethelize.

Two days later she wrote:

He has been asleep since 5 a.m. (when Nurse & I moved him). Dr Kendall says it may be the sedative medicine & if it is he may wake & go on a little. If it is not he thinks it will end tonight . . .

Yesterday he was awake all day – restless in the morning – but with his eyes open & seemed to notice us – I was with him (M resting) 9.30–1.30. He kissed me many times – sometimes put his arm round my neck or kissed my hand – He did not speak except yes & no in answer to questions or 'better' once – I gave him my hand once & said 'give me a kiss for Ethel' & he did. He had a happy look all day. He sat in the chair, very still after tea, & himself pulled the red hood over his head – I told him he looked lovely – He liked me to smile at him I think. He evidently enjoyed some champagne he had – I told him all the lovely things I could think of & I think he went to sleep listening to me . . . It's such a lovely evening the sun has been shining into his room all day.

Milicent wrote to Ethel on the same day. Her letter betrays nothing of the tensions in the household, and indeed as the end approached she did achieve a degree of calm:

Dearest Ethel,

Things get quieter & quieter. Norman is mostly asleep. It is very peaceful . . . It's a beautiful mild day. Ethne tells me Hilda gives you the news of us here. Alan returned on Monday – Ethne is very capable & kind.

'Hilda' is Hilda Pryor, the only one of Jack's six sisters to remain unmarried. She lived in a flat in Carlisle Mansions just above Ethel Portal, and had proved a friendly and helpful neighbour. It is interesting that Ethne concealed from Milicent that she herself was sending bulletins to Ethel, instead allowing Milicent to believe that Ethel received news through Hilda.

When the end came, Rose Playford was alone with NM. At 6.20 p.m. on 30 November, as Rose often proudly recalled, she witnessed 'S'Norman's last breathes'. On this day forty-seven years before he had asked Amy to marry him in Peterborough Cathedral; it was exactly forty years since General Ludlow had died suddenly at Yotes Court as he awaited the return of his 'darling Lilybel' from her holiday at Eastbourne.

Ethne's telegram was brought to Alan and Mary as they sat by their drawing-room fire at Lewes. 'His life was noble & it pains me to think how unappreciative I have been & how often I have caused him regrets,' wrote Alan in his diary. 'He loved me very much. I am thankful that Mary knew him & that he was so fond of her & that he knew a grandchild was coming.

'I shall miss him in all things. Always I have been able to refer things to him. He rejoiced in my few successes & patiently listened to my complaints. I feel as though a rampart & defence were thrown down that had stood between me & the world.'

The state of semi-calm Milicent had achieved collapsed at once. Three factors combined to enrage or distress her. On the first of these, she and Alan were in agreement. *The Times* published an obituary which contained factual inaccuracies and which, more importantly, cast aspersions on the quality of NM's scholarship: 'He knew much, had read widely and was a facile writer, but he lacked . . . deeper scholarship . . . He was excellent as a committee man. . .' Alan wrote a letter to *The Times* correcting the facts and 'shewing scorn of a writer who decried my father's learning'. This was followed by a letter from M. R. James, Provost of Eton, author of classic ghost stories, and an old friend of NM's:

Men who publish works on so large a variety of subjects as he did
rarely escape being suspected . . . of being superficial. But it has often
struck me as characteristic of the great scholars of Ireland . . . that
they are able to do work of first rate quality in most diverse fields;
and this . . . is true of Sir Norman Moore, who could write as an
expert on the history and topography of the City of London, on the
Irish language, and on medical matters ancient and modern . . . I
think, moreover, that I have never met any man whose erudition
was so varied, lay so readily to hand, or was so delightfully enlivened
by human and humorous touches, as Sir Norman Moore.

The publication of this thoughtful letter mollified Milicent.
But over the second bone of contention she and Alan came to (ver-
bal) blows. It was agreed that NM should be buried at Sedlescombe, but that all the rites of the Catholic Church should be
observed; further, that a requiem mass should be said for him at
St James's, Spanish Place, in London. When Bart's suggested a
non-Catholic memorial service, Milicent exploded with anger.
Alan asked Father Miller, the local Catholic priest, whether his
church had any objection to such a service. He said his church
highly approved, that anyone objecting ' "ought to be kicked to
the bottom of the sea" & that Catholics might attend'. Milicent,
therefore, was the one who ought to be so kicked, but she was
intransigent. 'Her attitude distresses me beyond measure,' Alan told
Mary, 'or would do so did I not regard her as half-mad.' When
Alan and Milicent went to Sedlescombe churchyard to discuss a
suitable grave site, the grave digger was late for their appointment.
Alan accepted his explanation that his 'missus' had insisted he finish
his dinner before the meeting, but Milicent detected an anti-Catholic
protest in the delay. Aunt Charley came to the rescue. Privately
telling Alan that she considered Milicent 'very much unhinged',
she gently worked at persuading her that a non-Catholic memorial service would be an appropriate and all-inclusive way of celebrating NM's long association with Bart's. The arrival of a telegram
from the Pope, and another from the King and Queen, helped to

placate her, and on 4 December Alan reported that she had 'hand-somely withdrawn' her objections.

The third problem took longer to solve. NM's will, in Alan's opinion, was unsatisfactory. His money had been left to Milicent and to Alan (Ethne was, with her knowledge, excluded, because the Pryors' wealth meant she was already well provided for), but there was nothing to say what should happen to personal posses-sions. 'If M. dies or goes mad & dies intestate,' Alan wrote to Ethne, 'all *our* things I mean private possessions that naturally should come to us would go to the Ludlows, as well as Hancox. Don't talk about this: the fewer people who know the better. You may to Miss Portal.' Ethne wrote to Miss Portal at once: 'there are so many little personal things – the portrait of NM's father, our mother's paintings etc not to mention books – of course M. may be considerate over these things, but there are moments when we fear she will not . . . As you will understand its not that Alan feels she will destroy or give away or sell things, but that he regrets he will not possess them until he is quite possibly an elderly man.'

Alan had a private meeting with his cousin Noel Wickham, who was also Milicent's solicitor. His mind was partly set at rest – without betraying professional confidence, Noel hinted that Milicent's own will was in order – but the issue of the personal possessions remained. Alan wrote to Milicent trying to put the idea into her head that he and Ethne might be glad of some mementoes, but, he told Miss Portal, 'her letters have a non-comprehending quality in them wh make negotiations difficult . . . her lack of understanding of other's point of view is amazing.' The matter was, for the moment, allowed to rest.

Father Miller conducted the burial service at Sedlescombe on 5 December. It was very unusual for a Catholic priest to officiate at an Anglican church, and it took some arranging. A private mass was heard at 8.30 a.m. in the oratory at Hancox – formerly Gilla's bedroom – and then the procession moved on to Sedlescombe, where NM was laid to rest in a grave lined with moss and ever-green by Weekes, the Hancox gardener. Welland the butler, a Catholic, carried the thurible. There was a large congregation and a great many wreaths, all carefully listed in *The Times*. Father Miller's address centred on the theme of charity, that 'great virtue' that the deceased had exercised all his life towards his fellow men. The mourners came back to Hancox; at the end of the day, wrote Alan, 'Milicent and I were left alone. The house was very still.' The next day Alan thanked the Hancox servants for all they had done: 'They were all as kind and helpful as possible. They could not have done more. Welland, Mrs Cole the cook, Mrs Perry, Rose Playford & Weekes the gardener.' Then he returned to Lewes; 'There was my dearest Mary, so glad to have me back.'

★

Friends and colleagues of NM published reminiscences of him in an assortment of papers and journals. A boyhood friend from Owens College, Henry Brierley, wrote in the *Manchester Guardian*, 'If unpleasant odours pervaded the lockers where we kept our books they were always traced to Moore's, where some specimen could be found awaiting dissection; and he was the only man I knew who understood falconry. How well I remember him leaving my home at midnight with a hawk on his wrist . . . to walk the forty miles to Lancaster.' In the opinion of Sir John Phillips, Fellow of the College of Physicians, NM 'did more for the [medical] profession than anyone else, and took less out of it'.

Letters of condolence poured in for Milicent, Alan and Ethne. Ethel Portal, alone and unwell in her London flat, without the consolation of religious faith, must have felt forlorn indeed. I think it highly unlikely that Mary knew the true state of affairs between Ethel and her late father-in-law, but she sensed that comfort was sorely needed, and wrote a most sensitive letter, which Ethel kept in her box of precious papers:

> I love to think that Alan gave his father pleasure up to the end. They used to be delicious together didn't they? And I am so glad I knew Sir Norman and so grateful to think how he welcomed me. You must be very sad but in the midst of it you too must have great

pleasure in the thought of how much happiness your friendship brought him, right up to the end. I was there when he dictated a birthday letter for you to Alan. He was astray about many things but he remembered your birthday and his loving good wishes weren't astray. I'm so proud to think there'll be some of him in my baby.

The intimacy that had developed between Ethne and Ethel during those last dreadful weeks developed into a mutual dependency. Though I'm sure it was never openly expressed, I'm equally sure that Ethne, older, more experienced and less saintly than Mary, did understand the true nature of Ethel's 'friendship' with NM. Ethne, always unconventional in her responses, was able to accept and even admire the depth of their love; less creditably, she perhaps also welcomed it as an undermining of Milicent. The day before the funeral, Ethne wrote to Ethel, 'M has gone to Hastings to buy a hat & see a priest. I shall go home tomorrow with Jack – I shall be so pleased to see him again he is so sane (& loves me). So are you – you know the big red sofa in this drawing room? And the little red stool like a wave which is its child? When I come to you I feel like that little stool.' The sofa has gone, but we still have the stool. In Ethel, Ethne sought a renewal of the maternal love she had lost with the death of Amy and of Jack's mother, her dear 'Mrs Muff', and that she had never been able to accept from Milicent. 'Doesn't it occur to you,' she wrote from Lannock in her Christmas letter to Ethel, 'that I might want to say THANKS to you? Not counting little boys, & husbands are included in that category, there are so very few people I love. Either my heart is cold, or very very small – I like rows & rows & rows, nearly everybody – But loving is so different.

'If I might be allowed to love you a little, dear Madame, what fun it would be. And I should say Thankyou very loud indeed.'

On 8 January 1923, which would have been NM's seventy-sixth birthday, Ethne wrote again: 'I feel I must celebrate Papa's birthday somehow, and much the best way is by writing to you . . . On the days I believe in Heaven I imagine Papa having such fun with Dr. Johnson: if only we could listen! Yr loving, though idiotic Ethne.'

Epilogue: An old silk nightgown

Alan and Mary's son was born on 24 February 1923 and named Norman Winfrid after his grandfathers. Norman is my uncle; his arrival in this chronicle brings it within the realm of living memory, which means that it is time to wind it up.

The baby's arrival helped to restore cordial relations between Milicent and her stepson, the healing process furthered by Mary's gentle tact. Milicent was delighted with little Norman, who says that throughout his boyhood she 'was very good to me. We had long talks about a whole range of subjects.' Norman turned out to be exactly the kind of grandson NM would have hoped for. His parents recorded his early sayings and doings – as they were to do for all four of their children – and from the minute he could talk, it was obvious that what interested Norman most was the natural world, most particularly birds.

Once the weight of NM's last illness had been lifted, Milicent regained her old buoyancy. She began to see that it was only natural that Alan should want some mementoes of his father. Alan, hugely relieved to find that NM's marvellous library was not to be broken up and distributed to various Catholic charities, offered to help Milicent in the Herculean task of sorting through his letters and papers. The labour remains uncompleted to this day.

An early sign of the welcome thaw in Milicent's attitude was her suggestion that Alan might like NM's writing desk, an article imbued with huge significance. Alan accepted with pleasure. When the furniture van carrying the desk arrived at his house in Lewes, Alan was startled – pleasantly so – to find that Milicent had stowed herself away and was curled up in the back, clutching a hot water bottle. She had been unable to resist the chance of a free ride.

★

It would be fair to say that, with NM gone, Miss Portal lost the will to live. She remained in close and affectionate touch with Alan and Ethne, and she let Alan know that, when she died, most of the contents of her flat would be left to him. She also left him an annual sum which, eventually, enabled him to live at Hancox. He could not have afforded to do so on his doctor's salary alone. On 9 June 1923 she wrote him a letter explaining her intentions. It concluded:

> Your father was the best friend I ever had: in fact he gave me quite a new idea of what friendship could be. He never spared himself. Weather, work, tiredness – nothing could prevent him from doing the kind thing, or coming to say the cheering word, & my gratitude to him & affection for him cannot be put into words. So it was his affection for you that gave birth to mine & very soon that became affection for your own sake. Since his death you have shown so much kindness to me to prevent my feeling cut off from those he loved best, that gratitude & affection for you are added to gratitude & affection for him – that includes Mary whom I love for her mother's sake & your sake & most heartily for her own dear sake.
>
> I believe I always thought that love is the strongest thing in the world. I think so more than ever now. And so I mean the best I can when I send my love to you both.

Ethel Portal had never believed that she would 'make old bones'; she died in her Westminster flat on 3 March 1926. She was sixty-four. She was buried at Laverstoke, in the churchyard above her much-loved River Test, just outside the park walls of the beautiful house where she grew up. Alan and Milicent both attended the funeral, which was packed with villagers and with former pupils of the village school she had endowed. Milicent wrote an obituary notice for the *Hampshire Chronicle*, recalling their Bethnal Green days. Alan pasted it into his scrapbook:

> Her vocation was . . . a general one, namely, to be kind to all . . . Poverty in the days in which she worked [in the East End] was very

different in degree and far more acute in comparison to what it is now, and Miss Portal probed it to its depths and did what she could to relieve it . . . So great was her popularity with the men of a Club which contained certain light fingered gentry . . . that she found it necessary to refuse the presents they offered her . . . which she had reason to believe had left their true owners' pockets unlawfully . . . Miss Portal drew others to her with the force of a magnet . . . Her literary taste, her keen mind, and her excellent memory made her society a delight to learned men . . . None who knew her can ever forget her, and all who knew her well will always love her.

That comment about being 'a delight to learned men' is perhaps a clue to the way in which Milicent reconciled herself to Ethel's relationship with NM. Her words impress me deeply. It is hard to believe that so generous a eulogy could have been written by a woman who had been obliged to share her husband with its subject.

*

Aunt Charley remained very close to Milicent. For the last few years of her long life she was mainly confined to a wheelchair in her flat near Hyde Park, but her interest in everything and everybody never diminished, and her beauty, says my mother, was still evident in her enormous bright brown eyes. On birthdays in my uncle Norman's family, cakes are ceremoniously cut with a special knife, a gift from Charley. The little ritual is both a homage to the memory of Charley herself and to the fact that she was a link with Aunt Barbara and Uncle Ben, who were, for Norman, 'my most inspiring recent ancestors'.

To Charley's distress, her two sons were often at loggerheads. Phil, who had taken part in several relief missions to Russia during and in the aftermath of the Bolshevik Revolution, wrote several novels under the pseudonym Christopher Rover; two of these, *Pandemonium* and *The Red Horse*, describe events in Russia. Phil's diplomatic career later took him to Rome and Bern as chargé d'affaires. In 1933 he married a Dalmatian physicist, Alice Prébil, who worked with Madame Curie and was instrumental in discovering Element 85. 'Phil's going to marry a *dawg*?' was Bella's reaction to the engagement. 'She can't possibly be odder than a Smith at its oddest,' wrote Alan to Ethne.

Val moved permanently to Switzerland in the 1950s, leaving Scalands empty and in disrepair. Alan composed a Latin epigram about it:

> *Autumni foliis et desilientibus aura*
> *Heu fortuna domus; cecedit, dic si Barbara luges?*
> *Semper pristinam videas per lumina diva.*

> Her house is falling with the autumn leaves.
> Alas, poor house, O say if Barbara grieves?
> We pray her own old house through God's eyes she perceives.

Barbara would be pleased to know that Scalands is now fully restored. The fact that one of its inhabitants is a female doctor would particularly gratify her, as would the survival of the brick fireplace on which her visitors painted their names.

*

Ethne stayed on at Lannock with Jack and their three boys. Her descendants still live at Weston; they unearthed Ethne's memoir and teenage diary, on which I have drawn so frequently for this book. In 1934, Ethne published a children's book, *The Blue Rabbit*; the hero is a little boy called Luke, to make up for the fourth son she never had – she had wanted a Luke to go with her three 'evangelists', Johnnie, Mark and Matthew, but a hysterectomy put paid to that. She illustrated *The Blue Rabbit* herself, but the publisher substituted a blander set of drawings. The book won a prize for children's literature; the runner-up was *Mary Poppins*. Unluckily for the family fortunes, Hollywood never interested itself in *The Blue Rabbit*.

Alan and Mary's marriage turned out to be as happy as everyone had hoped and predicted. They spent the first twelve years of their married life in Lewes, paying frequent visits to Milicent at Hancox, which became a second home for their children Norman, Hilary and my father Richard. By the time Milicent reached her mid-sixties the place was becoming too much for her, so in 1934 she made it all over – house, contents, garden and farm – to Alan. He and Mary spent the rest of their lives there; their fourth child, Meriel, was born after the move. Ever since, Hancox has remained central to the life of the extended Moore family.

On NM's death Alan had inherited the baronetcy; he carried the title, said my mother, with a proud but slightly guilty air, as if he did not deserve it. In his children's opinion he carried his self-deprecation too far, and paid what seemed undue reverence to his father's memory. He spent his last years wrestling with the family archive in his uncompleted attempt to write NM's biography. For such a tidy-minded man, his filing system was surprisingly chaotic. 'Most, but not all, of the letters in this box are before 1900,' reads one typical note in his handwriting. At a later date he has pencilled underneath, 'No, I was wrong.'

'Sir Alan and Lady Moore' were both active in village life, and are still remembered with great affection. I have never found anyone who had a bad word to say about my grandmother. The only shadow over their marriage was cast by her poor health. She died of a stroke, at Hancox, in 1950, aged only fifty-three. Alan, who outlived her by nine years, had never lost his powerful sense of the wonderful good fortune that had brought them together. My aunt Meriel remembers a rhyme he made up to commemorate the day of their engagement:

> Remember remember the sixth of November
> The day when my Mary said Yes
> For when all the town talks
> Of the day of Guy Fawkes
> It's the sixth of November *I* bless.

★

It was Milicent who had played a key part in bringing Alan and Mary together; it was Milicent who so generously handed over her beloved Hancox and rejoiced in their success in turning it into a real, living family home. For all the difficulties, the eccentricities, the unyielding Catholic fanaticism, Milicent emerges as a force for good in her stepson's life.

During the period after NM's death, in which she stayed on alone at Hancox, her Catholicism had become ever more ardent. Alan and Mary employed a nanny, Louise Williams, who stayed with the family for many years. 'Ony', as she became known, told me in her old age about her first visit to Hancox, when she was in charge of little Norman. They arrived after dark; she and Norman slept in the night nursery, the room next to Gilla's old room, now Milicent's chapel. Ony didn't know about the chapel. She lay awake, rigid with fear, listening to strange and untranslatable mutterings and mumblings and watching the flickering of candlelight under the connecting door. Unbeknownst to her, Milicent and Welland the butler were telling their rosaries. Next morning, said Ony, she looked out of the window and saw the daffodils, 'And I knew everything was going to be all right.'

Milicent continued her work for the Red Cross, and nursed at Darvell Hall, a large house near Glottenham which had become a sanatorium for tubercular patients. She continued to travel, often to Rome, and often in the company of old friends. An attractive characteristic of Milicent's was her ability to maintain friendships from every stage of her life, right back to the Yotes Court days. She saw a great deal of Charley, of Bella, and of Roddy, who, liberated by the death of Aunt Jenny, had moved to a cottage near Lionel and Agnes in Hampshire and enjoyed an active spinsterly existence, sketching, gardening, and having friends and relations to stay. We have Roddy's visitors' book, which is full of cheerful comments from guests and lists of birds and wildflowers seen in the area. Roddy died in 1937, having lived, as Alan put it, 'chiefly for others'.

Milicent was rarely to be seen without a novice priest to hand. The priests had practical as well as spiritual uses. After NM's death

Milicent, independent as ever, decided to learn to drive. She never mastered gears. 'She used to start by putting the car into a high gear and pressing the accelerator hard,' says Norman; 'the car did a kangaroo leap forward.' This problem made it difficult for her to pause at a junction – she would always stall – so she kept a fit young priest in the car who would jump out and flag down oncoming traffic so that she could sail over the junction unhindered. Her driving is still remembered with an amused shudder by some of the local Catholic congregation. One woman, who did not like to refuse lifts 'Milicent Lady' offered her to church, used to hope that if they were going to be killed, it would happen on the return journey, 'because then we'd be shriven.'

When Alan and Mary took over at Hancox, Milicent bought herself a house called Little Shepherds in the high street of Cranbrook, a pretty Kentish town about twelve miles from Hancox. She turned it into a Catholic centre for the area, which lacked a Catholic church; St Theodore's, which started as a local Catholic mission in the 1920s, used the oratory at Little Shepherds. Today St Theodore's has its own church, and serves Benenden, Staplehurst and the surrounding villages as well as Cranbrook. My father remembers the oratory as awe-inspiring in its gloom, a contrast to the lovely and cheerful garden at the back of the house. Milicent had a garden house built so that she could sleep out of doors. Even in old age she looked forward eagerly to resuming this habit each spring.

My father's younger sister, Meriel, however, '*loved* the chapel . . . specially the statues and pictures'. Meriel called Milicent 'Granny Cranbrook', but did not look forward to her visits with glee. 'I thought she looked rather odd. I think this was because she wore a hat when she came to tea. I remember . . . pointing out that she was wearing a hat at teatime in the parlour and being shushed. I think it may have been this occasion when we went into the tennis lawn together and, having seen her safely in, I left by the white metal gate, down the steps, having shut the gate firmly and saying "Now you stay there." '

Alan and Mary found it comic that at events such as hunt balls

Milicent would forcefully make her way to the top table as if by right. Milicent's sense of religious decorum was even stronger than her social etiquette. Alan and Mary had to tiptoe their way through theological minefields. When their daughter Hilary was confirmed, Milicent would only speak of it as 'the Plan for Thursday', as she considered Anglican confirmation invalid. She remained standing all the way through Meriel's christening in Whatlington church, lest anyone should think she was praying in an Anglican church. At Christmas dinner at Hancox, Meriel remembers 'Mummy saying that we shouldn't ask for the bit of the turkey called the Pope's nose because Granny Cranbrook would not like this.' At one such dinner, Meriel, then about nine, froze the conversation by asking, 'Why do we sing about the Virgin's womb?' (b pronounced, and vowel as in 'bombe'). Awkward pause. 'It sounds rather like wombat, doesn't it?' Everyone hurriedly agreed.

Despite all this, Meriel remembers that Milicent was treated as an honoured guest, and it is to Milicent's credit that she never attempted to interfere with the way Alan and Mary managed things at Hancox. During the Second World War, Milicent led civil defence instruction at Cranbrook. Mary commented to Meriel that this was very courageous. 'I took Mummy's word for it but thought Granny C. was quite lucky if it meant operating a stirrup pump for spraying water at a fire.'

Milicent's life continued to be full of energetic activity for more than twelve years after she left Hancox, but in October 1946 she suffered a stroke. She spent the severe winter of 1946–7 in St Augustine's, a Catholic nursing home in St Leonard's-on-Sea, where, though often semi-delirious, she called upon visitors to admire the sea view from her bed – a 'Mediterranean view', she said. On 8 January 1947, Alan spent the day there with her celebrating what would have been NM's 100th birthday.

Milicent died at St Augustine's on 9 February 1947, a month short of her seventy-ninth birthday. On her death certificate the cause of death is given 'l.a. Cerebral Thrombosis. ll.i. Previous cerebral thrombosis. 2. Heart block.' Her stepson Alan, says the certificate, was in attendance.

Little Shepherds was taken over by the Archbishop of Southwark. The many small legacies she left to Catholic churches and institutions show how fully she was occupied in propagating the faith. She left £1,000 to Bart's for naming a bed 'The Sir Norman Moore bed' in perpetuity, several small sums to friends, and £500 to her niece Eira, now married and living in Australia. The other two Ludlow girls, Anne and Sylvia, got nothing; Anne because she had disgraced herself in Milicent's eyes by getting divorced, and poor Sylvia, I suppose, because of her insanity. Milicent also left an annual bequest of £26 to Rose Smith, née Playford, for the rest of her life. My aunt Meriel recalls, 'Rose once said to me pointing to a rosary – "If I had my life again them beads would be my religion."'

★

All old houses have a character, an atmosphere, and it is not always a pleasant one. When people drive up to Hancox for the first time and see it looming through the dark pine trees, they often ask, 'Is it haunted?' The answer is not straightforward. No, it is not haunted, certainly not by malign, unhappy or restless presences seeking to inflict their woes on the living. Neither I nor anyone else, as far as I know, has ever sensed anything like that. But as I sit here writing, surrounded by the 'little bits of driftwood washed up from the vast illimitable ocean of the past', in NM's phrase, it does not feel right to say that Hancox is inhabited only by the living.

I find myself wondering why Milicent's house should feel so benign, so consistent in its atmosphere, so comfortable for all its discomfort. It has, after all, seen its share of family disharmony, infidelity, dashed hopes, insanity, disease and death. But for all the tragedies of Milicent's life and the difficulties of her character, she had a courage and an integrity that rose above everything, and somehow caused the negatives to drop away.

Her warm admiration for Alan's Mary was one of the blessings of her widowhood. When she suspected she was dying she wrote Mary a letter of wishes which strikes me as touchingly characteristic – valiant, uncompromising, and ending with a request that reveals the enormous importance of her marriage to her:

My Father's diaries – very puzzling to know what to do I'm the only living person who has many clues to what he writes . . . Some may deal with the health of my mother. I can't tell at present . . .

I want to be buried at Sedlescombe (even in the face of difficulty) in an <u>unlined</u> deal coffin or pine.

It's not in <u>my will</u> but I showed you once an old silk nightgown, the last of my trousseau and in which I'd like to be buried if it is available but I don't carry it about with me (!!)

Milicent was indeed buried, with NM, at Sedlescombe, but history does not relate whether the nightgown was ever found.

Bibliography

Most of the sources for *Hancox* were family papers, previously unpublished. However, Pam Hirsch's *Barbara Leigh Smith Bodichon* (Chatto, 1998) was invaluable.

Hester Burton's *Barbara Bodichon 1827–1891* (John Murray, 1949) is interesting, though not always accurate.

Eugenie Sellers Strong: Portrait of an Archaeologist by Stephen L. Dyson (Duckworth, 2004) tells the story of Aunt Charley's sister.

Gillian Gill's *Nightingales* (Hodder, 2004) provides fascinating information about the family of William Smith MP.

As does *Progress By Persuasion: The Life of William Smith 1756–1835* by Jenny Handley and Hazel Lake. (Privately published; contact hazel.lake@ btinternet.com)

Mark Bostridge's *Florence Nightingale* (Viking, 2008) arrived too late to influence *Hancox*, but I strongly recommend it. Finally,

Beryl Lucey's *Twenty Centuries in Sedlescombe* (Regency Press, 1978) is a useful local history; it is available from Sedlescombe Post Office.

Index

This index follows the text in designating Norman Moore as NM.

94 Gloucester Place: Ethel at 349; Ethne at 288; failing domestic arrangements 277; medical textbooks 245; Milicent at 3, 278, 294, 364; Rebecca's last visit 299

Addison's, Hastings 361
Ades family 9
'Alaniania' (Alan Moore) 67
Alcott, Louisa May 64
Alexandra, Princess of Wales 27, 39
Algiers 92, 171, 243–4
Amelie of Schleswig-Holstein, Princess 244
American Civil War 26
Amoore & Son, Hastings 205
Anti-Corn Law League 60, 62, 79, 427
Antony and Cleopatra (William Shakespeare) 328
Ardtornish 156, 186
Armistice, the 421, 443
Ashburnham 212
Ashburnham, Lady 37
Ashton, Joan 360–61, 374, 398
Ashton, Lady 373, 374, 406
Ashton, Lord 373, 374, 406

Banting, Mr 30
Barlow, Dr 165–7, 264
Bateman's 95, 439

Battle Ball 295
Battle Manor 5
Baxter, William (Ben's agent) 146
'beating the bounds' 5
Beech Green ,Withyham 318, 397
Belloc, Bessie: Barbara's marriage 126; Barbara writes to 111; closeness to Barbara 118; death 430; Gilla's death 386; as go-between 120; *Englishwoman's Journal* (renamed *Review*) 20; travels with Barbara 190
Belloc, Elizabeth 430–31, 436, 439
Belloc, Hilaire 430–35, 439
Bernhardt, Sarah 132
Bethnal Green 232, 235, 285; *see also* St Margaret's House, Bethnal Green
Beverley, Bishop of 78
Bishop, Miss (Ethne's headmistress) 266–7, 273, 288
Bismarck, Prince Otto von 32
Blackadder, Henrietta 173
Blandford Square 18, 20, 39, 118
Blue Rabbit, The (Ethne Moore) 462
Blythe, Isa(bella): death 236, 238; failing health 235; a life partner for Nannie 33; Nannie sets up home with 34, 89; popular with Leigh Smiths 171–2
Bodichon, Barbara Leigh Smith; *see* Leigh Smith, Barbara

Bodichon, Dr Eugène 172–5; American visit 92–4; character of 20; death 175; degeneration 169, 174–5; eccentric lifestyle 92, 148; lack of feeling 126, 128; mental health concerns 172–3; NM and 52, 92; obsessions 172

Boer War 375

Bonfire societies 324

Bonham Carter, Alice 133, 141, 201

Bonham Carter family 22, 176

Booton Rectory 96–7, 138

Brabazon, Hercules Brabazon: J. M. W. Turner and 90; loyal friend to the Leigh Smiths 135; Ludlow's sketching tour 278; paintings by 259, 432; proximity to Hancox 187

Brassey, Lady 26, 38

Brassey family 135, 397

Brede Lane furnace 6, 7, 8

Brede, River 13

Brierley, Henry 457

Bright, John 62

Brightling church 23, 96, 366

Brightling Place 359, 376

British Museum 83

British Nurses' Association 193

Brown, Eliza: Alan's mock interview 248–9; Amy's death 274; brother's death 259; Ethne's wedding present 350; and Gilla 244, 277, 294; Milicent dispenses with 301; NM and Milicent's wedding 292–3

Browning, Robert 170, 183, 200

Brown's *see also* Firbank: Ben's farmhouse 28; change of name 95; First World War 372–3, 407; an idyllic place for children 33; passes to Charley 431

Bruce Castle School 85

Bunyard's Old Nurseries 205–6, 208

Burke, Edmund 108, 426

Burmese War (1824–6) 16

Burnett, Miss 257, 272

Burrows, Mary *see* Moore, Mary

Burrows, Winfrid , Bishop of Chichester 437–8

Byng, Admiral 42

Caldbec House 210

Cambridge University 79–82, 259, 290, 306, 368–71

Campagne du Pavillon 92, 148

Campagne Montfeld: at Amy's disposal 241; Nannie buys 34; Nannie leaves 181; reasons for buying 170–71; warmth and beauty of 148, 170, 244

Carrig-O'Gunnel 57

Chandler, Lily 372, 386

Chapman, John 21

Chatham 377

Chichester Cathedral 446

Churchill, Winston 270, 357, 404

Church of England Temperance Society 3, 232, 252–6, 316

Church of the Annunciation 348

Clapham Cave 70

Clarke, Christopher 218

Clarke, Emily 218

Clarke, Louisa 29

Clarkson, Thomas 17

Cloth Hall, Ypres 382, 385

Coape Ludlow, Ludlow 194–203; Beech Green 318; changes name 2, 197; ill health 264; kindness 263; leaving Hancox 3; Milicent and NM 284–5, 302; money from Milicent 252; sketching tour 278

Coape Smith, Ludlow *see* Coape Ludlow, Ludlow

Coape Smith, Marianne 163, 193–4, 196

Coape Smith family 193–5, 196

Cobden, Richard 62
Collier, Mr 317
Colquhoun, Sir Patrick 34
Columba, Saint 176
Columbcille, Saint 105
Combe family 135
Connell, Pat 277
Convent of the Blue Nuns 263
cookery books 223–4
Cope and Nichols' art school 333
Corn Laws 60 *see also* Anti-Corn
    Law League
Corot, Jean Baptiste-Camille 20, 90
corporal punishment 32, 353–4
Cotman, John Sell 109
Crabbe, George 96
'Croteslei' 344
Crowham Manor 86–90; ancient name
    for 344; Amy bored by 84, 133;
    description 12; Ethne 88; Gilla
    and 318; lack of light 134;
    Milicent's birth and 36; NM visits
    139; problem for Roddy 277, 285;
    sale of 343, 344, 346; Willy and
    25, 27

Daily News 200
Dane Lodge 265–8, 270, 288, 289
Dann, George 11, 87, 139, 339, 427
Darvell Hall 464
Darwin, Charles 49, 105–6, 355, 434
Darwin, Emma 49
Darwin, Frank 80, 106, 220
Darwin, Henrietta 49
Daubigny, Charles François 90
Davos 10, 312, 314
de la Warr, Lord 2, 9
De l'Humanité (Eugène Bodichon) 92
Descent of Man, The (Charles Darwin) 105
Diana (ship) 41, 50
Dictionary of National Biography 192, 234
discomfort xxiii

Domestic Cookery 223–5
Dounton, Joan *see* Sackville, Joan
Dounton, John 5–6
Down End 242
Down House 49, 106, 434
Dulley, Father 387

East End (London) 231
East Sussex Lean Stock Society 210
Edmonstone, Lydia 77
Edmonstone sisters 74, 77
Edward VII, King 345
Egerton, Squire 182
Eira (ship) 145–6, 150–53, 182, 305
Eldorado SS 189
Eliot, George 20, 21, 23, 47, 126, 146
Elizabeth of Hungary, Saint 250
Elwin, Philip 80, 81, 96, 176
Elwin, Revd Whitwell 81, 96–7, 138,
    142, 250
Embley 174
Emilie (maid) 161, 175
Ems 30, 32, 35
Englishwoman's Journal, The 20, 93
Eton College 300
Evans, Sir Lacy 336
Evans, Marian *see* George Eliot
'Everything Book' (Ethne Moore)
    267, 270

Family Magazine, The 248–50, 273,
    315, 316
Fanny (nursemaid) 31
*Farmer's Labour and Team
    Journal, The* 214
fields, named 211
finials, staircase 315–16
Firbank 95, 96; *see also* Brown's
First World War 372–425
Fisher, Benjamin Clarke 56, 58, 69
Fisher, Rebecca *see* Moore, Rebecca
Fisher family 56, 57, 60

Fitzgerald, John 134, 142

Fitzgerald sisters 312, 315, 333

Fletcher, Dr 448

Flora Cottage 151–2, 182

Football (horse) 176

Fordcombe 43, 157

Four Men, The (Hilaire Belloc) 430

Franz Josef Land 145, 146, 151

Fraser's Magazine 105

Freefolk 398

Free Trade 62, 390

Free Trade Movement 79

Frewen, Hugh 357

Froebel, Friedrich 64, 69

Fuggle hops 216

Galton, Mary 272

Galway 104, 134

Garrison, William Lloyd 64

Gee, Dr 242

Girton College, Cambridge: Amy and 115; Barbara co-founds 20; Barbara visited by alumnae 178; Barbara's death 202; Barbara's painting at 93–4; Ethne and 296–7; Hitchin college 89–90

Gladstone, William Ewart 97, 437

Glastonbury Abbey 107, 110

Glenarm Castle 444, 447

Glen Columbcille 105

Glottenham Manor: Amy and 246; Ben at 27–8; Charley at 182; Christina Rossetti at 94; revenues 144; Scalands Gate 91; Willy employed at 86

Gloucester Place 193, 375; *see also* 94 Gloucester Place

Glover, Arthur: circumstances conspire against 164; family opposition 166–7, 195; Mabel and 161–6; Mabel starts to forget 175, 188

Goldie, Miss 168

Gore-Booth, Sir Henry 146, 155

Goring, Fred: brings Gilla's effects home 393; brother 400; Gilla's death 385; Gilla's friend 380; letter to NM 386, 391; recovery from head wound 393

Goring, Sir Foster 400

Gott, Benjamin 11, 12, 253–5

Gough, Deborah (née Fisher) 58

Grafton, HMS 411, 413–15, 418, 422–3

Grealey, Esther 200

Great Dixter 398

Great Exhibition 62

Greatorex, Miss 157

Green, J. R. 104

Greenwich 298

Grey, Captain 155

Grieg, Edvard 189

Guestling Lodge 36

Haig, General 382, 393

Halcyon (minesweeper) 386

Halliday, Georgina *see* Leigh Smith, Jenny

Halliday, Lionel 138

Handcocks, John 5

Handel Society 297

Harveian Oration 276

Hastings 39; Amy at school 49; Anti-Corn Law League 60; coaches for London 324; Marina 141, 186; Pelham Crescent 18; return 28, 31; summer holidays 87; Warrior Square Gardens 39; Willy's childhood 336

Haviland, Mary 358–64; approval of Gilla's career 369; family take note of 371–2; Gilla lunches with parents 379; letters 376; NM and Milicent's reactions 388–9

Haywards Heath convent 303

Healy, Michael 69

hedgerows 212–13

Helvig, Madame 264

Henderson, Caroline 63

Herford, William Henry 69–70

Hilder, Ben 336–7

Hill (Cambridge undergraduate) 80–81

Hill, Octavia 39

'History of Grandmama's Life' (Rebecca Moore) 72

History of St Bartholomew's Hospital (Norman Moore): a magisterial work 82; NM embarks on writing 312; NM works on 326, 351, 399–400; publication 416

'Hodgepodge' (Gillachrist Moore) 356, 392

Hooker, Dr 44

Hope, SS 151

hop-picking 41, 215–18

Hotel Beausite, Rome 257, 258

Hotel Continental, Paris 132

Howitt, Anna Mary 64, 66

Howitt, Margaret 423–4

Hoy 409

India 163, 202

'inebriates' 3, 4, 10, 11, 252–4, 295, 314

Ireland 104–5

ironworks 6, 7, 212

James, Henry 277, 400, 417

James, M. R. 454–5

Jebb, Miss 199

Jekyll, Gertrude 20, 90, 91, 135

Jenner, Sir William 118

Jesus College, Cambridge 155

Jeypore (Jaipur) 16, 163

Johnson, Esther 102

Jopling, Louise 236

Kahn, Miss 158, 167

King's Land 430, 431

kinkajous 262, 357

Kinslingby, Miss 177, 186

Kipling, Rudyard 95, 217, 439

Knole 6

Ladycross 301, 302

lampreys 213

Lannock Manor 350, 376, 462

Last Days of Mast and Sail, The (Alan Moore) 298

Laverstoke Park 234, 235, 327, 460

Lea Hurst 129

Leasowe Castle 413

le Grand, Louis 173

Leigh Smith, Amy *see* Moore, Amy

Leigh Smith, Barbara 89–103, 109–43; achievement and fame 20, 34; American Civil War stance 26; American tour 92–4; Amy and 49, 89–90; Amy, NM and 101–2, 109–10, 112, 114, 138; artistic abilities 43, 90; Bella's problems 21, 39; Ben feared by 140; Ben's attitude to Amy angers 37; Ben visits after stroke 117–18; concern for Harry 51–2; death 200; death of father 23; final illness 199–200; maids' concerns important to 116; marriage 92, 94, 126, 128; Married Women's Property Act 20, 64, 126; Milicent's birth 37; NM 51–2, 69, 98, 100; Portfolio Club 86; problems mount up 146–8; Rebecca's friendship 60; Scalands Gate 91; strokes 117–20, 134, 186; two companions 116; William Rossetti describes 48; women's rights 41, 50

Leigh Smith, Bella (daughter of Willy and Jenny): birth 133; engagement 286; motor cycle 439; overworked 365, 397–8; physical appearance 304; wedding 321–2

Leigh Smith, Bella (sister of Willy and
    others) 18–29, 31–9, 44–51;
    Barbara upset by 39; breakdowns
    19, 21, 26, 28, 33–4; courted by
    General Ludlow 22; Edmund dies
    35; final illness 44–7; gives birth
    for first time 24; marriage 23;
    Milicent born 36–7; Milicent's
    relations with 38; normal married
    life 25, 27; physical health
    problems 29; problems with
    Harry 32; siblings and 20;
    talents 19, 26
Leigh Smith, Ben 178–86; Amy
    considered a child still, 130; Amy's
    declining health 245; Amy's
    European tour 114; Arctic voyages
    50, 145–6, 151–5; Barbara fears
    140; Barbara's first stroke 117–18;
    Bella's wedding 23; birth of
    Milicent 37; Brown's 33–4;
    business brain 306; cab accident
    196; Charley Sellers 178–86, 279,
    291; chess with Bella 39; on his
    children 306; controlling Mabel
    166; death 366; dementia 306–8,
    356; employs Willy 86; estate left
    on death 367; family tensions 306;
    favourite poets 96; favouritism
    towards certain nieces 131–2, 139,
    156; a forceful personality 20–21,
    184; interference re Amy 140;
    later years 305; naming discovered
    lands 152; national hero 155;
    opinions of NM 99–100, 112;
    Sampson the polar bear 41;
    terracotta bust 144; Wellingtonia
    seed 43
Leigh Smith, Dolly 89, 150, 240–41
Leigh Smith, Jenny (Georgina) 84–90;
    Amy, NM and 109, 120, 121,
    141–2; Amy stopped from
    attending dances 135–6; baby
    Milicent pleases 37; background
    85; character 86; clothes 90;
    conservative outlook 49;
    death 449; and Dolly 241; Ethne's
    adolescence 247; Ethne's wedding
    348; First World War 398; Janet
    MacCreath 44; last pregnancy
    150; married life 84–5; physical
    appearance 87–8; Willyboy's
    death 395
Leigh Smith, Lionel: an atheist but 322;
    as a child 133, 136, 150; engage-
    ment 291; India 318, 365, 428
Leigh Smith, Nannie 170–75; Amy and
    238, 241, 257–9, 272; Amy and
    NM's concern 250; antipathy to
    NM and Milicent 290; begins to
    approve of NM 147; Ben and
    Charley disapprove of 178–81,
    184; on boy babies 150; Campagne
    Montfeld 34, 170–72; death 423;
    Ethne describes 304–5; fancy
    dress 25; financial generosity 193;
    First World War 398; gondolier
    183; grief for Isa 236; harangues
    for Amy 84; ill health 27; Janet
    MacCreath 44; life partner 33, 34;
    low opinion of men 111;
    own worst enemy 238; paints
    Milicent 50; will 424; women's
    rights 86
Leigh Smith, Philip: Bellocs and 430,
    431; Ben and 306; birth 220;
    Ethne dared by 311; Gilla and
    393–4; later life 461–2; signs up
    for service 377; Val and 185
Leigh Smith, Roddy: Amy and 176;
    Amy's bridesmaid 142; Charley's
    clothes 197; death 464; First
    World War 398, 406; ill health
    285–6; indulged by Ben 131–3;

physical appearance 49; a spinster's role 230

Leigh Smith, Valentine 305–10; birth 185; First World War 378, 398–9; health crisis 247; Mary Haviland 371–2; Scalands 364, 462; sells most of estate 431

Leigh Smith, Willy 86–90, 335–40; Bella's only visitor 25; conservative outlook 49; death and legacy 338–9; Edward VII and 345; gardening advice for Milicent 208; an Irishman? 104; lobbies for relief vessel for Ben 146; marries Jenny 84–5; opposes Amy and NM's match 120, 121, 142

Leigh Smith, Willy (Willyboy) 188–9, 343, 365, 395

Leigh Smith family *see also* Smiths (various): Brabazon a loyal friend to 135; Crowham 12; half-siblings 19; long-term residents of East Sussex 2; physical appearance 46; popularity of Isa 171–2; united 50

Lewes, George 20

Lifford 56–8, 63, 69

Limerick 54–5, 56

Linacre Lectures 351

Lincoln Cathedral 14

Little Britain 100

Littlegos 369, 370

Littlehampton 292

Little Shepherds 465, 467

Liverpool, Lord 60

Lloyd George, David 419–20, 421, 426

London and Middlesex Archaeological Society 103

Longden, Anne 18, 23

Longden, Dolly 18, 140, 366

Ludlow, Amabel *see* Ludlow, Mabel

Ludlow, Anne 220, 221, 370–71, 394

Ludlow, Edmund 16, 162

Ludlow, Edmund Villeneuve 28, 30, 32, 33, 35, 48

Ludlow, Eira Leigh 220, 221, 366, 370, 397

Ludlow, Harry: behaviour 30–31; birth 25–6; carefree letters 45; death 164; early drinking 51, 52; energy of 134; health problems 30; India 163; interests 51; mother's behaviour 28, 32; talents of 46; vocational training 163

Ludlow, John 220, 221, 370, 377, 410

Ludlow, Major General John 27–40, 43–8; Amy and NM 112; Bella's death 47–8; character 19; children 28; clashes with Barbara 39, 51; death 157–8, 454; diaries 22, 191; fruit cultivation 46; Guestling Lodge 36; health issues 149; a liberal parent 32; marriage to Bella 22–5; suttee abolished 16–17; Yotes Court 40, 45

Ludlow, Ludlow Coape *see* Coape Ludlow, Ludlow

Ludlow, Mabel 25–8; anxiety 46; Arthur Glover 161–6; Beech Green 318; chaperoned 160, 162; children 220; christened 25; energy of 134; 'family taint' xxiv; India 202; Flora looks after 278; marriage to Ludlow Coape Ludlow 2, 196–200; mental breakdowns 1, 3, 148–9, 167, 192, 202, 252, 278, 282; Milicent and NM 284–5, 303; mother's legacy 159; Paris 132; physical prowess 2; put out by birth of brother 27; second birthday party 26; setting up home with Milicent 186–7, 199; sixth birthday party 34; snobbish about NM 131, 284;

suicide attempt 165; Switzerland
32; twenty-first birthday 146;
writes play 50
Ludlow, Milicent *see* Moore, Milicent
Ludlow, Sylvia 220, 221–2, 370
Lusitania 399

MacCreath, Janet (Creathy): arrival at
Yotes 44; bedroom 218; brandy
for her health? 204; chaperoning
Mabel 160; death 231; Eastbourne
with Milicent 156; ill health 220;
Milicent feels obliged 231;
Milicent's upbringing 158; moves
to Crowham 167
Manchester 62, 73
Mario, Alberto 116
Mario, Jessie White 116–18
Married Women's Property Act 20,
64, 126
Marvell, Andrew 96
Maturin, Father Basil 250, 286,
302–3, 399
Mazzini, Giuseppe 116
McGill, Donald 226
McNaught Davis, Jim 368, 371,
387, 394
Menin Gate 385
Millais, John Everett 236
Miller, Father 455, 456–7
Mitchell and Co. (wine merchants) 204
Montreux 114, 115
Moore, Alan 402–58; 'Alaniania' 67;
Ashtons' ball 435; baronetcy 463;
Belloc family 430–34, 436; birth
150; birth of son 459; Cambridge
259, 290; Eton 300; fair-minded
judge of character 66, 422; *Family
Magazine* 248–50, 273, 315, 316;
finds NM fanciful 104; First
World War 377, 396, 402–23; joins
HMS *Grafton* 411, 413; married

life 462–3; Mary Burrows 438–47;
medical practice (various) 425,
431, 436; medical studies 297–8;
Milicent and 298–9; mock
interviews 248–50; nautical
passions 298; NM and Milicent
289; NM's death 454; *Q2* 407–9;
Val and 185, 310; visits to Hancox
11, 12, 13
Moore, Amy 94–145; boarding school
84; Brabazon 135; death 68, 274;
life at Crowham 12, 87–90, 133–4,
138; Roman Catholicism 237,
240, 250–51
Character and appearance: a face 'full
of love' 16; liveliness 125; natural
beauty attracts 115; need for
affection and attention 128;
physical appearance 49, 90;
vulnerability 125
Health : bath chair 242, 248; invalid
diet 265; lack of energy 115; ill
health (miscellaneous) 67, 123–4,
191, 204, 236; tuberculosis 143,
145, 265, 272
NM: 94–143; conditions placed on
letters received from 121;
conditions placed on seeing 120,
128; first letter to 95; photograph
for 110; pledges herself 114; sent
Wellingtonia seedling 112;
wedding 142–3
Other family members: Alan born 150;
Barbara feels she is stifled 48–9;
Barbara's illness 140; Ben
reappears 245; Dolly's legacy 140;
Ethne born 176; family love for
51; Milicent and 3, 10, 256–7;
Nannie and 238, 241, 257–9, 272;
Rebecca's atheism 237, 263,
Roddy and 176; warmth of
family life created by 238

Travel: Algiers 243–4; European tour 114; Ireland 104–5; Rome 256–60, 271–2; Venice 183–4

Moore, Charles 218, 223

Moore, Ethne: affection from father 239; Algiers 243–4; art 251, 296, 297; art school 333–4; birth 176; birth of children 396–7, 411; *Blue Rabbit* 462; Charley and 311, 452; as a child 192, 240; coming out 295; Crowham 87–8; Davos 312; Ethel Portal and 458; facts of life 245; Flora 296, 346, 347; Gillachrist's birth 237; Girton College 296–7; Jack Pryor 335, 340–43, 345–51; letters to her mother 259–60; music 297; new school 266–8; NM's approach 333; NM and Milicent 287–9, 458; 'Notes from the Danery' 274; Pryor family 260–62, 263; puts on weight 315; Queen Victoria dies 267–70; Rebecca embarrasses 61–2, 67; Roman Catholicism 273, 302–3, 334

Moore, Gilla(christ) 352–65, 373–97; Ben and 356–7; birth 220, 237–8; Cambridge 368–70; death 385, 386, 390, 443; education 300–301, 304; First World War 373–97; Mary Haviland 358–64, 369, 370–72, 376–7, 379; memorial tablet 401; NM and Milicent's wedding 293; NM continues to mourn 400; possible dyslexia 259; schooldays 317–19, 352–5

Moore, Mary 438–47; Alan describes his father 297–8; Ashtons' ball 435; birth of son 460; a good woman 464; Milicent and 468

Moore, Meriel 213, 466–8

Moore, Milicent 1–6, 9–16, 36–46, 156–65, 230–35, 252–60, 277–87, 326–34, 446–61, 464–8; artistic talents 46, 209–10; Bethnal Green mission work 1, 3, 231–5; death 466; diary extract 151; driving habits 465; Janet MacCreath 44, 156, 158, 231; later years 464–5; pet names for 327; Roman Catholic Church 291–2; Rose, her maid 222–3, 225; scrimping while travelling 204; Second World War 466; St Margaret's House, Bethnal Green 231–5; takes up residence at Yotes 40, 83

Character and appearance: an active life 365; cleanliness 294; moral scrupulousness 329; 'penurious extravagance' 204, 295–6; perplexing lack of warmth 160; physical appearance 230; a spinster's role 230

Early years: background 16; christened 37; school exercise books 41–2; six years old 84; sixteen years old 167–9;

Hancox: building work 13–14, 207–8, 218–20, 448; buying 15; crucial role xxiv; deep interest in 187; farming 210; first sets foot 5; fruit trees 206–7; gardens 206–8; hops 215, 217; lets to Temperance Society 3, 252–6; a responsible landlord 325; stationery requirements 205; supply of drink 204; vegetables 207

Health: chest infections 134–5; diphtheria 161; ill health (miscellaneous) 10, 134, 161, 311–12, 344

Other family members: accompanies Amy to Rome 252, 256–70; Alan

and 298–9; Charley and 310;
Ethne's coming out 295; Flora
158; godmother to Eira 220;
Mary Burrows 438; NM 53, 54,
277–93, 313, 451, 455; Rebecca
and 299; recovers after NM's
death 460; relations with mother
38, 159; sense of family 51;
setting up home with Mabel
186–7, 199

Moore, Norman (NM) 51–4, 69–83,
94–143, 271–84, 326–33, 447–62;
baronetcy 426–7; belief in God
105–6; Belloc and 434–5; birth 63;
books 65, 317; burial service
455–7; Burke's motto 108; buys
car 326; Cambridge 80–82;
clearing up after the inebriates 10;
confusion in his final days 450–51;
converts to Catholicism 250;
death 453; dinner parties 136;
Ethel Portal 327–33, 344–5; final
days 452–4; financial position
120–21; first visits to Crowham
139; friends 80; gardening
notebook 14; Hancox enjoyed
402; Irish folklore 56; Jonathan
Swift 102; letters 449–50; library
218; literary tastes 65–6, 102;
medieval chivalric ideal 103;
mentors 69; moves into Hancox
1; natural history interests 4; 'The
New Journal to Stella' 102, 106,
117, 123–4, 174; 'Nut Brown
Mayd, The' 103; Owens College
73; Parkinson's disease 447; a
personal manifesto 102; portrait
68; Scalands 91–2; school 69–72;
skiing 314; on smoking 313;
teenage walk to Limerick 58;
Times obituary 454; walks the
streets of London 400; Waterton
73–9; will 456; women, his
views of 125
Character and appearance: attributes
52; beard 239; high principles 107;
Irish character 104; 'larger than
life' xxv
Family relations: an affectionate father
239; Amy 94–143; Amy immerses
herself 129; Amy's illnesses a
financial drain 204; Amy's
wedding 142–3; anonymous
presents to Amy 109; Barbara and
51–2, 69, 98, 100; Barbara's stroke
117; on the Bodichons' marriage
126–8; chooses photograph of
Amy 110; Ethne and 333; Ethne
and Jack Pryor 341; examines Ben
307–8; General Ludlow's position
112; Gilla's death 386, 388, 389–92,
400–402; life at Dr Bodichon's
148; Mabel disparages 131, 284;
Milicent and 53, 54, 277–87, 293,
313; relations with mother 64–6;
status within family secured
192; writes every day to Alan
390–91, 408
Professional life: doctoring style 329;
Harveian Oration 276–7; *History
of St Bartholomew's Hospital* 82, 312,
326, 351, 399, 416; pensions
tribunal 415; President of the
College of Physicians 416;
professional activities 192–3;
retirement 351; Senior
Physician 315

Moore, Norman Winfrid 1, 79,
460, 465

Moore, Rebecca 54–68; background 52,
54–7; death 299; a long life
299–300; love of pretty things 61;
Milicent 299; NM's schooling 72;
petition for votes for women 64;

portrait 54; Robert Moore's
attraction 59; 'scientific atheism'
55, 237, 263, 299
Moore, Richard xxiv, 184
Moore, Robert 58–62, 79, 390, 427
Morris, William 14
mulberries 206
Munro, Alexander 21
Murray, John 105

Nation, The 116
Neale, Dr: *Eira*'s fate 152, 154, 155;
looks after Ben 305, 307, 366, 367
Nebula, The 314; *see also Family
Magazine, The*
Newcomes, The (William Makepeace
Thackeray) 16
'New Journal to Stella, The' (NM) 102,
106, 117, 123–4, 174
Newman, Cardinal 250
Newnham College, Cambridge 199
New Orleans 93
Niagara Falls 93
Nightingale, Fanny 130, 136–7
Nightingale, Florence: ambulances 117;
British Nurses' Association 193;
godmother to Eira 219; Lea Hurst
129; NM corresponds with 125;
related to Smiths 17; suttee
campaign 34
Nordenskiöld, Adolf Erik 145
Normanhurst 136
North Pole 145
Norway 189
'Nut Brown Mayd, The' (traditional) 103

oasthouses 218
Oratory School, Birmingham 318–19,
339, 350, 353–5, 363
Orkney 409, 411, 413
Orr, Kathleen 142
Osborne 393

Our Mutual Friend (Charles Dickens)
136
Owen, Wilfred 390, 425
Owens College 72–3, 79
Oxford House Settlement 230, 437

Paci, Santi 294, 314, 316, 326, 329
Paris 114, 132
Parkes, Bessie Rayner *see* Belloc, Bessie
*Pathological Anatomy of Diseases,
The* (NM) 193
Pathological Society 102
Peel, Sir Robert 60
Penshurst 34, 36
Petley Lodge 18
Phillips, Sir John 457
Piers, Thomas 7
Playford, Frederick 222
Playford, Mrs 222, 229, 326
Playford, Rose 222–9; alone with
NM at his death 454; cousin
drowns 394–5; long service for
Moore family 15; memories of
Gilla 358; Milicent's bequest 468;
skeleton staff 326
Pont de l'Arche 311
Poor House, Zennor 116
Portal, Ethel 327–33; death 461–2;
dines at Gloucester Place 349;
Ethne 458; Ethne and Jack Pryor
346; First World War 373–5;
France 344–5; heraldry 426;
illnesses 417, 447; letters to and
from NM 351, 450; letters to
soldiers and sailors 398; Mary
Talbot 437; Milicent and 233–5;
Milicent, NM and 291; NM and
327–33; NM dies 457; NM's last
days 451–4; summerhouse 352;
two years of romance 358; warm
support offered to NM 391
Portal family 234–5, 327

Porter, Mr 253–4

Portfolio Club 86

Post-Traumatic Stress Disorder 425

postcards 225–8

Prébil, Alice 462

Prussia 32

Pryor, Hilda 265–6, 270, 346, 348,
    453–4

Pryor, Jack 335, 340–43, 345–9,
    387, 411

Pryor, Marlborough 260, 262, 350

Pryor family 260–63, 340

Q2 (ship) 407–9

Quakers 54, 56, 74, 93

Quarterly Review 81, 97

Queenie (rocking horse) xxi

Rathlin Island 301–2

'Reasons for the Enfranchisement of
    Women' (Barbara Leigh Smith) 34

Revolution (magazine) 64

Rivers, W. H. R. 425

Robert Ker (ship) 58

Robertsbridge 1, 11, 337, 366, 373

Robinson, Dr 81

Rome 256–60, 271–2

Rose and the Ring, The (William
    Makepeace Thackeray) 281

Rossetti, Christina 94–5

Rossetti, Dante Gabriel 90

Rossetti, William 48

Rossetti family 20

Rother Valley 216

Royal Academy School 334

Royal College of Heralds 426

Royal College of Physicians 68, 276

Royal Geographical Society 155

Royal Oak, Whatlington 11, 87, 255,
    324, 326

Royal Sailors' Home, Chatham 377

Russell, Alys 387

Russell, Risien 305

Rutherford, May 168

Sackville family 6–7, 9

Sagitta HMS 396, 402

S. Ambrogio, Florence 278

Sampson (bear) 41, 145

Samworth, Joanna 26

Sayers family 320

Scalands Gate 94–6; Barbara designs
    and builds 20, 91; Ben acquires
    201; bullet marks 306; Charley
    at 182; fireplace signatures 90;
    Night School 147; NM visits
    91–2; open house for the Smiths
    188; studio 27; Val moves in 367;
    Val moves out 462; 'women's
    feast' 50

Scott, Sir Francis 327, 328

'scriptorium' xxiv

Seaford 302

'Seddlescombe Place' (drawing) 9

Sedlescombe 5, 13, 215, 216, 455, 468

Sellers, Charles 214, 223

Sellers, Charlotte (Charley) 177–85;
    Ben marries 177–80; Catholicism
    368; concerned re management
    of Ben's affairs 306–7; Ethne 311,
    452; Ethne's wedding 347; First
    World War in France 397;
    housekeeping 247; last years 462;
    marriage faltering 279; Milicent
    and 310

Sellers, Eugénie 177–80

Seven Weeks' War 32

ship's bell 317

Shoolbreds 187

Smith, Adams 29

Smith, Benjamin 17, 18–19, 23, 60

Smith, Flora: Ben stays with 247;
    dinner party 191; Ethne and 297,
    346, 347; Flora Cottage 152; loan

of carriage 193; Mabel looked
after by 278; Milicent and 158
Smith, Ike 222–3, 228–9
Smith, Julia ('Aunt Ju') 17, 18, 23, 91,
129–30, 169
Smith, Louisa Shore 136–7, 158, 163
Smith, Ludlow Coape *see* Coape
Ludlow, Ludlow
Smith, Rose *see* Playford, Rose
Smith, Shore 136–7
Smith, Valentine 146, 156, 186, 305, 367
Smith, William 17–18, 51, 192
smuggling 13
Spark, The 248, 251
Spitzbergen 145
St Bartholomew's Hospital: 'The New
Journal to Stella' 102; NM's
career 4, 52, 82, 100, 315; posts
held by NM 120; Roman tombs
103; Warden's House 143, 173,
176, 239
St Margaret's House, Bethnal Green 3,
231–5, 437
St Peter's, Wapping 240
St Theodore's 465
staircase 315–16
Stephen, Leslie 192
Stromness 409
Sussex Regiment, the Royal 378–85
Sussex Weald xxi, 213, 215
suttee 16–17, 34
Sutton family 222
'sweating' 231
Swift, Jonathan 102

Talbot, Mary 437–8
Test, River 234, 461
Thompson, Dr Reginald 117–18,
174, 200
Thompson, General Perronet 79, 117
Thorius, Raphael 276
Ticehurst, Dr 29, 36, 37

Ticehurst & Co, Battle 205
Times, The 395, 454
Toynbee Hall 231
Tryphena (typewriter) 117, 118
tuberculosis 10; *see also* Leigh Smith,
Amy: *Health*
Tuke, Doctor 34, 40, 165
Turner, J. M. W. 90

Una (journal) 64
Unitarians 17, 19, 141

Vaughan, Molly (Rebecca's nurse)
55–6
vegetable plots 207
Venice 183–4, 199
Victoria, Queen 42, 178, 267–70,
393, 428

Walker, Hannah 24
Wallace Collection 278
Walton, Fanny 36, 158, 163
Walton Hall 4, 73–5, 77, 78, 79, 284
Ward-Price, Leonard 368, 410
Warley Place 14
Waterton, Charles 4, 73–9, 250, 292,
313, 319
Watts, William 209, 210, 360
Wells, Arthur (architect) 219
Weston Park 260–62, 463
Whatlington 5, 215, 216, 323–4
Whatlington Benevolent Society 324–5
Whistler, Joan *see* Ashton, Joan
Whistler family 210
Wickham, Agnes 291, 318, 365
Wickham, Bill 125
Wickham, Dora 125
Wickham, Noel 456
Wilberforce, William 17
Williams, Louise ('Ony') 464
Willmott, Ellen 14, 125, 293, 402
Winter family 11, 252

'Wonderful Exhibition of Art
Treasures' (Rebecca Moore) 63
Wynne, Dr Walter 286, 321–2, 338

Yeats, John Butler 54
Yeats, W. B. 240
Yosemite Valley 112
Yotes Court 40–45, 131–2; coldness of
134–5; given up 165, 167; hops an
important crop 215; Mabel feels
capable of running 158, 160, 162;
Mabel's twenty-first 146; Milicent
prepared for Hancox 325;
Milicent takes up residence 83;
NM at 53; rented 1, 204; used by
Coape Smiths 194
Young, Sir Allen 151, 155
Young, Miss ('Youngster') 359, 361
Ypres 385, 386, 390, 393, 442

Zennor 116, 117, 126
Zwarzleene 393